D0787613

AGAINST COERCION

ELEANOR COOK

Against Coercion

GAMES POETS PLAY

STANFORD UNIVERSITY PRESS

STANFORD, CALIFORNIA

1998

Stanford University Press
Stanford, California

© 1998 by the Board of Trustees of the Leland Stanford
Junior University

Printed in the United States of America

Source acknowledgments and CIP data appear at the end
of the book

To Maggie, Markham, and Vera

Acknowledgments

Over the years, colleagues and friends have provided the conversation, encouragement, and enlightenment without which this book would not exist. I am especially and happily indebted to Alan Bewell, James Carscallen, John Hollander, H. T. and J. R. de J. Jackson, Jay Macpherson, Christopher Ricks, and David Shaw, and, for particular essays, Roberta Frank, Inge Leimberg, Herbert Marks, Jane and Michael Millgate, Mary Nyquist and Margaret Ferguson, Magdalene Redekop, John Serio and B. J. Leggett, and E. G. Stanley. I am most grateful to Helen Tartar of Stanford University Press for her literary acumen and unfailing good sense, to Pamela MacFarland Holway, and to my splendid copy editor, Peter Dreyer, master of griffin history and much more. Occasions for thinking and rethinking were provided by generous audiences at Boston, Cambridge, Indiana, McMaster, Toronto, and Westfälisches universities, as well as at Queen's University (Kingston) for the Dolman Lectureship, 1992–93. The Academy of Fine Ideas, the Association of Canadian College and University Teachers of English, the Association of Literary Scholars and Critics, the Canadian Comparative Literature Association, and the Modern Language Association also offered welcome occasions for testing ideas.

I am grateful to Tim Zuck for permission to reproduce his painting *Bird and Memorial*. Those familiar with the Nova Scotia landscape will recognize yet one more reason for its inclusion here.

Some of this work was done with the help of a Social Sciences and Humanities Council research grant, to which grateful acknowledgment is made. The little *jeu d'esprit* "The Flying Griphos" represents the first small published fruit of work done on the literary riddle with the support of the John

Simon Guggenheim Memorial Foundation and subsequently a Killam Research Fellowship; most grateful acknowledgment herewith, and to the University of Toronto for the Connaught Fellowship (honorary).

The support and encouragement of my family has been far above rubies.

Contents

Foreword

The inertia of language . . . is also the coercive force of language.

— GEOFFREY HILL, The Lords of Limit

This book is about poets' games, the serious games of all their indirections. Throughout, it is also about how these indirections speak to our entire lives in their historical moment, individual lives yes, but also the lives of empires and nations (Part I). In a more pointed sense, these games include the *ludus* of allusion (Part II) and the various games of Part III, from play within the wells of creation in the Godhead (chapter 11) through the play of riddles both large and small (chapters 13–15). Part IV offers practical criticism, because all larger readings here work out from particular evidence, and are tested in turn by particulars. Occasionally, I have included examples of prose fiction.

Why poems? First, my continuing delight in the sheer craft of the best practitioners. Some twenty years ago, I put myself to school with Wallace Stevens, although I didn't realize at the time that this was happening. After a while, I began to be able to answer the questions: just what makes this or that twentieth-century poem a good poem? How could I demonstrate such a thing? What's the state of the art now? What do apprentices, journeymen, and masters of the art work at nowadays? Underlying all these essays are my fascination in the bone with this art and a strong desire that we not throw away accumulated knowledge about its workings, "as if all history were deciduous" (Anthony Hecht, "A Birthday Poem").

Second, poetry is our most highly organized form of words. It encompasses more than other verbal constructions in the way of thinking and feeling and sensation, and also in the pleasure of language. Good poems offer our most energetic — and energizing — verbal artifacts. This means that poems have something to teach all other verbal disciplines about words. Poems work notably with fictive constructs (stories, fables, allegories) and with figuration (figures of speech, tropes and schemes), this last being poetry's special domain. Because we all live inside the stories of our own lives, and because we all live with the figurative power of words, good poems are invaluable.

The figurative power of words? Suppose we start with the often-repeated statement that poets are not original thinkers. To be sure, since "original thought" is nearly always defined in advance as nonpoetic. Philosophers and scientists are not original tropers or storytellers either. Poets know about these things, and we neglect the power of figures of speech and of fictive constructs at our peril. The best philosophers and scientists do no such thing. See, for example, Stephen Jay Gould: "We often think, naively, that missing data are the primary impediments to intellectual progress. . . . But barriers are often deeper and more abstract in thought. We must have access to the right metaphor."[1] Or consider Oliver Sacks's *The Man Who Mistook His Wife for a Hat and Other Clinical Tales*. One aim of that book is simply to undo the force of our unexamined metaphor "The brain is a machine," especially as applied to brain-damaged people. (" 'Deficit', we have said, is neurology's favourite word — its only word, indeed, for any disturbance of function. . . . What then of the opposite — an excess or superabundance of function?")[2] There are two possible responses to the brain-machine metaphor. One says: let's get rid of metaphor, period. The other, more experienced response says: let's look for a better metaphor or use more than one. We can't get rid of figures of speech even if we want to. Dead or alive, they're part of the language. Poets are the great experts in this area and so can alert us to their power. To their pleasure too.

This may come clearer if we recognize that poems are often answering the question "What is *x like*?" rather than "What is *x*?" "What is *x*?" usually elicits the answer "*x* is ——— [a noun]." Poems answer "What is *x* like?" by means of figuration and fictive construct, and such answers can be just as valid and useful as answers to the question "What is *x*?" See, for example, the parables of the New Testament, for they work this way. "The kingdom of heaven is *like* unto. . . ." "Who is my neighbor?" "A certain man went down from Jerusalem to Jericho, and fell among thieves. . . ."

Of course, poems proceed by indirection, not being political or forensic or ecclesiastical or didactic oratory. As with all the arts, the relation with the outside world is both necessary and oblique:

The relation between an artist and reality is always an oblique one, and indeed there is no good art which is not consciously oblique. If you respect the reality of the world, you know that you can only approach that reality by indirect means. The painter who throws away the frame and rebels at composition is not a painter any more: he thinks the world is himself. . . . He lacks that feeling of inadequacy which must precede every genuine act of creation.[3]

Art is a harmony which runs parallel with nature — what is one to think of those imbeciles who say that the artist is always inferior to nature?[4]

There is a process of rereading that I call to myself "putting pressure on a poem." With a good poem, whether in high or popular art, the pressure yields something. The poet has been there already, has thought of x, has felt y, has observed z, and will thereby direct the reader further. This might be in the area of lexis (diction) or grammar or rhythm or syntax or logic. Without this grace under pressure, a poem will ring dead. Even if a reader cannot say exactly why certain words in a poem resonate somehow, they nonetheless do. Often this is quite simply the result of hard work. Elizabeth Bishop held back some poems for years, waiting for just the right phrasing, and James Merrill remarked: "It can take me dozens of drafts to get something right, which often turns out to be a perfect commonplace. What a joy when it works — like fighting one's way through cobwebs to an open window."[5]

Language full of verbal energy gives us mental energy in turn. Once I was yawning and squirming my way through a graduation ceremony at which Mavis Gallant was to be the guest speaker. She rose and spoke a living English, whereupon boredom and fatigue vanished instantly for all of us. Our brains had been released from the forced labor of cliché, and energized by the true work and play of words.

Which brings me back again to the matter of coercion. Geoffrey Hill once wrote that "the inertia of language . . . is also the coercive force of language."[6] What such coercing inertia can do in a specific historical situation may be seen in Václav Havel's extraordinary 1978 essay "The Power of the Powerless." Havel knows about the power of words, for good and for ill:

In the beginning of everything is the word. It is a miracle to which we owe the fact that we are human. But at the same time it is a pitfall and a test, a snare and a trial. More so, perhaps, than appears to you who have enormous freedom of speech, and might therefore assume that words are not so important. They are. They are important everywhere. . . . Responsibility for and toward words is a task which is intrinsically ethical.[7]

— this little painting (a sketch for a larger one?)
has never earned any money in its life.
Useless and free, it has spent seventy years
as a minor family relic. . . .
Heavens, I recognize the place, I know it!
. . . How strange. And it's still loved,
or its memory is (it must have changed a lot).
Our visions coincided — "visions" is
too serious a word — our looks, two looks:
art "copying from life" and life itself,
life and the memory of it so compressed
they've turned into each other. Which is which?
Life and the memory of it cramped,
dim, on a piece of Bristol board,
dim, but how live, how touching in detail
— the little that we get for free,
the little of our earthly trust. Not much.
About the size of our abidance
along with theirs: the munching cows,
the iris, crisp and shivering, the water
still standing from spring freshets,
the yet-to-be-dismantled elms, the geese.

— ELIZABETH BISHOP, *"Poem"*

Introduction

This book works from the assumption that, while it is all well and good to read poems in the light of history, it's a pity if history doesn't get read in the shadow and play of poetry. Nowadays we are very aware of the ways in which historical and cultural contexts condition writing—for example, through socioeconomic forces, the process of book production, assumptions about appropriate roles for women or ethnic groups, and so on. But literary scholars and critics are also aware of the ways in which writing speaks back to the very history that conditions it. At least we should be aware. If not we, who?

Then, too, history as writing is a verbal discipline through which history as event is interpreted. Like other verbal disciplines, it can learn from the verbal disciplines of poetry and criticism. I'd go further and say that we learn most about words from poetry simply because it is our most highly organized form of language.

Attacks on aesthetics in the name of history are often themselves curiously ahistorical. When I read of "timeless aesthetics" (unspecified) and its nefarious hidden plots, I want to ask: exactly *whose* aesthetics, when and where? When I hear about formalism, I want to have a definition, and I want to know whether the author is distinguishing between the use of forms and the *-ism* in a given formalism. When I hear that some aesthetics conceals a political agenda, I want also to ask about politics that conceals—or, for that matter, manifests—an aesthetic agenda. And when I read increasingly clumsy, ill-informed remarks about formal effects, my heart goes out to the writer (assuming the remarks are made in good faith), who has been deprived of decent training in the great verbal traditions of the art of poetry. Some cultures, like St. Augustine's North African audience or Elizabethan England, value verbal ability. Others do not.

Of course, it is not possible to separate, with a high, thick wall, aesthetic and ethical and political questions, to say nothing of the various disciplines. And, of course, scholars and critics, as responsible citizens, must be concerned with social and political questions. There is always interpenetration among these areas, and should be. But if literary scholars and critics have nothing to offer by way of a specifically literary training, we should shut up shop and let properly trained historians and philosophers and sociologists and anthropologists take over literary analysis. Little wonder that they sometimes ask if there is any such discipline as literary criticism.

There is a little fable about this whole matter in the subtitle of Northrop Frye's *Anatomy of Criticism*.[1] For that subtitle is, baldly speaking, a lie. The full title of Frye's 1957 masterpiece is *Anatomy of Criticism: Four Essays*. But *Anatomy of Criticism*—that is, the entire book—is more than four essays. It consists of four essays plus a "Polemical Introduction" and a "Tentative Conclusion." What then is the title of the entire book? It is *Anatomy of Criticism: Four Essays*.[2] The four essays may be read as a simple 1-2-3-4 plus pre-1 and post-4, but they are more precisely read as four essays framed, informed, crossed by something different in kind, the introduction and conclusion. I take it that Frye's subtitle quietly and provocatively points toward the paradoxical structure of his book. For the book at once is and is not an anatomy of four essays.

Frye's framing narrative includes: (1) the function of criticism in 1957 (the introduction);[3] (2) the relation of literary criticism to other disciplines (the conclusion, first part); and (3) a view of the end of criticism (the conclusion, second part). In short, the introduction and conclusion focus on some theoretical and social functions of criticism, both immediate and long-term, as perceived by Frye in 1957. For, to quote the end of the conclusion: "No discussion of beauty can confine itself to the formal relations of the isolated work of art; it must consider, too, the participation of the work of art in the vision of the goal of social effort" (348).

There are, then, two ways of looking at *Anatomy of Criticism*. One reads that subtitle literally, confines the anatomy to the four essays, and reads *anatomy* in a dry-bones anatomy-lesson context. The second reads that subtitle paradoxically, works with the 4-plus-1 formula, and reads *anatomy* in both a dry-bones and a living-flesh context. Skeletons are found in laboratories and in graveyards, and one archaic meaning of the word *anatomy* is "skeleton." We also carry them around inside us, and they carry us too, although not in the most vital sense (see Richard Wilbur's fine poem "To His Skeleton"). Even in this most schematic of structures, the structure does not stand in isolation. The very subtitle of *Anatomy of Criticism* tells us as much.

But it tells us something more, for this argument works both ways. It tells us that the social and theoretical implications of criticism do not stand in isolation from anatomy either — that is, do not stand in isolation from "the formal causes of art" (29), which is the area where the four essays live.[4] For myself, these are the two areas of activity necessary for literary criticism: the study of "literary conventions" and the study of the "social relationships" of literature, including its material and efficient causes.[5] The study of literary conventions — that is, of anatomy — I think of as literary criticism proper. The study of the social relationships of literature I think of as the necessary responsibility of the critic at large. Neither should be cut off; neither should swallow up the other. As corollary, this also means that the metaphors connecting the two areas are very important, especially nowadays, when the power of figuration is so underestimated.

Metaphors connecting criticism proper and the wider social concerns of criticism offer a great though hidden challenge. They may indeed connect or they may break. They may casually assign a middle ground to poetry — say, between politics and aesthetics (but this is to assume a difference in degree rather than in kind). They may try to reconcile or they may prefer to rupture. The challenge in such metaphors is analogous to the challenge that every good artist faces when form must answer to matter and matter must answer to form. Frye and the deconstructionists alike drew attention to certain latent, and sometimes determining, metaphors of connection, even in such lowly parts of speech as prepositions. When we say we need to "go beyond" the study of literary discourse to the study of cultural practice, we have already decided how these areas are connected. Can we also say that in some circumstances we need a study of literary conventions that would "go beyond" cultural practice?

I want to argue that literary critics, of all people, should understand something of the immense discipline of form. "Going beyond" cultural practice might mean no more than formal self-examination, but with something of the rigor that any good poet uses. If we read, say, James Merrill's prose or Marianne Moore's or Seamus Heaney's, we apprehend a little of what Geoffrey Hill means by "a self-castigating craftsman's faculty."[6] Only those ignorant of an art suppose formal questions to be peripheral or morally neutral. And surely what we have to offer to other disciplines is precisely some sense of the demanding and shaping power of verbal forms, of the *serio ludere* of poetry.

Elizabeth Bishop's late poem "Poem" tells of a moment of inheritance, an aunt passing on a family keepsake, a small painting by her great-uncle. Suddenly, the poem erupts in astonishment as Bishop recognizes the Nova Scotia scene in the painting and starts to identify landmarks. This is an actual landscape seen and represented in painting, following the conventions of the day (her great-uncle was a member of the Royal Academy). It links uncle and niece in a moment of looking, a living historical moment passed on through the indirections of painterly art ("titanium white, one dab") and passed on to us in turn through the indirections of verbal art. Something about this poem, with its wonderful example of mimesis, memory, and the arts, caused Bishop to name it simply "Poem," not "A Poem" or "The Poem." Something of that simple family moment, transmuted through Bishop's alchemy into poetic form, has to do deeply with the art of poems.

I first thought of calling this book "The Little That We Get for Free," until this title's risible side occurred to me. Still, what we inherit, "we get for free," a small family keepsake, for example. Memory, too, "we get for free": "life and the memory of it," "the little of our earthly trust," "our abidance," living when and where we do. The word *abidance* means: "1: a state of abiding or staying: CONTINUANCE 2: COMPLIANCE (~ by rules)" (*Webster's*). Little wonder that Elizabeth Bishop liked the word, with its double meaning, and more.

The word *trust* also resonates with matters of continuance: life and the memory of it, dwelling in some corner of the world and also decidedly dwelling in our heads; life and the memory of it abiding by rules (some through necessity, some through choice), including the rules of a game. The same is true of paintings. The same is true of poems.

PART ONE

Empire, War, Nation

Eliot, Keynes, and Empire: *The Waste Land*

The Waste Land requires three maps for its place-names. One is a map of Greater London and the lower Thames, for the poem is a London poem even in its final form. One early plan, as Hugh Kenner has argued, conceived of part 3 as a vision of London through various Augustan modes, making of the city almost another character, and suggesting a geographical unity as focal point for the poem. At this stage, says Kenner, "the rest of the poem seems to have been planned around it [part 3], guided by the norms and decorums of an Augustan view of history."[1] Then Eliot wrote part 5, the vision of an urban apocalypse became dominant, and part 3 was cut accordingly.

The Waste Land is not only a London poem; it is also a European poem, or more precisely a Mediterranean poem. It was always so through the early drafts, and it became noticeably so when, in part 5, London was listed as the last in a series of five great cities, Jerusalem, Athens, Alexandria, Vienna, London. The poem therefore requires a second map for those place-names that are not from the London area, leaving aside the names of Ganga and the

Himavant. If those place-names are plotted on a map, they may be seen to ring the Mediterranean in the following sense. The northerly names are not seen as centers, in the way our twentieth-century eyes see them. Rather, they balance Carthage and Mylae to the south, and Jerusalem and Smyrna (now Izmir) to the east. This map coincides roughly with the Roman Empire at its most expansive, and also with the theater of war during World War I. The center of this second map is Rome.

This leaves us with the names of Ganga and the Himavant. The map that is useful here is a very simple and a very symmetrical one: it is Dante's map of the inhabited world.[2] The exact center of this world is Jerusalem. Ninety degrees to the east is the eastern limit, the mouth of the Ganges, which is also the eastern limit of *The Waste Land*. Ninety degrees to the west is the western limit, Gibraltar, or the western end of the Mediterranean, which is also the western limit of *The Waste Land*. Precisely halfway between Gibraltar and Jerusalem is Rome. We have thus three maps, one of a city, one of an empire, one of a world. They are not set side by side; that is, we do not make orderly progression from one map to the next in the poem. Rather, it is as if they were layered, and we read meaning from one map into another. Urban vision, imperial vision, world vision: each illuminates the other.

The English Augustans, Kenner observes, saw encouraging parallels between their London and Rome at the time of Augustus. Eliot's early plan for *The Waste Land*, mentioned above, was to develop satiric parallels between modern London and Augustan London. Kenner argues persuasively that Eliot "may well have had in mind at one time a kind of modern *Aeneid*, the hero crossing seas to pursue his destiny, detained by one woman and prophesied to by another, and encountering visions of the past and the future, all culminated in a city both founded and yet to be founded, unreal and oppressively real, the Rome through whose past Dryden saw London's future" (39–40). London was to be "the original Fisher King as well as the original Waste Land, resembling Augustine's Carthage as Dryden's London had resembled Ovid's Rome" (28). With the final revisions, however, the center of the poem became "the urban apocalypse, the great City dissolved into a desert" (46).

But I wonder whether the preeminent pattern for London from first to last was not Rome. Of course, in one sense all the cities in the final version of *The Waste Land* are the same: they are Cities of Destruction. But the poem nonetheless focuses on one particular city, London. Similarly, I think that the poem focuses on one prototype for London, and that the prototype is Rome, the center of the second map, and the center of the western half of the third map. Among these three maps, studies of *The Waste Land* have tended to concentrate on the first and the third, Eliot's urban vision and his world vision. But London in 1922 was still the center of an empire. What I want to concentrate on here is Eliot's vision of imperial apocalypse in *The Waste Land*, working from the hypothesis that a vision of Rome and the Roman Empire lies behind Eliot's vision of London and the British Empire.

Rome could provide a pattern for London in *The Waste Land* for good reason. The most obvious is that Rome was once both a great city and the capital of a great empire. In this, she is no different from those other great cities in part 5 that were also capitals of great, although very different, empires: "Jerusalem, Athens, Alexandria, / Vienna, London." This list is worth examining. Eliot preserves the chronological order of the flourishing of each empire. He lists three ancient empires in one line, two modern ones in the following line. The large gap between the three ancient and two modern empires is dominated by Rome, who—and here it differs from the other cities—held sway over all three old empires. The name of Vienna, capital of the Austro-Hungarian Empire, suggests a line of succession, for the Austro-Hungarian Empire saw itself as heir to the Holy Roman Empire, which in turn saw itself as heir to the Roman Empire. Eliot was explicit about part of this line of succession in 1951:

> For Virgil's conscious mind, it [destiny] means the *imperium roma-num*. . . . I think that he had few illusions and that he saw clearly both sides of every question—the case for the loser as well as the case for the winner. . . . And do you really think that Virgil was mistaken? You must remember that the Roman Empire was transformed into the Holy Roman Empire. What Virgil proposed to his contemporaries was the highest ideal even for an unholy Roman Empire, for any merely temporal empire. We are all, so far as we inherit the civilization of Europe, still citizens of the Roman Empire. . . . It remains an ideal, but one which Virgil passed on to Christianity to develop and to cherish.[3]

This is the older Eliot speaking. The younger Eliot was quite detached about Christianity, but Eliot always saw himself as heir to the riches of classical civilization, and especially Roman civilization. "Tradition and the Individual Talent" appeared in 1919, and in 1923 Eliot wrote: "If everything derived from Rome were withdrawn — everything we have from Norman-French society, from the Church, from Humanism, from every channel direct and indirect, what would be left? A few Teutonic roots and husks. England is a 'Latin' country" (*Criterion* 2 [Oct. 1923]: 104).

"For at least seven years, it would seem," writes Kenner, "an urban apocalypse had haunted Eliot's imagination" (42). To an imagination thus haunted, and brooding from 1919 onward[4] over material for what was to be *The Waste Land*, it might very well have appeared that the inheritance of Rome was disintegrating. "I am all for empires," wrote Eliot in January 1924, "especially the Austro-Hungarian Empire."[5] But the Austro-Hungarian Empire had just been broken up by the Treaty of Versailles in 1919. And Christianity, considered simply as a force in history, in the way Henry Adams saw it, might also be disintegrating. "The struggle of 'liberal' against 'orthodox' faith is out of date," Eliot wrote as early as 1916. "The present conflict is far more momentous than that."[6] The ghost of Rome prevails in *The Waste Land* because Rome evolved from the greatest of Western empires into a Christian one; because the various European empires that followed Rome, all the way down to the British Empire, retained something of this inheritance, including the association of church and state (at least, officially); and because Eliot at the time of *The Waste Land* sees the possibility that this inheritance and this association will come to an end in the disintegration of church and state and civilization as we know them. "Eliot . . . once said to me," Spender recalls, "that *The Waste Land* could not have been written at any moment except when it was written — a remark which, while biographically true in regard to his own life, is also true of the poem's time in European history after World War I. The sense that Western civilization was in a state which was the realization of historic doom lasted from 1920 to 1926."[7]

The decline of Western civilization and the parallel between Roman and modern civilization: this suggests Spengler. We tend to associate *The Waste Land* with Spengler, in general because of this sense of the decline of civilization, and in particular because Spengler's seasonal cycle so neatly fits Eliot's allusions to English literature in parts 1 to 4 of the poem. But Eliot's view of history in *The Waste Land* seems to me less Spengler's than that of Henry Adams, although Stuart Hughes reminds us in his *Oswald Spengler* that the Adams brothers were precursors of Spengler. (Eliot's own dismissal of Spengler is brisk: "These are only a few of the questions suggested by Mr. Perry's work; which compels more attention, I think, than the work of such abstract philosophers of history as Otto [*sic*] Spengler.")[8] In *The Education of Henry Adams*, Adams argues that Christianity is the last great force that the West has known, but that its strength is coming to an end. The twentieth century will see a major shift in civilization, like the last major shift, which began at about the time of Augustine. For Spengler, the modern cycle begins in 900 A.D., Augustine is not a pivotal figure, as he is for Adams, and Christianity is not the latest force the West has known. Our age, according to Spengler, parallels that of the shift from Greek to Roman dominance in the Mediterranean, and we are at the beginning of another "Roman" age. "*Rome*, with its rigorous realism — uninspired, barbaric, disciplined, practical, Protestant, *Prussian* — will always give us, working as we must by analogies, the key to understanding our own future" (*The Decline of the West* [1918–22], 1.10). Adams makes no such forecasts, being altogether more tentative, at least in the *Education*. But within what Eliot calls the "sceptical patrician," there lay a strong sense of apocalypse. Augustine's *Confessions* do not lie behind *The Education of Henry Adams* for nothing. In 1919, Eliot wrote a review of *The Education of Henry Adams* in which he makes no mention of Adams's view of history. But then, he makes no mention of the Maryland spring, which finds a place in "Gerontion."[9] (Odd that Eliot says "there is nothing to indicate that Adams's senses either flowered or fruited," while his subconscious tucked away that sensual, flowering Maryland spring for poetic use.) Nor does he mention Adams's image of the Hudson and the Susquehanna, perhaps the Potomac, and the Seine rising to drown the gods of Walhalla, nor the argument that *Götterdämmerung* was understood better in New York or in Paris than in Bayreuth. Yet in *The Waste Land*, Wagner's Rhine-daughters from *Götterdämmerung* are given equivalents in the Thames, and it may be that Adams suggested to Eliot the usefulness of *Götterdämmerung* in a poem about the end of things and about (in part) the life of a river. For Adams, the beginning of the end of the Roman Empire was the beginning of the age we know, and the coming change will not be the end of things, and thus not a true apocalypse. But his imagery and his sense of cataclysm are such that they would have fed an imagination already haunted by the theme of apocalypse.

So would Conrad, and so possibly would Henry James, two writers whom Eliot read and admired. Conrad, of course, enters into *The Waste Land*. Neither James in *The Golden Bowl* nor Conrad in *Heart of Darkness* looks ahead like Adams to a change in civilization such as the world has not seen in some fifteen centuries. But both books present a dark and troubled vision of empire, and both make use of a parallel between Rome and London. Here are the opening sentences of *The Golden Bowl*:

> The Prince had always liked his London, when it had come to him; he was one of the Modern Romans who find by the Thames a more con-vincing image of the truth of the ancient state than any they have left by the Tiber. Brought up on the legend of the City to which the world paid tribute, he recognised in the present London much more than in con-temporary Rome the real dimensions of such a case. If it was a question of an *Imperium*, he said to himself, and if one wished, as a Roman, to recover a little the sense of that, the place to do so was on London Bridge. . . .

Parallels between Rome and London were common enough at the turn of the century, but only rarely did they serve to set a question mark against the enterprise of empire itself, its uses as well as its abuses, its civilization as well as its corruption. Both *The Golden Bowl* and *Heart of Darkness* do this, al-though Conrad's reaction to the kind of power that underlies the rhetoric of empire is beyond even James's darkness: it is horror. Conrad offers us an ancient Roman view of Londinium at the beginning of *Heart of Darkness*, and a parallel between contemporary London and ancient Rome is implicit. His red-sailed barges in the Thames are also from the beginning of *Heart of Darkness*, and they are already present in the early drafts of part 3 of *The Waste Land*.

Something of the force of Conrad's great dark vision of empire on Eliot's imagination in 1919 may be seen in a review of Kipling that Eliot published two weeks before his review of *The Education of Henry Adams*.[10] In 1941, when Eliot wrote an introduction to his selection of Kipling's poems, he outlined sympathetically Kipling's idea of empire. It was for Kipling "not merely an idea . . . it was something the reality of which he felt." And Eliot went on to analyze Kipling's sense of the Empire as an awareness of respon-sibility. But not in 1919. Then, his reaction to Kipling's imperialism was contemptuous, and his sympathies clearly lay with Conrad, who provides the contrast to Kipling in the 1919 review.

> Both of the poets [Kipling and Swinburne] have a few simple ideas. If we deprecate any philosophical complications, we may be allowed to call Swinburne's Liberty and Mr. Kipling's Empire "ideas." They are at least abstract, and not material which emotion can feed long upon. And they are not (in passing) very dissimilar. Swinburne had the Risorgimento, and Garibaldi, and Mazzini, and the model of Shelley, and the recoil from Tennyson, and he produced Liberty. Mr. Kipling, the Anglo-Indian, had frontier welfare, and rebellions, and Khartoum, and he produced the Empire. And we remember Swinburne's sentiments toward the Boers: he wished to intern them all. Swinburne and Mr. Kipling have these and such concepts; some poets, like Shakespeare or Dante or Villon, and some novelists, like Mr. Conrad, have, in contrast to ideas or concepts, points of view, or "worlds" — what are incorrectly called "philosophies." Mr. Conrad is very germane to the question, because he is in many ways the antithesis of Mr. Kipling. He is, for one thing, the antithesis of Empire (as well as of democracy); his characters are the denial of Empire, of Nation, of Race almost, they are fearfully alone with the Wilderness. Mr. Conrad has no ideas, but he has a point of view, a "world"; it can hardly be defined, but it pervades his work and is unmistakable. It could not be otherwise. Swinburne's and Mr. Kipling's ideas could be otherwise. Had Mr. Kipling taken Liberty and Swinburne the Empire, the alteration would be unimportant.
>
> And that is why both Swinburne's and Mr. Kipling's verse in spite of the positive manner which each presses to his service, appear to lack cohesion — to be, frankly, immature. There is no point of view to hold them together.

Eliot is here working out the function of ideas as against the function of a point of view. (The distinction had appeared already in 1918 in his analysis of Henry James, the analysis that includes the well-known sentence "He had a mind so fine that no idea could violate it.")[11] But there is no doubt about Eliot's opinion of Kipling's idea as idea. In the later essay, it is Eliot's reaction to that idea that has changed. This time, he compares Kipling, not with Swinburne, but with Dryden, "one other great English writer who put politics into verse."

There is another work that I think entered into the making of *The Waste*

Land. It is a book contemporary with the poem; it sheds light on some of the allusions in *The Waste Land*, ties the poem to post-World-War-I history, and incidentally relates Eliot's work at Lloyds Bank to his poetry. It treats the theme of imperial collapse, and it uses Rome as an implicit example. It is John Maynard Keynes's *The Economic Consequences of the Peace.*

Eliot in 1951 observed that Virgil knew the case for the loser as well as the case for the winner. When he cut and revised the drafts of *The Waste Land*, he deleted several references to Virgil. The one specific reference he chose to retain is an allusion to Dido, a reference that stresses the price rather than the glory of empire. Virgil's Sibyl of Cumae knew the price of empire too. (Kenner notes that we are meant to recall Virgil's Sibyl, if we have any sibylline knowledge at all, when we see the ruined Sibyl of Cumae in the poem's epigraph.) In book 6 of the *Aeneid*, the Sibyl of Cumae warns Aeneas of the realities on which empires are founded: "bella, horrida bella et Thybrim multo spumentem sanguine cerno" (86–87). And the Tiber, running with blood, takes its place behind the great rivers of the poem, Cleopatra's Nile; the Rhine, so recently also running with blood; the Thames. Beyond that, it merges into the larger bodies of water that provided routes for the great maritime empires. All the cities of part 5 are associated with famous waters. And the great maritime empire of 1922, on which the sun never set, has behind it the great maritime empire of Rome, and behind that the greatest (we are told) maritime empire of them all, Phoenicia's, whose sailors and ships were a source of power for centuries, and a byword for good seamanship. (One of Phoenicia's sailors appears in parts 1 and 4 of *The Waste Land.*) At the naval battle of Mylae in the First Punic War, its erstwhile colony Carthage was defeated by Rome. In the Second and Third Punic Wars, Carthage was again defeated; in the Third War, Carthage was besieged, and, when the city had been taken, its citizens were slaughtered, the city leveled and sown with salt in order to make the soil sterile, and the site dedicated to the infernal gods. The Carthage to which Augustine came was a rebuilt Carthage.

The phrase "a Carthaginian Peace" would therefore mean a peace settlement so punitive as to destroy the enemy entirely and even to make sterile the land on which he lives. What it does to the victor is another question. In December 1919, John Maynard Keynes published *The Economic Consequences of the Peace*, in which he passionately denounced the Treaty of Versailles as a

"Carthaginian Peace." (He had resigned as representative of the British Treasury at the Peace Conference.) The book was widely read (according to Etienne Mantoux's *The Carthaginian Peace*, it had been translated into eleven languages and sold some 140,000 copies by 1924), and whether or how far the peace treaties were a Carthaginian Peace was widely disputed. Eliot, as the Lloyds representative "in charge of settling all the pre-War Debts between the Bank and the Germans, 'an important appointment, full of interesting legal questions', . . . was kept busy 'trying to elucidate knotty points in that appalling document the Peace Treaty.' "[12] Evidence that Eliot read *The Economic Consequences of the Peace* may be found in his article on Keynes in the *New English Weekly*, 16 May 1946 (29, no. 5: 47–48). In a "London Letter" in the *Dial*, March 1921, Eliot refers to the "respect . . . with which Clemenceau and Lloyd George bonified President Wilson." The view of the respect and the bonifying among the three men is Keynes's view. In Eliot's later remark, quoted above, "I am all for empires, especially the Austro-Hungarian Empire," the view of the Austro-Hungarian Empire is also Keynes's.

The phrasing in *The Economic Consequences of the Peace* evokes an apocalyptic foreboding and sense of nightmare very like that in *The Waste Land*.[13] Keynes wrote that he himself came to be "haunted by other and more dreadful specters. Paris was a nightmare, and everyone there was morbid. A sense of impending catastrophe overhung the frivolous scene . . . the mingled significance and unreality of decisions. . . . The proceedings of Paris all had this air of extraordinary importance and unimportance at the same time. The decisions seemed charged with consequences to the future of human society; yet the air whispered that the word was not flesh, that it was futile, insignificant, of no effect, dissociated from events." In the "hot, dry room in the President's house . . . the Four fulfilled their destinies in empty and arid intrigue." Clemenceau, "dry in soul and empty of hope, very old and tired," schemed on behalf of the "policy of an old man, whose most vivid impressions and most lively imagination are of the past and not of the future." Paris was a "morass," its atmosphere "hot and poisoned," its halls "treacherous." "Then began the weaving of that web of sophistry and Jesuitical exegesis." "In this autumn of 1919, in which I write, we are at the dead season of our fortunes. . . . Our power of feeling or caring beyond the immediate questions of our own material well-being is temporarily eclipsed." This is not Pound speaking, or Hesse: it is Keynes, who supports his plea with pages of detailed economic argument that would have interested Eliot professionally. ("I want to find out something about the science of money while I am at it: it is an extraordinarily interesting subject," Eliot wrote to his mother on 11 April 1917, just after joining Lloyds Bank.[14] And to Lytton Strachey on 1 June 1919: "You are very — ingenuous — if you can conceive me conversing with rural deans in the cathedral close. I do not go to cathedral towns but to centres of industry. My thoughts are absorbed in questions more important than ever enters the heads of deans — as *why* it is cheaper to buy steel bars from America than from Middlesbrough, and the probable effect — the exchange difficulties with Poland — and the appreciation of the rupee.")[15]

Ezra Pound saw London as another Carthage: "London has just escaped from the First World War, but it is certain to be destroyed by the next one, because it is in the hands of the international financiers. The very place of it will be sown with salt, as Carthage was, and forgotten by men; or it will be sunk under water."[16] But in 1922, I think Eliot saw London as primarily another Rome, who had brought a famous trading enemy to her knees. Commenting on the use of Mylae in *The Waste Land*, Cleanth Brooks notes that the "Punic War was a trade war — might be considered a rather close parallel to our late war."[17] And Keynes quotes Clemenceau's view that England in World War I, as in each preceding century, had destroyed a trade rival. The poem's one-eyed merchant and Mr. Eugenides from Smyrna with his shorthand trading terms are figures of importance in an empire.[18] "Money is, after all, life blood," Spender reminds us. The sense of doom in the 1920's "emanated from the revolutionary explosions and still more from the monetary collapse of central Europe."[19] Carthage is in *The Waste Land* not only because of its connections with Dido and Aeneas, *The Tempest*, and St. Augustine; not only as a colony of Phoenicia, Phoenicia who had given the Greeks most of their alphabet, which in turn was given to the Romans (by Greeks at Cumae?); not only as part of a great maritime empire. It is in the poem also because Carthage was Rome's great rival, as at the beginning of the *Aeneid*, and the relations between the two were a pattern for enmity so established that Keynes could use the phrase "a Carthaginian Peace" without further explanation. The argument for declaring the third war against Carthage (repeated again and again by Cato the Censor, with his famous refrain "Carthago delenda est") was the argument at the center of the controversy over the peace treaties: whether the reviving prosperity of a defeated trade rival could become a danger to the victor. In a poem of 1922, to introduce the battle of Mylae where the reader expects a reference to a World War I battle is to raise chilling questions. The line out of Baudelaire's Paris, which follows the spectral Mylae speech and ends part 1, does not help either, for those who had read Keynes: "You! hypocrite lecteur! — mon semblable, — mon frère!"

For a Carthaginian peace is one that slowly but surely deflects back upon the victor. It is a common argument that Roman life began to decline after the Punic wars. As long as Rome was in a state of war, Augustine writes near the beginning of *The City of God*, she could maintain concord and high standards of civic life. "But after the destruction of Carthage," he continues, quoting Sallust, "there came the highest pitch of discord, greed, ambition, and all the evils which generally spring up in times of prosperity" (2.18).[20] The argument was repeated by Lecky in 1877: "complete dissolution of Roman morals began shortly after the Punic wars" (*OED*, s.v. *Punic*, A.1). Keynes similarly argues his case as much on behalf of the victors as the vanquished: "they [France and Italy] invite their own destruction also, being so deeply and inextricably intertwined with their victims by hidden psychic and economic bonds." "If we aim deliberately at the impoverishment of Central Europe, . . . nothing can then delay for very long that final civil war . . . which will destroy, whoever is victor, the civilization and progress of our generation." For Rome the victor, and so long the victor that it must have seemed invincible, the eventual turn of time brings Alaric and Attila. Rome itself experiences destruction. St. Augustine, who telescopes history much as Eliot does, argues that the destruction of Rome is only fitting, for the outward devastation only matches the collapse of the inner fabric of society. "For in the ruin of our city it was stone and timber which fell to the ground; but in the lives of those Romans we saw the collapse not of material but of moral defences, not of material but of spiritual grandeur. The lust that burned in their hearts was more deadly than the flame which consumed their dwellings" (2.1). This is true not only of public life, but also of private. "Now a man's house ought to be the beginning, or rather a small component part of the city, and every beginning is directed to some end of its own kind. . . . domestic peace contributes to the peace of the city" (19.16).

No argument that Rome provides the preeminent pattern for London in *The Waste Land* can ignore the classic exposition of the *civitas Romae* and the *civitas Dei*, Augustine's *City of God*. Spender speaks of the implicit contrast in

The Waste Land of the two cities, and he is surely right about this.[21] The original drafts twice included references to an ideal city, although in the end Eliot omitted any explicit reminder of a *civitas Dei*. One reference was in part 3, and read as follows: "Not here, O Glaucon [originally Ademantus], but in another world" (l. 120), which is annotated in Valerie Eliot's edition of the drafts of the poem: "Adeimantus and Glaucon, brothers of Plato, were two of the interlocutors in *The Republic*. Appalled by his vision of the 'Unreal City', Eliot may be alluding to the passage (Book IX, 592 A–B), which inspired the idea of the City of God among Stoics and Christians, and found its finest exponent in St. Augustine" (127–28). As the poem's shape changed, the ideal city shifted. In a draft of the speech of Madame Sosostris in part 1, the following line is inserted in a bracket after the present line 56: "I John saw these things, and heard them"; the quotation, from near the end of Revelation, refers not only to John's vision of judgment, but more particularly to his vision of the New Jerusalem, which immediately precedes it. Eliot finally cut all references to an ideal city, because, I think, the developing theme of urban and imperial apocalypse refused to accommodate so firm a hope as that in *The Republic* or Revelation. What Eliot kept from the Johannine vision was the dark view of the earthly city or Babylon. The sense of an impending *dies irae* hangs over most of his poem.

Augustine's earthly city is, of course, Babylon also, together with Babylon's daughter, Rome ("Babylonia, quasi prima Roma . . . ipsa Roma quasi secunda Babylonia" [18.2]). And over Augustine's earthly city, the *civitas Romae*, there also hangs a sense of doom in *The City of God*. Rome had been forewarned of her destruction, writes Augustine, by Sibylline prophecy, and the same prophecies warn her of the final apocalypse. Augustine is one of the Church fathers responsible for the conversion of Virgil's Sibyl into a Christian prophetess, and, if Virgil's Sibyl of Cumae lives behind the Sibyl of Cumae in *The Waste Land*, so also, I think, may the later Christian Sibyl. "The Sibyl of Erythrae or, as some are inclined to believe, of Cumae . . . is evidently to be counted among those who belong to the City of God," writes Augustine (18.24). And he goes on to quote in full the Sibylline oracle that prophesies a day of judgment, using sources from both the Old and New Testaments, the oracle especially famed because its initial letters form an acrostic in Greek that spells *fish*, one of the common symbols for Christ in the early Church.[22] There are other fates for the Sibyl than the fate Petronius portrays and Eliot quotes, although they offer no comfort to the inhabitant or the reader of *The Waste Land*. The Sibyl may find her way into the words of the *dies irae* ("teste David cum Sibylla"), and her verses might be called the fifteen signs of the judgment and sung in some places as late as 1549.[23] Whatever evidence is chosen, this Sibyl is associated with the collapse of Rome and also with the final apocalypse and the day of judgment. In 1921, Eliot was considering poetic treatments of the day of judgment at least enough to make clear how not to treat it: some poets, he wrote in the Spring issue of *Tyro*, "could imagine the Last Judgment only as a lavish display of Bengal lights, Roman candles, catherine wheels, and inflammable fire-balloons. *Vous, hypocrite lecteur. . . .*"

Eliot's dark vision of the earthly city may be close to Augustine's dark vision of the *civitas Romae*, but it goes without saying that for Augustine the activities associated with any Fisher King, like those in *The Waste Land*, would be evidence only of superstition. *The City of God* includes references to such activities only to attack them. The belief, for example, that the Delphic Apollo might have inflicted sterility upon the land is mere superstition (18.12); so are fears of an evil spell cast upon the land that motivate the fertility rites (7.24). It is likewise superstition that inspires the familiar proverb "Pluuia defit, causa Christiani sunt" ("No rain! It's all the fault of the Christians" [2.3]). Welldon's edition of *The City of God* notes that Augustine makes use of this proverb frequently, and it is a proverb that, read with varying degrees of irony, may be applied very handily to *The Waste Land*.[24]

In an apocalyptic mode, the world may seem split into the sweetness of a visionary, ideal, and virtually unattainable world and the sordidness of an actual, present, and virtually inescapable world. There is no middle ground, and practical, temporal concerns and governance are left to others. This kind of painful contrast is what gives *The Waste Land* its poignancy. It is the viewpoint of someone not at home in the world, a peregrine, like Augustine. Augustine was an outsider in more than one sense: not only was his over-whelming allegiance given to another world, but he was a provincial in the Roman Empire, one of the *peregrini* or resident aliens during his stay in Milan.[25] In *The Waste Land*, he takes his place among those other great exiles or provincials who perhaps understood their city and their empire all the better for having been exiles or provincials: Ezekiel, Ovid, Dante. And Eliot? One of Eliot's quotations is from the psalm of exile, with its passionate love of

Jerusalem, and its cry, "How shall we sing the Lord's song in a strange land?" The cry echoes behind the homeless voices of *The Waste Land*.

But the Jewish voices were able to utter this psalm or to include an Ezekiel. In the twentieth century, there remain only fragmented voices, a desiccated Sibyl. The apocalyptic mode in *The Waste Land* moves toward its own destruction in the disintegration of the uses of language. Augustine, whose etymology is highly idiosyncratic, thought that the name Babylon was connected with the name Babel. Babylon may thus also be called "confusion," and "punishment in the form of a change of language" is the fate of a Babel or of any Babylon or of any Rome — a punishment some readers may feel Eliot demonstrates with peculiar force. (Another twentieth-century example of this punishment had been seen at the Peace Conference, where the difficulties of negotiating had been compounded by the fact that only Clemenceau, among the Four, spoke both French and English.)

The dangers of abandoning the middle ground of practical, temporal affairs are all too apparent. At the end of *The Waste Land*, there is a turning, or rather a returning, toward this middle earth, and away from exile or private grief. The apocalyptic mode is useful, but not for long. It provides an ideal, but no working pattern for living in this world. A working pattern without an ideal may very well collapse sooner or later, but an ideal with no working pattern can find terrible ways to translate itself into action, or can find itself readily outmaneuvered and paralyzed. Augustine does not ignore the question of how to live in the earthly city. And Keynes, at the end of *The Economic Consequences of the Peace*, tempers his own dark vision with practical suggestions for relieving the nightmare.

The Waste Land, in the end, retains its geographical unity, but the unity becomes far more complex. London as a city forms one focal point. The maps shift, as we muse on the poem, and London becomes a center of empire, another Rome. Do they ever shift again, so that London and Rome become Jerusalem, the center of Dante's world? Never, in the old sense, and not until "Little Gidding" in a mystical sense, and by this time the center may be anywhere, "England and nowhere. Never and always."

TWO

Schemes Against Coercion:
Geoffrey Hill, Elizabeth Bishop, and Others

... the inertia of language, which is also the coercive force of language.

— GEOFFREY HILL[1]

French-English Scheming in 'The Mystery of the Charity of Charles Péguy'

Geoffrey Hill's grave and moving tribute in his 1983 poem *The Mystery of the Charity of Charles Péguy* is moving in a particular way for a Canadian. Hill has chosen to work with French words so as to make them part of his English poem. This includes work with schemes in the oldest English sense of the word—that is, rhetorical schemes such as a rhyme scheme. It is one of the strengths of poetry that even such apparently small and purely poetic effects can speak to large matters in the hands of a master craftsman.

I cannot recall anything like Hill's schematic work with French and English. James Joyce's multilingual wordplay is different in kind. Other multi- or bilingual effects for the most part read like novelties, as do variations on macaronics. A. M. Klein's pleasing little poem, "Montreal," is of this last sort.

> O city metropole, isle riverain!
> Your ancient pavages and sainted routs
> Traverse my spirit's conjured avenues!
> Splendour erablic of your promenades

> Foliates there, and there your maisonry
> Of pendant balcon and escalier'd march,
> Unique midst English habitat,
> Is vivid Normandy!

(A. M. Klein, The Complete Poems [1990])

Even skillful polyglot rhymes by Pound or Eliot seem to me more limited, because they are scarce and so often used for ironic effect. What Hill has achieved is of another order.

Take, for instance, his opening French-English rhyme (1.1–2):

> Crack of a starting-pistol. Jean Jaurès
> dies in a wine-puddle. Who or what stares. . . .

Hill closes part 1 as follows (stanza 8):

> The brisk celluloid clatters through the gate;
> the cortège of the century dances in the street;
> and over and over the jolly cartoon
> armies of France go reeling towards Verdun.

"The brisk celluloid clatters through the gate." Throughout this first part, we read about war and see images of war in our mind's eye, notably of the 1914–18 Great War. For a moment, we may hear horses in that verb *clatter*, the horses of a cavalry troop from World War I going through a gate, until another reading takes over, and we know we are watching a film about the war. (A gate on a movie projector is the hole through which light is projected.) Hill has made a little allegory of the act of reading, reminding us that reading is always reading-through, just as seeing is always seeing-through. We read and see through the evidence we have, and perforce through the schemata we have learned, for example, from film.

Hill is working with pun and enjambment as well as rhyme effects. This is a reel of film and the armies also appear to reel. Then, too, the word *cartoon* is a noun, we assume, until enjambment surprises us, and it turns out to be an adjective, as we ourselves stride over the end of the line (poetic, not military) to the start of the next line: "Jolly cartoon" modifies *armies* grammatically, but also semantically and in a most disjunctive way. The rhyme on *cartoon . . . Verdun* is similarly disjunctive. "Violent contrariety of men and days" reads line 1 of stanza 7. Violent contrariety of adjective and noun, and of rhyme also.

"Jolly cartoon / armies" reflects the way that old films look to our eyes. We know these films record actual human beings, like us, flesh-and-blood soldiers, many of whom died at Verdun. Yet they *look* cartoonlike, jerking along like animated Walt Disney figures, because our eyes have now been trained by far more advanced techniques in filmmaking. (Hill does not say so, but this advance in our movie-watching eyes has occurred at the same time as a decline in our poetry-reading eyes. And how many people who assume filmmaking techniques are worth studying also assume that poetic techniques are worth studying?) We can play and replay those reels of film, making the dead march toward their death over and over again. For them it happened once, and they were gone. The *oon . . . un* near rhyme at the end extracts *dun* from "Verdun," and we may hear an echo of the verb *to do* moving over to *done* in a final reel for those cartoon armies. For us, this is what we call history, something we can watch from the outside.

In the opening rhyme too, Hill can make us see early twentieth-century men and also see our own act of seeing.

> Crack of a starting-pistol. Jean Jaurès
> dies in a wine-puddle. Who or what stares
> through the café-window. . . .

Hill has so phrased the question that we do not know whether Jaurès's dead eyes stare through the window, or whether the assassin stares in at what he has done, or whether spectators stare in at the sight, or whether some spirit of the age stares. His preposition *through* covers all these cases: the victim, the assassin, the spectator, the spirit. The reader may imaginatively take the place of each one, although chiefly the reader is a spectator from the outside. But Hill can make us feel a little uncomfortable in this role. His questions bend far away from common movie thrills:

> Did Péguy kill Jaurès? Did he incite
> the assassin? Must men stand by what they write . . . ?

By his rhyme, Hill has linked noun and verb, *Jaurès* and *stares*. In a classic essay, "One Relation of Rhyme to Reason,"[2] W. K. Wimsatt suggests that rhyming the same parts of speech might be called "tame rhyme." Rhyming different parts of speech is more effective, to judge from the example of Pope, than rhyming a noun with a noun or a verb with a verb. Wimsatt does not offer a reason for this, perhaps because it is self-evident. Two different parts of speech can more readily set up a little plot or allegory, even a core sentence. That is what happens here. There are actually two possible core sentences: "Jaurès stares" and "stares [at] Jaurès," with the assassination acted out in this small rhyming drama of staring.

There are only so many tropes for the process of reading or seeing, and the window is one of the best known. We see through its transparent glass; our seeing is framed; we can also see ourselves reflected, at a certain angle, and our reflection may lie over what we see like some ghostly second presence. The window through which we see what is represented, yet the window that also shows us ourselves in the act of looking; the transparency and the mirror: this makes a fine trope for reading. In a piece of film, the process is reversed. The shadowy images on a strip of film can be seen through, and so superimposed on a present scene. All these metaphors of seeing-through and inside-outside caution us against any easy inside-outside model of reading.

There is another effect of this opening rhyme of a French and an English word. In this English poem about French matters, yet also about deeply English matters, the question of how to handle another language is inescapable. Think of it as a practical problem. You are going to write about a Frenchman, a French poet, a French poet good enough to be published in a Pléiade edition. What will you do about his language? A few stray quotations? How will French proper names enter your text? How will an English tongue pronounce them? What will you say to the hovering spirit of this dead writer whom you are recalling, as you choose your English words and measure their distance from a French sense of things? Will you remember that the English language is also French, in the sense that French has been widely interwoven in English since 1066?

Hill has thought through this problem before he begins, for there the problem is, in the first main scheme of his poem, "Jaurès . . . stares." Pronounce these words and hear how each one pulls the other a little in its own direction. I concentrated earlier on the signification connecting these words, when developing the possibilities of a core sentence, "Jaurès stares" or "stares [at] Jaurès." Now listen how the name *Jaurès* sounds when it is pulled toward *stares*. It is flattened, anglicized, and we hear a foreigner pronouncing the name. Or rather, we hear someone like us pronouncing this name, and it is heard as one of those foreign names about which we are uncertain, or which we are poorly trained to utter.

But listen to the corresponding effect with the word *stares* if we pull it a little toward *Jaurès*. Turn the *r* of *stares* into a French *r*, and lengthen the *-res* a little so that *stares* approximates a disyllabic word. Does this not evoke, if only slightly, a stage figure, someone picturesque, perhaps a little comical? Instead of a parallel neutral response to an anglicized *Jaurès*, do we not find a stereotype of the foreigner, the non-English speaker, emerging from its hiding-place in our minds? And if this is so for a British reader of Hill's poem, what are we to say of a Canadian reader, because French is not a foreign language in this country, but one of the two official languages of Canada. When we hear English-Canadian speakers flatten and anglicize French words, and then hear a corresponding French-Canadian treatment of English words, do we hear these in the same spirit?

Every section of Hill's ten-part poem includes French-English rhyme. Of twenty-two examples, thirteen are proper names, and Hill's work with them is instructive. He rhymes on the name *Péguy* only in part 8 (apart from the muted rhyme in the title), and he rhymes on the name *Chartres* in part 10 in a remarkable use of closure. I have not included the word *France* in this count, because we pronounce that word in its anglicized form. Suddenly to insert the French *France* in an English poem, unless there is a clear signal to do so, would be to introduce M. le Snob himself. Still, we are not allowed to forget altogether the difference between the French *France* and *France* in Hill's poem:

> . . . proud tears,
> proud tears, for the forlorn hope, the guerdon
> of Sedan, "oh les braves gens!", English Gordon
> stepping down sedately into the spears.

> (5.49–52)

English Gordon. "English Gordon," General Gordon, is indeed one epitome of Englishness in the Victorian era (see Lytton Strachey's *Eminent Victorians*). But in this poem so full of French names, Hill is also reminding us that this one is pronounced '*Gor-don* and not *Gor-'don* . The rhyme-word '*guer-don* similarly has an English pronunciation, although it derives from Old French.

So there are signals not to forget altogether about the sound of *France* as pronounced by a French person. And these signals in turn show us another way that schemes can work.

Here are the first three examples in which *France* is a rhyme word:

> . . . the old soldiers of old France
> crowd like good children wrapped in obedience. . . .
>
> *(2.13–14)*

> To dispense, with justice; or, to dispense
> with justice. Thus the catholic god of France. . . .
>
> *(6.1–2)*

> . . . name your own recompense,
> expecting nothing but the grace of France. . . .
>
> *(8.18–19)*

These are all compound rhymes, rhyming a multisyllabic word with two or more monosyllabic words. (This effect is sometimes called mosaic rhyming.) Hill does remarkable work with this type of scheme, as for example in part 1, stanza 4:

> Did Péguy kill Jaurès? Did he incite
> the assassin? Must men stand by what they write
> as by their camp-beds or their weaponry
> or shell-shocked comrades while they sag and cry?

Weaponry sounds professional and impersonal. "Standing by" weaponry, when the metaphor is literalized, includes standing at attention during inspection, also standing by or near when weaponry is in use and, to retain the sense of the metaphor, remaining faithful to it. Remaining faithful to the purpose of weaponry in war means using it to kill, which in turn means that others fall by it, so that the impersonal word *weaponry* rightly calls out for a rhyme like "sag and cry." The dactylic stress of *weaponry* makes the second verb, *cry*, fade a little, with *sag* coming first, and *cry* itself sagging a little. Hill's poem is full of such work with compound rhymes, where a rhyme scheme begins to function as a trope.

The rhymes on *France* are all compound, apart from the last example. If we hear the ghost of a French *France*, the effect is very striking. For all three compound rhyme words also exist in cognate form in French. And in French, the rhyme would be full (or true) rhyme. If we make a little allegory of this, as Hill's scheming encourages us to do, we hear a ghostly French linking, a true and not a part linking, of *France* with *obedience, recompense,* and *dispense*: *France, obéissance, récompense, dispense*. (*Obéissance* has a wider meaning that includes "allegiance"; *dispense* includes exemption from military service. The words repay attention.)[3] The last rhyme on *France* is part of Hill's conclusion, and it is very different.

> J'accuse! j'accuse! — making the silver prance
> and curvet, and the dust-motes jig to war
> across the shaky vistas of old France,
> the gilt-edged maps of Strasbourg and the Saar.

> *(10.33–36)*

Monosyllable with monosyllable now, and for the first time, a full rhyme, so that the ghostly French pronunciation is kept back in "prance/France." Nor is there any cognate French word for "prance." It comes from — but where does it come from? Here the *OED* fails us:

> Prance . . . origin obscure: see *Note* below. . . . *Note*: The phonology and spelling of *praunse, pranse* . . . suggest French origin but no corresponding or allied word is recorded in French. Danish dialects have *prandse, pranse*. . . . These resemble the Eng. word; but their age and history are unknown [both eds.].

There are many full rhymes on *France*, as any rhyming dictionary will tell us. Mine gives twenty, apart from *prance*. Hill wanted this word, I think, because this scheme adds to his earlier troping on *France*. Now it is a full rhyme, so that we hear two terms, rather than the potential four terms of a near rhyme. Yet even so, we hear a ghost in the missing etymon for the English word *prance*. Behind modern *prance*, there should be a ghostly French parent or sibling *praunce*. So it was with *obedience, recompense,* and *dispense*. This time, the pull toward French comes in the English word itself, and what seemed simply English *France* turns out to be the French *France* a little too. Hill's conclusion quietly takes its leaves of etymological and cognate linguistic ghosts in a very fine turning of earlier effects.

What about French words other than proper names? Here I want to move away from rhyme and consider patterns of accents and italics. To quote T. S.

Eliot on punctuation: "Verse, whatever else it may or may not be, is itself a system of *punctuation*; the usual marks of punctuation are themselves differently employed."[4] So also with accents and italics. Hill uses an *accent aigu* on *café* (see above) and follows this immediately with a more noticeable accent on another hard-*c* word, a *circonflexe* on the word *crêped*. How do we decide when to retain and when to drop an accent on a word from another language? Like rhyme, these things may mean nothing at all in a piece of writing except what dictionary A or B says, or perhaps that the author doesn't know or care what dictionary A or B says anyway. What do we do with such a word? The usual convention is to italicize, and that is quite straightforward. The difficulty comes when a word is in process of being assimilated. At some point, we stop italicizing and use roman, but we may retain accents, at least for a while. The word *élite* sometimes keeps its accent and sometimes does not. In Hill's poem, it does. How often do we still retain accents on *café* and *crêpe*? Hill does, and on the word *châtelaine*. On the other hand, he hardly ever italicizes French words, even those that are entirely French and come over into his English text without quotation marks. The effect, to my eye, is twofold. First, we easily accommodate French words, where appropriate, in an English poem, without making them stand out in their lines, stepping forward in an italic uniform instead of the decent roman uniform that most of our words wear. Second, Hill reminds us quietly but repeatedly that the English language (like all languages) cannot claim ethnic or national purity. Without thinking of origins, we call a certain fabric "crêpe." Decisions to italicize or not, to add accents or not, are small printing decisions that can do much poetic work.

In these words, we see in little the diachronic history of words, *parole* as against *langue*, where some words began as foreign words, became more familiar, dropped italics and retained accents, dropped accents and became fully assimilated—all smoothly, or so we like to think. In fact, our peaceable word-histories encapsulate other kinds of history. The Anglo-Saxon and French branches of the Germanic and Latinate languages did not intermarry because of a love match or a tranquil arranged match. They married because of William the Conqueror. The *Oxford English Dictionary* is a history of warfare, among other things. Hill's war poem makes us think about the condition of words in this context. He does not allow us the comfort of carelessness, as though the proper condition of all words were to attain pure Englishness and forget the fact of other languages. For him, the condition of language requires alertness, perhaps skirmish, perhaps battle. So it should be, say the poets — Eliot, for instance, in his military metaphors in *Four Quartets*:

> . . . And so each venture
> Is a new beginning, a raid on the inarticulate
> With shabby equipment always deteriorating
> In the general mess of imprecision of feeling,
> Undisciplined squads of emotion. . . .
>
> *("East Coker," pt. 5)*

So it should be, Hill implies, because "the inertia of language . . . is also its coercive force."

Hill's meditations on questions of honor and warfare are also meditations on language, or rather not also, but necessarily, for language is part of the world of swords. There is a little schematic parable of words and swords in part 6 that tells us as much:

> Here there should be a section without words
> for military band alone: "Sambre et Meuse",
> the "Sidi Brahim" or "Le Roi s'Amuse";
> white gloves and monocles and polished swords. . . .

The first line reads like a stage or filmmaking direction, or a direction to the reader. We hear the referential force of Hill's musical titles, and we listen to the unheard tunes of those fancied military marches. We smile, because of course we are hearing words, not music. Then we come over the white space at the end of this stanza, as over a parade-ground or wordless place, with the pleasures of military marches in our ears. We do end on *swords*, of course, with a fine reworking of the old *words/swords* rhyme, a rhyme that is to be "without words," or so we are told. Words and swords may be in antithesis, as in the proverbial pen that is mightier than, etc. Words are sometimes said to be stronger than monumental brass, the might of kings, and so on, especially by poets, especially when they are young. Hill does not allow such ready assertions; he has opened his poem by questioning the relation of words and swords. ("Did he incite / the assassin? Must men stand by what they write / as by their camp-beds . . . ?") Swords are never without words in one sense: the word *sword* has *word* built into it.

So then, we walk across that white space (and over the page, as it happens, in the book), and what do we find? A fine celebratory day, with military ceremony and dress uniforms and light band music? Not quite:

> Here there should be a section without words . . .
> white gloves and monocles and polished swords
>
> and Dreyfus with his buttons off, chalk-faced
> but standing to attention. . . .

The scheme of *words/swords* is still in our heads when someone moves "to snap the traitor's sword." This is another kind of military ceremony, another relation of words and swords, the possible undoing of one by the other — not the glory but the shame. "Must men stand by what they write / as by their camp-bed or their weaponry . . . ?" "Stand by," "standing to attention." Who or what stood by or stood to in the Dreyfus affair?

The military tunes are still in our heads two stanzas later when we read "Drumrap and fife." This is not a section evoking fife-and-drum military tunes, not a portion of the film without words. There are words, all right, and Hill has built a French-English rhyme with his usual precision: *fife*, the pleasing fife of some military band, plays only a near rhyme on *Juif*, a repeated *Juif*:

> Drumrap and fife
> hit the right note: "A mort le Juif! Le Juif. . . ."

In French we can hear another rhyme, *fifre/Juif*, and that ghostly near rhyme becomes a deadly little trope for the whole of the Dreyfus case.

In his closing stanzas, Hill returns to some of the rhymes in part 1, including a rhyme on the sound of *stares*. The burial detail comes to gather Péguy's body on the battlefield,

> his arm over his face as though in sleep
>
> or to ward off the sun: the body's prayer
> the tribute of his true passion, for Chartres
> steadfastly cleaving to the Beauce, for her,
> the Virgin of innumerable charities.

The scheme of *a* and *b* rhymes, whether *abab* or *abba* or *aabb*, here merges the twofold scheme, and with a memory of the opening stanza, also a stanza of death: "prayer . . . Chartres . . . for her . . . charities." All the rhymes are near rhymes, and of great force. *Prayer* rhymes with *for her*, the rhyme pulling *prayer* toward two syllables, as if the word were a homonymic pun, both a petition and a petitioner. Or rather as if the prayer as petition (whether in Péguy's final moments or earlier) had given way, as it must, to the petitioner as body. *Prayer* also rhymes in its first syllable with *Chartres*, providing the extraordinary ghost rhyme of *cher*, which then also echoes behind *charities*. *Chartres* is rhymed with *charities*, "charities" in the old sense, taking on the force of *caritas*, or Christian love, while the sound of the first syllable, *char-*, also rhymes on *prayer*. The body and prayers of Péguy, the cathedral, the object of Péguy's prayers in one sense and then in a larger sense: all these are intertwined in these ghostly schematic effects. We hear, as it were, a living voice joining the dead, who are nonetheless alive and echoing behind our words.

We begin with an old film, and we end there too, and with maps and history books. Hill comes from staring at the old movies of war to an act of prayer, and then in the last two stanzas to the intertwined French and English "éloge and elegy" that is his poem.

Scheming and Troping

Schemes. I have been showing how such patternings can lay out fables and allegories. Perhaps schemes, in their heart of hearts, desire to be something other. Perhaps they are themselves schemers, and the scheme they have in mind is how to get to be a trope. *Scheme* in this sense, the oldest meaning listed in the *Oxford English Dictionary*, is marked as now obsolete, surviving in general use only in terms like *rhyme scheme*. But as we recover a little of the rhetorical knowledge lost in the nineteenth century, we have gained a few rhetorical terms beyond the old standard grade-school *onomatopoeia*, *alliteration*, and the like. *Trope* is one such term, and can be variously defined. When it is one of two classes of figures of speech, then the term *scheme* also comes on stage in its wider, older rhetorical sense as the other of the two classes.

A scheme in this sense is a figure of speech in which ordinary meaning is not overtly changed — for example, alliteration or chiasmus (*xyyx*) or rhyme. A trope is a figure of speech (some prefer to say, a figure of thought), such as metaphor or metonymy, in which ordinary meaning is overtly changed or turned. (The root meaning of *trope*, from τρόπος, is "turn.") The word *overtly* is important in both these definitions. In schemes, what the *OED* calls "signification" (class 3 of a word's meaning) does not alter when some surface arrangement is made. Of course, meaning in a wider sense is affected. If you find a rhyme of *moon/June*, it says to you: see this inept poet. Or: see this ironic poet. Or just possibly: see this courageous poet. That too is meaning. In tropes, signification does alter, so that the *OED* will assign *fig.* to well-known tropical meanings. But schemes are those "patternings of elements of language . . . which carry no meanings per se."[5]

This is not the place to consider very far why figures that are meaningless per se should be interesting. One answer is mnemonic. Rhymes or alliteration help us to remember, and so are useful ("Thirty days hath September . . ."; "*I* before *e*, except after *c* . . ."). Richard Wilbur says that rhyme "also has the virtue of meaninglessness," but "is a device of great formal and magical value." "Meaninglessness" can "suggest comparisons and conditions . . . with the same briskness and license with which a patient's mind responds to the psychologist's word-association test."[6] Meaninglessness is not devoid of meaning then. Roman Jakobson implies as much: "Whatever the relation between sound and meaning in different rhyme techniques, both spheres are necessarily involved." Or again: "Valéry's view of poetry as 'hesitation between the sound and the sense' is much more realistic and scientific than any bias of phonetic isolationism."[7]

Here are a few quick examples of how schemes can work.

Tony Harrison, punning on *justified* in a poem called "Self Justification," offers "blank printer's ems" in the spaces around the word *eloquence*. This provides a justified right margin (in the only lines so justified in the poem):

> Their aggro towards me, my need of them's
> what keeps my would-be mobile tongue still tied —
>
> aggression, struggle, loss, blank printer's ems
> by which all   eloquence   gets justified.
>
> ("Self Justification," in *Selected Poems* [1984])

The conventions of printing stand in for other conventions of language that Harrison's tongue learned, then mastered, then turned to its own uses.

Or see Seamus Heaney's stanza on learning letters in elementary school:

Two rafters and a cross-tie on the slate
Are the letters some call *ah*, some call *ay*.
There are charts, there are headlines, there is a right
Way to hold the pen and a wrong way.

("Alphabet," in *The Haw Lantern* [1987])

Heaney, working with the sight and sound of the letter *A* (two possible sounds, actually), builds *ah* into his first noun ("rafters") and *ay* into his rhyme words. Again the conventions of poetic line breaks provide a scheme, here the word *right* on the right-hand edge. The word adds a syllable to the third line, whereas line 4 comes one syllable short — both acceptable variations. The lines would be entirely regular if the word *right* moved to the left-hand edge at the start of line 4, and the rhyme shifted to *abbb*. But how would we pronounce "*ay* . . . a . . . way"? Ah. Both Harrison and Heaney remind us of the conventions of the Queen's English, including its relation to matters of class and dialect, but also including its play and pleasure.

John Hollander's "Looking Ahead" ends thus:

In the tunnel now . . .
Hurtling on through the dark tube in which there is only
One direction, the way out. All this comes from looking
Ahead, seeing well what is there, and having to put
Something — in this case there are only our own eyes — in
The way of that final evening of all the odds.

("Looking Ahead," in *Harp Lake* [1988])

Hollander has punned on the word *evening* at the end of his poem, with *evening* as part of an even-odd set of contraries playing against *evening* as the end of the day. In this poem, evening is also a figure for death. That much is obvious. What may not be obvious is the play with a metrical scheme. The poem is written in thirteen-syllable lines, one of a series built this way. If we read *ev'ning* as the end of the day, we elide the second *e* and end with twelve syllables — that is, with an even-syllable line that is not even with all the other lines. But if we read *evening* as a gerund, we pronounce it as a three-syllable word and end up with a thirteen-syllable line: uneven syllables but an even line in the metrical scheme of things. The scheme becomes a double trope of death as ev'ning and death as evening, with attendant paradoxes.

Gjertrud Schnackenberg closes an elegiac series of poems in memory of her father, a historian, by describing William of Normandy:

> He swivels and lifts his visor up and roars,
> *Look at me well! For I am still alive!*
> Your glasses, lying on the desk, look on.

> ("There Are No Dead," in *Portraits and Elegies* [1982])

Schnackenberg encloses her two final lines within the scheme "Look at . . . look on." The scheme quietly weights the two prepositions, simply by contrast. *Look at* must take an object, but *look on* may be transitive or intransitive. In life, the glasses were a means of looking at and looking on, but now, with the peculiar pathos of objects once belonging to those we have loved, they "look on" without an object. "On . . . on," the closing line echoes, following its closing word. The glasses lie on the desk in a second sense, lying by offering a false surmise.

David Ferry's "The Guest Ellen at the Supper for Street People" is in the form of a sestina, with a set scheme of six repeated end-words. Here is the first stanza:

> The unclean spirits cry out in the body
> or mind of the guest Ellen in a loud voice
> torment me not, and in the fury of her unclean
> hands beating the air in some kind of unending torment—
> nobody witnessing could possibly know the event
> that cast upon her the spell of this enchantment.

> (in *Dwelling Places* [1993])

We usually translate the New Testament lexis of the "unclean spirits" into our own vocabulary, clinical, abstract, detached, psychological, sociological. It comes as a shock of recognition to see how well the ancient words suit a contemporary world. Ferry is a master of repetition, here and elsewhere. Repeating the end-word *unclean*, as a sestina's scheme requires, he brings together ancient and modern tormented souls throughout. His scheming does not "update" older English translations of biblical language, but rather enlarges our own poor language for such a state.

Finally, the visual schemes of James Merrill's posthumous poem "b o d y." The poem opens by asking us to look at the spaced characters of the title, characters that are actors and letters at once, and also provide a stage, into the bargain. The upright lines of *b* and *d* become the sides of the stage. The *o* becomes a moon, entering stage right as a half-moon or half of the letter *b* (stage directions are given from the actor's perspective), rolling across the stage as the full moon of the letter *o*, and exiting stage left as the half-moon of the letter *d*.

> Look closely at the letters. Can you see,
> entering stage right, then floating full,
> then heading off — so soon —
> how like a little kohl-rimmed moon
> *o* plots her course from *b* to *d*
>
> — as *y*, unanswered, knocks at the stage door?

> ("body," in *A Scattering of Salts* [1995])

b: birth. *d*: death. *y*: why? One lunar cycle stands in for a human life. (The old trope of the moon as eye also comes into play.) Now, when I see newspaper listings of the dates of the full and half-moon, with their familiar graphics, I often see Merrill's title too: "body." This visual scheme offers a trope of — well, of everything, all in one short word and ten lines. It is a virtuoso legacy that Merrill has bequeathed us.

Elizabeth Bishop, "North Haven"

Elizabeth Bishop's exquisite elegy for her friend Robert Lowell includes a remarkable scheme in the last line of stanza 4:

> The Goldfinches are back, or others like them,
> and the White-throated Sparrow's five-note song,
> pleading and pleading, brings tears to the eyes.
> Nature repeats herself, or almost does:
> *repeat, repeat, repeat; revise, revise, revise.*

How is this scheme working? First, as a mimesis of birdsong, "the White-throated Sparrow's five-note song," mimesis in the sense of miming. Italics mark the line as something quoted or heard, or remembered as such, like the italicized first stanza of "North Haven." In nature, this song starts on a given pitch with one or two clear sweet whistles, then moves to a different pitch and repeats three quavering notes. Where I hear it, the second pitch is a minor third above the first note. But wait. Bishop's scheme mimes a six-note and not a five-note song. Ah well, we say, poetic licence. But Bishop doesn't let us away with this. See her closing stanza addressed to Lowell himself:

> You can't derange, or rearrange,
> your poems again. (But the sparrows can their song.)

Well, but, *can* they? Clearly, in this poem, it matters, now that Bishop has made a point of it. And she was a good amateur ornithologist, as well as an acute observer of the creaturely world at large. In fact, the authorities turn out to be not quite unanimous on the song and the way it behaves.[8] For one thing, the number of notes can vary somewhat.[9] Then, too, "as every birdwatcher knows, the song of each species usually follows a set pattern, but there is enough flexibility within the pattern for regional and individual variation."[10] I suppose a considerable variation could sound a bit "deranged," although mostly we register local variation as a rearrangement. (Is there a chance that white-throated sparrows go in for six-note songs in North Haven?)

Second, and most important, this simple scheme functions as a figure for the entire tradition of elegy, even as it marks Bishop's own revision of that entire and repeating tradition. How can this be, in so short a space? Bishop makes her birdsong emblematic of all Nature: "Nature repeats herself, or almost does." The point is anticipated in "The Goldfinches are back, or others like them." A similar line break and conjunction in lines 1 and 4 serves to emphasize the point. The first time I read the end of this stanza in the *New Yorker*, I thought, "She's done it, she's said it, and in poetry, in elegy itself." This was because of some lines that had stuck in my head years before, from Moschus's ancient "Lament for Bion," which stands at the beginning of elegy in the Western tradition:

> Ay me! when the mallows and the fresh green parsley and the springing crumpled anise perish in the garden, they live yet again and grow another year; but we men that are so tall and strong and wise, soon as ever we be dead, unhearing there in a hole of earth sleep we both sound and long.[11]

But as any gardener knows, mallows and parsley and anise don't live yet again, not the selfsame plants. Parsley is a biennial, so the roots live one year, although the stems and leaves are different. Only the roots of perennials remain, and as for annuals, nothing at all stays except for the seed. We usually let this go as an understandable trope, if we bother with it at all. (Even Tennyson, who grieved over nature's care of the species and carelessness of the individual, followed the old topos: "The seasons bring the flower again" [*In Memoriam* 2.5].) Bishop, an excellent naturalist, shows a faithfulness to the creaturely world throughout her work. So here she revises the ancient lament, and within the elegiac tradition itself, but how quietly and how extraordinarily simply. Nonetheless, she is altering the complex genre of elegy itself by her quiet acknowledgment, repeating it, yes, and revising it too. "Nature repeats herself, or almost does." This is how genres change, over the centuries: *repeat, repeat, repeat; revise, revise, revise.*

Third, the song, "pleading and pleading, brings tears to the eyes." Certainly, the beauty of the song, which is sweet and plaintive, and somewhat like an oboe to my ear, and which is often a harbinger of returning spring — certainly the beauty of this song can bring tears to the eyes. What is the sparrow pleading for? Most immediately, this is a mating song. Thus the logic of stanza 5. A whole train of thought interposes between the last line of stanza 4 and what follows:

> Years ago, you told me it was here
> (in 1932?) you first "discovered *girls*"
> and learned to sail, and learned to kiss.

Both spring birdsong and Lowell's (1932?) discovery of "*girls*" have to do with the world of generation, a world hard to avoid in elegy. Bishop touches on this side of Lowell's life obliquely, and with the tact of true friendship. Her small scheme embodies this world too. Children "*repeat, repeat, repeat; revise, revise, revise*" their parents and grandparents. Repeat, obviously, but also and happily, revise; nobody wants a clone for a child.

Fourth, Bishop's scheme works retrospectively for stanza 3, the flower stanza:

> Hawkweed still burning, Daisies pied, Eyebright,
> the Fragrant Bedstraw's incandescent stars,
> and more, returned, to paint the meadows with delight.

Here, the diction or lexis alerts us, by its archaic tone in so conversational a poem, that an older language is present ("pied," "paint the meadows with delight"), and so it is. Bishop is alluding to Shakespeare's spring song at the end of *Love's Labor's Lost*. Her scheme of *"repeat, repeat, repeat; revise, revise, revise"* is also a scheme for the workings of allusion, where we always both repeat and revise. Allusion repeats older words, obviously. It also always revises, even if minimally, in that it takes words out of their original context and puts them in a new dwelling place.

Fifth, the scheme reminds us that birdsong is often a figure for the voice of a poet, here Bishop's voice. After some words from Shakespeare's spring song, the poem turns, as if reminded of song, to birdsong, ending stanza 4 by itself breaking into song. Bishop has shaped her grammar so that *"repeat, repeat, repeat; revise, revise, revise"* can be indicative or imperative. "Pleading and pleading": what does elegy plead for, if not the impossible, and that is a return, a repeating of the presence of the dead loved one. The little scheme, read as imperative, seems to sing to Lowell in the voice of the poet as white-throated sparrow: *"Live."* Like all elegies, this one is an exercise in memory, and memory herself both repeats and revises, including a repetition of bird-song as poetic voice.

Sixth, and parenthetically, this sparrow is singularly appropriate for Bishop as a figure for her own poetic voice. For I think she might have known something else about the white-throated sparrow: "Males [among the song-birds] do most of the singing. . . . In a few species, including the . . . White-throated Sparrow, both sexes sing."[12] In an elegy in memory of a dearly loved friend, who once placed her among the best four women poets of the day, her song also smiles a little in this unheard troping.

Seventh, at the end, the white-throated sparrow's song is made parallel to Lowell's revising of his own work. Now the scheme breaks in two over the semicolon, and we see its full elegiac force. As long as bird or man is alive, the song can be changed. Once dead, the song and words can only repeat in our heads, revised by us, to be sure, but never again by the originator. No more can he change himself:

> You can't derange, or re-arrange,
> your poems again. (But the Sparrows can their song.)
> The words won't change again. Sad friend, you cannot change.

The whole nub of grief and solace in elegy is caught by Bishop's simple scheme. Grief lies in the word *repeat*, cut off from any revising from the dead.

Yet solace also lies in the word *repeat*, as elegy turns away from a nadir of grief to some form of continuing life, whether in a younger generation or in some continuing tradition. Revising does go on, although by others.

Finally, the scheme is itself a scheme of schemes, for this is how they work. We lay out schematic patterns all at once, spatially. Rhyme: *abab*. Chiasmus: *xyyx*. And so we consider a *moon/June* rhyme without regard to sequence. I myself felt free to play with the backwards order of *stares/Jaurès*. Yet it matters immensely in a poem that rhyme-word 1 comes first and rhyme-word 2 second. Schemes themselves are partly defined by sequential order in a way that tropes are not. (Refrains, for example, repeat the selfsame words, yet we do not hear them in the selfsame way because of the intervening stanzas.) Thus it is that a poet who uses schemes to exploit the possibilities of sequence can be especially powerful. Hill's schemes work so well because he is reflecting precisely on sequence: on history, war, belief, cause and effect. So is Bishop: on the sequences of a life and of poems. In her scheme for the white-throated sparrow's song, she has gone to the heart of the matter, and given us, very simply, a scheme of schemes: *"repeat, repeat, repeat; revise, revise, revise."*

THREE

Fables of War in Elizabeth Bishop

Reader, looke
Not on her Picture, but her Booke.[1]

"Paris, 7 A.M."

"Paris, 7 A.M." is a 1930's poem shadowed by war just as surely as Auden's
"September 1, 1939." Elizabeth Bishop lived in Paris during the winter of
1935–36; the poem was written by September 1936 and first published in
February 1937.[2] Because we currently bend our attention so assiduously to
Bishop's personal affairs, we catch very little of the feeling for which a Paris
apartment building is the objective correlative. Yet the correlation is just
right. It is a fine example of the indirection of poetry, as described by James
Merrill: "You hardly ever need to state your feelings. The point is to feel and
keep your eyes open. Then what you feel is expressed, is mimed back at you
by the scene. A room, a landscape. I'd go a step further. We don't *know* what
we feel until we see it distanced by this kind of translation."[3] If we look at
Bishop's poem with care, we can perceive a much-neglected aspect of her art:
her engagement with public questions.[4] Such engagement is more evident in
two remarkable poems also having to do with war and peace, "Roosters" and
"Brazil, January 1, 1502." Even so, we tend to underestimate Bishop's intel-

ligence and imaginative force in her fables that speak to the public realm, always indirectly.

"Paris, 7 A.M." invites an exercise in explication, for the poem is virtually unread. Here are the first six lines:

> I make a trip to each clock in the apartment:
> some hands point histrionically one way
> and some point others, from the ignorant faces.
> Time is an Etoile; the hours diverge
> so much that days are journeys round the suburbs,
> circles surrounding stars, overlapping circles.

David Kalstone, so often Bishop's best critic, saw how "the clock faces of the opening lines . . . merge into the map of Paris, the Etoile with its dispersing circles."[5] The Place de l'Etoile is round, like a clock-face, with avenues radiating out from it, diverging, so that it does appear starlike, especially on a map. The poem draws us toward a map of Paris, which tells us there are twelve avenues diverging out from the Place de l'Etoile, and thus one for each hour of the day, if we make a clock of l'Etoile. These avenues, with a little wiggling, do extend out into the suburbs so that, for imaginary clock hands going round l'Etoile, days are "journeys round the suburbs." The hour hand would sweep through two huge circles each day, and the minute hand through twenty-four circles. Hence line 6: "circles surrounding stars, overlapping circles."

Time and place provide our usual coordinates on waking and rising. So does observing the weather, as in lines 7–8:

> The short, half-tone scale of winter weathers
> is a spread pigeon's wing.

Not the iridescence of tones on a pigeon's throat, as when the sun glints on the damp slate roofs of Paris, and "les irise leurs ardoises gorge-de-pigeon," as Proust has it.[6] But instead, Paris winter skies, a short chromatic scale (punning on the word *tone*), bluish gray through to slate. (Overlaid winter clouds lapping each other do look like feathers on a pigeon's wings.) The skies are lying over us, not like a bowl in Anacreon, a bowl to tip and drink (a sunny sky, presumably), and not even like Stevens's white bowl sky in "The Poems of Our Climate." More like what we call a leaden sky. More like Dickinson's cap of lead: "A Cap of Lead across the sky / Was tight and surly drawn" (no. 1649).[7] For Bishop goes on to give her bird wing the sense of a dead weight, a sense emphasized by the irregular line-break.

Winter lives under a pigeon's wing, a dead wing with damp feathers.

The second stanza is more easily read, following the poem's imperative instructions: "Look down into the courtyard." The eye then moves across to "the mansard roof-tops where the pigeons / take their walks" and down into the inner courtyard:

> . . . It is like introspection
> to stare inside, or retrospection,
> a star inside a rectangle, a recollection:
> this hollow square could easily have been there.
> — The childish snow-forts, built in flashier winters,
> could have reached these proportions and been houses;
> the mighty snow-forts, four, five, stories high,
> withstanding spring as sand-forts do the tide,
> their walls, their shape, could not dissolve and die,
> only be overlapping in a strong chain, turned to stone,
> and grayed and yellowed now like these.

The hollow square becomes a memory place, with triple end-rhymes, triple early rhymes, and one internal rhyme, all suggesting the associative process of the journey back. Introspection, retrospection, recollection. *Stare, star, square* (with *stare* shortening to *star* in a pararhyme, echoed by *square* in a full rhyme repeated by the end-word *there*).

Bishop uses precise descriptive language for the memory of childhood snow-forts evoked by this early-morning gaze at a Paris apartment building. (But she says "childish" not "childhood," a small, passing dislocation that suggests larger ones to come.) Snow-forts do become ice-forts by the end of a long cold Nova Scotia winter, the ice "grayed and yellowed" like Paris stone, and also "withstanding spring." Snow-forts hardened to ice merely shrink in the spring, so that their walls become "overlapping" (the word Bishop also chose for the clock hands in stanza 1) and only in real warmth finally "dissolve and die." A "flashier winter" is easily recognized by a North American accustomed to cold bright winters, especially one who then endures a raw, damp, gray Paris winter. The word *flashier* also works to limit any sentimentalism about childhood memories.

In Bishop's work, the pacing of a poem often tightens suddenly as it approaches its close. So here, the third stanza begins unexpectedly:

> Where is the ammunition, the piled-up balls
> with the star-splintered hearts of ice?

It is true that snow-forts come with their own kind of ammunition, piled-up snowballs, and snowballs can turn icy or be made icy. But something more is going on. "Star-splintered hearts of ice" returns us once more to Paris and the Etoile, and to 1936.

At the center of the round Place de l'Etoile is the rectangular Arc de Triomphe with a hollow square inside. It is not a fort; it is a triumphal arch. But it is assuredly a memory place, and it lies at the heart of Paris. It celebrates military victories from Napoleon's time onward. The names of 558 generals are inscribed there; an unknown soldier was buried beneath it in 1920. Of the twelve avenues radiating out from the center, starlike, one for each hour of the day, six bear the names of military heroes, three of battle sites where Napoleon was victorious against the Prussians or Austrians. The magnificent and familiar Champs-Elysées (the Elysian Fields) has as its opposite counterpart, the avenue de la Grande Armée. The twelfth street is anomalous in that it is named for a writer, Victor Hugo, although his given name is oddly appropriate to the place.

What does it mean to ask the question, "Where is the ammunition?" in the winter of 1935–36, the winter Bishop lived in Paris? What does it mean to look at the shape of a typical Paris apartment building, to remember the look of childhood snow-forts (built for childhood snow battles), then to remember the look of the map of Paris with its own central battle memorial?

The third stanza continues:

> This sky is no carrier-warrior-pigeon
> escaping endless intersecting circles.
> It is a dead one, or the sky from which a dead one fell.

What *is* a "carrier-warrior-pigeon"? No one asks, but I became curious. Can pigeons be warriors? Yes, indeed. They were used in both world wars, and an American pigeon was even decorated for work over a battleground in France in World War I.[8] And what about a "carrier-warrior-pigeon / escaping endless intersecting circles"? How can we now escape those circles in the sense of the searchlights of war? In the winter of 1935–36, a "carrier-warrior-pigeon" is not fanciful. It is precise descriptive language. (A first test for Bishop is always, I think, the test of ordinary representation, very precise.) Dead things falling out of the sky—planes, birds: these are not "surreal" images. They are the nightmare images of actual war.

Pigeons belong to the dove family, and Bishop owned two white doves in Paris. "I am sending two pictures we managed to get of the doves the other day; one . . . shows Mr. Dove bowing to his wife with stiff knees and his throat puffed out. They are presenting quite a problem just now, as the mating season is coming on just as we are about to start traveling again. . . . I was so pleased . . . [with] a copy of your [poem] 'Pigeons'" (to Marianne Moore, 4 Feb. 1936).[9] Pigeons are ubiquitous in Paris, but they can look a little strange walking on the Arc de Triomphe. For the dove is the bird of peace, but the massive Arc de Triomphe is covered with the bird of war, the imperial eagle. Enwreathed eagle motifs separate the lists of battles on the monument's columns, and a great metal eagle is set into the pavement near the center. Bishop had a war nightmare "late in the thirties": "Tanks, lost in crowds of refugees, bombardments, etc. Last night I dreamed I heard cannon and that I was explaining to someone . . . that it sounded exactly like the cooing of doves amplified 2 thousand times and 'stretched out' . . . and that there was some connection with that and the Peace Dove."[10]

Bishop's first collection, *North and South*, is unmistakably a war volume,[11] even though "none of these poems deal directly with the war," most having been written before 1942. Many of the poems grow out of the gathering menace of the 1930's. Consider again "Paris, 7 A.M." Time is passing, circling around the Arc de Triomphe. The clock hands, moving, slice a long thin triangle between each avenue, a long splinter, a star-splinter (so to speak) whose point pierces the heart of Paris, l'Etoile. (Or is it hearts of ice?) And by synecdoche, each cannonball or bullet.

It is the winter of 1935–36. Economic conditions in Europe are very bad, and nationalism is in full flower, a deadly combination. Hitler has been in power nearly three years. "Like so many of my contemporaries," John Lehmann wrote of 1935, "I was haunted by the feeling that time was running out for a new world war. 'How to get out of this trap?' I noted in a journal at the time. . . . How to defend oneself, to be active, not to crouch paralysed as the hawk descends?"[12] In his excellent book on literature and politics in the 1930's, Samuel Hynes notes that if the decade is plotted as a tragedy, the peripeteia would be 1936: "In that year, Hitler reoccupied the Rhineland and the Treaty of Versailles was finished, Abyssinia surrendered and the League of Nations had failed, the Rome-Berlin Axis was formed and the German-Japanese pact was signed. And, most emotional and implicating of all the year's events, the Civil War in Spain began."[13] Doomsday in the form of a second world war "had become a commonplace." By 1936, "war was a part of ordinary consciousness" (ibid.). World War II would start for Czechoslovakia in 1938, for most of Europe in 1939, and for the Commonwealth, including Canada (and Bishop was part Canadian), in 1939 also. In a letter dated by the editor as of January 1937, Bishop submitted a poem called "War in Ethiopia" for publication: "I don't know who the other poets you're gathering are, or what the material is likely to be like — but in case it's all 'social consciousness,' etc., and you'd rather keep up a united front, I am sending 'War in Ethiopia.' Of course, it is very out-of-date, and I am not sure whether my attempts at this kind of thing are much good, but I should like to have you see it, too, and tell me what you think."[14] The poem is apparently lost.

And so to the ending of "Paris, 7 A.M.," with its questions:

> When did the star dissolve, or was it captured
> by the sequence of squares and squares and circles, circles?
> Can the clocks say; is it there below,
> about to tumble in snow?

There may be a memory here of Hans Christian Andersen's tale "The Snow Queen," where a glass splinter lodges in the heart and turns it to ice, but in the end is dissolved (rather easily) by a tear of love. (The young couple return from a world of ice into warm spring and a beloved house, where the clock measures ordinary time, and where it all started when they met across a roof.) Bishop said of her 1936 story "The Baptism" that she was trying to produce an effect something like Hans Christian Andersen's.[15] And three poems after "Paris, 7 A.M." in her collection, she placed a fairy tale from Grimm, shot through with terrible wartime imagery, "Sleeping Standing Up."

Bishop has laid out three possible fables of war, all pertinent to the 1930's, and I daresay later. (Of course, later uses of the fables would have to be troped differently, so the fables themselves would be altered.) The first is a fable of peace: the ice in the heart dissolves, as in normal late spring, as in snowballs, as in "The Snow Queen." The second is a fable of appeasement:

l'Etoile of military valor and glory dissolves or else is captured. The third is a fable of war, with or without military glory: snow-forts become stone, snow-balls become cannonballs, hearts become ice, a war perhaps lost (l'Etoile captured like a prisoner).

"Can the clocks say?" Bishop asks. In stanza 1, they have ignorant faces, presumably because they cannot tell time properly; their hands diverge. Time will tell, we like to assert. But tell what? As Auden would write later:

"Time will say nothing but I told you so."

Bishop's poem is sometimes described in puzzlement, if at all, as "surreal."[16] Its method is not in the least surreal, but if readers are genuinely reminded of surrealism, this is because Paris in the mid 1930's was "surreal." Surrealism, Hynes argues, "provided a parabolic method for the social nightmares of the time."[17] In another context, Bishop herself spoke of "glimpses of the always-more-successful surrealism of everyday life."[18]

In "Paris, 7 A.M.," Bishop lays out possible fables, but I hear no preference other than the desire to see clearly, and so to try to evade the trap of which John Lehmann speaks. In the remarkable poem "Roosters," written some five years later, Bishop's fables of war do suggest a response, although not an easy one.

"Roosters"

"Roosters" is a more fully read poem, yet its chief challenge remains, as it should. It is handed over to the reader at the end, and it places us even while we attempt to place it. Bishop's great challenge here lies in her art of juxtaposition, the juxtaposition of two rooster fables. The poem is a diptych, first, of the barnyard rooster, strident, strutting, aggressive, warlike; and second, of Peter's rooster whose portentous third crow recalled his denial of Jesus, and whose image adorns many a church steeple.

The poem begins with aggression, "in the gun-metal blue" of early dawn: "cruel feet," "stupid eyes," "uncontrolled traditional cries," "terrorize," "gloats," "screaming." Colorful roosters mark the landscape like pins in a military map. The poem challenges their challenge, and the first section ends in what the Battle of Britain (raging in 1940–41) would call "dogfights," those fights in the sky between airplanes — here, cockfights:

> Now in mid-air
> by twos they fight each other.
> Down comes a first flame-feather,
>
> and one is flying,
> with raging heroism defying
> even the sensation of dying.

Then comes the second fable, with no transition but a space:

> St. Peter's sin
> was worse than that of Magdalen
> whose sin was of the flesh alone;
>
> of spirit, Peter's,
> falling, beneath the flares,
> among the "servants and officers."

The quotation marks apparently need explaining: they simply indicate a quotation from John's Gospel, just after Peter's first denial:

> Then saith the damsel that kept the door unto Peter, Art not thou
> also one of this man's disciples? He saith, I am not. And the servants
> and officers stood there, who had made a fire of coals; for it was cold:
> and they warmed themselves: and Peter stood with them, and warmed
> himself.
>
> *(John 18:17–18)*

The sense of "falling, beneath the flares" links Peter's fall with that of the fighting cocks and of warplanes. The spirit also has its battles and defeats.

> Old holy sculpture
> could set it all together
> in one small scene, past and future:

It is more than we can do. Peter's sculpted tears "gem" the cock's spurs, for Peter, repenting,

> still cannot guess
> those cock-a-doodles yet might bless,
> his dreadful rooster come to mean forgiveness.

And it *is* odd how contrary the uses of this bird are, perhaps especially odd for someone both a bird-watcher and a reader, like Bishop. How can one bird be a figure for both war and forgiveness?

The challenge is handed over to the reader at the end of the poem. Here is the last stanza, which follows four stanzas of exquisitely colored, tranquil sunrise:

> The sun climbs in,
> following "to see the end,"
> faithful as enemy, or friend.

Bishop's quotation makes the sun itself a character in the crucifixion story, where Peter (this is before the threefold denial) "went in, and sat with the servants, to see the end" (Matt. 26:58) — words Bishop said she always felt "to be extremely poignant."[19] In Christian iconography, the standard role for the sun is that of Christ, as in George Herbert's poem "The Sonne," playing on the English-language pun of *son* and *sun*.

Bishop's "sun climbs in" — *in*? The sun climbs the sky or (we say) peeps in a window. I wonder if Bishop, a formidable punster, had in mind "peters in." For we do say that things "peter out," so why not the sun at the end of a day? I owe this thought to Anthony Hecht:

> Day peters out. Darkness wells up
>   From wheelrut, culvert, vacant drain;
> But still a rooster glints with life,
>   High on a church's weather-vane;
> The sun flings Mycenaean gold
>   Against a neighbor's window-pane.[20]

Logically, at dawn of day, the sun would "peter" (rather than peer?) in. And especially at the dawn of Peter's day, when he stayed "to see the end." Bishop's sun is no Christ but a Peter — the follower, the friend and disciple, the betrayer and enemy, the bitterly repentant, the forgiven.

What end has the sun followed to see? As its natural self, the end of the day and beyond that, the end of all of us, some day. As part of a poem enacting itself, the end of this poem. Thereby also, the end of these very fables, which is to say how wars and forgiveness will play out in human history. As Peter, the sun has followed to see the end of a story that is already completed, the crucifixion story.

But if the sun is Peter, who then is Christ, or is anyone? Who for all that are the "servants and officers," also quoted from the crucifixion story? Who are these others, unless we ourselves, as we are also sometimes Peter? What lies ahead is a trial, a death sentence, the execution of an enemy of the state. What follows then? Forgiveness is one option, here a human option and not a divine one. The sun is a follower, its faithfulness lighting up the path to the end, the end that we choose. It is neither the state nor the accused, neither killing nor forgiving. Insofar as the sun is a synecdoche for nature, then nature neither executes nor forgives. This is also true of Bishop's natural creatures, the roosters, and in both fables.

Bishop is gesturing toward the uses and the abuses of fable. When we justify wars and aggression by troping them as natural, the question is: whose nature? When we trope forgiveness in the figure of a cock, the question is: what forgiveness? This last question was Eliot's too. "After such knowledge, what forgiveness?" In "Gerontion," the knowledge is at once historical and carnal and spiritual. Historical in the references to World War I and the negotiations at Versailles, carnal in the back-and-forth of history as harlot and harlotry as history, spiritual by implied absence. Eliot wrote two years after a war ended, and Bishop in the midst of a war, a more difficult problem. Eliot is explicit about the question of forgiveness in relation to military victory and defeat. Bishop is implicit. Nonetheless, we have been unusually slow to acknowledge what Bishop's juxtaposition asks: what form of forgiveness, if any, enters the making of peace after a war, whether the war is military or domestic, public or private, social or individual?

The end of the poem holds us to Peter's unfinished story, to be completed by us according to what fable we choose. And choose we must, most painfully in times of war. Bishop's art of juxtaposition allows no easy answers.

"Brazil, January 1, 1502"

> Januaries, Nature greets our eyes
> exactly as she must have greeted theirs.

This is about as packed as things can get in twelve words and two pentameter lines. "Januaries": neat, memorable and unusual (not "in January"), and of course an ongoing parallel with the date in the title, when Europeans discovered what was named Rio de Janeiro. A new place and a new year. "Nature" capitalized and personified. And each new season greeting us (who are "we"?) as if we were explorers seeing a landscape for the first time. Then the epigraph:

> . . . embroidered nature . . . tapestried landscape.
>
> —*Landscape into Art*, by Sir Kenneth Clark

Epigraphs work variously. This one is spare, two phrases only, grammatically parallel, each adjective a past participle. Bishop chose to include her source as part of the epigraph, so that we see Clark's title offering a metamorphosis, but in one direction only, the art-making direction. Bishop, however, has so selected the quoted phrases as to offer a two-way metamorphosis. We cannot tell from the phrases whether nature and landscape look sewn or woven, or whether an embroidery or tapestry is depicting nature and landscape. As such, the phrases tell us that the act of seeing is not simple. Actual nature and landscape can look as if it were embroidered or tapestried. More important, we actually see them through pictorial conventions, through what E. H. Gombrich called "schemata" in his remarkable book *Art and Illusion*. "And have you read *Art & Illusion* by one Gombrich? — it is fascinating," Bishop wrote to Robert Lowell in July 1960.[21]

I want to return to three matters in Bishop's great poem: first, her gradual unfolding; second, the ending; third, the most difficult phrase in the poem, "Just so." Here is how the poem starts to unfold after the first two lines:

> Januaries, Nature greets our eyes
> exactly as she must have greeted theirs:
> every square inch filling in with foliage —
>
> . . . .
>
> solid but airy; fresh as if just finished
> and taken off the frame.

We accept Bishop's first two lines because in a sense they are true. Nature stays constant, or constant enough despite despoiling, so that we can look at it as if through the eyes of those first explorers. But wait. That is not what Bishop says, and that is the part she will show to be quite untrue. It is Nature who greets us in the same way. It is we who do not greet, let alone even see, Nature in the same way. Far from it.

Still, we can start with a world that looks newly created, as the New World did to the European explorers, as Nature does each new spring and summer (January in South America). Bishop follows the order of creation in Genesis. The first stanza goes up to day four, sounding as if God the Embroiderer or Weaver had just finished his innocent vegetable world and taken it off the frame. In fact, it was a commonplace, a topos, to think of God as Maker in this and other ways. "God . . . appears now as weaver, now as needleworker, now as potter, and now as smith. . . . 'God as painter' is an old topos, which first appears in Empedocles and Pindar and which is transmitted to the Middle Ages through Clement."[22] And the word *frame* signifies more than a weaver's or an embroiderer's frame. It can also be "applied to the heaven, earth, etc., regarded as a structure" (*OED*, both eds., *frame* [substantive], 8). We are familiar with it from Shakespeare and perhaps from Milton or Wordsworth: "this goodly frame, the Earth" (*Hamlet* 2.2.310); "Almighty, thine this universal Frame" (*Paradise Lost* 5.154); or the closing lines of Wordsworth's *Prelude*:

Prophets of Nature, we to them will speak . . .
Instruct them how the mind of man becomes
A thousand times more beautiful than the earth
On which he dwells, above this frame of things . . .
In beauty exalted, as it is itself
Of quality and fabric more divine.

— *The Prelude* (1850), 14.444–54

Bishop has started by exemplifying the epigraph, so that we see with double vision: a landscape in a work of art, and a landscape that looks like a work of art. Which is which? We don't know. The first stanza is full of leaves and flowers, colors and textures, relative size. Or rather not full of, but "filling in with," just as our own eyes are being filled in. ("Fill me in," we say; the *OED* [2d ed.] gives 1945 as the first recorded date of this idiom.) It is full — filling in — with the color and texture and size of objects. It belongs to the element of air. It also belongs to the embroiderer's or weaver's world ("solid but airy"). The colors sound like skeins of embroidery thread ("blue, blue-green and olive"); "a satin underleaf turned over" must surely be worked in satin stitch. Commentators who are grumpy about details of color can never have been inside a good needlework store or a painter's studio, or else they haven't enjoyed the experience. Commentators who take this exclusively for domestic needlework want to recall the "Circa 1492" exhibition at the National Gallery of Art in Washington, with its huge, magnificent Portuguese tapestries, several celebrating military victories.

From the third day of creation, when the earth brought forth grass and herb and tree, and the fourth, when sun and moon and stars arrived, we move to the fifth day of creation with Bishop's second stanza. In line 5, we also move on in time to a symbolically weighted landscape and to awareness of Sin.

> and perching there in profile, beaks agape,
> the big symbolic birds keep quiet,
> each showing only half his puffed and padded,
> pure-colored or spotted breasts.

Keep quiet because they are embroidered or woven? Keep quiet because they don't yet need to call out in warning? They can mutely remind us of choices anyway, by their "pure-colored or spotted breast," punning on "immaculate" and "maculate." (The wordplay is found elsewhere in Bishop: see "Seascape" or her housewalls in "Song for the Rainy Season.")

"Still in the foreground there is Sin," the poem continues. Now we read even the vegetable world differently. Those lichens, for example,

> threatened from underneath by moss
> in lovely hell-green flames,
> attacked above
> by scaling-ladder vines, oblique and neat,
> "one leaf yes and one leaf no" (in Portuguese).

The lichens are in the position of poor humanity on this middle earth, pulled between hell and heaven. That scaling-ladder vine, allegorical in its very name (Jacob's wonderful ladder or some proud Tower of Babel?), introduces a dialectic of yes and no, heaven and hell, up and down.

And yet — and here we slide forward a century or two or more, or else into a very different pair of sixteenth-century eyes — and yet, the "five sooty dragons" exemplifying sin in line 10 turn out to be only lizards after all in line 18. Another explanation of things — sex, not sin — has come into play. There is heat but not hell-fire heat. And there is a wicked tail but not a dragon's tail.

> The lizards scarcely breathe; all eyes
> are on the smaller, female one, back-to,

> her wicked tail straight up and over,
> red as a red-hot wire.

The word *wicked* still resonates a little by its association with sin and dragons. But I think we hear it chiefly in the modern colloquial sense: very bad or mischievous, here intensely sexual. The stanza has closed on a marked shift in tone. ("Madame Sosostris, famous clairvoyante . . . With a wicked pack of cards" [*The Waste Land*, ll. 43–46].) To the dialectic of up and down, we now add back and front, under and over. It's been there from the start ("a satin underleaf turned over") but not like this. This world, like embroideries and tapestries, has an overside and an underside.

"The lizards scarcely breathe." Bishop has brought us out of needlework and into a mimesis of the actual world, scarcely breathing. And so it is that we arrive at the third stanza, and with it, the high point of creation on the sixth day: mankind.

> Just so, the Christians . . .
>   . . . came and found it all.

The poem until now has been still, all movement arrested, soundless. Now sound begins: creaking armor in line 3, then a tune being hummed in line 12 ("L'Homme armé," a popular tune that was the basis for some 30 masses from the fourteenth to the sixteenth centuries), and finally the voices of the women — or are they birds? — on which the poem ends. The third stanza gathers up earlier kinds of seeing: light ("glinting"), texture ("hard as nails"), size ("tiny"). The dialectic of heaven and hell is relegated to the Mass, and an old dream governs all: "wealth and luxury," plus, says the poem, "a brand-new pleasure" — a phrase to cause shudders.

> Directly after Mass, humming perhaps
> *L'Homme armé* or some such tune,
> they ripped away into the hanging fabric,
> each out to catch an Indian for himself, —
> those maddening little women who kept calling,
> calling to each other (or had the birds waked up?)
> and retreating, always retreating, behind it.

And so the New World begins.

"Never again would birds' song be the same, / And to do that to birds was why she came," Frost wrote of Eve. And to do that to birds was why they came, we might add of these Christian warriors. If these women are like animal creatures, then sin does not enter into it, to say nothing of Petrarchan love conventions (as in ll. 5–6). (There were debates, in fact, about whether or not aboriginal peoples were human. The papal decree on the matter was proclaimed in 1537 by Paul III. In 1502, the jury was still out.) And what of "those maddening little women who kept calling"? For a moment, the enjambment just might imply some enticement, but no, they are "calling to each other." "Maddening" is very much the idiom of someone drawn on by what he projects into those elusive calls. As with the word *wicked*, the tone of "those maddening little women" matters a good deal. They did retreat, of course, those women, always retreat, those who were lucky enough not to get caught. "I finally had to do something with the cliché about the landscape looking like a tapestry, I suppose," Bishop wrote to Lowell in February 1960.[23]

Tapestries are silent, and so is this one, this poem that is a tapestry and mimes a tapestry. Yet tapestries can speak in their way. There is a very famous one in Western literature, also made by a woman, whose story ends a little later than this one. I wonder how far Bishop had it in mind, and I think the question is how far and not whether. It is Philomela's tapestry, in which she tells the story of her violent rape by Tereus, her sister's husband, after he severed her tongue to prevent her speaking. (This is "the voice of the shuttle," Sophocles' memorable phrase, quoted by Aristotle from Sophocles' lost play on Philomela and Tereus [*Poetics* 16.4].) She and her sister wreak a terrible vengeance, killing the small son and serving him in a dish to his father, Tereus. Tereus pursues and nearly kills both sisters. All three are metamorphosed into birds: a hoopoe, a swallow, and a nightingale. In the best-known account, Ovid's, the cries of the mutilated girl precede the device of the silent-speaking tapestry and the vengeful slaughter of Tereus's son. The calling of birds comes at the end. Here, the two moments are collapsed into one. But the Christian warriors with their swords are hot in pursuit. That white space at the end of the poem is waiting for quite another sound.

This would help to account for Bishop's quiet insistence on the armor. Here is Ovid at the end of his story:

With drawn sword he pursues the two daughters of Pandion, as before with drawn sword he cut out the tongue of one. As they fly from him you would think that the bodies of the two Athenians were poised on wings; they were poised on wings.

(Loeb ed.)

The Latin is better with its wonderful sounds and use of enjambment:

> . . . pennis pendere putares:
> pendebant pennis. . . .

(6.667–68)

Ovid has so shaped his lines that the metamorphosis happens over the line break, in the split second our eyes take to move leftward again.

When Tereus himself is changed into a bird,

> Upon his head a stiff crest [*vertice crista*] appears, and a huge beak stands forth instead of his long sword. He is the hoopoe, with the look of one armed for war [*facies armata videtur*].

Or, in Golding's better translation of 1560: "all armèd seemes his face."

If we did not know better, we might suppose that Bishop's Christians took their name, not from the Greek but from Latin *crista* (crest): as on a bird, as on armor, as (rarely) in sexual use ("a tuft on the head of animals; most freq. of the comb of a cock . . . the crest of a helmet, plume . . . the clitoris" [Lewis and Short, *A Latin Dictionary*]). And if we suppose Bishop was unaware of this, we should look again at "Roosters":

> . . . *gallus canit;*
> *flet Petrus . . .*

The cock crows; Peter weeps. A cock's comb is called *crista galli*, and so sounds like a juxtaposition of Christ and Peter's terrible rooster. It is as if the very name of the cock's comb, described earlier in another lexis altogether ("fighting blood . . . excrescence . . . a most virile presence") — as if the very name could echo forever in Peter's mind as a reproach.

Bishop's slow unfolding matters when we come to read her difficult phrase "Just so," the phrase that starts stanza 3 and brings the poem up to the moment of its title. "Just so" briefly suggests the analogy of those Christians and the lizards that immediately precede them. Both are in protective mail, hard as nails. (*Mail* means both "armor" and "the scales of some animals.")

"Hard as nails," with the double meaning of "in good physical condition" and *callous*, echoes *mails* to my ear.) This reading offers an easy stance: them, not us. Then memory and logic take over, and we recall lines 1 and 2 of the first stanza, where "Nature greets our eyes / exactly as she must have greeted theirs," the Christians' eyes when they found Brazil. Although this is the only reference to a "we," it forbids us to stand outside what is happening. This second analogy, them and us too, might give more pause than it usually does.

The two analogies for "just so" contain the story of all that we have seen, all that has happened up to certain moments of arrival: the Christians', ours. What nature is it that we see and that they saw? Is it innocent vegetable nature, fresh "as if just finished"? Is it nature in a Christian scheme of things, full of symbolic correspondences, itself created good, but fallen or about to fall? Or is it a nature that is heir to the eyes of some nineteenth- and twentieth-century scientists, where lizards are lizards, and the female in heat explains a lot?

We all inherit our "just so's," but we also choose them, more or less consciously. This happens in the very act of seeing, and it perforce influences action. The phrase "Just so" precedes action. The Christians have come, have seen, but have not yet finished conquering. As with "Paris, 7 A.M.," as with "Roosters," fables are there for us to choose: innocent vegetable nature, fallen redeemable nature, Darwinian nature, dreams of wealth and luxury and a brand-new pleasure, a Mass built on the popular song "L'Homme armé" although presumably also including "Dona nobis pacem," and finally swords and retreat, and a memory of swords and retreat going back to the earliest Western legends — and the making and memory of all these things in needlework, in poems.

FOUR

Faulkner, Typology, and Black History in *Go Down, Moses*

Typology and her sisters belong to a large family whose members often seem to step forth as identical twins or to bear the same name but have different identities.

— EARL MINER, *Literary Uses of Typology* (1977)

Like the patriarchs of old our men live all in one house with their wives and concubines, and the mulattoes one sees in every family exactly resemble the white children.

— *Mary Chesnut's Civil War Diary* (1861)

We are first cousins, aren't we? Didn't Adam and Eve have two sons?

— *Unidentified Savannah black woman* (1865)

I

"The modernist is likely to err by underestimating the importance of typology for literature," Earl Miner remarked in 1977.[1] Readers of early American literature are not likely so to err, thanks to a recovery of typological knowledge. A generation ago, biblical typology was a sadly esoteric subject for most literary scholars. As Sacvan Bercovitch observed in 1972, "Nothing more clearly reveals the parochialism of colonial studies than the fact that in 1948, when introducing Jonathan Edwards' *Images or Shadows of Divine Things*, Perry Miller felt it necessary to explain the nature and meaning of typology."[2] And not only colonial studies. In 1957, Northrop Frye noted crisply: "Biblical typology is so dead a language now that most readers, including scholars, cannot construe the superficial meaning of any poem which employs it."[3] This despite the fact that Erich Auerbach's important essay "Figura" had been available in German since 1944.[4] By the 1970's, literary scholars were working extensively on the subject of typology, work that has continued to this day, so that we have now largely retrieved what biblical scholars never wholly lost: the knowledge of how typological reading variously works, lines of argument about such a method, and its manifold implications.

But how useful is such knowledge for the reading and writing of modern literature?[5] More than we suppose, to repeat Earl Miner's point. I want to offer one example where we have neglected specific biblical typology, to our loss: Faulkner's *Go Down, Moses*. This example will sound surprising, for *Go Down, Moses* has not lacked commentary on its types, in various senses of that word, and notably on Isaac McCaslin. Yet I want to show that we have not sufficiently considered Faulkner's work with specific figural typology, for Faulkner has brought together, as we have not, the typology of biblical patriarchal families and Southern patriarchal families. I want to argue, not only that Faulkner makes essential use of specific biblical typology, but also that he undermines it, that he offers in effect a heterodox typology or at the least radically questions orthodox typology. He does this by applying typology's own principles to itself in a kind of historical reenactment of typological brothers. Such a use of typology — not parody but heterodoxy — may be found in writers other than Faulkner. It is something we have not fully reckoned with in American literature.

The history of typological interpretation is long, disputed, and fascinating, and I shall not enter into its intricacies, but I do need to review briefly some terms and some lines of argument. To offer an elementary handbook definition: biblical typology is a method of biblical interpretation in which a person, thing, or event in the Old Testament is read as the foreshadowing type of a person, thing, or event in the New Testament. The New Testament figures are read as the fulfilling antitypes of the Old Testament's types. The method is derived chiefly from St. Paul, although the principle may be ascertained elsewhere in the Bible and has its roots in Judaism. The principle is neatly and memorably put by St. Augustine: "In vetero novus latet; in novo vetus patet" ("In the Old, the New lies latent; in the New, the Old stands patent"). The force of such examples lies in the conviction that Jesus fulfills the Messianic prophecies of the Hebrew Scriptures, the prophecies so emphasized in the intertestamental period.[6] An allegorical method of reading biblical types is sometimes subsumed within the phrase "biblical typology," but more usually not.

Our reading of types is perforce influenced by an expansion of the word *type* in the eighteenth and especially in the nineteenth centuries, for the nineteenth century, with its passion and genius for taxonomies, found the word very useful, and it invented the word *typology*. The allegorical sense of type expanded beyond biblical figures to a wide general reading, more loosely connected with the Bible, if at all. And the word *type* also came to be used analytically and inductively as a system of categories. The first method is biblical and figural; we move from type to antitype, shadow to fulfillment. The allegorical method, whether biblical or expanded, might be called Platonic or Neoplatonic. The third use of *type* might be called Aristotelian, in the sense of being inductive. Today, the later meanings of the word *type* have overtaken the older meanings (appropriately enough, considering how biblical typology works). When the *MLA Bibliography* classifies books and articles under "Typology," it uses the word in the later senses of *type* (5 through 7 in the *Oxford English Dictionary*) and *typology* (3, *OED*). For the older sense (1, *OED*), it adds the adjective *biblical*.

The lines of dispute in typological reading are well known, and I shall briefly mention only two. One question (more pressing in earlier times) is whether or how biblical typological principles can properly be extended into postbiblical times. In one sense, they cannot, and we might better have devised other terms for a postcanonical sense of type and antitype. Yet the word *type* was used of postcanonical history, albeit over the protests of Samuel Mather.[7] And the nineteenth-century development of *type* and *typology* ensured that such use would continue. A. C. Charity suggests *sub-fulfilment*,[8] a useful word despite its curious general effect, and certainly more useful than the loaded phrase "progressive revelation." "Progressive revelation" works to blunt the uniqueness of revelation, and, when it is part of the notion of progress so favored at the end of the nineteenth century, it effects a blunting of the bluntest kind.[9]

A large area of dispute concerns the distinction between allegorical reading and typological reading. To quote Frye: "Typology is not allegory: allegory is normally a story-myth that finds its 'true' meaning in a conceptual or argumentative translation, and both testaments of the Bible, however oblique their approach to history, deal with real people and real events."[10] Typological reading assumes a "historical framework of revelation."[11] The two methods may shade into one another, especially with certain books of the Bible, but, although there is an overlap in allegorism and typology, ignoring the differences can be misleading.[12] This is to summarize very loosely what is a complex matter. But we do need to keep the broad distinction in mind and to watch our own allegorizing tendencies. We also need to remember that reading historically is no simple matter. One useful suggestion comes from Charity when he asks us to remember the existential function of typology's historical grounding: "Biblical typology . . . is an analogy between actions. If we speak of men or even of things as 'types', we do so legitimately only in so far as we think of them as acting or as involved in action" (*Events and Their Afterlife*, 58, 136).

For readers of modern literature, the difficulty is not simply that typology is no longer practiced as it once was, that we have no Edward Taylor. The difficulty is, I think, twofold. First, we tend to blur different kinds of typological reading, a blurring that is understandable enough, given that the methods shade into one another, and given the force of our nineteenth-century inheritance. Second, when we do work with specific figural typology, we sometimes treat it as a static pattern. We lose the sense of dialectic or of action in typology. We lose the force of typological imagining.

Our readings of *Go Down, Moses* have not yet asked enough questions about Faulkner's biblical typology. When Ike McCaslin explicitly casts himself as a follower of the Nazarene, we examine his actions and motives against that ideal model he has chosen. We read the angle of difference between his viewpoint and Faulkner's. And we consider generalizations about the possibility of any such imitation of Christ. But we do not muse upon the implications of specific figural typology, even when Faulkner has christened this Christ-follower Isaac. Ursula Brumm's excellent pioneering work on biblical typology and American literature does treat Faulkner, for example, but she is chiefly interested in how a Christ figure functions in *Light in August*, *A Fable*, and *Go Down, Moses*.[13] I want to show how specific figural typology works more widely, indeed, is necessary, for a fuller reading of *Go Down, Moses* — not a synchronic application of typological knowledge, but a sense of the working of a typological imagination, and in the end a sense of the limits of typology, together with the challenge of historical narrative.

II

One of the puzzles in *Go Down, Moses* is an apparent error in the last episode of the book, the title story "Go Down, Moses." Old Aunt Mollie, mourning the death of her grandson Samuel Beauchamp, wails repeatedly: "Done sold my Benjamin. Sold him in Egypt."[14] But the reader knows that it was not Benjamin who was sold into Egypt; it was Joseph. So also, in *The Sound and the Fury*, Benjamin is "our lastborn, sold into Egypt," "Benjamin the child of mine old age held hostage into Egypt. O Benjamin."[15]

Faulkner was once asked about this apparent error, and his laconic reply is wonderfully evasive and challenging:

Q.   Why is it that Mrs. Compson refers to Benjy as having been sold into Egypt? Wasn't that Joseph in the Bible? Is the mistake yours or hers?

A.   *Is there anybody who knows the Bible here?* [emphasis added]

Q.   I looked it up and Benjamin was held hostage for Joseph.

A.   Yes, that's why I used them interchangeably.[16]

How else to respond? Faulkner once said of the Old Testament, among a few other books: "I've read these books so often that I don't always begin at page one and read on to the end. I just read one scene, or about one character, just as you'd meet and talk to a friend for a few minutes."[17] If you have lived with a book so long that parts of it are like old friends, if its phrases enter your own writing, what else is there to say to the student who looks it up — and gets it wrong? For it is Simeon who is held hostage in the end, held by Joseph in lieu of Benjamin (see Gen. 42–45). Benjamin does indeed repeat the journey into Egypt, under duress and to his father's desperate fear. But this time the outcome is different.

It is certainly possible to use Joseph and Benjamin interchangeably as "types" in the general or allegorical meaning of the word. Such a combined Joseph-Benjamin type would be marked by a forced journey into Egypt, with the threat (realized for one but not the other) of being sold into slavery. And this forced journey, for such a Joseph-Benjamin type, would be caused through the agency of brothers (actually half-brothers), either through jealousy and betrayal or through the force of circumstance and a desperate hope. (Egypt as the "house of bondage" is, of course, the type for the condition of slavery, as in the spiritual that gives Faulkner his title.) The emphasis in such a Joseph-Benjamin type would be on what is general and common to the two stories, the "interchangeable" features: a forced journey into Egypt, the agency of brothers.

Samuel Beauchamp evokes two other memories of Benjamin. For in Genesis, Benjamin's mother, Rachel, who is also Joseph's mother, dies when he is born; so also does Samuel Beauchamp's mother in "Go Down, Moses." In Genesis, Benjamin is likened to a wolf in his father's last prophetic blessing: "Benjamin shall ravin as the wolf: In the morning he shall devour the prey, And at night he shall divide the spoil" (49:27). When Faulkner calls Samuel Beauchamp, executed for murder, "the slain wolf" (p. 382), he is using a metaphor from the world of hunting that is so important in his book; he is also echoing a simile from the Old Testament story of Benjamin. In the Genesis account, Jacob especially cherishes the two sons borne by his beloved Rachel. When Joseph is sold into Egypt by his jealous half-brothers, Jacob, supposing him dead, cherishes Benjamin all the more. In the later hostage drama, Joseph, now master, plays on this fear as part of his testing of his brothers, in a repeat performance of his own betrayal. But this time the brothers prove to be brotherly, and in the end Joseph saves them all.

For Aunt Mollie, Jacob's terrible fear has come true. Her Benjamin is dead, so that Samuel Beauchamp appears to function as an ironic, perhaps parodic, variation on a general Joseph-Benjamin type. This, Faulkner's narrative may tell us, is what happens now when you go or are sold into Egypt. You do not become a ruler like Joseph; you are not rescued like Benjamin. So read, this use of an interchangeable Joseph-Benjamin type offers another example of modern parodies of old typology.[18]

Faulkner directs us toward other Old Testament names in *Go Down, Moses*. There is the "Moses" of the title, of course. Most prominently, there is the name of his central character, Isaac McCaslin, so christened as the son and heir of an older couple. Faulkner also mentions, in passing, the names of Ham and of Esau. And he uses the Nazarene from the New Testament, Ike's chosen pattern for his life. The Nazarene is very appropriate typologically, both as a canonical and a postcanonical biblical type. The sacrifice of Isaac, turned aside at the last moment, is one of the dominant types of the Old Testament; it finds its fulfilling antitype in the crucifixion of Christ, the Nazarene. And Ike sees his simple way of life and the sacrifice of his patrimony as patterned after the Nazarene.

How does Ham enter Faulkner's novel? He functions as the general type for blacks, in the way he commonly functioned when biblical authority was sought for enslaving or oppressing them.[19] The use of the curse on Ham as a proof text for slavery extends that curse from the time of the flood to the modern era. This is so standard an interpretation that Cass can refer to it elliptically in passing. In *Absalom, Absalom!* a crude variation is given as a matter of course: "niggers, that the Bible said had been created and cursed by God to be brute and vassal to all men of white skin."[20] And the distinction between bondage and servitude only underlines the force of the biblical curse as it was typologically interpreted. Sam Fathers endures the sense of bondage rather than of servitude. His Indian blood is a burden, but a different kind of burden.[21] Typology can be put to many uses. Ike, of course, will have nothing to do with the common interpretation of the curse on Ham: "There are some things He said in the Book, and some things reported of Him that He did not say" (260).

As for Esau, he is proverbially the man who sells his birthright for a mess of pottage. He is also the firstborn who loses his patrimony because of the guile of his mother and his twin brother, to his father's great sorrow. Isaac's patriarchal blessing to his heir, once given, cannot be revoked, and Jacob gains it by trickery. Isaac McCaslin is anxious not to be seen as an Esau in one sense, the Esau who sells his birthright for a mess of pottage. The Nazarene provides the true type for his action, he insists. He denies that he "reneged, cried calf-rope, sold my birthright, betrayed my blood" (109). We might note, however, that, like Esau, he is a great hunter.

Readings of *Go Down, Moses* have worked chiefly with general or allegorical types, and rightly so — to a degree. I want to pursue another line of enquiry, one with more radical consequences, and one that I think Faulkner meant us to pursue. Suppose we pay attention to Faulkner's specific figural typology. I have already mentioned how Ike's own name is appropriate in figural and in postcanonical typology. Faulkner's title works this way too. The title, twice used, once for the novel and once for the last episode, is an allusion to a spiritual that is built on typological principles. In practice, it was read both specifically and generally. If we read from Old Testament into New, Moses' deliverance of the Israelites from Egyptian bondage becomes the type for which the antitype is Christ's deliverance of the Christian from sin. (Thus a boatload of the dead at the beginning of Dante's *Purgatorio* thankfully sing "In exitu Israel de Aegypto" [2.46; see Ps. 114:1].) When blacks sang this song in a spiritual sense, they were using specific biblical typology. When they sang it as a pattern for eventual deliverance from slavery, they were extending biblical typology to include the tribulation of their own time. Slaveholders were certainly aware of these two senses, and sometimes deeply suspicious of the second.[22]

Let me come back to Joseph and Benjamin, and to one important fact about them. They are brothers. They are full blood brothers, and they are also half-brothers to Jacob's other ten sons. So is Ham a brother; so is Esau a brother. So, for all that, is Isaac a brother. For the characters in the patriarchal stories, the fact of being a brother is crucial in their family stories. In *Go Down, Moses*, an intermittent background pattern of Old Testament brothers plays against the dominant foreground pattern of Faulkner's own stories about brothers. And these Old Testament stories of brothers include stories of rejection and betrayal. The patriarchal line does not descend smoothly: "And when Esau heard the words of his father, he cried with a great and exceeding bitter cry, and said unto his father, Bless me, even me also, O my father. . . . And Esau said unto his father, Hast thou but one blessing, my father? bless me, even me also, O my father. And Esau lifted up his voice, and wept" (Gen. 27:34, 38). For three generations, there are rejected brothers: Ishmael, Esau, and (temporarily) Joseph. The patriarchal stories treat the "theme of the rejected 'brother'" that is also central to Faulkner's work. (The phrase is Robert Penn Warren's: "Faulkner's theme of the rejected 'brother' is at the very center of his drama and the character with mixed blood is mandatory.")[23]

We know how Faulkner pairs the white and black descendants of Lucius Quintus Carothers McCaslin. Tomey's Turl is the black half-brother of the twins Uncle Buck and Uncle Buddy. Zack and Lucas "could have been brothers, almost twins" (47); they "lived until they were both grown almost as brothers lived" (55). Roth Edmonds, when young, accepts Henry Beauchamp as "his black foster brother" and the phrase *foster brother* is repeated twice more in the same paragraph (110). Isaac McCaslin is not explicitly paired with a black descendant, but I think that Faulkner implicitly provides him with one. For Ike and Tennie's Jim are of an age, as a glance at the McCaslin family tree will show. Ike would have grown up with Jim, just as the other white McCaslin descendants grew up with the descendants of the black half-brother. I suspect that Faulkner had Tennie's first three children die in infancy so that Jim and Ike could be paired this way.

When Ike repudiates his patrimony, he does so in order to purify himself of a tainted inheritance. In one sense he repudiates his own name. He wants to live like the rejected brothers: like Ishmael (in the wilderness), like Esau (the skillful hunter). He has been born on the winning side, so to speak, the late child of older parents, an Isaac and not an Ishmael. By his own act of repudiation, he intends to bring himself closer to the losing side, to the black McCaslin line rather than the white, the Ishmaels to his Isaac. His own acknowledged pattern for acting this way is the Nazarene, Christ, who himself was said to be "despised and rejected of men":[24] "not in mere static and hopeful emulation of the Nazarene . . . but . . . because if the Nazarene had found carpentering good for the life and ends He had assumed and elected to serve it would be all right too for Isaac McCaslin" (309). Blacks felt the Nazarene to be very close to them, closer even than Moses, to follow Eugene Genovese, "by virtue of the low earthly station the Son of God chose as His own."[25] Frederick Douglass alludes to the same passage from Isaiah quoted above, the "suffering servant" chapter, in his slave narrative. Slaves "were in very deed men and women of sorrow, and acquainted with grief" (Isa. 53:3).[26]

Now, Christ as a general pattern (even a "type") to be imitated is one thing. Certainly, Christ is an heir who by birthright is entitled to all that the world has to offer, but an heir who chooses to sacrifice himself in his life and death. Ike takes this sacrifice as the pattern of his act of repudiation, and, insofar as we agree that Christian doctrine and story can find temporal fulfillment (or subfulfillment), we must accept Ike's sacrifice as valid in principle, whatever we think of it in practice. It is a compulsion to perform publicly and in his own person some act to ally himself with the rejected, with those in servitude, with those who have lost. We may think this *imitatio Christi* is inappropriate, or we may think that someone like Cass represents a truer, if unacknowledged, following of the Nazarene. In any case, the Nazarene constitutes the pattern to be emulated (or the antitype to be imitated) in a postcanonical typology.

As general types, Ham and Isaac and Esau and Joseph and Benjamin also have clear and well-known functions. But the story Faulkner is telling introduces a radical and disquieting question. What happens to rejected brothers in specific figural typology under the new dispensation of the Nazarene? The answer is well known. In his Epistles, Paul continues to reject them. Christ is said to be of the lineage of Isaac and Jacob, not of Ishmael and Esau, for all his sympathy with those who are outcast. This is understandable, of course. Because Paul wants to establish Jesus as the fulfillment of Jewish messianic hopes, he is hardly likely to parallel him with the rejected brothers in the patriarchal stories. This would amount to an attack on the legitimacy of patriarchal succession. But Faulkner's narrative seems to me to suggest a deep skepticism toward this orthodox typology, insofar as orthodox typology disregards rejected brothers.

In the patriarchal stories, it is Joseph who breaks the pattern of brother set against brother. Betrayed by his own jealous half-brothers, he nonetheless rescues them years later, and the reunion of the family is one of the great reconciliation scenes of the Bible. Benjamin, the younger brother of the pair in this generation, does not eclipse Joseph. Although Joseph eclipses his older half-brothers in one sense, he does not eclipse them as heir. All twelve of Rachel's and Leah's sons establish the twelve tribes of Israel. To quote Regina Schwartz: "Only when they [Joseph's brothers] achieve the awareness that they must be their brothers' keepers — the insight Cain so dramatically denied — are they qualified for divine enfranchisement. Cain is condemned to exile, but Joseph teaches his brothers to become the Sons of Israel."[27] Here the pattern of rejected brothers seems to be ended.

I think it is precisely because the story of Benjamin in Egypt marks the end of three generations of rejected brothers that Faulkner uses it at the end of *Go Down, Moses*. Faulkner did not use Joseph and Benjamin interchangeably in order to stress the similarities in their stories. This reading takes us only so far and makes little aesthetic sense of Faulkner's substitution. He used Joseph and Benjamin interchangeably in order to stress the differences in their stories and to stress that his Benjamin's story has tragically become Joseph's early story. There has been no reconciliation in Lucius Quintus Carothers McCaslin's patriarchal line of legitimate heirs and rejected brothers. Rejection and thereby a form of slavery go on, even after Emancipation.

Ike McCaslin is the namesake of the Isaac who was grandfather to both Benjamin and Joseph. He is the namesake of the man who, in old age, was deceived into blessing the wrong son, and so deprived his firstborn. Ike McCaslin fathers no children. But Faulkner does provide him with a black "brother." In that rending interview in "Delta Autumn," Ike repeats the name of his black brother, "Tennie's Jim." And Faulkner gives Ike a chance to extend his blessing to the flesh and blood of Tennie's Jim, to a woman who is the age that Ike's own grandchild might have been. But neither an Esau nor a Jacob receives Ike's true blessing. (Granted that Ike is incapacitated by the shock of a seeming parallel of old and new intimacies between the black and the white McCaslins. The parallel holds only so far.) It is as if the biblical Isaac had a chance to bless the grandchild of an Esau and the great-grandchild of an Esau and a Jacob. (Tennie's Jim bears the name of Jacob. The English name *James* comes through Latin *Jacobus* and through Greek from the Hebrew name that is transliterated as *Jacob* in the English Bible.) But Faulkner's Ike has no true blessing to give. This is why the scene of Isaac's refused blessing just precedes the last episode, with its tragic then elegiac conflation of Benjamin with Joseph, and the consequences for the sojourn in Egypt that the spiritual "Go Down, Moses" knows all too well.

I wonder also (I am less certain of this) whether the patriarchal stories may provide a useful background for the opening episode "Was," where the only Moses of *Go Down, Moses* appears. This Moses is a hunting dog, who, as it happens, is not needed in this parody hunt-and-rescue from a parody Egypt. (And it is very much a matter of parody here, not of heterodoxy.) Brothers (twins, in fact, like Esau and Jacob) open the book, together with the question of what it means to love God. (The names Amodeus and Theophilus bear one signification, lover of God or beloved of God.) Uncle Buddy shows the strength of cunning, Jacob's strength, in order to rescue Uncle Buck, who is a hunter like Esau, although not very skillful. For Uncle Buck has come within an ace of being caught by a bed-trick, as Jacob was by Leah and her father. Eventually, of course, he will become an Abraham of sorts by fathering Isaac. Tomey's Turl shows consummate skill in hunting and great cunning. There is certainly no easy inference from all this. The lovers of God are mixed characters in a mixed comedy. However, if Faulkner's memorable tale of the ancients in "Was" can be read in this way, then *Go Down, Moses* is loosely yet significantly framed by the patriarchal stories and their typological implications. This would go some way toward establishing the book as a novel rather than a short-story collection.

Faulkner allows this story of rejection one brief alleviating counterpattern. In the last episode, "Go Down, Moses," Miss Worsham appeals to Gavin Stevens, saying, "Can nothing be done? Mollie's and Hemp's parents belonged to my grandfather. Mollie and I were born in the same month. We grew up together as sisters would" (375). We look at that group of mourners, to which Gavin Stevens is an outsider, in a new light: the black woman, the white woman who grew up like a sister with her, together with the black brother and his wife, all grieving, no bond broken. Faulkner's story of brothers is unlike the patriarchal stories in one way, for in Genesis the women play crucial roles. In *Go Down, Moses*, the white McCaslin women have virtually no role to play. If Faulkner makes Miss Worsham a true "sister," he also makes her an outsider to the McCaslin family, with no complicating blood relations between her and Mollie. And if he does offer a brief alleviating counterpattern of "sisters," it comes at the very end, when the bond of brothers in *Go Down, Moses* has been irrevocably shattered. Neither Old Testament patriarchy nor New Testament revision offers any hope to that rupture.

III

Typology itself is the story of "brothers," Old Testament and New, older and younger, law and grace. Here, too, the older brother in the person of the Hebrew Scriptures is set aside, abrogated, in favor of the younger. Not rejected. But made a forerunner to the greater glory of the younger brother, who is the ordained fulfillment. The typological method is grounded in the anticipation and realization of messianic hopes, and, if those hopes are accepted, it matters little whether one is a forerunner or a follower. As method, typology of course owes something to the patriarchal stories themselves, for St. Paul chooses as analogy for his typological reading the patriarchal stories in which the younger brother is the true heir and the older brother is set aside. So, also, the younger new covenant is offered as the true heir, and the Hebrew Scriptures offered as the old covenant, now abrogated.[28] Yet for the older brother, the Hebrew Scriptures, the sense of being rejected remains, since the condition for not being rejected is to become the Old Testament — a different book, even if the two texts are identical word for word.

There are two kinds of typological question in Faulkner's novel. The first is the possibility of any enactment in history of the pattern or general type of sacrifice set by Christ. Who sacrifices exactly what in any *imitatio Christi*? This is a question that would present itself if Ike were called John Doe, born to young parents, and without black cousins. How can Ike's desire be translated into action in family life or in the civic realm over a span of 50 years and more? The New Testament kingdom is said to be not of this world. The kingdoms of this world constitute one of the three temptations for Christ, and he explicitly refuses the use of temporal power. Rather, he prefers to ally himself with the lowly and the outcast. How may a kingdom that is not of this world be related to the kingdoms of this world, both large and small, national and regional and familial? The relation of the power of the Gospels to temporal power is a perennial problem for Christian apologists. And Faulkner's own interest in this problem is evident, notably in *A Fable*. The problem of how spiritual power is translated into temporal terms is, of course, central to the history of Southern slavery. It is a theme of the *Narrative of the Life of Frederick Douglass, an American Slave*. And ongoing work in social history has returned to this perennial problem once again.[29]

Ike wishes to mark the wrongs done to his black cousins, to unweave history or at least to stop the ongoing shuttle. He wishes also to mark the wrongs done in his region and in his nation, for his own family history, like much Southern family history,[30] is interwoven with the history of slavery and the Civil War. Or perhaps these histories should be read as family histories, as strife between brothers, in the way Goethe read the patriarchal stories of the Old Testament.[31] "Two nations are in thy womb, and two manner of people shall be separated from thy bowels; and the one people shall be stronger than the other people; and the elder shall serve the younger" (Gen. 25:23): thus the prophecy to Rebecca, mother of Esau and Jacob, wife of Isaac. The historical books of the Old Testament are full of stories about the legitimacy of origins, the rule of law, the relation of a people to the land, the concept of a promised land, kinds of marriages and families, and the strife between brothers. And all of these are themes in *Go Down, Moses*. "To me," said Faulkner, "the New Testament is full of ideas and I don't know much about ideas. The Old Testament is full of people, perfectly ordinary normal heroes and blackguards just like everybody else nowadays, and I like to read the Old Testament because it's full of people, not ideas."[32]

Yet Faulkner was hardly ignorant of the ideas of the New Testament, including its ideas of the Old. This leads me to the second typological question, one that belongs specifically to *Go Down, Moses* and to figural biblical typology. It is this: does biblical typology reach its limit as a guide to a spiritual life with the pattern of the elder and rejected brother? (In literary terms, what are the possible relations between figural typology and narrative action based on the patriarchal stories?) When such brothers are in the comfortable mists of patriarchal history, with their destinies sealed, well and good. But suppose they are present, here and now. What guidelines does biblical typology now offer to someone with a sense of outrage and of justice like the young Ike McCaslin's? Allegorical or general reading isolates an Isaac or an Esau from his narrative functions, his family history, his relations with brothers and sisters. He becomes a type or allegory of this or that quality, in a synchronic reading. Specific figural typology is more diachronic, and it focuses precisely on heirs and successors.[33]

Faulkner was not the first Southern writer to see in the stories of the patriarchs a type for one kind of Southern family life. Mary Chesnut's diary records just such a perception; one example is given in the second epigraph to this essay. I use the word *stories* deliberately, for the term *patriarch* was common enough in descriptions of Southern family life. Its function was often to claim legitimacy for a benign, authoritative family structure. Mary Chesnut may be heard implicitly responding to someone like Thomas Cobb, who wrote in 1858: "In short, the Southern slavery is a patriarchal, social system. The master is the head of his family. Next to wife and children, he cares for his slaves."[34] She does so by turning, like Faulkner, from the general type to the type in action, from an allegorical use of type to the recorded narrative, here from the patriarch to Leah and Rachel: "Mr. Harris said it was so patriarchal. So it is — flocks and herds and slaves — and wife Leah does not suffice. Rachel must be *added*, if not *married*. And all the time, they seem to think themselves patterns — models of husbands and fathers."[35] And she responds more than once, repeating the names of Leah and Rachel (72, 276). In 1864, in a reported conversation, she is reminded of Hagar and Ishmael, against whom she sets David and Bathsheba (587). Her use of the patriarchal stories is far from precise; indeed, she somewhat generalizes the type of wife, handmaiden, and so on.[36] Her difficulty and pain should not be skirted, yet it remains true that, in the end, "the main victims were the slaves."[37] Certainly, that was Frederick Douglass's view. He thinks not only of slave women but also, like Faulkner, of brothers. It is often more humane for the master and father to sell his children, he writes, "for, unless he does this, he must not only whip them himself, but must stand by and see one white son tie up his brother, of but a few shades darker complexion than himself, and ply the gory lash to his naked back" (*Narrative*, 49–50).

Writing on Southern history uses terms and allegorical types taken from the Old Testament. It does not appear to make much use of the stories of Old Testament patriarchal families and the relations between brothers or between women found therein. This includes the writing on miscegenation I have seen.[38] Mary Chesnut knew how to read more fully the stories of the patriarchs, for all that her reading was limited. And the unidentified Savannah black woman of my third epigraph used the typology of brothers, extending it back to the first human family.[39] She has something to teach us about the reading and uses of the past. So does Faulkner. But then, we might have learned already from the blacks' widespread and highly intelligent use of biblical typology. "Biblical figures must come alive, must be present, must somehow provide a historical example for modern application," as Eugene Genovese says. Part of that "somehow" lay in the uses of typology, as for example, and prominently, in the spiritual "Go Down, Moses." Although Genovese does not use the word, it is typological thinking that bridges the "gap" he remarks between the God of the Old Testament and of the New, between Moses and Jesus.[40]

In *American Counterpoint*, C. Vann Woodward comes close to Faulkner's comprehension. There, he juxtaposes remarks on miscegenation, patriarchal families, and blood kin in the slave quarters: "Miscegenation also flourished . . . in the old South as well. . . . The incontrovertible evidence of this walked in and out of some of the finest mansions of the Old South, but was rarely mentioned in polite circles." After quoting Mary Chesnut on Leah and Rachel and patriarchal families, he goes on to analyze acutely and sympathetically the lives of white women in such families. He then turns to the cost for others:

> Blood, sweat, and tears went into the fulfillment of paternalistic codes about the care and welfare of "the servants," sleepless nights ministering to distress in the quarters, and all that. But the fact remained that these people, blood kin along with them, were excluded, shut out resolutely from basic human ties, hopes, aspirations, opportunities. The ultimate horror might be the tragedy of Charles Bon in *Absalom, Absalom!* or that of Joe Christmas of *Light in August*. But the ultimate cost has never been reckoned.[41]

In *Go Down, Moses*, Faulkner sets up patterns of type and antitype, but his narrative ends by implicitly questioning the standard Pauline line of inheritance. Nor does he follow the patriarchal line of inheritance. He accepts neither the New Testament's interpretation of the Old nor the Hebrew Bible's interpretation of its own narrative. What he does is to go back to the powerful patriarchal stories that he knew and loved, and from them to retell stories of rejected brothers and accepted heirs. Then, as defiant as Emily Dickinson, he implants the question of why some brothers were disinherited in favor of other brothers, and why the New Testament accepted such types for its antitypes. The result is to question our whole sense of type and anti-type, including the patriarchal narratives used by St. Paul as analogies for typological thinking — including also the term *patriarch* in Southern history. I hear no answer in Faulkner to this questioning. I hear complex stories of "perfectly ordinary normal heroes and blackguards" whose lives may be enlarged or burdened by the great ancient stories and ideas. And I hear Dickinson, in her refusal of orthodox typology: "Old Man on Nebo! Late as this — / My justice bleeds — for Thee!"[42]

FIVE

"A Seeing and Unseeing in the Eye": Canadian Literature and the Sense of Place

There is a society for the study of literature written in Canada that calls itself the Association for Canadian and Quebec Literatures/Association des littératures canadiennes et québécoises. When I once objected to this name on the ground that a federalist could not belong in good faith, I was told that it avoided the awkwardness of hyphens. Ever since, I have been interested in hyphens and hyphenated conditions, especially in relation to Canadian literature.

Preface: The Placing of Hyphens

Apart from the political difficulty of the phrase "Canadian and Quebec," is it useful as a nonhyphenated equivalent for writing in English and in French? Well, no. This association is not at all the same as an association for English- and French-Canadian literature (alphabetical order). Or as an association for

French- and English-Canadian literature (chronological order, beginning with Marc Lescarbot, chronicler of the short-lived Acadian colony of Port-Royal, whose play was performed there in 1606). For where does the present association place the work of Antonine Maillet, voice of the Acadians, scholar of Rabelais, and creator of the memorable cleaning woman La Sagouine? Acadians know what it means to be excluded, whether by deportation or by current categories. (The 1755 deportation is the subject of Longfellow's *Evangeline*, and the return from exile the subject of Maillet's *Pélagie-la-Charette*, which won the Prix Goncourt in 1979.) One possible name would be the Association for Canadian Literature in the French and English Languages; this, of course, would shift the categories.

La Sagouine reflects on categories when the census taker appears in order to "cense" her. Here she is, in the Acadian French that Maillet has done so much to record and keep alive — "un langage d'avant l'Academie":[1]

Ta natiounalité, qu'ils te demandont. . . . C'est malaise à dire.

Je vivons en Amarique, ben je sons pas des Amaricains. Non, les Amaricains, ils travaillont dans des shops aux Etats, pis ils s'en venont se promener par icitte sus nos côtes, l'été, en culottes blanches pis en parlant anglais. . . . Nous autres je vivons au Canada; ça fait que je devons putot être des Canadjens. . . . Ben ça se peut pas non plus, parce que les Dysart . . . ça vit au Canada itou [mais] ils sont des Anglais, pis nous autres, je sons des Français. . . . je pouvons pas dire ça: les Français, c'est les Français de France. . . . Je sons putot des Canadjens français. . . . Ça se peut pas non plus, ça. Les Canadjens français, c'est du monde qui vit à Québec. Ils les appelont des Canayens, ou ben des Québécois. . . . Pour l'amour de Djeu, où c'est que je vivons, nous autres? . . . En Acadie, qu'ils nous avont dit, et je sons des Acadjens. . . . je sons les seuls à porter ce nom-là. . . . [mais] les encenseux . . . ils avont eu pour leu dire que l'Acadie, c'est point un pays, ça, pis un Acadjen c'est point une natiounalité. . . . je leur avont dit de nous bailler la natiounalité qu'i' voudriont. Ça fait que je crois qu'ils nous avont placés parmi les Sauvages. . . .

Ils te disont ben que t'es un citoyen à part entchere; ben ils pouvont point noumer ta citoyenneté. T'es pas de trop, peut-être ben, mais t'as pas ta place au pays.[2]

The single most important statement about Canadian cultural identity is by Northrop Frye. La Sagouine is a living example of his argument:

When the CBC is instructed by Parliament to do what it can to promote Canadian unity and identity, it is not always realized that unity and identity are quite different things to be promoting, and that in Canada they are perhaps more different than they are anywhere else. Identity is local and regional, rooted in the imagination and in works of culture; unity is national in reference, international in perspective, and rooted in a political feeling.[3]

La Sagouine has no problem of identity. (This malady is not as widespread in Canada as some suppose.)[4] What she has is a problem of unity, of her place in the country:

> The essential element in the national sense of unity is the east-west feeling, developed historically along the St. Lawrence–Great Lakes axis, and expressed in the national motto, *a mari usque ad mare*. The tension between this political sense of unity and the imaginative sense of locality is the essence of whatever the word "Canadian" means. Once the tension is given up, and the two elements of unity and identity are confused or assimilated to each other, we get the two endemic diseases of Canadian life. Assimilating identity to unity produces the empty gestures of cultural nationalism; assimilating unity to identity produces the kind of provincial isolation which is now called separatism.[5]

La Sagouine has no desire for isolation. It is just that others have not seen her. La Sagouine is here, in this place, yet not fully here. She has and makes a powerful sense of the place called l'Acadie, a place that both is and is not on a map. (True places never are, said Melville.) Yet the census taker finds her hard to place and so makes her wonder about her "place au pays." She is a useful starting point for this essay, which has to do with two different, although related, senses of place. The first is *place* in the more usual meaning of the sights and sounds, smells and tastes, the textures of a place, the sensing of its natural landscape, its streets and buildings, its inhabitants. The second is *place* as category — of cultural identity, of the various filters through which we see and read actual, palpable place.

Canadians tend to be aware of categories, of hyphenated conditions. Founded by two imperial powers, situated between the two current superpowers: for us, such awareness is natural enough. In our writing, too, we are aware of categories, of how things get put together. An older, fuller literature has a sense of something already put together (with all the concomitant problems for the artist). The British poet Geoffrey Hill writes of an England put together so long ago that one can forget it was put together. A Canadian finds his extraordinary poem *The Mystery of the Charity of Charles Péguy* especially interesting because of the way Hill relates French and English (peoples and languages) by rhyme and word root and hyphen. His poem enriches our sense of how we place ourselves: how we come together, stay apart, form bonds, break bonds. It challenges unexamined notions of oneness and of fragmentation, just as Frye's remarks do in a different way. Words do not fit neatly into French-English, as if that hyphen were an international boundary. But then international boundaries do not divide neatly. Very few human things do, Hill's poem reminds us.

In Canadian literature there is much less sense of a place already put together than in British literature. Rather, there is still a sense of getting things together, not so much in narrative or argumentative plotting as in form. It turns up in the strong schematic skeleton of much Canadian writing, whether the anatomy is neatly carved or experimentally pieced together. Here are the bones, here is how they may be put together, here is how these bones may live, may be articulated. It turns up in the often-remarked absence of realism in its pure form. (Realistic Canadian work tends to turn into magic realism or into mythically informed realism.) It turns up in the often-remarked Canadian gift for irony and satire and self-mockery. (The late George Ferguson, the crusty editor of the *Montreal Star*, used to say that what *this* country needs most is a good five-cent bullshit-filter. That is yet another use for a hyphen.) Such characteristics mark a self-consciousness about the sense of place.

A word on the phrase "sense of place" before going on to particulars. These are not precise rhetorical or logical words in the way that a synecdoche or a syllogism is. They are not to be found in the glossary of Northrop Frye's *Anatomy of Criticism* or in the analytical index of *PMLA* (Publications of the Modern Language Association of America). Nonetheless, they remain among those enduring, useful, general words or phrases on which we center certain kinds of observation. And this phrase can provide a useful way of introducing or reviewing literature that comes from a certain area. I am speaking, of course, about "sense of place" in the first and usual meaning noted above, as when Dame Helen Gardner says she would recognize the garden of

T. S. Eliot's "Burnt Norton" if she were brought blindfolded to the place. Or as when Browning, visiting Italy, laughed aloud in pleasure at recognizing a sorb tree because of Shelley's poem "Marenghi." This is the imaginative (and so, the precise and memorable) fixing of a landscape in words. We inherit this topographical sense most immediately from eighteenth-century English loco-descriptive writing, and our mimetic expectations for a sense of place are still much governed by those eighteenth-century conventions. This remains true, even though modern writing is altering our codes for perceiving place.

For we do not see or read place except through some code, some filter, some set of categories. It is always worth stepping back to consider, as best we can, how these filters or categories place us in the very act of our seeing and reading place. Categories are best understood, not just as pigeonholes where we put things after seeing or reading them, but as problem-solving models without which we can hardly see or read at all. (See Alastair Fowler on genres, for example.)[6] And we all know, thanks to E. H. Gombrich's *Art and Illusion*, how schemata filter our seeing, how there is no such thing as Ruskin's innocent eye. This second sense of *place*, the place that conditions place (so to speak), is the subject of the last part of this essay.

The Seeing of Our Places

A sense of place usually has to do with landscape, whether rural or wild or urban. "The aim of poetry is to saturate every terrain, every city, every village, so that every American child might find a native landscape invested with language. This was, after all, the normal condition for the European child. The *genius loci* lives only where poetry creates it." This is Helen Vendler speaking of American poetry.[7] The aims of Canadian writing resemble the American in this, although Canadians also live with the knowledge of vast northern terrains that resist saturation. What sense of place may be found in major or representative writers in Canada? This will give a mental set, a schema. And if ordinary mimesis is not found, this too gives information: what is not seen can be as important as what is seen. (One says this knowing that later generations will see where we are blind and will miss some of our seeing, "and least will guess that with our bones / We left much more, left what still is / The look of things.")[8] What sense of place, then, may we find in our various terrains and cities and villages where our writers have invested them with articulate presence? To take a handful of excellent writers from the last generation or two and ask this question is to begin to make a map. Everyone has a mental map; this is a personal one.

Consider the world of Hector de Saint-Denys-Garneau, who died in 1943 at 31 (French Canada's most eminent poet, said Etienne Gilson). Usually, the middle ground is altogether missing. The space of his poems is occupied by large foreground figures and a large sky; the middle ground is empty. So also in the work of the painter Jean-Paul Lemieux; the foreground figures commonly break the margins of the painting and look directly out with haunting eyes; the background is a vast sky. The angle of viewing varies; sometimes it makes the foreground figures huge, as if seen by a child; their presences overwhelm. In Lemieux's paintings, as in Saint-Denys-Garneau's poetry, we have the self and space. *Regards et jeux dans l'espace* is the title of Saint-Denys-Garneau's first collection. Here the tension of holding self and space in relation is extreme, and sometimes snaps. The double (there are a lot of doubles in Canadian writing) walks with the poet to the corner, then goes the other way (in "Accompagnement" we hear: "Je marche à côté d'une joie"). Absence of community is a felt thing.

> Mes enfants vous dansez mal
> Il faut dire qu'il est difficile de danser ici
> Dans ce manque d'air
> Ici dans l'espace qui est toute la danse.
> Vous ne savez pas jouer avec l'espace
> Et vous y jouez
> Sans chaînes
> Pauvres enfants qui ne pouvez pas jouer. . . .[9]

In the end, the tension split altogether, and Garneau retreated into silence, unable to put things together in his work. His close friend, the remarkable essayist Jean Le Moyne, accused clerical Quebec of having killed the poet—of having killed him through a hatred of life, a fatal dualism that ignores Easter and hates women. Le Moyne's passionate attack is against a clericalism whose power waned with the Quiet Revolution of the 1960's. (There were other attacks too: Claire Martin's memoir *Dans un gant de fer* [1965] is one of the best known.)

This changing sense of Quebec alters the very look of the landscape, for we live not just in a territorial country but also in a country of the mind. It is not just the look of Quebec's church buildings (whether active or deserted or converted to other uses), of its shrines and clergy, that is informed by Saint-Denys-Garneau's poetry and Le Moyne's essays. It is the look of the very air of Quebec, its great spaces, the dance lines cut by hills or by buildings. Le Moyne's ample imagination abhors confining boundaries and holds itself open, for example, to Henry James, to music. (Glenn Gould knew and loved the music essays in Le Moyne's collection *Convergences*, where the essay on Saint-Denys-Garneau also appears.) Walls are metaphysical as well as physical, and these mental walls and boundaries are a most important part of a general sense of place. Mental boundaries and walls and hyphens come before the physical ones we construct. They are the cause (formal, perhaps teleological) of the physical ones.

A similar tension appears in the work of Saint-Denys-Garneau's cousin Anne Hébert, where the self wanders not so much under a great sky and against a huge landscape as in a domestic scene. But the self is equally alone. As with Garneau, there are bones, a parceling out of the body, of detached hands that no synecdoche will make whole, of bones with no desire for flesh: "Je suis une fille maigre / Et j'ai des beaux os" (from "La Fille maigre": "I am a thin, thin girl / And I have beautiful bones. . . . I polish them ceaselessly"). The self wanders the ancestral home and from a mirror pulls a ghost, a dead damp possessing spirit, clinging like seaweed or like a lover ("Vie de château"). "The first voices of our poetry speak to us of unhappiness, of solitude," Hébert once said.[10]

In the back-and-forth of active looking, which is also a possessing of the landscape, one sees the manor houses of Quebec differently after one reads Hébert. One sees differently those beautiful long houses on the north shore between Quebec City and Montreal with their steep-sloping roofs. They not only become invested with the nostalgic charm of Robert Laroque de Roquebrune's classic memoir *Testament de mon enfance*. They also become invested with the ghosts of a certain past, like the river of Hébert's well-known short story "The Torrent." Canada is a land of violent contraries. (Perhaps that is why we value the peaceable kingdom, the middle way, the rituals of courtesy.) When Hébert plays with her familiar contraries in her novel *Les enfants du sabbat*, we find a more sophisticated, funnier treatment of John

Updike's theme in *The Witches of Eastwick*. More is at stake in Hébert's book; these are her own hauntings, treated in fine black farce, convent life alternating with *cabane* (shanty) life, the whole thing ludicrous and powerful. She holds and turns those inimical and similar worlds back and forth, making actual Quebec ghostlier and more real all at once.

One modern form of this Quebec may be found in the powerful, violent work of Hubert Aquin, to which I shall return. An ardent Quebec nationalist (that is, a separatist), Aquin is an urban writer, more Gnostic than Gothic, a French Canadian with a hunger for absolutes, a hunger thwarted and diverted, never sublimated.

For the sense of place in a more everyday Quebec, we might turn to Roch Carrier, whose short story "The Hockey Sweater" is a Canadian favorite. This is also the story of any Canadian country boy: the old Eaton's store catalogue (not Sears), the hockey (not baseball, not soccer). Carrier said in a recent interview that ice was meant, first, for hockey and, second, for keeping meat. The paintings of William Kurelek, a primitivist of rare genius, show a prairie boy's sense of this world of snow and ice, meant for play. This world is all one, Quebec or Manitoba. It is Rabelais against morbidity. "The same degree of morbidity is quite common among us," wrote Le Moyne, but against this, Rabelais keeps turning up, for Carrier as for Maillet. (If the conjunction sounds odd, we might compare U.S. Southern writing.) Satire, self-mockery, humor: these are strategies for survival, and even for a kind of celebration, as well as art forms. (But then, art forms *are* strategies for survival.) And satire, self-mockery, and humor are the kinds of literature in which Canadians shine.

Quebec's vital Jewish presence is caught in Mordecai Richler's fiction, and we in turn may catch the look of it as we walk Montreal streets. So may we with the work of A. M. Klein. The poems one returns to are precisely those that give a sense of place: Jerusalem alive in Canada, late-winter sugaring troped as a modern type of crucifixion, the rocking chair (used as a title for one collection), evoking those front porches on which one sits and watches. "Political Meeting," Klein's memorable poem about the conscription crisis, shows another kind of watching:

> The whole street wears one face,
> shadowed and grim; and in the darkness rises
> the body-odour of race.

"Rises . . . race." All the poem's risings come to rest on the tension of that closing near rhyme. The political meeting is in a room with a crucifix: what rising thence? Klein's Quebec is not simply a place of picturesque sights and sounds, sugar bush and rocking chairs. It is a place of conscience too. So also, Jewish Montreal, evoked by Richler, by the poets Irving Layton and Louis Dudek, by the scholar Leon Edel.

The Montreal of F. R. Scott, the distinguished jurist and poet, is a Montreal of sights and sounds and conscience in another way. It is a Montreal of crisp, elegant wit. Scott has an eye for satire and a passion for justice, whether he is defending *Lady Chatterley's Lover* or spotting funny bilingualisms. Scott works in areas mastered by W. H. Auden — fine occasional verse, satiric quatrains:

> I went to bat for the Lady Chatte
> Dressed in my bib and gown.
> The judges three glared down at me
> The priests patrolled the town.

Or, from "Bonne Entente":

> The advantages of living with two cultures
> Strike one at every turn
> Especially when one . . . sees on the restaurant menu
>   the bilingual dish: Deep Apple Pie
> Tarte aux pommes profondes.

On the other hand, Mavis Gallant's Montreal stories of Linnet Muir, in *Home Truths*, are imagined through the eyes of someone who knows struggle from the inside out. It is a different Montreal: "One day, standing at a corner, waiting for the light to change, I understood that the Sherbrooke Street of my exile — my Mecca, my Jerusalem — was this. It had to be: there could not be two, It was *only* this. . . . Reality, as always, was narrow and dull."

To return again to the Atlantic region is to return to Newfoundland (part of Canada since 1949) and to the Maritimes (including the region of Acadia). It is to see the North Atlantic through the eyes of E. J. Pratt, whether in the fine narrative poem *The Titanic* or in shorter poems like "The Shark." Pratt knows the everyday heroisms of seagoing life.[11] His whole sense of place is heroic, where heroism is an outward struggle, not a fight "against the trolls within" (Ibsen's phrase, put to such good use by Robertson Davies in his novel *The Manticore*). Pratt is Saint-Denys-Garneau turned inside out. He has the Newfoundlander's genial and exuberant imagination, together with an intelligence about the world of everyday society and action. All this informs his best work: the wartime parable *The Truant* (which spoke so strongly to the young Northrop Frye); *The Titanic*; and the best of his narratives, *Brébeuf and his Brethren*, on the martyrdom of the French Jesuit missionaries in what is now Ontario. Pratt's type of heroism and his favorite genre of narrative poetry are both out of fashion. The genre is just now coming back into favor, although not in the old way of telling. The type of heroism is too recent to exercise the historical imagination, although we still sometimes look at seascapes and landscapes with Pratt's eyes. But his instinct for the inclusive myths of this country was unerring.

The Maritime sense of place is not the same as the Newfoundland sense, for all that it shares a knowledge of the sea. It is not just the look of the countryside. It is the voice of that countryside, as distinctive as a New England voice. Elizabeth Bishop has heard it in her fine poem "The Moose," for which Canadians owe her a special debt. That voice, quiet and as sardonic as the occasion demands, belies any bucolic placidity. Thomas Chandler Haliburton, the nineteenth-century Maritime judge and creator of Sam Slick, also heard that voice. He is every Canadian's forefather, just as Sam Slick is every Canadian's typical Yankee salesman. Sam is the master of what we now call the soft sell; Haliburton called it "soft sawder."

The map of Ontario is now filling rapidly, thanks to the work of Robertson Davies and Alice Munro and Margaret Atwood. Thanks also to the continuing work of the poets, who began to fill the map earlier. James Reaney's poetry and drama, for example, trace the alphabet of southern Ontario; they are possessed by a fury of pastoral vision to set against false pastoral. Reaney writes a series of Spenserian eclogues, *A Suit of Nettles*: it is anserine rather than ovine. He also knows, as did Milton and Pound, the force of place-names. (Canada is a land of extraordinary place-names: the Indian names with their mysterious etymology, improbable names like Moose Jaw, anglicized French-Canadian names like Bien Fait, pronounced "bean-fate," names of sheer delight like Saskatoon and Saskatchewan.) Margaret Avison's work belongs here ("Nobody stuffs the world in at your eyes / The optic heart must venture"). So do the unforgettable cadences of Jay Macpherson

("And Memory, alas to me / A half-regained Eurydice / Is veiled and cannot speak"). So does George Johnston's light verse with its dark touches that leave a sense of something unspoken and sinister, as James Merrill puts it.[12] ("Don't be nervous, Mary Anne, / Don't be nervous, dear! / Carry a little water can / To catch the quiet tear.")

Ontario is a seemingly placid province, especially in its southern areas: the Golden Horseshoe metropolitan region rounding the end of Lake Ontario, the rolling rich agricultural land, the five different Great Lakes (huge inland waterways with their own lacustrine lore). The sudden change to rock and evergreens along the border of the Laurentian Shield introduces the country of those knowledgeable in the ways of wilderness, the resort country, the mineral and lumbering country, the country of countless lakes, the country now oddly browning as pollution rains down from what Marianne Moore called "the sequestered brilliance of Canadian skies."[13] This is a tourist-poster, an industrial-appeal Ontario. To see the place through its writers can give a sense of vertigo. Can these bones live so? Are some apparently placid Ontarians possessed by such mythic energy? Nonsensical stereotypes of the stolid northerner can be deceptive. (For an excellent attack on climatic arguments for national character, see Carl Berger's essay "The True North Strong and Free.")[14]

To an outsider, the world of Robertson Davies, to say nothing of James Reaney's, may appear essentially as fantasy. I suppose the world of William Faulkner could also appear to be fantasy. Yet we know how the satire of Stephen Leacock's best book, *Arcadian Adventures with the Idle Rich*, regularly repeats itself in actual academe, stock exchange, church, and social scene. A new university in Montreal, in fact, took on the name of Leacock's much-satirized fictional university, Concordia. Those who come from small Ontario towns read Davies's apparently fantastic Deptford trilogy and more recent novels with fascination. "How does he know?" they ask. And one drives through those towns, with their barbershops and festivals and churches and few prominent houses and local newspapers, wondering, wondering. So our sense of place in many a town and village in Ontario has been changed, has come alive, with knowledge that is both welcome and unwelcome. In many a city too, although Ontario's cities have not as yet the articulate presence of well-imagined Montreal.

Davies has a strong sense of the religious texture of Canadian life, which has never succumbed very far to American deism or to American fundamentalism. (PBS's series on fundamentalism addressed a U.S. phenomenon.) It is worth noting that Canadian writers are generally informed about such things as the main Protestant denominations, their doctrines and influence. This has nothing to do with personal belief. Atwood's sure touch in her novel *The Handmaid's Tale* tells her that someone in an Anabaptist tradition would never collaborate with an oppressive state religion. Gallant's Linnet Muir thinks: "Even in loss of faith, they [her parents] were unalike, for he was ex-Anglican and she was ex-Lutheran and that is not your same atheist — no, not at all."

The prairies speak differently in different seasons. Prairie writing is exuberant, hyberbolic, and it is also the contrary, brooding and meditative — like the landscape, one wants to say, knowing such analogues are false ones. A child's vision, says Eli Mandel, a child yearning for a true home. Mandel's bleak Estevan poems are paradoxically rich in Jewish presence. W. O. Mitchell writing in the tradition of Twain and Leacock, Rudy Wiebe finding a Mennonite voice, Gabrielle Roy speaking for the Franco-Manitobans — all make a prairie place for us. In Roy's story "Ely! Ely! Ely!" the dark, vast, flat land engulfs a passenger set down at the end of a long train, a train that has made a special stop for her. That railway line (*railroad* is American) is metonymically Canada itself, for demographically Canada has the shape of Chile, although its territory is third in area only to Russia and China. Under the huge dome of a prairie sky, the elements take on mythic force. Westerners hear Aeolus differently from Ontarians. ("The Wind, Our Enemy" is Anne Marriott's title for a poem about prairie drought.) The towns are peopled by outsize, mythic characters, as in two novels: Margaret Laurence's typic old woman, Hagar, from *The Stone Angel*, Robert Kroetsch's new Odysseus from *The Studhorse Man*.

Interior British Columbia is inhabited by haunting presences from Sheila Watson's novel *The Double Hook*, which has gone on speaking to younger writers for years. As a well-known man of letters says, "Mrs. Potter, the old fisherwoman, and James, her son and murderer, and Greta, her daughter . . . move in and out of a bright mythological light and yet, at the same time, in outward appearance, are the kind of cattle-raising people one might encounter any day riding on the back roads of the Cariboo country."[15] The mountains and the West Coast we have seen for some time through Emily Carr's autobiographical writing in *Klee Wyck*, as well as her painting; through the fiction of Ethel Wilson; and through the poetry of Earle Birney and P. K. Page. And now through Joy Kogawa's *Obasan*, that beautiful, unbearable novel of the deportation and dispossession of Canadians of Japanese origin. As her grandmother is cremated on a pyre in the British Columbia forest, Naomi thinks of other bones in that vast countryside. Some of her grandmother's bones and ashes are joining this soil, inextricably a part of this country she has tried to make her own. Vancouver, the mountain ghost town, the huge forest, the little settlement, the sugar-beet farm worked by forced labor — all are seen anew.

Our most extraordinary literary imagination does not work with poetry, prose fiction, or drama. It belongs to an essayist, the one who wrote *Anatomy of Criticism: Four Essays*. It belongs, most of us would say, to someone who has a genius for category, someone hardly to be associated with the country called Canada. Yet Northrop Frye is also of his time and place in a profound way that is sometimes hard for outsiders to grasp. One example is his speaking and writing voice, which can indeed be placed regionally by those familiar with the area. Here is that Maritime voice, as described by the daughter of two other Maritimers:

> The things that intimidated other people did not intimidate me. The deadpan delivery, the irony, the monotone, and the concealed jokes, may have seemed odd to those from Ontario, but to me they were more than familiar. In the Maritimes they're the norm . . . and no Maritimer could ever mistake a lack of flamboyance for a lack of commitment, engagement, courage or passion. Light dawned when I found out Frye had originated in New Brunswick.[16]

The speaker is Margaret Atwood, who has heard the regional sense of identity in Frye's voice. The reader hardly needs to be told to remember Atwood's own writing voice as well. That Maritime perspective informs Atwood's central Canada too.

Can we say that the person who writes an epic criticism is our epic poet? It is Robert Kroetsch who has suggested this idea,[17] knowing how Frye's sense of place allows us to walk around inside it with no sense of restriction. More than any writer of this country, Northrop Frye has taught us how to see.

I want to end this section by observing how important local context can be, for Canadian as for other writing. It is true that in some writing "whereabouts is as immaterial as in Kafka."[18] Yet how do we know this unless we know something of the whereabouts? John Bayley also writes that "Chekhov's 'Lady with the Dog' could only have taken place as it did where it did," an assertion that comes out of his knowledge of the time and place.[19] I make the point because Canadian writing is sometimes read in ignorance of its context — worse, in ignorance that it might have a context that matters. Three examples where context does matter, where our ordinary "sense of place" needs more detail, follow.

The first is *Le déclin de l'empire américain*, a popular Quebec film by Denys Arcand. Its eight men and women dance out their roles (sexual, cultural, professional), balancing, reversing, together, apart. We see a dance of modern love and work. But the film is also profoundly Québécois. It opens thus: "Il y a trois choses importantes en histoire. Premièrement, le nombre. Deuxièmement, le nombre. Troisièrement, le nombre." Arcand does not say what his characters know very well, since they are members of a department of history at a Quebec university: these are well-known sentiments of the prominent Quebec historian Michel Brunet.[20] One must read the title, not just generally, but also in the context of a Quebec that knows something about empires and their effects. *Déclin* shows decline, questions decline (depending on whether Quebec is inside or outside *l'empire américain*), echoes Gibbon, and puns on *déclin* as a decline in numbers, in the birthrate.

For a second example, try this: read "Les offensés," a poem by Anne Hébert; then read the English translation by Geoffrey Hill, titled "Homo Homini Lupus." The poem takes on a different context; it becomes a Hill poem, although in French it remains an Hébert poem. This is one of the most interesting effects of translation (one thinks of translations of the classics, say, of Catullus's "Vivamus mea Lesbia" rendered in English by Ben Jonson). Since Hébert went utterly unidentified in the English periodical *Agenda*, where Hill's translation appeared, readers might not be aware of her context.[21]

For a third example, take the last novel by Hubert Aquin, *Neige noire*, translated as *Hamlet's Twin*. This novel-cum-script may seem simply the sophisticated revision of *Hamlet* that it patently is. Its incest, ritual murder, lesbianism may seem the near-parodic outdoing of current conventions of violence that they patently are. The place, Montreal: what has this to do with

Aquin's Montreal in *Neige noir*? When read in context — say, against Saint-Denys-Garneau and Le Moyne — the novel alters. It becomes the Gnostic parable, the heretical defiance of Quebec and Canadian myths (above all, of Christianity) that it also patently is. Gnostic diction in the new-creation closure alerts us. We recall the ritual slaying with eating of flesh and remember the crucifixion. We recall the incest and remember the father-son story, here a modern father-daughter story. We recall James Joyce, who also saw that *Hamlet* could serve as a God-the-Father/God-the-Son story. Quebec remembers its fathers, and crucifies the daughters who cleave to those fathers, and goes out to make a film about it all. The new world, monstrously heretical to orthodoxy, can only arise from Fortinbras of Norway, here Eva. Aquin superimposes a Scandinavian, a Hamlet's, North on Montreal — or disinters it from Montreal. This is not the cheerful-northern, the hard-primitive sense of place, not the North of the novel *Maria Chapdelaine*. Aquin has a nihilist ferocity; he is intelligent, unrelenting, unsparing. His artistry is sophisticated almost as a matter of course. (You want postmodernism? Nothing easier.) How to look at the places of our seeing after this? Aquin's work shames any easy seeing. It tells us we must earn our sense of place.

The Places of Our Seeing

I have been tracing how Canadian literature makes a "sense of place," in the usual meaning of that phrase — its ways of putting and holding things together, the sometime violence when they will not stay together, the consciousness of a massive, powerful land. The placing of Canadian literature itself has been changing at astonishing speed over the last two decades. Now, a body of Canadian writers, not just individual writers, is generally accepted in and beyond this country. It took American literature until the early decades of this century to reach this invaluable stage, and many a recent debate over Canadian literature has replayed old arguments about American literature at that time. The early activities of the "CanLit" industry caused some smiles, but we should say of it what Seamus Heaney says of the Celtic Twilight in Irish literature: "Although it has long been fashionable to smile indulgently at the Celtic Twilight, it has to be remembered that the movement was the beginning of a discovery of confidence in our own ground, in our place, in our speech."[22] And Marie-Claire Blais has warned against "the modesty that can be disastrous for a writer."[23] One wants acceptance of a nation's literature in order to stop thinking of it as such, and to get on with helping and preserving the best possible reading and writing.

I want to end by returning to a more general sense of *place* — that is, place as category. And I want to come back to the question of "seeing and unseeing," as, for example, with La Sagouine, and to the question of hyphens.

In any seeing and unseeing in the eye, one wants to ask about motes and beams. If Canadian literature is finding a place for itself, it is also still learning of communities unvoiced or ignored. Thus the work of Maillet and Kogawa. There is yet another community that we are only just beginning to see, although it has been here all the while. It has a lot to do with our sense of place, our sense of putting things together here, in this particular place. It has to do with the fact that this is neither a new country nor an empty country. It has been inhabited just as long as most other countries. (So has Australia, as Judith Wright points out.)[24] It is just that we have not seen the inhabitants, just as the "censor" could not see La Sagouine, as men may not see women, as Americans may not see Canadians. They are here, in this place, yet not fully here, not here in the sense that others are here. Their tragic history, like the tragic history of the eighteenth-century Acadians, is part of this place. Their legends of this country preceded any stories of our own. This is not to prescribe any one specific action; it is to prescribe awareness.

I am speaking of the native population, of course, both Inuit and Amerindian. To see our terrain through Inuit or Amerindian stories is to shift our sense of place, to see it already inhabited by *genii loci*, just as Europe was inhabited for the European child. It is to take on a burden of knowledge and another sense of place, to remember Indian teenagers who commit crimes in order to get to the comforts of jail, to remember a Winnipeg doctor who stitched a string of Indian beads into an incision on the body of an Indian woman as he sutured it. (What an awakening was there: coming out of anaesthetic into the clear, tangible evidence that she had trusted her body to a healer and found the contempt of a white man.) When one's land is at once more theirs, and less, how does one possess it?

Writers have always been aware of this community (the work of the Confederation poet D. C. Scott, Al Purdy's poem "Lament for the Dorsets," Leonard Cohen's novel *Beautiful Losers*, Rudy Wiebe's novel *The Temptations of Big Bear*, Robert Kroetsch's "Stone Hammer Poem," and the poetry of Susan Musgrave and John Newlove). But general awareness, here as elsewhere, is still deficient. Nonetheless, a 1987 *Illustrated History of Canada* (edited by R. Craig Brown) begins with some 80 pages entitled "When Two Worlds Met." And M. T. Kelly's novel *A Dream Like Mine*, a 1987 Governor-General's Award winner, treats the Ojibway. There are ways of not seeing a place, but such unseeing can be hazardous. Frye observed in a 1986 interview that "you can't found a culture on a pure destruction of another culture; otherwise you'll be haunted by guilt feelings all the time. You have to establish some kind of continuity with it. The moment when the indigenous people seem to be at their last gasp . . . is the point at which cultural backlash begins, just as it has done in French Canada."[25]

Another kind of seeing and unseeing in the eye is made possible through the work of Alice Munro. (I am reading *unseeing* here in Wallace Stevens's second sense: that of unlearning an old way of seeing.)[26] A non-Canadian may not realize the particular effect that some of Munro's work has on a Canadian. To hear part of oneself voiced for the first time — this is an extraordinary experience. And to sense a very good writer still actively growing — one holds one's breath, wishing only to let her mind move upon silence. Munro sees the stories of money that possess some imaginations, especially men's. She sees them, not inimically, but as a matter of fact, knowing the dangers, the excesses, but knowing also the day-to-day work, what it maintains, as well as what it does not maintain. So too with the stories of love that possess some imaginations, especially women's. She sees them, not naively, but as a matter of fact, knowing the dangers, the excesses, but knowing also the day-to-day work, what it maintains, as well as what it does not. Stories of money and stories of love both go into making a sense of place. Both kinds of story are schemata through which the landscape is seen and inhabited. Both possessed the first explorers of this country, as Champlain's presence in her remarkable story "Meneseteung" suggests. It would be easy to exploit the differences in these schemata and to write a simple female-versus-male, love-versus-business, ecology-versus-industry, native-versus-European narrative. But Munro refuses easy either-or hyphens. She reads the land-as-woman metaphor in no easy self-congratulatory way. In "Meneseteung," the grapes, the river, the violence done to the town whore, the unspoken contract in looking at her nakedness: all these things make a sense of place, past and present, where a burden of knowledge yearns for relief, as just before the menstrual flow, until the words come coursing like the river Meneseteung itself.

So Munro suggests a new seeing and unseeing in the eye, a seeing that might include more fully a woman's perspective. One can work out the simile of Canada as a female: the occluded partner whom strangers find more exotic than do close relatives. (Atwood also works with this analogue.) We might wish our large partner on the American continent to see more fully from a Canadian perspective and not to assume too readily a Canada in the role of supportive, placid, reliable, flatterable partner, providing essential goods and services, taking care of dirty jobs, in the supporting, the unnoticed, role.

More and more, our sense of place makes us watch metaphors and narratives, for these govern our decisions about living in a place, about changing a place. If, all too often, place has been seen by males using female metaphors (as Annette Kolodny argues in her critical work *The Lay of the Land*), can females themselves speak out of their sense of place, as it were, for place? Someone as good as Munro will see with piercing clarity the old exploitations, yet refuse an easy either-or, female-versus-male, love-versus-money categorization. She can see the "male" (business) and the "female" (domestic, and in early settlements, artistic) senses of place. In "Meneseteung," Munro plays on two meanings of the one word *speculation* to hold before us two senses of place in one: "Would she herself, knowing that there was salt in the earth, discover how to get it out and sell it? Not likely. She would be thinking about the ancient sea. That kind of speculation is what Jarvis Poulter has, quite properly, no time for."[27] Munro might show us a truer sense of place, teaching us to know one particular place, to acknowledge viewpoints we have ignored, to acknowledge the shame as well as the glories of this place.

I began with a question about hyphens and hyphenated conditions, and that is where I want to end. Northrop Frye argues that hyphens may not be so deleterious, after all, when we are thinking about cultural identity and national unity. We can make the tug in identity-unity or local-national into a creative tension rather than a schism. I have introduced a number of hyphens into the last few paragraphs, literally and metaphorically: female-male, Canadian-U.S., native-latecomer. And I noted earlier a certain self-consciousness in

Canadian literature about how things get put together, about the hyphens, so to speak, latent in all our unities. Canadian writing has a few general characteristics, such as the tendency toward satire, self-mockery, and humor. But to me, these general characteristics are not the most interesting and useful area of Canadian literature to explore. To me, the most interesting and useful area of Canadian literature — whether in its rhetoric or its dialectic — is the area of the hyphen, including the metaphorical hyphens within this country. In a world where all our imagination and intelligence is needed to deal with such hyphens, the best of this country's writing, French and English and other, essay and prose fiction and drama and poem, has something important to say.

For most of us our sense of place is still new, still being put together, but we all put it together as against a deluge.

PART TWO

Culture and the Uses of Memory: Allusion

SIX

Questions of Allusion

We hear it in news broadcasts, we use it ourselves. ("Not with a bang but a whimper." "The centre cannot hold.") And we all know about the man who complained of a performance of *Hamlet*: well acted, but the play was nothing but a tissue of quotations. Has anyone ever counted? Line for line, *Hamlet* must be the most quoted, alluded to, echoed — and what verb, by the way, *should* we use? Which is one way of starting to think about allusion.

Allusion may seem a small matter, and yet it shows in little what we choose to remember from the past, what we "would not willingly let die," as Milton puts it. Allusion keeps certain words alive, or it tries to. "At Laguna Pueblo . . . many individual words have their own stories. So when one is telling a story, and one is using words to tell the story, each word that one is speaking has a story of its own, too. Often the speakers or tellers will go into these word-stories, creating an elaborate structure of stories-within-stories."[1] Just so. All words have stories, and good poets know these stories better than anyone, for they know words as they know people. Allusion is one type of word-story, one way of remembering word-stories.

In ordinary usage and in elementary literary handbooks, the words *allusion* and *reference* are synonymous. We talk of "alluding to" the character of Hamlet or the story of David and Bathsheba, even though we repeat no words at all from Shakespeare or the English Bible. In critical usage, it's handy to distinguish allusion from reference, allusion here involving the precise verbal repetition of sentences, phrases, words, even syllables. ("To be or not to be." "Thou art the man.") This includes play against the original wording, for we need to know the original words in order to enjoy the play. (See Margaret Atwood on "Meanie, meanie.")[2] It's also useful to distinguish specific allusion (which has a single origin) from what might be called general allusion, for example, to a formulaic saying ("Once upon a time," "Amen"). This matters because good allusive practice often brings a weight of context to bear, and we want to know what context.

Sources are different from allusions, just as source-hunting (the old *Quellenforschung*) is different from the study of allusion. And not all uses of memory are equal. See, for example, Milton on the unthinking citation of sources, as if such citation in itself guaranteed authority: "men whose learning and belief lies in marginal stuffings, who, when they have like good sumptors laid ye down their horseload of citations and fathers at your door . . . ye may take off their pack-saddles, their day's work is done."[3] It's this kind of allusion-dropping that can give allusion studies a bad name, as can some source-hunting. Sources differ from allusions in that a reader is not expected to recognize a source or to enjoy the pleasures of inference. In *The Waste Land*, where allusion functions as both a subject and a method, some of Eliot's notes provide sources, while others point to the origin of allusions. Notes on Chapman's hermit thrush and Shackleton's expedition offer sources; words from, say, Shakespeare or Marvell are allusions. *The Waste Land* focuses on memory, when it can bear to do so, memory that is not quite right. Some memories seem too loud, while others seem to be evaded. Or else memory is lost, especially communal memory. Allusion is part of this whole process of remembering and not remembering and misremembering, of speech and silence.

Literary critics often place allusion in the large domain now known by the term *intertextuality* (introduced by Julia Kristeva and the Tel Quel group). *Intertextuality* is the commodious term for reading a given work as the nexus of all the other verbal works that surround it and inform it. In theory, such surrounding is infinite, for one word leads to another. In practice, choices are made, by poet as by theorist. The Italian classicist Gian Biagio Conte suggests that we all accept the term *intertextuality* but seek to redefine it. For him, intertextuality is the "equivalent to the less technical 'poetic memory,' " an admirable starting definition.[4] It has to be said that most writing on intertextuality is singularly unhelpful for the practical reader or the student of poetics. Such writing tends to adopt what Carlo Ginzburg calls an "anatomical" method as against a "semiotic" or intensely inductive method.[5] The good God loves details (Warburg's saying), and so do lovers of good writing, especially poetry. At the same time, many books on allusion in author A or author B are vague or reductive in their implied plots of allusive action, and careless in their terminology. Only the rare critic manages to write about the principle and the practice of allusion with equal rigor and imagination and tact. Conte is one such and, among English-speaking critics, Christopher Ricks and John Hollander are two more.

In his critical readings of allusion, Ricks works through narrative, a narrative plot of inheritance. To quote: "Most allusions of subtlety and efficacy are likely to be related in some important way to inheritance." His argument is given *in nuce* in two articles on Dryden and Pope and on Tennyson, and expanded in his article on allusion in J. L. Austin.

Hollander's 1981 book *The Figure of Echo* works with a rhetorical taxonomy designed to move us away from the simple either-or model that still governs much hearing of allusion: either allusion as simple tribute or allusion as simple irony. It is not that this doesn't happen. It is that so much more may, and in the hands of a major artist often will, be happening. *The Figure of Echo* also distinguishes very usefully between quotation, allusion proper, and echo. (The word *allusion* commonly gets used for the whole process, as well as in the quotation-allusion-echo taxonomy, and I haven't found any way out of this, except to keep the context clear.) Quotation would be signaled as such, by quotation marks, attribution, placement in an epigraph, and so on. Allusion I should define as what a likely reader would likely hear in a given time and place. Echo ranges from strong through clear to faint, where the reader may be hearing things, as we say.[6]

For allusion proper, consider Eliot's poem "Mr Eliot's Sunday Morning Service." We need to have in our ears the cadences of the 1611 English Bible (the King James version, and part of the common tongue for 350 years and more), because the force of Eliot's allusion lies in a change of rhythm. "In the beginning was the Word, and the Word was with God, and the Word was God. The same was in the beginning . . ." (Tyndale's 1534 words, actually). Against this, Eliot plays the rhyme and rhythm of his quatrains (*abcb* rhyme and tetrameter rhythm):

> Polyphiloprogenitive
> The sapient sutlers of the Lord
> Drift across the window-panes.
> In the beginning was the Word.
>
> In the beginning was the Word,
> Superfetation of τὸ ἕν. . . .

Eliot tends to work with *forte* allusive effects, as here, where the contrast is obvious. The unobvious artistry consists of repetition. (Repetition is another type of echo, schematic echo, as in rhyme schemes or refrains.)[7] The first allusion (line 4) is like a fragment, detached from the Sunday morning reading from the Gospels, and drifting across the mind. The second allusion, once stanza 1 has established the rhythm, begins to beat the 1534 sound of "In the beginning . . ." into a 1918 mould. We hear "In the beginning was the Word, / The Word was with God, and what then?" Except that Eliot doesn't waste lines this way; he assumes "what then," and moves at once to the history of dogmatics.

A much quieter example, at the *piano* end of the spectrum of echo, and so unnoticed, occurs in the opening lines of *Paradise Lost* (17–19):

> And chiefly Thou O Spirit, that dost prefer
> Before all Temples th' upright heart and pure,
> Instruct me. . . .

I think Milton must be remembering the full text from the Beatitudes in Matthew, in a glancing echo, glancing toward personal loss and restoration. The full beatitude reads: "Blessed are the pure in heart, for they shall see God." Milton will turn directly toward the subject of his own blindness in the magnificent Invocation to Light (3.1–55). Here, where he is speaking of the fall and restoration of all mankind, direct reference to personal suffering would be inappropriate. Allusion and especially echo offer ways of indirection to the writer.

How to describe in critical terms the process of alluding? Conte suggests that we think of allusion as trope. He proposes metaphor as the trope "most closely analogous to allusion," with a further division into simile for allusion that involves "intentional confrontation."[8] Hollander takes us further, I think, in suggesting metaphor ("echo" in this context is metaphorical, not acoustic) and metalepsis (a figure with a hidden term which interpretation recovers). Metalepsis has the advantage of working with a temporal sequence rather than spatial patterning (which latter is how most figures work — that is, synchronically). As poetry takes place in the tension between synchronic and diachronic, any figure mapping this is most helpful. English-speaking critics have taken a good deal of interest in metalepsis as the interpretive trope of allusion. (Those who have worked with it should not miss Ricks's punning conjunction of *leap* and *meta-* in his essay on Austin — and the figure of metalepsis does leap over this and that, although not etymologically.)

Matters of allusion touch on a good many areas. Some questions are simply spurious. For example, allusion is not a matter of high art versus popular art. The spirituals of Southern African-Americans use biblical allusion in a sophisticated way. Pitting high art against popular art often has more to do with the attitude of the reader or a given historical moment. James Merrill has remarked that "Some readers (I am among them) are flattered by an author's assumption that they've read the same poems as he, or know by heart the same music. Others complain of elitism. This means we can't expect them to consult a reference book."[9]

Allusion studies no longer vex themselves much over the spurious question of plagiarism (spurious in this context). "'Tennyson suspected of plagiarism!' I once heard Browning say. . . . 'Why, you might as well suspect the Rothschilds of picking pockets.'"[10] Or there is Eliot's brisk and accurate summing-up: "Immature poets imitate; mature poets steal" ("Philip Massinger," in *Selected Essays*). Eliot is using the verb *imitate* in the modern reductive sense. For a fuller sense of the role of imitation, we might turn to classical or Renaissance theories of *imitatio, aemulatio*, and the radical revision that only a major author will effect.[11] Or to art history.[12] Academics themselves practice imitation. And allusion, where words are taken over from other writers, usually better ones, is a fine discipline for any writer. Misuse it, and it will turn on you, as in cheap proof-text uses of citation, where the citation can turn and bite the citer.

There are other genuine questions of allusion. For example, questions of different cultures living within a dominant culture. How will Amerindian writers allude, supposing they are working in the English language? Allusions alive in English are fine, but what of allusions in their native language and to traditions little known? Or, another example, suppose a writer wants *not* to use some kinds of allusion? How to empty a given poem of certain echoes, vibrations, implications? This is not the simple matter that most anti-allusive writing assumes. Words do come with their own stories, and unwanted echoes will reverberate in the work of the ignorant.

Or there are questions of audience. Nowadays, even an allusion to the best-known soliloquy in Shakespeare's best-known play may fall on deaf ears. The title of Richard Howard's 1989 collection *No Traveller* rang no bells when announced. But the book itself? The two framing poems are spoken from beyond the grave, or near it, and with ghostly force. Spoken (it had to be) from that undiscovered bourne from which no traveler returns. One hardly needed (I'd have thought) the jacket illustration, *The Isle of the Dead*, to confirm this. And how finely the allusion plays on the mystery of poetic voicing. No traveler does return, so the dead here must find their voice through Howard, who does return. (Re-trope too.) No traveler returns, but Howard does, so is he something other in this book? A magus? A masked persona? Or is he "No-Traveller" who returns? Or perhaps he has not altogether returned, not as a tourist-traveler anyway, for this is true of all of us who hear what the ghostly voices of the dead, our dead, have to say to us. No review I saw mentioned the allusion (even one by a conservative who likes to inveigh against public ignorance and against theory) and I've heard the title misquoted in the plural (by an academic admirer, up on theory). What a curious time it is just now for poets.

Further questions of allusion would include: What happens to an allusion when it becomes detached from its original? How or when does it then develop proverbial force (raising the further question of generic transformation in free-floating allusion)? And (very important) what terms do we use to connect our own words with the alluding words? (*Connect*? Well, splice, interweave, join somehow, and there is always a conditioning metaphor involved, dead or alive.) Allusion also offers fine case studies for comparing the literary uses of language with other uses, philosophical, legal, commercial, and so on.[13]

Marilyn Butler has praised allusion studies while also criticizing them. I sympathize with a wariness of their directing attention too exclusively to one area. Yet I'd want to rephrase her warning: "It's the glory of twentieth-century criticism to have uncovered a network of echoes, verbal allusions, minimalist quotations, that both establishes poetry as a rich private language and seals it off from more prosaic public discourse. . . . plot, a more democratic language [than diction], readily suggests real-life correlatives — change, action, revolt."[14] Whatever criticism may uncover, poetry is virtually never a private language, sealed off. (The exception would be poetry deliberately written in order to exclude some readers.) Some poetry will have a smaller audience than other poetry, but this has to do with the size of a given public audience, not with public versus private. This, too, varies somewhat according to the historical moment.

Most of all, diction cannot be set so readily against plot, because all verbal plots use words, for better or for worse. And words of allusion can just as readily suggest "real-life correlatives — change, action, revolt." To be sure, Butler is speaking of the effects of certain criticism. But it is unclear whether she thinks poetic allusions should be differently established or that they have now been established as she describes, "private . . . and seal[ed] . . . off from more prosaic public discourse."

Not so long ago, in a certain country, charges of seditious libel were laid against the following statements: "Woe unto them that decree unrighteous decrees . . . to take away the right from the poor of my people." "And they [the blessed, this time] shall build houses, and inhabit them; and they shall plant vineyards, and eat the fruit of them. They shall not build and another inhabit; they shall not plant and another eat." The charges of seditious libel were laid in 1919, and the country, I regret to say, was my own. The occasion was the Winnipeg General Strike. Unfortunately for studies in allusion, the case never came to trial, presumably because someone informed the Crown that these sentences came from Isaiah (10:1–2 and 65:21–22). The Crown entered a *nolle prosequi* on all charges.[15]

Or take the following text from Matthew:

Come unto me all ye that labour and are heavy laden, and I will give you rest. Take my yoke upon you, and learn of me; for I am meek and lowly in heart: and ye shall find rest unto your souls. For my yoke is easy, and my burden is light.

(Matt. 11:28–30)

The words are very well known. They provided Milton with the phrase "his mild yoke" in the sonnet on his blindness. They provided Handel with a text for *The Messiah*. I think Wordsworth heard them, when, in 1805, he spoke of his friend Beaupuy's revulsion against the poverty around him in prerevolutionary France (*The Prelude* [1805], 9.519–24); by 1850, he had included the word *meek* along with his earlier *lowly* (ibid. [1850], 9.523–24). In the twentieth century, at a time and place when it cost, Dietrich Bonhoeffer used these words from Matthew at the end of his introduction to *The Cost of Discipleship*: "May we withstand our foes, and yet hold out to them the word of the gospel . . ." and he quoted the entire passage above.[16] "Real-life correlatives"?

SEVEN

The Language of Scripture in Wordsworth's *Prelude*

Wordsworth opens his 1805 *Prelude* with a strong biblical allusion to "a house / Of bondage" (5–6). ("And Moses said unto the people, Remember this day, in which ye came out from Egypt, out of the house of bondage" [Exod. 13:3].) By 1850, he had cut this allusion, and in fact all biblical allusions (allusions properly so called) until the very end of the 270 lines added before his original first line ("Was it for this . . . ?"). The opening lines in the 1805 and 1850 *Prelude* are suffused with Milton's words, but by 1850 they have been emptied of any strong scriptural allusion, the very language of authority for Milton.

Then Wordsworth hands us a problem, for he seems to get it wrong:

> Unprofitably travelling toward the grave,
> Like a false steward who hath much received
> And renders nothing back.
>
> Was it for this . . . ?
>
> *(The Prelude* [1805], 269–71, and [1850], 267–69)[1]

The problem is not in the allusion itself, which is to the parable of the talents in the Gospels. That is sufficiently well known, and to this day.

> When I consider how my light is spent
> Ere half my days in this dark world and wide
> And that one talent which is death to hide
> Lodged with me useless. . . .

> *(Milton, sonnet 19 [ca. 1652])*

> But who would credit that, that one talent
> dug from the claggy Beauce and returned to it
> with love, honour, suchlike bitter fruit.

> (Geoffrey Hill, *The Mystery of the Charity of Charles Péguy* [1983])

If allusion is precise verbal repetition, what are we to say of Wordsworth's allusion to the parable of the talents? W. J. B. Owen rightly objects: "A reference [allusion?] to the parable of the 'unprofitable servant' (Matt. 25:14–30), who did not, however, receive 'much,' but only one talent, compared with the five and two received by his more enterprising colleagues."[2]

Yet Wordsworth was also capable of very precise and suggestive allusion. Take, for example, his allusions to Virgil's *Aeneid* and to the second Epistle of Peter. In book 6 of *The Aeneid*, the Sibyl forewarns Aeneas, "facilis descensus Averno" (6.126, easy the descent to hell). But to climb out, "hoc opus, hic labor est" (6.129, this is work, this is labor). The lines are, or were, very well known, and often imitated. Here is Wordsworth in both the 1798–99 and 1805 *Prelude*: "Hard task to analyse a soul, in which . . ." (262 and 232). I doubt that we would hear the Virgilian echo except for Milton: ". . . down / The dark descent, and up to reascend, / Though hard and rare" (*Paradise Lost* 3.19–21) and "Sad task and Hard" (ibid. 5.564). By 1850, Wordsworth decided to revise this line, raising the volume of his echo: "Hard task, vain hope, to analyze the mind / If . . ." (228–29). This is remarkable work. Wordsworth has come closer to Virgil than Milton did, by means of his compacted sounds: "*hoc opus* . . . hope." It is as if a contraction of Virgil's *hoc opus* into *hope* might suggest too lively a hope (Aeneas and Milton climbed out, and don't we all?), so that Wordsworth must invent an echo-verse that forewarns us of its own conditional emptiness: "vain hope . . . if . . ."[3]

The handling of allusion is expert: it rebounds from Virgil through

Milton, works with two languages, and works also with the repeated sound of a schematic echo (*hoc-opus*-hope). But it is the context that tells. Allusion can bring a weight of context to bear, and here the entire famous prophecy to Aeneas is pertinent, both to psychological and to political readings of Wordsworth. Consider: a lost father that Aeneas yearns to see, a river of blood (Wordsworth's phrase, of the Terror [10.584], and itself a Virgilian phrase, "Et Thyrbrim multo spumantem sanguine cerno" [6.87]), the movement downward to darkness and the struggle up again to light, Milton's use of the lines, and possible implications about beginnings.

As for 2 Peter, both the 1805 and 1850 *Prelude* allude to "the dog / Returning to his vomit" (1805, 9.934–35; 1850, 9.362–63; and see 2 Peter 2:22). Manuscript revisions show some struggling with the lines, and one editor comments: "The passage troubled WW in his final revisions, perhaps on grounds of taste . . . despite the biblical origins of the dog."[4] But the manuscript does not show Wordsworth putting off the dog, so to speak. On the contrary. He added lines to the beginning of this verse paragraph that emphasize the allusion: "Depressed, bewildered thus, I did not walk / With scoffers" (1850, 9.321–22). These words expand words from Peter, "there shall come in the last days scoffers, walking after their own lusts" (3:3). The manuscript shows *scorn* and *scorners* several times, but not *scoffers*, so Wordsworth may have wanted (also or instead?) the well-known opening to all the psalms: "Blessed is the man that walketh not in the counsel of the ungodly . . . Nor sitteth in the seat of the scornful" (Ps. 1:1) — better known than Peter on scoffers, and including *blessed*, a key word for *The Prelude*.

How could someone this good with allusion be so apparently clumsy at the start of his major poem? After all, he did write in 1831: "Again and again I must repeat, that the composition of verse is infinitely more of an art than Men are prepared to believe, and absolute success in it depends upon innumerable minutiae. . . . I could point out to you 500 passages in Milton upon which labour has been bestowed."[5]

Owen is quite right to object about the steward, but then on second glance Wordsworth is right too. Owen is right that no steward appears in the parable, but rather an unprofitable servant. And he is right that the unprofitable servant did not receive much. The person who received much was a steward, as Wordsworth says, but from another parable, one that ends with the sobering admonition: "For unto whom much is given, of him shall be much required" (Luke 12:48). "Like a false steward who hath much received / And renders nothing back." Jonathan Wordsworth briefly noted the second parable a few years ago, but it is worth pausing to note how apt both parables are.[6] Wordsworth has compacted two parables about stewardship, a double weight of unfulfilled vocation. The two patterns of unfulfilment just preceding in *The Prelude* correspond to the two patterns of unfaithfulness in the parables: "a timorous capacity from prudence, / From circumspection" (241–42), that is, burying a talent. Or "vacant musing, unreproved neglect / Of all things, and deliberate holiday" (253–54)—the mild Wordsworthian form of getting drunk and beating the servants, which is what the unfaithful steward does once his lord has gone away. Or, rather, not mild for anyone whom such parables reproach. (They chastened Coleridge. On the taking of opium: "Not to speak of ingratitude to my maker for wasted Talents.")[7] We might observe that Wordsworth uses no verbal echo of Milton's famous sonnet, as if he had no right as yet to claim so large a rendering back.

This is the only biblical allusion (again, allusion properly so called) in all of books 1 and 2 of the 1850 *Prelude*. And it turns out to be most appropriate and carefully worded. The question then becomes why it is comparatively quiet, unlike the "house of bondage," and why Wordsworth's narrative is paced so as to come to scriptural language only at the very end of his 270 introductory lines. To answer that, we need to look more widely at Wordsworth's allusive practice in *The Prelude*.

If there is only one biblical allusion proper in books 1 and 2 of the 1850 *Prelude*, there are a number of biblical echoes. They are there from the beginning in 1798–99, and I believe unheard. And they are enough to make the pious mind quiver, as Wordsworth was quite prepared to do. See, for example, his allusion to Shakespeare just preceding a biblical echo. Here is Shakespeare, in the concluding couplet of sonnet 116:

> If this be error and upon me proved,
> I never writ nor no man ever loved.

Here is the young Wordsworth:

> If this be error, and another faith
> Find easier access to the pious mind. . . .

> > (*The Prelude* [1798–99], 2.465–66; [1850], 2.419–20)

Editors may find this allusion inappropriate, but it is precisely the marriage trope that matters. It allows Wordsworth to hint that a marriage metaphor is just right for the state of mystical transport between his youthful self and the natural world. Shakespeare's sonnet opens:

> Let me not to the marriage of true minds
> Admit impediments. . . .

His lines require us to emphasize the adjective *pious* in Wordsworth:

> If this be error, and another faith
> Find easier access to the *pious* mind. . . .

Not the *true* mind, but the pious mind. As for impediments, one impediment for the true mind can be precisely the pious mind, the pious mind with other models of the marriage trope for what goes on between the self and the natural world. In 1815, in a well-known letter on these same intense youthful feelings, Wordsworth wrote to Catherine Clarkson: "The impediment you may meet with . . ." — another pious mind, hers was.[8]

"If this be error," Shakespeare's couplet begins. "If," Wordsworth goes on,

> If in my youth I have been pure in heart,
> If, mingling with the world, I am content
> With my own modest pleasures, and have lived
> With God and Nature communing . . .
> The gift is yours. . . . thine, O Nature!
>
> > (*The Prelude*, 1798–99, 2.473–92; 1805, 2.444–62;
> > 1850, 2.427–47)

"Blessed are the pure in heart, for they shall see God": thus one of the Beatitudes from the Sermon on the Mount. The pious mind might well be startled at Wordsworth's implicit claim. Even the blind Milton, who echoed the text very quietly when he opened *Paradise Lost*, did not make such a claim (". . . Thou O Spirit, that dost prefer / Before all Temples th'upright heart and pure, / Instruct me . . .").

Yet it is blessedness that matters most for Wordsworth, I think. In the two-book *Prelude* of 1798–99, forms of the word *bless* appear midway through the second book, then begin to accumulate as Wordsworth moves toward his ending with retrospective acknowledgement. "Blessed the infant babe — /

For my best conjectures . . . blest the babe" (2.267–69). "I at this time / Saw blessings spread around me like a sea" (443–44, of age seventeen). "If in my youth I have been pure in heart" (473). "If . . . I yet . . . retain . . . a faith . . . The blessing of my life, the gift is yours" (486–91). The last lines are addressed to Coleridge: "so haply shall thy days / Be many, and a blessing to mankind" (513–14). When Wordsworth reshaped his first two books, he kept the closing passages on blessedness. He also chose to open with blessing, so that *The Prelude* familiar to us begins: "O there is blessing in this gentle breeze." The layered memories of books 1 and 2 are now themselves wrapped in blessing, for the last line remains "Be many and a blessing to mankind."

How does the language of scripture echo and allude through one sustained passage, say the revolutionary books 9 and 10 of *The Prelude*? How might such echo and allusion modify current readings of Wordsworth, including the political Wordsworth?

To my ear, there are no specific biblical allusions at all in book 9, although there is one remarkable echo. It is true that all quotations, allusions, and echoes, not just biblical ones, are singularly muted in this book. General rather than specific echo, however, there is in plenty, of which more later.

In 1805, Wordsworth spoke of his friend Beaupuy's revulsion against the poverty he saw around him in prerevolutionary France (*The Prelude* 9.519–24):

> . . . I with him believed
> Devoutly . . .
> . . . that we should see the earth.
> Unthwarted in her wish to recompense
> The industrious, and the lowly child of toil. . . .

By 1850, this had been revised (9.523–24):

> Unthwarted in her wish to recompense
> The meek, the lowly, patient child of toil. . . .

"For I am meek and lowly in heart." How likely is it that Wordsworth is recalling this? As in all the range of echo, context matters, and this is a powerful one for Wordsworth's purposes.

Come unto me all ye that labour and are heavy laden, and I will give you rest. Take my yoke upon you, and learn of me; for I am meek and lowly of heart, and ye shall find rest unto your souls. For my yoke is easy, and my burden is light.

(Matt. 11:28–30)

In book 10, as the Revolution changes in kind, so also does Wordsworth's allusive practice. There are a good many more allusions in general, as if the mind recalls inherited words more in times of crisis than in times of promise. Wordsworth alludes to three Shakespearean tragedies, the first two, *Hamlet* and *Macbeth*, having to do with murder and with voice. So do the biblical allusions. They are as follows: to Pentecost, to John the Baptist (a reference actually), to Paul's sermon on Mars' Hill (I claim), and, most important, to 2 Kings and Elijah's translation to heaven. All four have to do with voice as prophetic or apostolic. All four have to do with a crucial time, even a revolutionary time. They have to do with personal voice, yes, but personal voice now called to speak to a community, and beyond that, to a world not always receptive. The first two examples are skewed from the original in the Bible, the third is adapted, while the fourth and most important is claimed as an inheritance. Or rather it reclaims an inheritance known instinctively in book 1.

The "gift of tongues" (139; 1805, 122) alludes to Pentecost (Acts 2:3–4). The phrase is not incongruous in itself, but incongruity there is. At Pentecost, the gift of tongues was given to the new small revolutionary group of apostles, who would radiate out from that center into "all the world," as the narrative in Acts puts it. But Wordsworth, watching the momentum of events in France, says he "could almost / Have prayed" that the gift of tongues be given to those *outside* the center of revolutionary fervor. It is as if the Gentiles, not the apostles, were to be granted the gift of tongues, because among the apostles,

> The best lack all conviction, while the worst
> Are full of passionate intensity . . .

— Yeats's better-known and better rephrasing of Wordsworth's lines "The indecision on their part whose aim / Seemed best, and the straightforward path of those / Who in attack or in defense were strong / Through their impiety" (1805, 130–33).

We might hardly notice this small skewing of allusion except for the much louder incongruity of Wordsworth's next biblical words, a reference to the Precursor and the Deity. This time, readers and editors are given pause. Either Wordsworth is decidedly inept or something unusual is going on, for what follows the Precursor is worse, not better. Patriotic love gives way to false patriotism, "Like the Precursor when the Deity / Is come Whose harbinger he was" (307–8; 1805, 307–8, ". . . he is"). Wordsworth, I think, is simply implying that John the Baptist knew whereof he spoke, whereas not all precursors do. When it is bliss to be alive, when hope is rapidly dawning, better must follow good—or so we like to think. Wordsworth's apparent ineptitude allusively speaks to inept thinking that too often takes on the wrong prophetic role. It may also forget that John the Baptist was guillotined, in a manner of speaking.

The next biblical echo should, I think, be rapidly reclassified as an allusion (375–76; 1805, 375–76):

> . . . even thinking minds
> Forgot, at seasons, whence they had their being.

"For in him we live, and move, and have our being; as certain also of your own poets have said." Paul's reported phrasing has entered the common tongue, but it is not an example of general biblical diction. It is used once only in the 1611 Authorized Version, and in a well-known passage, from Paul's sermon on Mars' Hill in Athens (Acts 17:22–31). This time, the allusion is adapted and not skewed, and once again context tells. The sermon takes place in Athens, center of arts and learning, as Paris also was in Wordsworth's time. It opens: "Ye men of Athens, I perceive that in all things ye are too superstitious," Paul here preaching against the altar to the unknown God, and quoting Greek poetry. Wordsworth's "blessed name" is that of "Liberty," in whose name these things are done, and he refers, not to French poetry, but to the words of a patriot and champion of liberty just before she was guillotined on 8 November 1793, Mme Roland. (Her words, translated, were: "Liberty, what crimes are committed in thy name!")

Some 50 lines later comes Wordsworth's loudest biblical allusion: "So, did a portion of that spirit fall on me" (448–49; 1805, 410–11, "some portions"). "I pray thee, let a double portion of thy spirit be upon me": the petition is from Elisha to Elijah at the time Elijah died, or rather was translated—Tyndale's word, in Heb. 11:5, for being caught up into heaven and so never tasting death. Among the biblical ancients, only Enoch and Elijah were so translated. Elijah replies:

> Thou hast asked a hard thing: nevertheless, if thou see me when I am taken from thee, it shall be so unto thee. . . . And . . . behold, there appeared a chariot of fire . . . and Elijah went up by a whirlwind into heaven. And Elisha saw it, and he cried, "My father, my father! the chariot of Israel." . . . And . . . he took up also the mantle of Elijah that fell from him.
>
> *(2 Kings 2:10–13)*

The story of the prophetic mantle and the chariot of fire is a powerful story of vocational calling. What matters most in *The Prelude*, I think, is not so much the mantle or the chariot or the confirmation by sight or the call to a father. What matters most is that Wordsworth takes on Elisha's voice at all, and his occasion for doing so. Wordsworth's note on the "Immortality Ode" reads: "I used to brood [when a child] over the stories of Enoch and Elijah, and almost to persuade myself that, whatever might become of others, I should be translated, in something of the same way, to heaven."[9] We know little about Enoch except that he is said to have "walked with God" (Gen. 5:22, 24) and to have been "translated that he should not see death" (Heb. 11:5). When Wordsworth writes, "I walked with Nature," in *The Prelude* from 1798–99 on (1805, 2.377; 1850, 2.358), I hear a faint echo of Enoch, itself translated into Wordsworth's terms. This is an echo so quiet that it might even fall into the category of private echo—that is, an echo meant chiefly for the poet's own ear.

Answering an adult call to vocation meant moving to the role of an Elisha rather than an Enoch or Elijah. It meant seeing death, here death through the terror of a Revolution gone mad.[10] To all the discussions of prophetic voice in connection with the Romantics, we might add the question: What prophet? What apostle? To discussions of the steadily higher mountain peaks in *The Prelude*, culminating with Mount Snowdon and an apocalyptic moment of transfiguration, we might add the counterpattern of descending the mountain or speaking down from it to a people. The Beatitudes are from the Sermon on the Mount, Paul's sermon is from Mars' Hill. If natural heights are places of vision, nonetheless the vision must be translated. The prophet inspired on the mount also speaks on the mount. The poet is "uplifted" (10.449) so that he can speak out, not just receive into himself. Wordsworth seems here to accept his task: not to be translated into heaven like Enoch and Elijah, but to translate a visionary life, its sight and darkness both, into human community.

What follows in book 10 are references rather than allusions: to deluge (480), to the recollection of a "rainbow-arch" (495) that came before the deluge. With Robespierre's death and the end of the Terror, tension eases.

These are specific allusions and echoes. We might apply the term *general allusion* to those words that are well known, but get detached from their original. General allusiveness is more complicated than we might suppose, and its taxonomy, including the crossing-over area from specific to general allusion, could use some work. Quite different things may be happening with general allusion. Try the following examples from the 1850 *Prelude*: "Wherefore be cast down" (3.82), "puffed up" (5.282), "broad highway" (5.348), and "The plain straight road" (11.71), "potter's clay" (5.531), "lively hope" (7.49), "the mighty City" (7.723), "the dead letter . . . the spirit" (8.296), the "great deep" (9.83), "His hour being not yet come" (8.356, not of Jesus). (All these examples, by the way, are present in the 1805 *Prelude*, except for 11.71, 7.49 [1805: "cheerful hope"], and 10.83.) The problem lies in deciding what context may be at work.

Some examples cut across more than one book of the Bible, and we need to be wary about reading one context only. "Puffed up" and "wherefore be cast down" are examples. Then again, some words have detached themselves from their context, as with the proverb of the dog returning to its vomit in Peter's epistle, itself taken from Proverbs. Some words retain their context faintly if at all: "lively hope," "potter's clay" — this last used more than once but always with the creator as potter and the creature as clay. The letter and the spirit have come over into common usage, and any allusive sense is probably dissipated. The "mighty City" is in Revelation, but may or may not be heard as an echo. It is a question of how often Wordsworth's epithets for *city* resonate with those refrains of the doomed city in Revelation. ("Babylon is fallen, is fallen, that great city.")

We also need to listen for tone, including the humorous turning of biblical allusion by the devout and others. When Wordsworth says, "His hour being not yet come" (1850 *Prelude* 8.356), we respond, Ah, yes, biblical allusion. And it is true that "Mine hour is not yet come" is said by or of Jesus several times in the Gospel of John. It is also true that Wordsworth says of his son John: "He is making steady advances in the practice of Composition, to which he had never been trained — I made many attempts to put him upon it, but always failed; his time was not yet come."[11] Common usage, yes, but then the sentence itself is used more widely in John's Gospel. ("A woman when she is in travail hath sorrow, because her hour is come" [John 16:21].) Did Wordsworth know this? Likely enough; John's Gospel was a favorite.

Wordsworth's method of re-echoing, translating, and dispersing these biblical words is gradualist, accruing, leading from or to the place of allusion. He is remarkable in working over the full scale of quotation, allusion, and echo, both in specific and general allusiveness. Biblical words approach, enter, become part of everyday language almost imperceptibly sometimes. It is a method whereby things fit and are fitting: "fit converse," "if here the words of Holy Writ / May with fit reverence be applied" — the word *fit* itself fitting *Writ* by internal rhyme.

In this attention to detail, Wordsworth's larger concerns may be seen writ small. For as Geoffrey Hartman has taught us in his remarkable *Wordsworth's Poetry, 1787–1814*,[12] Wordsworth prefers to naturalize the literary, concealing it within a language like that of everyday life. "The problem for Wordsworth," to quote Alan Bewell, "is that he is not simply a poet of nature, but also 'a prophet of nature.' "[13] He must somehow also retain the language of prophecy. Given this problem, his preference for echo over allusion, as for a gradualist use of biblical phrasing, seems very natural.

Blake, of course, would have nothing to do with such a method of alluding. He wishes to "cast off the rotten rags of memory by Inspiration . . . To take off his filthy garments, and clothe him with Imagination . . . To cast aside from Poetry all that is not imagination." Yet even here, the casting off may not be in quite the spirit that Harold Bloom supposes. When Bloom asks, "Why should Blake's memory of Milton's poetry be one of 'the rotten rags of Memory'?"[14] I want to hazard the answer: because of Isaiah and Bunyan, and see also Browning. (The three B's, Bunyan, Blake, and Browning, make up a Nonconformist line of descent.) For Blake may well be alluding to a once well-known passage from Isaiah: "All our righteousnesses are as filthy rags" (Isa. 64:6). Filthy rags, that is, if we want to count them as merits in the eyes of God. In the first paragraph of *Pilgrim's Progress*, Christian is said to be "clothed in rags" and the supporting text is this one. Browning's Pope in *The Ring and the Book* refers to "these filthy rags of speech" (10.372). And Browning's Mr. Sludge, the medium, from the poem of that name, inquires, in his antinomian way: "Are we merit-mongers, flaunt we filthy rags?" (986). Such a reading of Blake's allusion would alter our sense of just how he casts off the memory of Milton's poetry, and also does not cast it off. If Milton's works are a righteousness of a sort for Blake, he nonetheless cannot claim any merit because of them. Salvation comes through his own faith, or Inspiration.

Wordsworth's gradualist approach and temperament may disguise the kind and degree of revision in his work. Blake's iconoclastic approach and temperament may disguise the kind and degree of continuity in his work. If we polarize the hearing and writing of allusion, we might find ourselves with these two models: one gradualist, one iconoclastic; one with the authority of tradition, one with the authority of the inner light. Mapping by limits has its uses, though such polarizing can give a false picture.

To return to the word *blessing*, Wordsworth's use of *blessing* to enclose books 1 and 2, his schematic echoing of "blest/best/blest" for the infant babe, his allusion to "Blessed are the pure in heart": all these cause us to listen for later forms of the word *bless*. It appears at the start of the excised Julia-Vaudracour story, for example,[15] and is used of Beaupuy. More than one of Wordsworth's biblical allusions draw on passages in which the word appears — for example, the parable of the false steward ("Blessed is that servant"). (Is it more frequent in the "prophetic and lyrical parts of Scripture," the "grand store-houses" of the "poetical imagination," as Wordsworth called them?)[16] The word *blessed*, sometimes *blessedest*, also runs like a refrain through the love letters of Mary and William Wordsworth.[17] How Wordsworth, how anyone, may journey from early blessedness to later is the burden of the whole *Prelude*. It is a journey (as Wordsworth saw it) from receiving blessing to giving it.

Allusions can have this re-echoing effect, both between poems and within a single poem, where words are dispersed and begin to tell their own stories. As with the word *blessing*, so with other words: *unprofitable*, *pure*, *peace*, and so on. As Wordsworth builds toward his ending, all these words are gathered up and re-echoed. And the whole metaphor of travel introduced at the beginning ("Unprofitably travelling toward the grave") is revised. Wordsworth, so remarkable an ambulatory poet, is unusually sensitive to tropes of walking, running, traveling.

In the allusions of *The Prelude*, Milton is Wordsworth's great original. Wordsworth alludes to Milton ten times more often than to the next contender.[18] In comparison, there is little specific biblical quotation, allusion, and echo. But the language of Scripture carries a special weight, and it is carefully disposed, with attention to pacing, to kind, and to degree. In delaying his opening biblical allusion until the two parables of stewardship, Wordsworth's revision suggests he is deferring the language of Scripture until we grow into it, so to speak. Experience first, then recognition of how this language might speak to our experience. So also with the end of the 1850 *Prelude* (14.124–27). Just as Wordsworth deferred his first biblical allusion, so also here, looking back over his entire poem, he only now allows specific mention of words of Holy Writ:

> Hence, amid ills that vex and wrongs that crush
> Our hearts — if here the words of Holy Writ
> May with fit reverence be applied — that peace
> Which passeth understanding. . . .

Wordsworth has repeated words of Holy Writ from book 1 on, so that his parenthesis might give an irreverent reader pause. (We aren't to apply earlier words? We've been misapplying them? Only certain words should be applied?) But on second thought, there is a question, after all, of just where "here" is. The word *peace* was marked at the beginning: "Long months of peace (if such bold word accord / With any promises of human life")" (1805, 1.26–27; 1850, 1.24–25). It is marked at the end, this time drawing from a biblical benediction (Phil. 4:7). "Here" in one sense is the whole of *The Prelude*, the retrospective sense of how Wordsworth would have us read his poem and read Holy Writ.

EIGHT

The Senses of Eliot's Salvages

". . . le sens du poème dépend de la structure musicale aussi bien que de la structure intellectuelle."

— T. S. ELIOT (1952)[1]

We usually read "Dry Salvages," Eliot's title for the third of his *Four Quartets*, as yet another place-name in his series, repeat his annotation, and let it go at that. The annotation we owe to John Hayward:

> I took Dry Salvages — for you omitted the inverted commas that might have suggested to me that it was a place-name — to be in some sense a reference to what the sea gives up — the torn seine and the dead, and, by extension, memories of a dead life and so on; supporting this interpretation with a vague conviction (unchecked by the dictionary) that insurance companies recognize "dry" salvage and "wet" salvage, the former being more valuable than the latter.[2]

Troubled by Hayward's initial query ("Dry Salvages in a quotation?"), Eliot had first tried inserting the phrase *Les trois sauvages* under the title, then adding quotation marks around the title, before deciding on the present headnote:

(The Dry Salvages — presumably *les trois sauvages* — is a small group of rocks, with a beacon, off the N.E. coast of Cape Ann, Massachusetts. *Salvages* is pronounced to rhyme with *assuages*. *Groaner*: a whistling buoy.)

Eliot's annotation has had one unfortunate effect: it tends to remove the strangeness of his title, so that we do not pause over its words. His first and strong preference was to leave the title unexplained:

"The Dry Salvages" *is* a place name (rhymes with "rampages"). It is ("Les trois sauvages") the name of a group of three rocks off the eastern corner of Cape Ann, Massachusetts, with a beacon: convenient for laying a course to the eastward, Maine or Nova Scotia. *It happens to have just the right denotation and association for my purpose* [my emphasis]; and therefore I am the more disturbed by your comment. It doesn't matter that it should be obscure, but if it is going to lead people quite on the wrong track, then something must be done. I don't like the idea of a note of explanation. Please advise.

The denotation points us toward the rocks on the Massachusetts coast, but the association? The beacon, the sea, the Gloucester fishermen, the Eliot family connection, a name with local flavor? All these associations, however, could be suggested by the quite unmysterious title "Cape Ann," Eliot's title for one poem in his "Landscapes" series. Or, more precisely, suggested by the title Hayward offered, " 'The Dry Salvages,' Cape Ann." "Cape Ann" would have required no headnote and would hardly have elicited tangential speculation on marine insurance. What is gained by "Dry Salvages" rather than "Cape Ann" as title for the third quartet? We should lose the implicit pun on *salvages*, but how great loss would that be?

A crucial loss, I think, but not (or not only) for the reasons put forward by Hayward and Northrop Frye. Frye heard the pun in 1963: "The beauty of the great reverie on the sea (*Ib*) does not conceal the sense of terror and waste, manifest in the grotesque junkpile of 'dry salvage' (the pun is implicit in the title) it spews up on shore."[3] To this we might add the presumably wet salvage that the river bears, "its cargo of dead negroes, cows and chicken coops." And Hayward rightly widens the pun figuratively to include mental salvage or memories, a use anticipated in "Rhapsody on a Windy Night" ("The memory throws up high and dry / A crowd of twisted things").

Eliot's headnote makes two nonreferential points about his title. One gives a presumed derivation from *les trois sauvages*; the other gives the correct pronunciation of *salvages*, for the stress falls on the second syllable, not the first, as we might assume from *salvage* in the singular. To shift the stress is to bring the word closer to *salvation*, and to remind us of the (perhaps odd) thought that one Latin root, *salvare*, gives us both the words *salvage* and *salvation*. Logically, this makes sense, but the connection of *salvage* with what is discarded or wrecked is very strong (see Frye above). The dissociation of *salvage* from *salvation* remains in spite of all the force of the Gospel narratives. Rocks that are "salvages," however, readily suggest the biblical metaphor of the rock of salvation, in this quartet in which the "dominant imagery is of rocks and the sea."[4]

As for the derivation of *salvages* from *sauvages*, Eliot's cousin, Rear-Admiral Samuel Eliot Morison, tells us that this is spurious, *salvage* being simply an obsolete form of the English word *savage*. New Englanders, in preserving the archaic form, *salvages* (Eliot would say, in anglicizing *sauvages*), kept the word closer to *salvare* and also closer to its own Latin origin, *silvaticus*, from *silva*. *Salvage, savage, salvation*: it is a strange trio, but suggestive. We begin the New World quartet with a possibly savage god as it might be comprehended by savage minds, say those of the "salvage-men from the New World" (*OED*, *savage*, 5b). The "leaden periphrases"[5] of the opening lines assume that what is savage simply needs civilizing or saving. Yet savage-civilized and savage-saved are contraries, not opposites. Thomson's Selvaggio in "The Castle of Indolence" is both savage and a savior, *savage* here bearing the Spenserian sense of "rough unpolished" (2.5.3) and also vigorous. Thomson twice makes a Selvaggio-save connection:

> Come, come, sir Knight! thy children on thee call;
> Come, save us yet, e'er ruin round us close!

> *(2.31.3–4)*

> Thrice happy he! who without rigour saves.

> *(2.34.9)*

We might read Eliot allegorically: how do we treat what is "savage" within us and outside us ("the river is within us, the sea is all about us")? As "salvage" (waste) or "salvage" (to be saved) or Selvaggio (a force that may work for salvation) or *salvatio* (a saving force)? (*Salvare* and *salvatio*, incidentally, are both late Latin, and most examples in Lewis and Short are from Christian writers; neither word is listed in the Oxford Latin Dictionary. The adjective *salvus, -a, -um*, is used in classical Latin.)

I offer all this echoing of puns, derivations, and cognates because I think that Eliot's headnote points us toward the punning and etymological and multilingual life of his title. "Salvages" not only refers to a place, but also has a life of its own, with interesting relatives; the wordplay, far from diminishing Eliot's sense of place, enhances it. One allusive echo in particular is essential for a full reading of Eliot's title.

Readers carrying Eliot's poems in their heads may already have moved from *silvaticus* and *silva* to recall Milton's phrase "sylvan scene,"[6] which so darkly enters *The Waste Land*, and of course the "dark wood" from "East Coker":

> In the middle, not only in the middle of the way
> But all the way, in a dark wood . . .

This is an English rendering of Dante's "Nel mezzo del cammin di nostra vita / mi ritrovai per una selva oscura," extended from the beginning of a journey through the entire journey; the allusion is strengthened by the repetition of "in the middle way" later in the same quartet. Dante's "dark wood," like his "middle way," has entered English literature many times. Someone sensitive to Dante's own schematic echoing may hear how his word *selva* in line 2 of the *Inferno* is itself re-echoed in line 5, with the noun repeated, then expanded into an adjective, so that we hear like a refrain the triple echo "selva . . . selva selvaggia." Joyce hears the Dantean wood without ellipsis: "Ah, how wonderful that was to get up early in the morning . . . and enter the misty regions of my emerging epic, as Dante once entered his selva oscura selva selvaggia."[7] And Milton hears how Dante's *selva oscura* and also his *selva selvaggia* may be echoed in English poetry, although he restricts his phonetic echoing:

> O might I here
> In solitude live *savage*, in some glade
> *Obscur'd*, where highest *woods* impenetrable . . .
>
> (*Paradise Lost* 9.1084–86; emphasis added)

Affecting private life, or more *obscure*
In *savage wilderness*, wherefore deprive
All earth . . . ?

(Paradise Regained 3.22–23; emphasis added)[8]

Standard Milton editions and commentaries have not observed this Dantean resonance, although it makes excellent sense in both *Paradise Lost* and *Paradise Regained*.[9] In *Paradise Lost* 9.1084–86, for example, Milton re-places Adam in a fallen nature; the Dantean echoes implicitly suggest that this is an allegorical landscape of sin, but equally that it is the possible start of a pilgrimage back to Eden. Prelapsarian "savage" introduced us to the forest of Eden ("that steep savage hill," 4.172), but here we see the word itself fallen from a savage-sylvan association to a savage-barbaric association, language, like the woods, participating in the general fall.

If we come to "Dry Salvages" with the Dantean allusions from "East Coker" still in our heads, along with the Italian original, and if we hear the reverberations of salvage, *sauvage, salvare,* savage, *silvaticus, silva,* sylvan, and so on, then we cannot but hear a Dantean re-echoing in Eliot's "Dry Salvages." In part 4 of this quartet, Eliot quotes part of the opening line of the last canto of the *Paradiso,* "figlia del tuo figlio." The pilgrim Dante hears this petition voiced by St. Bernard at the end of his journey, after the darkness of the "selva oscura . . . selva selvaggia" has given way to the darkness of hell, then to the very different shadow of "la divina foresta spessa e viva . . . alla selva antica" (*Purg.* 28.2, 23), then to the great vision of light that will inform Eliot's own closure in *Four Quartets.*[10] To begin with Dante's *selvaggia* from his first canto and culminate with "figlia del tuo figlio" from his last canto makes sense in this quartet, which "is all transit, comings and goings, with the attendant temptation of choosing our direction and attendant danger of getting lost."[11] To shift from the *selva oscura* of the quartet of earth to a watery *selvaggia* in the quartet of water also makes sense. We may even hear Dante informing Eliot's own remarks about his title: "It doesn't matter that it should be obscure ['selva oscura'?], but if it is going to lead people quite on the wrong track ['la dritta via era smarrita . . . la verace via abbandonai'?] then something must be done."

Finally, given Eliot's ear for Latin resonances,[12] I wonder if a "salve-vale" echo is not playing through part 3 of "The Dry Salvages" with its repeated "Fare forward, travellers! . . . 'Fare forward. . . . Fare forward. . . . 'Not fare well, / But fare forward, voyagers." *Salve* means "hail" or "good day" or "fare well" or "farewell." We may know it from "Salve Regina" or perhaps from the funeral salutation of Aeneas in his abrupt, final parting from the dead:

> nos alias hinc ad lacrimas eadem horrida belli
> fata vocant: salve aeternum mihi, maxime Palla,
> aeternumque vale.
>
> *Me the same grim destiny of war summons hence to other tears: hail thou for*
> *evermore, noblest Pallas, and for evermore farewell.*
>
> (*Aeneid* 9.96–99, Loeb ed.)

Here *salve* and *vale* mark the end of a journey, whose finality is beautifully rendered in the chiasmus of "salve aeternum . . . aeternumque vale" (the sounds of *vale* are anagrammatically included in *salve*). The reiterated *aeternum* opens its line, and the period then closes with *vale*, an eternal *vale*. Halfway through the journey that is "The Dry Salvages," Eliot gives us several journeys, beginning with ordinary train trips and ending with a faring forward to the field of battle, where "fare well" all too often moves to "farewell," like the history of the word itself. *Salve* and *vale*, like the more familiar *ave valeque*, seem a natural pair. Yet something different may be set against these pairs — for instance, the earthly paradise, whose properties of birds, woods, water, and valleys are found within the four words, *ave, salve, vale*, and the conjunctive *-que*, in Joyce's "Aves Selvae Acquae Valles!" (*Finnegans Wake* 147.6–7). This exuberant punning, which makes Eliot's wordplay look restrained, plays on a *salve-selva* near-homonym, and of course much else as well.

What I hear in Eliot's text is counsel not to move toward a Virgilian mode of farewell, as we move forward to our farewells. At the end of the *Purgatorio*, Dante must take his leave of Virgil before he can complete his own journey of salvation. Of these cantos, Eliot said, "In a way, [they] are those of the greatest *personal* intensity in the whole poem" ("Dante" [1929]). Here is Dante's cry, on finding Virgil vanished:

> Ma Virgilio n'avea lasciati scemi
>   di sé, Virgilio dolcissimo patre,
>   Virgilio a cui per mia salute die' mi;

> *But Virgil had left us bereft of himself, Virgil sweetest father, Virgil to whom I gave myself for my salvation;*

(*Purg.* 30.49–51, trans. Singleton)

My interest is in that extraordinary word *salute* in line 51, variously translated as salvation (Singleton, Ciardi, Sinclair), good (Sayers), weal (Carlyle-Wickstead), and safety (Cary). At this moment, such a word in such a line is a generous and beautiful tribute to Virgil (more generous than some of the warily orthodox translators are); it is confirmed by Beatrice, who repeats the word *salute* in line 137 (variously translated by the same authors as, respectively, *salvation, saving, salvation, to save, salvation,* and *preserving*). Latin *salus, -utis,* may mean safety or salvation or salutation. Dante's *salute* comes in his great salutation and calling-out to Virgil, so that we may hear a play on *saluto,* with *salute* transforming a Virgilian *saluto,* a *salve valeque.* Not *salve* but *salute,* we might say, paraphrasing Eliot. Not farewell but fare forward. (It may even be important that Dante avoids a *salve-vale* formulation precisely where we expect one, such avoidance just suggesting a revision of Virgil, one more to add to those so finely observed by John Freccero.)[13] Eliot's counsel of "fare forward" rather than "fare well" similarly defines his kind of journey in a salutation revised by salvation — a salutation that itself orders our hearing of the earlier complex of *salvare* echoes.

Wallace Stevens, three years after the publication of "The Dry Salvages," heard — and disliked — what Eliot was doing. ("After all, Eliot and I are dead opposites.")[14] Stevens's phrase, "obscurer selvages" ("Esthétique du Mal"), evokes Eliot but even more loudly recalls the "selva oscura . . . selva selvaggia" of Eliot's source, and brilliantly re-puns on *selvaggia.* For *selvage* has a Germanic not a Latinate root, apparently coming from *self* and *edge;* one old form among many is *salvage.* Stevens echoes sound in his "obscurer selvages," but dislocates denotative and associative meaning by decentering Dante. For Dante's "selva oscura . . . selva selvaggia" is not in the middle of life's way for Stevens, but on the edge of things, the selvages. Eliot's poem is, if anything, obscurer.[15] I do not know whether Eliot was aware of Stevens's encoded *riposte,* but, if he knew of it, he must at least have been pleased that it made use of a Dantean weapon.

This complex of quotations, allusions, and allusive and fainter echoes should go some way to answer F. W. Bateson's charges that Eliot's allusions in

Four Quartets are not functional. I am less certain how far it answers difficulties with voice and diction in parts of "The Dry Salvages." But if the poem depends on the "degree to which his [the reader's] own sense of the process is animated by Eliot's words,"[16] then it can only be strengthened by a sense of the associative process at work. For all the associations with *salvages*, and especially the *selva-selvaggia* echoes, expand to enrich our sense of different kinds of journeying. They allow us to read backward in a renewed way, hearing Dantean echoes in Milton and possible wordplay in Dante himself.

They are also self-descriptive. We reflect on what in language is saved or salvaged ("most allusions of subtlety and efficacy are likely to be related in some important way to inheritance").[17] Or savage or saving ("What we remember saves us," says W. S. Merwin in his poem "Learning a Dead Language"). We reflect on the faring forward of words, and our possible farewells to them. Both Eliot's and Stevens's allusive echoes seem to belong to John Hollander's category of metaleptic echo, Stevens's being radically revisionary as Eliot's are not. Eliot's metalepsis takes up and widens "an inheritance, a various poetic inheritance."[18]

His most specific tribute to that inheritance is in part 2 of "Little Gidding," with its dead master who is both one and many, whose truths are severe but whose unheard farewell is a kind of benediction in its tranquillity: "He left me, with a kind of valediction, / And faded on the blowing of the horn." The language of hallucination and poetic echoing itself gives way here to the language of denotation. (The re-echoing of a Virgil-Dante farewell is deliberately deadened in the precise and austere phrase, "kind of valediction," and the echo from *Hamlet* appears only to fade itself in new hearing.) So also, all Eliot's associations with *salvages* may themselves give way to the language of denotation when we turn back to the "Dry Salvages" as those rocks Eliot knew. In the end, Eliot's "denotation and association" seem to me inseparable.

NINE

Wallace Stevens and the King James Bible

"Last night was house-cleaning night with me. I went through my things . . . and threw away a pile of useless stuff. . . . One of the things was my Bible. I hate the look of a Bible. This was one that had been given to me for going to Sunday-school every Sunday in a certain year. I'm glad the silly thing is gone."[1] Thus Wallace Stevens, in 1907, aged 27. You might not guess from this that the same Wallace Stevens had written in his journal in 1906, quoting Ps. 19: "I wish that groves still *were* sacred — or, at least, that something was: that there was still something free from doubt, that day unto day still uttered speech, and night unto night still showed wisdom" (*L*, 86 [5 Feb. 1906]).

These two quotations may serve as emblems of two sides of Stevens that will persist through most of his life. One is mischievous, sometimes iconoclastic, given to polemic, especially active in the presence of high-toned old Christian women, even more so in the presence of what Stevens called "the spirit's own seduction" (*L*, 438, 28 Jan. 1943). The other yearns for the sublime and feels the force of the ancient words. One pulls against the other. "Behold, I make all things new," says the Book of Revelation (21:5). "Crispin beheld and Crispin was made new," says the mischievous Stevens in "The Comedian as the Letter C," part 1. Or, "Our God whom we serve is able to deliver us from the burning fiery furnace," says the Book of Daniel (3:17, varied 6:17, 6:20). "The Got whome we serve is able to deliver / Us . . . Click, click, the Got whom we serve is able / Still, still to deliver us," says a voice in Stevens's "Examination of the Hero in a Time of War." His "Got" is a Germanic God, one *t* short of the Gott of the Luther Bible, and so perhaps an English-language pun, this being a wartime poem where "Got you" might mean rescue or might mean killing. Stevens is quite capable of so grim a pun. But then: "Feed my lambs," says Christ to Peter, in a pastoral injunction, repeated in his *Adagia* by the Stevens who yearns for the sublime, and applied to the poet's vocation. "(Poet,) feed my lambs." "Feed my lambs (on the bread of living)."[2]

These two tendencies are familiar enough to us. By and large, they work separately, as an either-or, in Stevens's earlier use of biblical allusion. In the 1930's that begins to change, as he develops a different approach, an approach that he will bring to perfection in the 1940's. The Stevens who desires the sublime will present a set of traditional arguments, topoi, genres, rhetorical figures, dominant polarities. (These are often presented in compact, elliptical, even enigmatic ways.) Then the mischievous or iconoclastic Stevens will decreate this pattern.[3] But then Stevens will move beyond, in order to retrieve what, after much testing, will hold. And what is retrieved and holds is different in kind, not just in degree, from what has preceded it. This is a pattern that is true of Stevens's use of allusion in general; it is so with the words of Milton as much as the words of the English Bible.

One poem (or part of a poem) in which this happens is the seventh canto of the 1947 poem "The Auroras of Autumn." But first, a few remarks about allusiveness and about Stevens's biblical knowledge in general. Our own notions of allusion sometimes pull between two poles, rather like those two sides of Stevens that I have outlined above. That is, to quote John Hollander, "allusions tend to be treated as innocent, ironic, or, at best univocally significant."[4] Hollander's poetics works with a rhetorical taxonomy designed to get beyond the polarity of innocence versus irony. Studies of allusion may also work usefully with a narrative plot rather than a rhetorical taxonomy, a plot in which allusions make up a narrative of inheritance.[5] Both these ways of reading allusions are helpful for "Auroras of Autumn" as a whole and the seventh canto in particular.

As for Stevens's biblical knowledge in general, I take it that I no longer need to argue the case that he did possess considerable knowledge of the language of the English Bible in its most familiar form, the 1611 King James or Authorized Version. By now we have heard too many biblical words echoing in Stevens's poetry and prose to doubt such knowledge.[6] Among many examples, variations on "I am that I am" in *Notes Toward a Supreme Fiction* are familiar. Less familiar examples include the following: "The poet must always desire the pure good of poetry just as the sinner desires only the pure good of the blood of the lamb. Without thee, O Sophia, what value has anything?" (*L*, 625 [1948]; see Rev. 7:14, 12:11). Or: "What light requires a day to do, and by day I mean a kind of Biblical revolution of time, the imagination does in the twinkling of an eye" (*NA*, 61–62 [1943]). Stevens refers to a biblical day, but he alludes to biblical resurrection and final revelation, transferring the agency from God to the imagination. "We shall not all sleep, but we shall all be changed, In a moment, in the twinkling of an eye" (1 Cor. 15:51–52). Or, of "poets and painters alike today" (1951): "the validity and serious dignity that become them as among those that seek wisdom, seek understanding" (*NA*, 175; see Prov. 4:7).

Stevens's mother used to read her children a chapter of the Bible each evening at bedtime, although, "often, one or two of us fell asleep" (*L*, 173 [25 June 1912]). Stevens, we assume, was one of the sleepers, since he found himself having to consult the library in order to be sure who Saul was ("confound my ignorance") (*L*, 176 [11 Aug. 1912]). Yet he clearly knew passages from the English Bible, and not only because some were then part of the common tongue. He was even familiar with at least one text from the Luther Bible: "I wish I could tell you how much I enjoyed getting your letter. It was like going to the Evangelical Church in Reading and hearing old Dr. Kuendig preach in German on the text 'Ich bin der Weg, die Wahrheit, und das Leben'" (John 14:6).[7] And although he might dislike the look of a Bible, and cheerfully throw his away, he cherished some books among the 66 of the Protestant Bible. Psalms and Proverbs were special favorites. "'I am a stranger in the earth.' — You see, I have been digging into the Psalms — anything at all, so long as it is full of praise — and rejoicing. I am sick of dreariness" (*L*, 141 [3 May 1909]). Or, in 1922, thanking someone for the gift of a carved Chinese figure: "The old man is so humane that the study of him is as good as a jovial psalm" (*L*, 231 [28 Oct. 1922]). (Stevens is surreptitiously introducing a god from another pantheon into Yahweh's domain, this also being the reason for the adjective *jovial* in the phrase, "jovial hullabaloo among the spheres," in "A High-Toned Old Christian Woman.") In 1947, he spoke of Eccles. 12:6 ("Or ever the silver cord be loosed, or the golden bowl be broken . . ."): "these images . . . relate to reality and . . . give us the pleasure of 'lentor and solemnity' in respect to the most commonplace objects" (*NA*, 78). And the Ecclesiast himself enters "An Ordinary Evening in New Haven," canto 19. Stevens wrote in 1909, "I am not pious" (*L*, 140 [3 May 1909]), and this remained true all his life. He also argued that the poetic imagination is one thing and the biblical imagination is another (*NA*, 143–44 [1948]). Nonetheless, the ancient words spoke in various ways to his "magnificent agnostic faith," to use Geoffrey Hill's precise and just phrase.[8]

Of course, we need to keep a sense of proportion in all this. We might want to plot the frequency of biblical allusion throughout Stevens's work. We might want to consider the proportion of such words and phrases in comparison with other words and phrases that lived in that capacious imagination (say, from Shakespeare). We might go on to consider how often biblical allusions rebound from, say, Milton and Wordsworth. And we should distinguish from specific biblical allusion the use of general biblical diction, as well as references to characters or stories. Revising of biblical genres (for example, apocalyptic writing or wisdom literature) and awareness of methods of biblical interpretation (for example, typology) argue more for Stevens's extraordinary capacities than for any specialized knowledge. In his specific allusions, we should map the angles of Stevens's own responses with great care, as always with allusion, acknowledging that such responses can range from a surprisingly rough-and-ready ironic reversal through to the more usual subtlety and force. And we should guard against the simplistic tendency in our own reading of allusion mentioned above.

Canto 7 of "The Auroras of Autumn" opens with three questions:

> Is there an imagination that sits enthroned
> As grim as it is benevolent, the just
> And the unjust, which in the midst of summer stops

> To imagine winter? When the leaves are dead,
> Does it take its place in the north and enfold itself,
> Goat-leaper, crystalled and luminous, sitting
>
> In highest night? And do these heavens adorn
> And proclaim it, the white creator of black, jetted
> By extinguishings, even of planets as may be,
>
> Even of earth, even of sight, in snow,
> Except as needed by way of majesty,
> In the sky, as crown and diamond cabala?

To begin with the third question: the allusion to the opening verse of Ps. 19 is commonly acknowledged. "The heavens declare the glory of God; and the firmament sheweth his handiwork." Stevens changes the verbs from the assertive mood to the interrogative (and we should work out various possible answers to his three questions). He changes the verbs *declare* and *show* to "adorn / And proclaim" (here, etymology may matter, Latin *clarare* as against Latin *clamare*). He changes "the heavens" to "these heavens" (a signal to watch all deictics in this canto). A good poet's allusions will bring a weight of context to bear, and it is worth considering all of Ps. 19 in relation to this canto. After all, Stevens quoted the second verse in the 1906 journal entry given above, and quoted from memory, I assume, since he substituted the word *wisdom* for the Authorized Version's *knowledge*. The entire psalm includes the desire for innocence "from the great transgression" (whatever that may be), and Stevens will move to innocence in cantos 8 and 9.

What do critics usually make of this allusion? If anything, we make an ironic reversal that sets Stevens's auroras against a biblical heaven. (The auroras are unpredictable in their occurrence and in their trajectory, unlike the stars and the planets; they come in the autumn and in the north, but no one can predict exactly when or where; they make an allegory of death and not of eternal life.) It is true that, for 25 years and more, Stevens has moved against the topos of the starry night declaring the glory of God, that topos drawn from the Bible and figuring in Kant and in Coleridge. But considered conceptually, why could the auroras not just as well declare the glory of God in some way? And considered rhetorically, isn't this allusion rather uninteresting, just a fillip reminding us of Stevens's doctrinal position? It is hardly surprising that some commentators simply ignore the allusion, when its point seems obvious and a bit dull.

We need to look again at the two preceding questions. In the opening question, the allusion to "the just and the unjust" must have been heard, although it is not commonly noted. The context is important. Once again, there is a heaven, or rather your Father which is in heaven, this time from the Sermon on the Mount, from the Gospel of Matthew. (Stevens appears to have had Matthew on his mind at this time; his 1948 essay "Effects of Analogy" includes a text from Matthew, a quotation by Jesus of a pastoral verse in Ezekiel.) The phrase "the just and the unjust" comes from one biblical vision of a heaven, with a Father who sends the gifts of sun and rain on both the just and the unjust, and so, says Jesus, gives us a pattern for the near-impossible commandment "Love thine enemies" (a commandment unlikely to have been much quoted in 1947). And Stevens's parataxis is very odd. How do we align *grim* and *benevolent, just* and *unjust*?

Stevens's second question does not make use of allusion, but of its quieter sister, echo, and although the echo has not been noted, I judge it loud enough to be called allusive echo.

> . . . When the leaves are dead,
> Does it take its place in the north and enfold itself,
> Goat-leaper, crystalled and luminous, sitting
>
> In highest night?

"In the north": yes, we say, the northern lights; "enfold itself": yes, we say, enfold itself like the serpent that opens this whole poem, effective descriptive language for the auroras; "crystalled": a figure of descriptive accuracy again. But Stevens's mind is running on yet another biblical heaven, and this time an appropriately apocalyptic one.

> And I looked, and behold, a whirlwind came out of the north, a great cloud, and a fire infolding itself. . . . [4]
> And the likeness of the firmament upon the heads of the living creature was as the colour of the terrible crystal, stretched forth over their heads above. [22] And above the firmament that was over their heads was the likeness of a throne. . . . [26]

These verses are from the opening chapter, the wheel-within-a-wheel chapter, of the Book of Ezekiel, when "the heavens were opened, and I saw visions of God." Ezekiel is the earlier partner, the begetter, the type, for the last book of the Bible, the Apocalypse. Both give us scenes of judgment, when the heavens are opened, and one gives us the last judgment. In the Apocalypse, it is the Lamb, come in judgment, that sitteth upon the throne, a Lamb as grim as He is benevolent (to use Stevens's adjectives). Incidentally, I don't know whether a full display of the northern lights would ever have been visible as far south as ancient Babylonia, where Ezekiel was captive. I myself have seen the smaller white displays often enough, but a full display only once — and it's a memorable sight (with a crown, by the way, as in lines 12 and 18). Perhaps some miracle-debunker has already suggested that Ezekiel's vision was a display of the aurora borealis, although not to my knowledge. If you ever should see a full display, you might want to look again at the first chapter of Ezekiel. "A wheel within a wheel a-rolling, / Way in the middle of the air" catches it very nicely.

In the sixty-eighth year of his life, then, and two years following the great conflagrations of World War II, Stevens looks up at the auroras of autumn. Three different biblical heavens inform his sight in this canto: first, the merciful heavens, with the perhaps impossible injunction of radical love toward one's enemies, and the puzzle of whether justice can work without being grim, and benevolence without being unjust. Second, the thrones of heaven, Ezekiel's and by extension Revelation's, the apocalyptic heavens, terrible and judging. And third, the singing heavens, declaring the glory of God, and explicitly questioned by "these" heavens.

In the midst of these heavens is a somewhat incongruous creature, a "Goat-leaper." This creature is *not* Capricorn, *pace* several commentators. Or rather it is Capricorn only at one remove. Capricorn is etymologically a goat-horn and not a goat-leaper. My observation may seem niggling at first glance, but poetry is nothing if not the art of the precise. Why a goat-leaper, then, rather than a goat-horn? There is a good deal of leaping in this canto, to be sure, and it makes appropriate descriptive language for the auroras. But there is also an uncommon amount of goatishness, more than we have realized. Here are the stanzas that follow the four given above:

> It leaps through us, through all our heavens leaps,
> Extinguishing our planets, one by one,
> Leaving, of where we were and looked, of where

We knew each other and of each other thought,
A shivering residue, chilled and foregone,
Except for that crown and mystical cabala.

But it dare not leap by chance in its own dark.
It must change from destiny to slight caprice.
And thus its jetted tragedy, its stele

And shape and mournful making move to find
What must unmake it and, at last, what can,
Say, a flippant communication under the moon.

The etymology of *caprice* in line 20 has been noted; it derives from the word for *goat*. The etymology of the word *tragedy* has not been noted; the etymon, *tragos*, although much disputed, has long been defined as "goat-song" — whence Shelley's preface to Hellas, "the only *goat-song* which I have yet attempted." And there is one more piece of goatishness. Although French speakers may not be familiar with this term, *Brewer's Dictionary of Phrase and Fable* (s.vv. *merry dancers*) does say that one French literary phrase for the northern lights is, in fact, *les chèvres dansantes*, the dancing goats — goat-leapers, we might say.

This points us in the direction of the biblical story of the sheep and the goats — once more from Matthew, and, like the phrase "the just and the unjust," found only in Matthew (25:32, 33). For consider who ought to sit upon a throne in the heavens in a Christian apocalypse: it is the Lamb. To see the auroras as a Christian vision of the Apocalypse is to see the Lamb, enthroned and terrible in judgment, dividing the sheep from the goats. Well, but suppose a French imagination sees those leaping northern lights as dancing goats. Suppose it refuses the goat-song of tragedy, its mournful making, and prefers the goat-leap of caprice, the "flip" of *flippant*. Suppose it refuses the last-judgment division into the just and the unjust, the sheep and the goats. Suppose it celebrates, not a grim goat but a leaping goat — even a horny goat, a Capricorn, since the goat is after all a figure for lechery, and the verb *leap* also has a sexual meaning in biblical and Shakespearean and other usage. See Touchstone to Audrey, in Shakespeare's *As You Like It* (3.3.7–9): "I am here with thee and thy goats as the most capricious poet, honest Ovid, was among the Goths" (pronounced "goats"). *Capricious* is glossed in the Riverside Shakespeare as meaning "ingenious, full of witty conceits; with play on Latin *caper*, 'he-goat,' which further suggests the sense 'goatish, lascivious.'" A caper in English is, of course, a leap. Stevens might well say, with James Joyce: "Anyhow I am now hopelessly with the goats and can only think and write capriciously." And he might even go on to vary the biblical text, as Joyce does: "Depart from me ye bleaters, into everlasting sleep which was prepared for Academicians and their agues!"⁹ — a thought to give pause to academics.

A whole series of associations, then, works retrospectively to undo the jetted tragedy of goats, their black destiny. It moves to restore goats from a destiny in the dark to a leap toward their own nature, so to speak: caprice, capriciousness, a capriole, a caper, dancing lustiness, witty conceits, leaping. This canto comes to be dominated by the Goat, or rather the Goat-leaper, as against the enthroned Lamb. But the force of destiny and of the dark inhibits the goatish imagination from taking a leap — a leap of faith, we might say, not a leap in *the* dark (where we know what destiny would decree), but a leap by chance in its *own* dark. ("Necessity and Chance / Approach not mee," says Milton's God [*Paradise Lost* 7.172–73].)

The story of the sheep and the goats is one topic of biblical pastoral.¹⁰ Stevens is, I think, implanting an antipastoral here, an eg-logue as against as ec-logue, reaffirming the place of the goat in pastoral,¹¹ and thereby separating out New Testament pastoral from classical pastoral, where goats enjoy life. He is moving against the entire great force of Christian pastoral tradition, a tradition that could sometimes speak to Stevens about his vocation, as in the quotations from the *Adagia* given above. His flippant communication under the moon suggests the "serious burlesque" (the phrase is Hazlitt's) of a countergenre.¹² If Stevens were writing in the 1920's, and writing such a poem as "A High-Toned Old Christian Woman," he would stop with a set of contraries, and run all the risks of binary oppositions, of not moving out of the black-and-white, the sheep-and-goats axis. If he were writing "The Comedian as the Letter C," he would stop with a decreation of genre and countergenre, of general pieties. Not so in the 1940's. Not so in the white canto with the flippant communication under the moon in *Notes Toward a Supreme Fiction* (part 1, canto 3). Not so here. Stevens sets up polarities (and the actual auroras do center on the two magnetic poles, north and south, negative and positive respectively). Then he steps aside and dismantles them, in a Joycean move. But he will not stay there. As he writes two years later in "An Ordinary Evening in New Haven" (17.17–18):

> The serious reflection is composed
> Neither of comic nor tragic but of commonplace.

And so he goes on, in canto 8 of "The Auroras of Autumn," beginning thus:

> There may be always a time of innocence,
> There is never a place.

This move to the question of innocence introduces a far larger matter than I can treat here. What might be observed is that Stevens is retaining something of pastoral in his return to innocence, for all that he may have suggested an antipastoral or anti-Christian pastoral in canto 7. This innocence will be not under the care of a shepherd or even a goatherd, but of a woman, a mother. It will not be in a sheepfold, to say nothing of being enfolded in the heavens (like that grim benevolent imagination) or even in the enfolding of an actual mother, and alas, not even in the active memory of such enfolding. (One of Stevens's most poignant lines in this poem reads: "The necklace is a carving not a kiss," a line punning gently and sadly on an embrace as a necklace.) No, the enfolding is earthly, domestic, a being-at-home, in a northern latitude of America.

This short exegesis raises other questions as well. Most puzzling to me is why Stevens introduces a question of the just and the unjust, and why he wants to retrieve an innocence of the earth. This is a poem that speaks powerfully of (and perhaps to) an older person imagining the facing of death. How does it also speak of and to the year 1947, the time of a realignment of wartime allies, of the new nuclear age, but also a time free at last of the shadow of World War II?[13] Why, at this date, does Stevens come back so strongly to a time of innocence?

I have argued for a three-part movement in Stevens's mature use of allusion — here his reading of the skies through an older, sacred text. Suppose we take this three-part movement and make a little allegory of it for our own critical practice. The first type of critical reading would take the text on its own terms, follow its apparent intentionalities, offer (I suppose) something like a New Critical reading, fully exploiting ironies and ambiguities. The second reading would deconstruct all this: not simply reversing the hierarchy of sheep and goat, but stepping outside that duality and making (what else, for a deconstructionist?) a "flippant communication" and making it (where else for a deconstructionist?) "under the moon," in the realm of mutability.

But then comes the crux, the turn, the difficulty for us, as for Stevens. It is the decision of what to retrieve, to hold to, in readings of the past, in our inheritance. Struggles with this question absorb us now in our critical lives — struggles to avoid too naive an innocence, too self-righteous an irony, or too facile a recovery from the past. These are hazards against which good art warns us, and not least that of Wallace Stevens in his strategies of biblical allusion.

TEN

Birds in Paradise: Revisions of a Topos in Milton, Keats, Whitman, Stevens, and Ammons

The Mockingbird as a Figure of Echo

In 1813, when Byron adapted Goethe's Song "Kennst du das Land," he took the liberty of adding a singing bird:

> Know ye the land . . .
> Where the citron and olive are fairest of fruit,
> And the voice of the nightingale never is mute . . . ?
>
> — *"Bride of Abydos"* 1.5, 9–10

This is hardly an intrusion; birdsong seems to belong so naturally to an earthly paradise that Goethe's omission of it may appear stranger than Byron's addition. In 1949, Wallace Stevens also added a bird to his Goethean earthly paradise, this time not the expected nightingale but a New World bird, the mockingbird. And although the mockingbird is a prodigious singer, who can reproduce numerous songs, Stevens, like his admired Goethe, makes no clear reference to birdsong. His enigmatic earthly paradise opens canto 19 of "An Ordinary Evening in New Haven":

139

> In the land of the lemon trees, yellow and yellow
> Were yellow-blue, yellow-green, pungent with citron-sap,
> Dangling and spangling, the mic-mac of mocking birds.[1]

(505–7)

Stevens's poetry, as so often, refrains from ready interpretive, and here even tonal, indicators.[2] Why mockingbirds, and in what sense do they mock? Should we read simple irony (mock in derision)? Or ambiguity (mock in derision and/or mime)? And what do we do with the apparent nonsense syllables *mic-mac*?

The mockingbird offers a reader almost too much possibility rather than too little. To follow its natural history: *Mimus polyglottos* is a bird of the Western Hemisphere and enters the English language only in 1649, according to the *OED*. It thus does not appear in Spenser or Shakespeare, or, as it happens, Milton. It is by far the most skillful of the American Mimidae, and it is the state bird of Stevens's once-loved Florida.[3] The song is generally admired. To follow its literary history, we may go back to 1732, when an English visitor made the bird a figure of echo, heavenly echo, in a loco-descriptive poem anticipating Thomas Jefferson's view that the nightingale is a "third-rate singer" compared with the mockingbird:[4]

> But what is He,* who perch'd above the rest,
> Pours out such various Musick from his Breast!
> His Breast, whose Plumes a cheerful white display.
> His quiv'ring Wings are dress'd in sober grey.
> Sure all the Muses, this their Bird inspire!
> And he, alone, is equal to the Choir
> Of warbling Songsters who around him play,
> While, Echo like, He answers ev'ry lay
>
> . . . .
>
> Oh sweet Musician, thou dost far excel
> The soothing Song of pleasing Philomel!
> Sweet is her Song, but in few Notes confin'd;
> But thine, thou Mimic of the feath'ry Kind
> Runs thro' all Notes! — Thou only know'st them All,
> At once the Copy — and th'Original.[5]

*The Mock-Bird

Wordsworth called the mockingbird's song merry, in contrast to the song of a melancholy Muccawiss (*The Excursion* 3.946) — thereby demonstrating that he had never heard a mockingbird, whatever his experience of Muccawisses. Sir Richard Burton, a better ornithologist, abducted one to an Arabian *locus amoenus* in one of his notes to *The Arabian Nights* — a well-justified eastward *translatio*.[6] Ruskin used one for fierce anti-American polemic.[7] Longfellow's mockingbird in "Evangeline" (1847) preceded by twelve years Whitman's justly famed singer in "Out of the Cradle Endlessly Rocking":

> Then from a neighbouring thicket the mocking-bird, wildest of
>   singers,
> Swinging aloft on a willow spray that hung o'er the water,
> Shook from his little throat such floods of delirious music,
> That the whole air and the roads and the waves seemed silent to listen.
> Plaintive at first were the tones and sad; then soaring to madness
> Seemed they to follow or guide the revel of frenzied Bacchantes.
> Single notes were then heard, in a sorrowful, low lamentation;
> Till, having gathered them all, he flung them abroad in derision,
> As when, after a storm, a gust of wind through the tree-tops
> Shakes down a rattling rain in a crystal shower on the branches.[8]

Whitman made explicit what is latent in most of these writers: the mocking-bird, like all songbirds, gives us an image of voice, especially the poet's lyrical voice.[9] And the earthly paradise is partly defined for the poet as a true place of singing voice. Conversely, any place of singing seems to take on something of the earthly paradise, even if only in memory.

That last phrase is one whose burden we know well in the twentieth century, especially if we follow arguments about post-Miltonic loss of voice.[10] Is nonironic birdsong from an earthly paradise now possible? Yeats's paradisal bird scorns common bird or petal (he does not, of course). Eliot's thrush offers deception (unavoidable deception, to be sure).[11] Should we then hear Stevens's birds as late, faint, American echoes of the once-powerful singing bird in an earthly paradise? A tribute to his forerunner, Whitman, as the first line is a tribute to Goethe? And should we assume simple irony or, at best, ambiguity? My general literary history thus far seems to offer little more guidance than this.

Yet the mockingbird is an extraordinarily suggestive figure for matters of belatedness, presence or absence, and allusion. As both New World bird and mimic, it is by definition belated, and would be even in paradise. As a mimic that imitates what is not necessarily there, it gives us a figure for the dialectic of presence and absence. Allusion itself works with paradoxes of presence and absence, so that if Harold Rosenberg's remark were a riddle, we might answer at once, "Mockingbird song": "the true ghostly principle of historical revival . . . the thing alluded to is both there and not there."[12] If an ironic or ambiguous reading is not altogether wrong, it certainly seems inadequate. So read, Stevens's text seems to remain closed or to give off dead sound. So read, what we hear is lack of resonance, a curiously muted text. Why use so potentially rich a figure only to deaden or mute our responses?

It is time to return to the nonsense-syllables that govern the mockingbirds: *mic-mac*. Stevens opens his canto with the possibility of referential reading: the allusion of line 1 points to Goethe's "Land wo die Zitronen blühn," and, insofar as it denotes actual rather than typical landscape, it is Mediterranean. "Mic-mac," two lines later, suddenly blocks referential or even typical reading, except to the most stubbornly ingenious, who may use the Algonquian meaning of *mic-mac* ("allies"). (So read, yellow lemons and/ or citrons are the "allies" of these birds, a logical if dull reading. To formulate this reading does, however, show us why Stevens says "yellow and yellow": this way, he doesn't have to identify the fruit as either lemon or citron.)[13] Lower-case *mic-mac* reminds us that the mocking-bird is a mi-mic, and thereby that language has conventions of mimicry as well as conventions of depicting, that the word *mimesis* is used of both, and that the two kinds of convention may coincide or divide, or perhaps are indivisible.[14] (The mockingbirds mime and/or depict yellow, pungent fruit or the words of yellow, pungent fruit.) Since the *mocking* part of the bird's compound name tells us all this anyway, Stevens's nonsense-syllables seem to function as emphasis. Any nonsense-words block referential reading. These not only block; they also point to questions of mimesis inherent in the mockingbird, questions that we might ignore in a strongly referential reading.[15]

As for phonetic effects, *mic-mac* reminds us that onomatopoeia can give meaning, again through convention. We hear *tick-tock* as clock sounds, *click-clack* as light machine sounds.[16] Here, we logically expect something like *snick-snack*, since the syntax suggests we read "fruit" (or "fruit which is subject for song") for "mic-mac." Yet the sounds seem inappropriate, as if Stevens were deliberately, if slightly, grating our ears, just where we expect the usual lyrical sounds of a land of lemon trees. If the semantic associations of *mic-mac* point us toward questions of mimesis, the phonetic effects encourage an allegorical question: have the standard properties of this topos become only so much machinery? *Mic-mac-mock*: the sequence plays with all these questions and itself becomes a small refrain, an internal echo.

Our ears now alerted, what can we hear? Some of Stevens's poetry is best read through its echoes as well as its allusions, and I want now to follow an echo sounding faintly through these opening lines. Although it is at first faint, it is persistent; it may be connected with other echoes in "An Ordinary Evening in New Haven"; it is logical. And if we pursue it far enough, we may hear new readings of other poets.

This echoing is of Milton, and we begin to hear it when we follow the direction of Stevens's *mic-mac* and ask the following question: What mimics may be found, and where, in the earthly paradise? If we ask this question of the greatest earthly paradise in English, one Stevens echoes and alludes to elsewhere in his work, we find a curiously logical answer. For there is one mimic only in all of *Paradise Lost*, and it turns up where it ought to, that is, in the land of the citron trees. (*Citron*, like *mimic*, appears only once in *Paradise Lost*: 5.22, 5.110.) But the mimic is not a bird or birdsong. It is fancy, mimic fancy — which, to be sure, may give a dream of birdsong. This seems unhelpful at first. Surely Milton's nightingale is the true paradisal bird, whether in Eden or as image for his poetic voice in the Invocation to Light. And surely Milton's nightingale is the forerunner of Whitman's mockingbird, or American nightingale. Why introduce questions of mic-mac or mimicry? Because, I think, Stevens heard how Milton's mimic fancy introduced a false nightingale into Eden in Eve's dream: "the night-warbling Bird, that now awake / Tunes sweetest his love-labor'd song" (5.40–41). Because this mimicking false nightingale can raise questions about truth and falseness and poetic voice and earthly paradises. And because Keats heard all this too.

Keats's great ode not only engages with Milton's nightingale; it also engages with questions of fancy, cheating fancy. Leo Spitzer, in his fine essay on Whitman's "Out of the Cradle Endlessly Rocking," heard how Whitman substituted a New World bird for the "hackneyed nightingale" and "synthesized" the "motifs" of the earthly paradise.[17] His approach is strongly synchronic, and it suggests no specific verbal revisions. Perhaps that is why Whitman's own echoing of Milton and Keats is rarely heard. In any case,

our histories of romantic allusiveness all too often do not make this transatlantic trip. But Stevens did, as we may hear in his 1931 poem "Autumn
Refrain" (*CP*, 160). And at least three other American poets have connected a
Keatsean topos with Whitman.[18] In Stevens's poem, the re-hearing of birds
is said to be stilled, even as Stevens echoes earlier language about birds and
singing:

> The skreak and skritter of evening gone
> And grackles gone . . .
>
> . . . .
>
> Some skreaking and skrittering residuum
> . . . grates these evasions of the nightingale.

> (1–2, 10–11)

Not only is the oaten pipe of evening gone; we can't even sing like grackles,
can't even grate on our scrannel pipes of wretched straw. The *scr — grate*
combination is Milton's, and the evasions are of Keats's and Milton's nightingales both, and surely of Whitman as well. For Stevens's "yellow moon of
words" (l. 4) echoes Whitman's "yellow half-moon . . . The yellow half-
moon enlarged . . . the yellow and sagging moon" ("Out of the Cradle,"
ll. 10, 135, 155). Whitman's words find a "key" word, "the key, the word up
from the waves" (l. 179).[19] Stevens finds only the musical "key" (l. 13) to his
stillness.

The line of succession, then, from Milton through Keats to Whitman is
not new to Stevens. If Stevens is echoing Milton in canto 29, it is worth
pursuing the line of succession, the movement from Milton's nightingale and
mimic fancy through Keats's nightingale and cheating fancy to Whitman's
mockingbird. How might this literary history of a topos work?

"Inescapable Romance, Inescapable Choice of Dreams"

In Milton's land of the citron trees, mimic fancy gives Eve a false dream — or
so Adam says by way of comfort to a distressed Eve.[20] He does not mention
that mimic fancy may also give true or prophetic dreams, but the reader
knows perfectly well, if Eve does not, what this dream foreshadows. If false
when dreamt, it will become true enough. And what is it that mimic fancy has

mimicked in Eve's dream? The nightingale, the "Full Orb'd . . . Moon," and a temptation like Eve's first speculating temptation to self-absorption, but also like her future fall. She ends the story of her dream this way:

> suddenly
> My Guide was gone, and I, methought, sunk down,
> And fell asleep; but O how glad I wak'd
> To find this but a dream!
>
> $(5.90-93)^{21}$

Let me juxtapose lines from another earthly paradise in which fancy is also a deceiver, Keats's "Ode to a Nightingale," whose lines on fancy are sometimes ignored or trivialized by commentators: "Adieu! The fancy cannot cheat so well / As she is fam'd to do, deceiving elf."[22] Consider, in terms of setting and action, the following sequence in both Eve's dream and Keats's ode: nightingale, moon, flight, fall, sleeping, waking.[23] Let me now juxtapose one other nightingale scene, Milton's magnificent Invocation to Light, from which Keats takes his best-known allusion to Milton, "Darkling I listen." Here again are nightingale, flight, waking; no moon, for Milton is blind and his own "Orbs" are "quencht" (the "Full Orb'd" moonlight of Eve's dream deceives while Milton's blind orbs enlighten); no fall (the hazard of poetic falling will come later); no sleeping.

If we follow the curious logic of Stevens's "mic-mac of mocking birds," we may hear these juxtapositions. We may even hear Eve's dream itself echoing and turning Milton's own vision in the invocation to light. We may also hear it echoing and turning all the invocations, which consistently use figures of singing, of flight, of darkness and light, and of birds and winged creatures closely associated with poetic voice. "Darkling, I listen to Milton's darkling," Keats might well say,[24] and I listen to Milton's entire invocation. But also to all the invocations and not just one;[25] to Eve's dream as well as Adam's. And if the Imagination is Adam's dream (he awoke and found it truth, says Keats), what for Keats is Eve's dream? She awoke and found it false, and, alas, made it true — or so Milton says.

Is Keats's "vision" a true dream, an Adam's dream, from which he awakes to find it truth? And is his "waking dream" a false dream, an Eve's dream, a dream of mimic or cheating fancy, from which he awakes to find it false? Surely Keats's last question recalls two types of dream, Adam's and Eve's both, yet without accepting the Miltonic dialectic of true versus false.[26] Rather, Keats questions such a division.

We might pursue the question of Keats's echoes of Milton by considering tropes of poetic flight. In the invocations, Milton flies, the flight figuring his epic voice.[27] Once, but I think once only, he makes explicit the possibility of fall that is implicit in all flight. Like Bellerophon (he does not mention Eve), he could fly too high, tempted to overweening and improper voice.[28] Marvell's tributary poem centers on precisely this danger and precisely this trope. "The lofty . . . sometimes imagine they are flying," as A. R. Ammons says,[29] and Marvell, much as he admires Milton's flight, may be suggesting a lower trajectory for him.[30] Milton, however, claims that the true Muse preserves him as Calliope cannot, for Calliope is an "empty dream" (7.39). "Was it a vision, or a waking dream?" asks Keats, whose bird sings, then flies away, but whose own represented flight is ambiguous, and who never claims to sing (all the while singing, or writing). And Keats's word *forlorn*, echoing Adam's, surely also echoes the warning, terminal *forlorn* of a fallen poetic voice: "Lest . . . I fall / Erroneous there to wander and forlorn" (7.17–20).[31]

Yet Poesy does fly in Keats's ode, if not Keats himself, and it flies on Miltonic wings, "viewless wings." "See, see the Chariot," says Milton of Ezekiel's chariot, which is hailed but then declined as a vehicle, he himself preferring a "transporting Cherub" or a "viewless wing." Thus Milton, aged 21, in "The Passion," just before falling into silence, his imperfect control of language allowing it to wander inappropriately into the groves of classical elegy—precisely that place where Keats, aged 23, will find voice and complete his poetic flight. Keats finds voice by hearing a place where Milton's voice is equivocal, as, in my earlier examples, he found voice by hearing multiple echoes from very different Miltonic places.

I have followed the logic of Stevens's and thereby Keats's echoing, and it has proven not to be arbitrary; it does not depend on a coincidence of plot. Nor is it trivial; the Miltonic echoes center on those matters on which Keats's ode is centered, matters of immortality and voice and the everyday world. If Keats were working with a Miltonic dialectic of true and false, he would know how to judge cheating fancy. But he is not. No logos governs his fancy; it is not judged that way, but then neither is it validated that way. What Keats implies through his echoes is that Milton's dialectic is itself an imagined thing. He must then ask the reader what imagination is, and what this poem is — a "vision" or a "waking dream."

What, then, of Whitman? Whitman's mockingbird to my ear recalls Longfellow's, yet also sets it aside, as Keats's ode, stanzas 2 and 3, recalls and sets aside eighteenth-century ease and disease topoi for a nightingale ode. I think Whitman's language for his bird comes first and foremost from Keats. We need to know that the mockingbird is also called the mock nightingale. We need also to hear the echo of Sophocles' metonymy for Philomel (the "voice of the shuttle") in Whitman's second line ("out of the mocking-bird's throat, the musical shuttle"), although his bird is deprived of a desired mate. Most of all, we need to hear Keats's "Thou wast not born for death, immortal Bird" echoing against Whitman's repeated "death, death, death . . . ," the key "word of the sweetest song and all songs." Keats preserves song, although not himself, from death. Whitman introduces death into the emplotment of the bird; adds another element, the sea; disperses the melodious plot along a shoreline, edged with "hissing melodious."

Keats's Miltonic topos of the earthly paradise lies behind Whitman's night scene of calling—evocative and vocational at once—with American nightingale, moon, waking after sleep, but no flight or fall except the cadences of song. (Particularly Keatsean are the month of May, midnight, the play of shadows, the stress on darkness, the words *twittering* and *ecstatic*.) Waking is unequivocally affirmed: "my tongue's use [was] sleeping . . . I wake . . . my own songs awaked from that hour." The tropes of flight—of flying or fleeing—are conspicuously omitted. Birdsong rises and falls, and "from these fitful risings and fallings, I heard. . . ." Elsewhere, Whitman can say in simple explicit simile, "I fly like a bird," but not here. His remembered self is stationed strongly on earth, on that Long Island shore, with no pastoral flowers "at my feet" ("Ode to a Nightingale," l. 41) but instead the sea "rustling at my feet."[32]

As for mocking, the full-throated Whitman here mocks only reductive readings of an American poet as mere overhearer and mimic of nightingale song. (Disabling self-mockery comes in a counterpoem, "As I Ebb'd with the Ocean of Life": "the real Me stands yet untouched, untold, altogether unreached, / Withdrawn far, mocking me with mock-congratulatory signs and bows" [28–29].) "My brother," Whitman chants to the bird, joining it in death, overgoing it in song, with the natural world mated or matched (to use Gombrich's word)[33] in revised tropes of voice.

Thus far, I have been working with the history of a topos: birds in an earthly paradise as an image of voice for a poet. The topos includes matters of singing, flight, waking or sleeping, dreaming, death. I began with the curious logic of Stevens's echo, and I have pursued other echoes from Milton through Keats to Whitman wherever such echoes made sense. My pursuit has been from rhetoric toward argument. That is, I have made use of verbal echo to try to illuminate processes of debate within and between these poems.

My argument might now proceed in various directions. A historian of ideas, for example, might go on to speak of different concepts of death.[34] A strongly referential reader might point to Whitman's descriptive accuracy,[35] and go on to develop an argument about what Walter Ong calls the "irreducibility of voice,"[36] or about "utterances that occur of their own accord," or seem to, such utterances being one mark of the lyric mode, according to Gerald Bruns.[37] (Birdsong, like lyric poems, appears to be more spontaneous than it is. It has to do with mating and territory, except apparently for the song of the wonderfully named "ecstasy flight" and for mockingbird song, which continues after the mating season.) Logocentric readers might observe that authority of voice ultimately comes from the logos, and that birdsong is exemplary rather than authoritative (thus Dante or Milton). Deconstructionist readers would continue to keep their play well away from the old controversy between song and the logos. To quote Northrop Frye: "A good deal has been said about the deferring of written language to the spoken word: much less has been said about the deferring of written poetry to music, especially in lyrical poetry, where the very word lyric implies a musical instrument."[38]

But I want to return to where I began. I want now to consider not so much how rhetoric helps us read argument as the other way around. That is, I want to consider the rhetorical strategies of Keats and Whitman and Stevens when they echo or allude to their great predecessors.

Metalepsis

Paul de Man speaks of allusion as an "intertextual trope . . . in which a complex play of substitutions and repetitions takes place between texts."[39] John Hollander demonstrates that at least two kinds of trope are in play, metaphor and metalepsis.[40] When Keats transfers Milton's "viewless wing" to his own pastoral grove, when he alerts us to one and all of Milton's nightingales in "Darkling I listen," he changes Milton's context, making us hear Milton in his own terms. We know in a general way what happens to words when we move them from one context to another. This is familiar "mockingbird" strategy in uses of quotation, allusion, and echo — least interesting as simple irony and most interesting as truly "complex play." And writers of genius can change the context itself through such maneuvers. Each of my examples draws attention to its own way of changing Milton's context.

With "viewless wings," we have an example of an echo rebounding from one author to another, and an example of another metaleptic strategy. Metaleptic echo goes back to an earlier voice, leaping over or transuming, middle echoes of this earlier voice. Author C revises Author B's dominant word or phrase by setting Author A's quietly against it.

We may see such a strategy at work in two examples from Keats's ode: " 'Tis not through envy of thy happy lot" and "the viewless wings of Poesy." When Keats writes, " 'Tis not through envy of thy happy lot," he is returning Milton's comparative adjective *happier* to *happy*, thereby also restoring Ovid's place of the Muses. Milton alludes to the haunt of the Muses in the invocation to light: "where the Muses haunt / Clear spring, or shady Grove" (3.27–28). He also evokes it in book 4, this time through a delicate revisionary echo of Ovid: "I chiefly who enjoy / So far the happier Lot, enjoying thee," says Eve (4.445–46). "We have indeed a happy lot [*gratam sortem*] were we but safe in it," says one of the Muses (*Met.* 5.272, Loeb ed.).[41] *Happier* is used by Eve to affirm the superiority of her lot in the earthly paradise. But *happier* also resounds back against its Ovidian source, for Ovid's whole scene of attempted seduction, flight, and fall is a prototypical temptation scene, to be read against Eve's temptation in *Paradise Lost* and Christ's in *Paradise Regained*.[42] Keats alludes to the haunt of the Muses in the phrase "the true, the blushful Hippocrene" (to which he does *not* say he prefers Zion's flowery brooks), but he has already evoked it in line 2, through his own delicate revisionary echo, which moves back through Milton to Ovid.

" 'Tis not through envy of thy happy lot" comes to our ears with Miltonic reverberations because of Milton's phrase "happier lot," because the sin of envy is so markedly a Satanic sin, and because Keats chooses to cluster forms of *happy* in Miltonic fashion just after this line.[43] But Milton does not combine *envy* with "happy lot" or "happier lot" or even "lot." It is, in fact, Dryden who does this, Dryden, gifted with so fine an ear for memorable Miltonic phrasing:[44] "happy thy lot," says Eve to Lucifer in *The State of Innocence* (4.1), and to Adam, "I envy thee that lot" (5.1). Keats leaps over or transumes Dryden in this example of transumptive or metaleptic echo.

At the same time, another metalepsis may be fancied rather than heard, and might best be described as follows. Suppose there were an audience with Ovid's poetry, rather than Milton's, fresh in their heads. Such an audience would hear the Ovidian echo as dominant, and Milton's "happier lot" would then be transumed. This is not what happens, but Keats's extraordinary handling of the Miltonic echo just suggests the possibility of a very different line of development from Milton's of the Ovidian topos of a place of song. This second metalepsis is fainter and antihistorical (now, anyway) because Milton's words dominate our cave of echo. But Keats's ode raises the possibility of this fainter metalepsis becoming dominant in time, or dominating for the first half of this ode. See, they return, Keats might say of Ovid and the old haunts of the earthly paradise, the *sors grata* that Keats loved. See, they return, Keats might also say of Sophocles and his earthly paradise, for Keats declines the chariot of Bacchus rather than the chariot of Ezekiel (l. 32), preferring transport on "viewless wings" (l. 33). Both these lines, not just the second, revise Milton's "The Passion." The point of the first revision is to reassociate with the place of the nightingale what Sophocles says belongs there (*Oedipus at Colonus* 677–80) and what Milton banishes from his place of song (*Paradise Lost* 7.32–37) — the revels of Bacchus.[45] To be sure, they return only to be excluded, yet they are excluded "not by dismissal . . . but by being put gently by," to quote Helen Vendler.[46] The exclusion is quite un-Miltonic. (Just as un-Miltonic is Keats's explicitly heterodox rereading of the Book of Ruth in lines 66–67, lines whose beauty tends to mask their heterodoxy. After all, the most famous text in Ruth is written precisely against *nostos*, against being "sick for home.")[47]

Recent critical interest in the phrase "viewless wings" has centered on the echo of "viewless winds" from *Measure for Measure* rather than the actual Miltonic phrase "viewless wing."[48] So loudly is the echo sounding in our ears that it is heard as allusion. I find this critical movement of great interest, for it marks a historical change in our way of hearing that I think Keats's own strategies encourage. For me, the Miltonic phrase retains its primacy for reasons given above. But I also hear how Keats's Shakespearean echo works to undo Milton's own revision of Shakespeare's phrase. ("Viewless winds" is part of a vision of death; "viewless wing" is transport to heaven.)

In her richly suggestive essay on this ode, Helen Vendler deals chiefly with Shakespearean echoes, developing the argument that Keats is engaged with the question of "natural music" (or "the pure world of sound") as a possible model for lyric art; that he rejects this model because it posits an art with no conceptual or moral content. I would use the terms *melos* and *logos* (logos as both "word" and the "Wisdom" Vendler cites), and I would urge letting Milton enter this debate, as I think he did for Keats. It is Milton who most powerfully treats the old question of possible (not necessary) tension between melos and logos, and one place he implicitly does so is in the Invocation to Light, where Keats found his word *darkling*. (I am not, of course, arguing for any simple anti-Milton and pro-classics-and-Shakespeare position.) And I infer that Whitman saw very plainly this debate between logos and melos — and death.

Considering the pattern of metalepsis, we might ask if Whitman reaches behind Keats in order to set Milton quietly against Keats. We then note that Whitman, working with Keats's ode, reintroduces into the place of song precisely what Keats has shorn from Milton's — that is, dimensions that are for Keats beyond the human and earthly: hell, bird as angel (*messenger* is Whitman's word), bird as demon. Whitman's alternative "demon or bird" (l. 144) and his anaphoric "never more" suggest that his demon bird owes something to Poe, but the presence of a demon bird at all owes even more, I think, to Whitman's Miltonic amplifying. (Whitman, of course, revises the word *demon*, humanizing Poe's Gothic as he humanizes Milton's transcendent.) It may be that Whitman's streaming tears, his verb *lave*, and his sense of himself as a genius of the shore are a turning of the end of *Lycidas*, with the sea's laving as a marine baptism into a new singing life. As *Lycidas* also lies behind Keats's "Ode to a Nightingale," Whitman may be said to restore the full topos of that pastoral to the topos of birdsong in the earthly paradise — opening out the enclosed garden of the earthly paradise to take in the sea (and death), and adding the sea's voice to the bird's. After all, it is words of the sea, "perilous seas forlorn" — "that perilous flood," as Milton says at the end of *Lycidas* — that toll Keats back to his sole self.[49] Whitman's "solitary" self hears bird and sea in a very different relation. The sea becomes another figure of voice within (not against) the earthly paradise.

With Whitman, the process of doubly rebounding echo is somewhat different than it is in Keats. First, Whitman does not allude; he echoes. Second, because he does not allude, and because even possible allusive echoes are not strongly so, we cannot point to a specific phrase and trace its revisions as particularly as in Keats's ode. Third, Whitman revises Keats by means of Milton but he also revises Milton, going back to an earlier text than Milton's and reading it in a way Milton did not. That text is the English Bible, which gives Whitman his cadences and also some of his phrasing. ("Sounds and sights after their sorts" is richly resonant because "after their sorts" recalls the survival and new-creation narrative of Noah's Ark in Genesis, while also recalling Keats's synaesthesia, for instance, where sounds and sights are not mated after their kind, but crossed.) In Whitman's revisions, a pattern of metalepsis may be seen generally in the ways I have shown, but in specific tropes it is not as clear as in Keats.

With Stevens, we return to allusion (Goethe), allusive echo (of Whitman), and, faintly, ingeniously, but unavoidable once heard, echo (of Milton):

> In the land of the lemon-trees, yellow and yellow
> Were yellow-blue, yellow-green, pungent with citron-sap
> Dangling and spangling, the mic-mac of mocking birds.

Milton's citron trees (which also lie behind Goethe's *Zitronen*),[50] Milton's mimic, Milton's nightingale are all evoked here. So also is the ghost of Philomel — evoked by Stevens's syntactic implication that "mic-mac of mocking birds" signifies fruit eaten by the birds, or subject of song by the birds. For the correct etymology of *Philomel* is "lover of fruit" rather than the sentimental favorite, "lover of song" (not φιλω-μέλος but φιλω-μῆλον). Stevens's birds suggest their origins through their eating habits, which are philomelic, and their singing habits, which are also philomelic — like Milton's own:

> Then *feed* on thoughts, that voluntary move
> Harmonious numbers; as the wakeful Bird
> Sings darkling.

> (37–39; *my emphasis*)[51]

It may also be that "They rolled their r's, there, in the land of the citrons" (l. 7) not only for the obvious reason that they speak a Mediterranean Romance language, and the less obvious reason that Stevens is punning on "voluble," but also because of Milton. "He pronounced the letter R . . . very hard," says John Aubrey in his "Minutes of the Life of Mr. John Milton."

Stevens's canto is not a shoreline poem like Whitman's. Rather, he separates the topos of the earthly paradise out again into a dialectic of here and there, dark and light—a dialectic that is paradoxically more like Milton's than like Whitman's. His mariners must voyage to reach their "longed-for land." He does not work, like Whitman, toward raising the here and now to the condition of an earthly paradise. Whitman is present in more ways than one in "An Ordinary Evening in New Haven," but something in Stevens reacts here against Whitman's dialectic, or perhaps his lack of dialectic. Stevens revises that powerful image of voice, Whitman's mockingbird, even as he acknowledges the figure as culmination of a tradition of birds in the earthly paradise. His retroping of Whitman's bird works like Keats's retroping of Milton: we hear Whitman differently.

In these revisions, we hear, not a head-on engagement in argument, but an undoing from within, a re-hearing of how the earlier writer unwove and rewove figuration, and from that re-hearing yet a new weaving. In familial terms, we might say that the child takes the heritage of the grandparent to set against the parent's strength.[52] This is a way of acknowledging the "special status" of one root (to use Thomas Greene's metaphor), but it also offers a specific way to "move out" from it.[53] It resembles Christopher Ricks's sense of allusion as inheritance, but tries to account for certain kinds of revisionary allusion.[54]

Conclusion

Such methods are demonstrable in contemporary writing, for example, in A. R. Ammons's poem, "Hermit Lark":

> Shy lark! I'll bet it took a while to get you
> perfect, your song quintessential, hermit lark,
> just back from wherever you winter: I learn my real
>
> and ideal self from you, the right to sing
> alone without shame!
> water over stone makes useless brook music; your

music unbearably clear after rain
drops water breaking through air, the dusk air
like shaded brookwater, substanced clarity!

I learn from you and lose the edginess I speak of
to one other only, my mate, my long beloved, and
make a shield not so much against the world,

though against its hardest usages, as
for tenderness's small leeways: how
hard to find the bird in the song! the music

breaks in from any height or depth of the spiral
and whirling up or down, jamming, where does it
leave off: shy bird, welcome home, I love your

song and keep my distance: hold, as I know you
won't, through the summer this early close visitation
behind the garage and in the nearby brush:

you will pair off and hiding find deeper
shyness yet: be what you must and will be:
I listen and look to found your like in me.[55]

In this birdsong poem, we may hear Shelley and Keats, and Eliot too, among others. The whole poem is governed by the title, "Hermit Lark," about which we should know that there is no such bird. Ammons is referring to a hermit thrush and also recalling Eliot's hermit thrush, that *grive solitaire* out of Quebec but also out of Whitman. For Ammons's poem also shows a pattern of doubly rebounding echo. Against the loneness of Eliot's hermit voice, Ammons goes back to what Eliot did not acknowledge, Whitman's work, for bird and mate.[56] Whitman he also revises: both bird and speaker have mates, and it is the human one who is called, in Whitman's phrase, "my mate." Bird and man, two home-makers and "maks" (I hear a submerged pun), are lovers of solitariness. "Solitary me listening . . . I listen" said Whitman to Keats's "Darkling I listen," to Milton's "Sings darkling."

Stevens heard it all: "Their dark-colored words had redescribed the citrons." This is how canto 29 closes, and it was once the closure of the entire series "An Ordinary Evening in New Haven." Certainly, Keats's famous *darkling* is a dark-colored word that redescribes Milton's citrons (taking citrons as a synecdoche for the earthly paradise). Stevens's extraordinarily rich canto is a small history of the earthly paradise, both personal and general. It is personal in its evoking of Goethe, Whitman, and Milton—a compound farewell tribute to Stevens's masters, appropriately offered at the threshold of his own remembering of the earthly paradise. Keats was also a master for Stevens, and I have followed the logic of Stevens's metaleptic echoing in order to recover Keats's place in a line of succession. For Keats is transumed, not echoed, in stanza 1. It is in stanza 2 that we return to the ordinary world, an ordinary evening in New Haven. It is only right that now we hear Keats, and through a Spenser-Keats line of succession:

> In the land of the elm trees, wandering mariners
> Looked on big women, whose ruddy-ripe images
> Wreathed round and round the round wreath of autumn.
>
> *(508–10)*

The "wreath of autumn" is a conventional metonymy, beautifully presented here in a chiastic scheme of echo. Spenser gives us an early and memorable example of Stevens's topos: "Then came Autumne . . . Upon his head a wreath that was enrold / With ears of corn . . . And in his hand a sickle he did holde, / To reape the ripened fruits the which the earth had yold" ("Mutability Cantos" 7.30.1–9). But it is Keats who is unavoidable whenever this topos is used, and Vendler has shown how "To Autumn" is diffused through Stevens's work.[57]

Stevens's land of the lemon trees and land of the elms—the earthly paradise and the here and now—are one and the same, "except for the adjectives" (l. 518). They are not separated by the fall according to Milton. The old dialectic is not encompassed, with little sense of separation, as in Whitman. Stevens is closest to Keats in this canto, which assumes Keats's "Ode to a Nightingale" and evokes Keats's "To Autumn." "As the wakeful Bird / Sings darkling . . . how blows the Citron Grove . . . kennst du das land wo die Zitronen blühn, / Im dunkeln . . . Darkling I listen . . . the song of my dusky demon and brother . . . Their dark-colored words had redescribed the citrons."

PART THREE

Poetry at Play

ELEVEN

Melos Versus Logos, or, Why Doesn't God Sing?
Some Thoughts on Milton's Wisdom

The Word was from the first . . . I have called Him a New Song.

— CLEMENT OF ALEXANDRIA

Music was the negation of sentences, music was the anti-word.

— MILAN KUNDERA, *The Unbearable Lightness of Being*

I am wrong, of course. God does sing, as witness my first epigraph. Or at least, he sings (or is Song) occasionally. But he does not sing within the canonical text of the Bible: he speaks, and his word comes, saying.[1] Perhaps, of course, he no more speaks than he sings, since "everything [was] wrought by God through the Son [Logos] in the Holy Ghost," to follow the much-used formula of Athanasius.[2] This means that I should rephrase my question and ask why the Logos, the second Person of the Trinity, speaks and does not sing. Or (moving out from canon to tradition) why it speaks so much and sings so little. Why are its creating and authoritative acts conceived as speaking acts and not singing acts? God composes, of course: he composes eternal harmony, and he plays upon the instrument that the universe is, metaphorically, in his hands. But others make his music, while he speaks his word. And he *is* the Word or the Logos, while he is not canonically, and seldom elsewhere, the Melos, not the Sound or Note or Song.

The question may sound trivial. Yet if the human logos or word can have by analogy (or by whatever means, and the means are disputed and important) some relation with a divine Word, then it has a significance that other terms, such as *melos* or *song*, lack in lacking this relation. And if one is a musician or a poet, and also a Christian in the Augustinian tradition, this matters a great deal. (Singing, by metonymy, may be poetry, as in Milton's "my advent'rous Song.") My question may sound both trivial and churlish to a strongly Platonic tradition, with its fine meditations on *musica speculativa* and its sense of world harmony. To such a tradition, Augustine is troublesome, since, for all his love of Platonism, he decisively rejects it.

Nowadays, we hear a good deal about the logos, sometimes with little sense of its history, which may be deliberately or just casually ignored. Yet historical tensions or lacunae within the interpretation of the logos are worth considering in these ante-Nicene days — ante-Nicene because of our sundry disputes over the logos and our sundry readings of ancient texts. My example raises a further question. The logos is now sometimes associated with masculine (i.e., rational) discourse, so that feminine discourse must choose between separatism and a renewed federalism (to speak in Canadian terms). The contraries of logos and melos may be conceived as masculine and feminine modes of discourse, if we observe how the language used of melos, as against the language used of logos, tends to be the language used of women, as against the language used of men. I am aware that this is a wide generalization, that the long history of the logos is exceedingly complex, and that I am arguing by analogy. Nonetheless, the point stands, and the question becomes how far the analogy holds, and what it can tell us.

I began to think about this matter because of a coincidence in the rhetorical strategies of Milton and Karl Barth. These two powerful representatives of a logocentric tradition, separated by some 300 years, desire to find (and know the strategic importance of finding) a divine origin for music in Scripture. Both Milton in 1667 and Barth in 1947 take the Wisdom figure of Prov. 8:22–31, who is said to rejoice or play during or before creation, and both extend the word for "rejoice" or "play" to musical playing. The passage from Proverbs is well known:

> The Lord possessed me in the beginning of his way,
> Before his works of old . . .
> Then I was by him, as one brought up with him:
> And I was daily his delight,

Rejoicing always before him;
Rejoicing in the habitable part of his earth;
And my delights were with the sons of men.

(King James Version)

Here is Milton, in the invocation to book 7 of *Paradise Lost*, lines 1–12:

Descend from Heav'n *Urania*, by that name
If rightly thou art call'd, whose Voice divine
Following, above th'*Olympian* Hill I soar,
Above the flight of *Pegasean* wing.
The meaning, not the Name I call: for thou
Nor of the Muses nine, nor on the top
Of old *Olympus* dwell'st, but Heav'nly born,
Before the Hills appear'd, or Fountain flow'd,
Thou with Eternal Wisdom didst converse,
Wisdom thy Sister, and with her didst play
In presence of th'Almighty Father, pleas'd
With thy Celestial Song.[3]

Milton's grammar in lines 9–12 does not say that the rejoicing or playing of Wisdom includes musical playing or Celestial Song. But his unobtrusive phrase "with her" merges Urania's song with Wisdom's rejoicing or playing. Whatever Wisdom may be — and it would be the height of folly to inquire into God's activities before Creation, as Milton says in the *Christian Doctrine* (1.7) — this mysterious personification of the Godhead offers a way of associating music and poetry with the divine. ("Poetical personification" is Milton's term for the Wisdom of Prov. 8.)[4] Here at least, song is not what it is elsewhere, almost without exception: a creaturely activity — sometimes, to be sure, an activity of the highest creatures, but nonetheless creaturely. For Wisdom, if made, is not made as angels or the universe are made.[5] She is an agent of creation and part of the Godhead. She is in Scripture. And she plays.

In 1947, in the first essay of *Die Protestantische Theologie im 19. Jahrhundert*, Karl Barth speaks of Prov. 8:27–31 and goes on to talk about music:

There is as we know a passage in the Bible according to which something like a conversation of the eternal harmony with itself takes place, just before the Creation, with a similar reference to playing [*eines Spielens*], i.e.,

Prov. 8:27–31: ". . . then was I by him, as a master workman: and had delight continually, playing always before him; playing in the habitable parts of the earth; and my delights were with the sons of men" [*und spielte vor ihm allezeit und spielte auf seinem Erdboden*]. Would it not be the revelation of a supreme will for form, a will for form manifesting perhaps only in this sphere its utmost absolutism, if the music of the eighteenth century sought to culminate the wisdom born of the Creator in its results and in the abandonment and superiority which cause us to forget all the craftsmanship behind it? Be that as it may, all earlier music is still too much involved in the struggle to subdue the raw material of musical sound, and it must be said that the later music, from Beethoven onwards, desired and loved the world of sound too little for its own sake, to be capable of looking upon it in the same unequivocal way as a game [*als Spiel*]. The music of the eighteenth century, the music of absolutism, plays [*spielt*], and for this reason it is in a peculiar way beautiful and that not only in its great exponents but in its minor ones too.[6]

Barth's moving, ingenious argument uses a similar strategy to Milton's, although a more self-conscious one. Music may be thought of as a beautiful game or play (whether or not eighteenth-century European music is unique in the way that Barth claims). Wisdom is said to play before God. Such a notion of play ought also to include the play or game that is music. Of course, the pun on *play*, in German as in English and Latin, helps greatly in this argument. What helps most of all is the Hebrew pun on *play*, and both Milton and Barth could read the original text in Hebrew.[7] The King James Version's Prov. 8:30–31 uses the word *rejoicing* and the Junius-Tremellius Bible, which Milton generally follows, uses *laetificans*, as W. B. Hunter observes.[8] But Harris Fletcher tells us that Milton's word *play*, like the Vulgate's *ludere*, "translate[s] the Hebrew with more care than had his English Version. The Hebrew reads מְשַׂחֶקֶת. This is a piel participle with feminine ending of the verb שׂחק, and clearly means *playing* or *sporting*." Fletcher's useful commentary does not mention that the Hebrew itself suggests the possibility of musical play, at least in a secondary or punning meaning. As Fletcher himself points out, "The same verb, in the same stem and with the same meaning, occurs in Prov. 26:19; I Chron. 15:29; I Sam. 18:7; II Sam. 6:5; and *passim*. The meaning *ludere* or to play is perfectly clear in these passages." He does not say that three of his four examples are associated with musical play.[9]

What marks the tradition of Milton and Barth is its strict adherence to the biblical text, and the strict line it draws between creator and creature. Someone less strict can simply expand the metaphoric possibilities of the Bible in order to merge Word and Wisdom and Song, as Clement of Alexandria does. (He is altogether a cheerful merger, as he also merges man and God, this no doubt being one of Milton's "thick-sown heresies.")

> The Lord fashioned man a beautiful, breathing instrument, after His own image; and assuredly He Himself is an all-harmonious instrument of God, melodious and holy, the wisdom that is above this world, the heavenly Word . . . we were before the foundation of the world. . . . We are the rational images formed by God's Word, or Reason, and we date from the beginning on account of our connexion with Him, because "the Word was in the beginning." Well, because the Word was from the first, He was and is the divine beginning of all things; but because He lately took a name — the name consecrated of old and worthy of power, the Christ — I have called Him a New Song.[10]

The seventeenth-century heir to Clement is Calderón, as E. R. Curtius has shown. Curtius is unsympathetic to Milton's "rigorism," and sees Calderón's syncretic "Logos as poet" as "a Christian solution to the problem of the Muses." It is a solution also informed by the useful figure of Hebrew Wisdom in Prov. 8:22–31.[11]

How strict Milton is about these matters, we may see by his diction for the activities of God in *Paradise Lost*. God speaks, beholds, calls, says, sees, names, makes, and so on — all biblical verbs for his activities. But some things God does not do. He does not "charm" in either the magical or musical sense, although creatures, fallen and unfallen, may do so. All the language of magic is kept away from his activities. When Northrop Frye speaks of "the charm that created order out of chaos" or "the Word of God itself, which pronounced the original spell to keep chaos away,"[12] it sounds a little strange until we recognize a romance strategy of charm versus counter-charm. So also Collins, when he makes Wisdom into a Fancy figure, breathing "her *magic* Notes aloud" ("Ode on the Poetical Character"; my emphasis). But this is not a strategy that Milton allows himself in his later poetry.[13]

Prov. 8:22–31 is of great importance for Milton. It resounds through his work more often and more profoundly than we have realized. I want to consider briefly how it echoes through several lines of *Paradise Regained* before moving on to its extended use in *Paradise Lost*. For, as we shall see, the relation of Wisdom to Adam and Eve is as significant as her relation to Urania. In *Paradise Regained* 4:331–34 Milton extends the implications of the invocation to book 7 of *Paradise Lost*. The words of Prov. 8:30–31 echo through Christ's reply to the last temptation:

> Or if I would delight my private hours
> With Music or with Poem, where so soon
> As in our native Language can I find
> That solace?

Christ in his "private hours" chooses the true "solace" of Hebrew rather than classical music and poem, which as solace would be a harlot's solace, at least in this context. For in Prov. 7 may be found Wisdom's opposite, Madam Folly, in all her harlotry, including a harlot's "solace" (Prov. 7:18). The contrast would be even more pointed for readers of the popular Geneva Bible, where Eternal Wisdom "toke my solace in the compasse of his earth" (Prov. 8:31). *Paradise Regained* is intimately involved with Wisdom and wisdom literature, both thematically and formally, so that Milton has good reason for using a specific echo. If I am right about this, then Milton has here extended the "delight" that Wisdom gives in Prov. 8:30 to the delight of music and poetry. An earthly delight it may be (this is the incarnate Word speaking) but the echo affirms the pleasure of the Godhead in these things, as in the invocation to book 7 of *Paradise Lost*. And indeed, that invocation anticipates Milton's later explicit argument that even the best of classical song and wisdom is illusion in comparison with biblical. It echoes but revises Horace's ode "Descende caelo . . . Calliope" (3.4.1–2), which also invokes a Muse to give general (not just political) "wisdom and order" (to use the title in Loeb). Milton opens, "Descend from Heav'n *Urania*," and closes, "thou are Heav'nly, shee [Calliope] an empty dream." It is appropriate that he petition Wisdom's sister to "govern" his song.[14]

In book 9 of *Paradise Lost*, Milton plays throughout the temptation scene with a subtext of Prov. 7 and Prov. 8, of the harlot Folly against eternal Wisdom. We know in a general way how Eve and then Adam undo wisdom and harmony. But Milton is specific and forceful. Eve, having eaten the fruit, plays with thoughts of usurpation: "Nor was Godhead from her thought," as "to herself she pleasingly began" (9.790, 794). Just as God was "pleas'd" with Wisdom and Urania, so Eve speaks "pleasingly" but "to herself" in a parody of the self-sufficiency of the Godhead (809–11):

> thou [the Tree] op'n'st Wisdom's way,
> And giv'st access, though secret she retire.
> And I perhaps am secret. . . .

Milton's conjunction *though* shows how grim this parody is. It is not that the sexual possibilities of the passage from Proverbs have been exploited, as if in a Kabbalistic or Gnostic reading.[15] It is that Wisdom will be opened no matter how secretly she retires, and retires from, not with, whoever would "possess" her, to use the biblical word. A sense of sexual violation is part of the general sense of violation in this passage, and it foreshadows in a paradoxical way the first fallen sex in Eden, when Eve will be only too open of access, with nothing of her old "sweet reluctant amorous delay" or "obsequious Majesty." The same dialectic of worldly wisdom against heavenly wisdom, of worldly secrets against heavenly mystery, continues through the temptation scene. We may map diction from Prov. 8:27–31 all through book 9: *delight, play, solace* and, of course, *wisdom, wise, sapience.* Milton places just before the fall the figure of the author of Proverbs, proverbially wise Solomon: "the Sapient King / Held dalliance with his fair *Egyptian* spouse" (9.442–43). Sapience can hold such dalliance and still be wise, though, as with other figures in book 9, a fall will come later. (Solomon is also remembered as someone seduced from his faith by heathen wives.)

As soon as Adam eats the forbidden fruit, he too is implicated in the violation of Wisdom and the move toward harlotry. His famous wordplay on taste (*sapor*) involves "Sapience," Eve's first word for wisdom in her address to the Tree — all Wisdom now reduced to this merely clever play. "Now let us play," says Adam, and the language of fallen playing echoes through this passage (1027–48): *toy, disport, amorous play, play'd.* We are meant to hear a rhyming echo of Eve's "amorous delay" in the "amorous play" of this un-delayed sex, with no sweetness (musical or other) in the play. It is not just the use of the words wisdom and sapience, or this rhyming echo, that suggests Milton's deliberate reversal here of Wisdom's heavenly play. His judgment is very clear (1042–44):

> There they thir fill of Love and Love's disport
> Took largely, of thir mutual guilt the Seal,
> The solace of thir sin.

"Come, let us take our fill of love until the morning; let us solace ourselves with loves." This is the harlot of Prov. 7:18. Milton's readers would easily call up the entire context of Dame Folly in her harlotry and Eternal Wisdom in her rejoicing or play or solace in order to read the violation of Wisdom here. The context is strengthened in the next sentence, for, just as "they rose,"

> So rose the *Danite* strong
> *Herculean Samson* from the Harlot-lap
> Of *Philistean Dalilah*. . . .

> *(1059–61)*

Samson, like Solomon famous for his wisdom with riddles, has like Solomon been seduced and betrayed by a woman, and so rises fallen, as we always rise from any "harlot-lap." (There is a pun on lap and *lapsus*, fallen.) Milton's grammar is very clear: both Adam and Eve are like Samson. Nonetheless, readers have insisted on identifying Eve with Dalilah and Adam with Samson,[16] thus falling precisely into Adam's later sin. (Milton is so sensitive to lapses in our fallen wisdom that his figuration may be a deliberate testing of the accuser in all of us, and a foreshadowing of Adam's later blame of Eve before God.) For Adam only later turns on Eve; here he assumes a mutual guilt, unlike the careless reader of the harlot lines above. From Godhead to harlotry then: the fall has undone Wisdom just as Raphael forewarned.

For Adam is told that he must learn to govern, and by Wisdom, which is potentially in danger from Adam's "transport," "touch," "passion," and sole weakness: "here only weak / Against the charm of Beauty's powerful glance" (8.528–59). In Adam's own self, and between Adam and Eve, a hierarchy must be kept (549–56):

> what she wills to do or say,
> Seems wisest, virtuousest, discreetest, best;
> All higher knowledge in her presence falls
> Degraded, Wisdom in discourse with her
> Loses discount'nanc't, and like folly shows;
> Authority and Reason on her wait,

As one intended first, not after made
Occasionally.

Raphael is appropriately admonitory (562–64, 589–91):

be not diffident
Of Wisdom, she deserts thee not, if thou
Dismiss not her

. . . .

true Love . . . hath his seat
In Reason, and is judicious.

Adam, in defense, moves away from the terms of his first perplexing to a reaffirmation of his "delight" (Wisdom's word) in "Union of Mind, or in us both one Soul; / Harmony . . . / More grateful than harmonious sound to the ear" (600–606). He gently rebukes the angel's high-minded pronouncement on carnal intercourse (598–99) so that Raphael has to rephrase it (622–23). Hierarchy includes mutual education, while harmonious order prevails. Potential discord is still only a passing shadow.

Here I want to depart from orthodox reading and raise a further question. Would Milton have said of his own art what Adam says of Eve? His celestial song also touches the senses and may transport and is itself a thing of beauty. Does his art keep "Adamic" wisdom superior over "the charm of Beauty"? Or is it in his art as in the Godhead, where Urania and Wisdom are sisters and play together — and are sometimes identified with the Logos. There are two harmonies here, the hierarchical harmony of unfallen Adam and Eve, and the sisterly harmony of Urania and Wisdom. The potential discord between Adam and Eve is the potential discord between the Word as Adamic wisdom (higher knowledge, Love with his seat in Reason)[17] and the Word as song and play, as Urania and Wisdom. Should the word as "Adamic" wisdom always govern the word in its melic and playful and charming and touching and beautiful — its "Eve-like" — functions? The same question arises every time the trope of marriage is used for the processes of Milton's art: what marriage?

When we turn back to book 4 and the first appearance of Adam and Eve, we may hear Milton preparing us for Eve's fall from wisdom. Yet his hierarchy sounds arbitrary. For Eve begins by sharing with Adam "the image of their glorious Maker . . . / Truth, Wisdom, Sanctitude severe and pure"

(4.292–93). But within 200 lines, this first image is altered, and wisdom undergoes what we now call gender-marking, as Eve acknowledges "How beauty is excell'd by manly grace / And wisdom, which alone is truly fair" (4.490–91). The association of wisdom with what is masculine becomes even more marked after the fall:

> From Man's effeminate slackness it begins,
> Said th'Angel, who should better hold his place
> By wisdom, and superior gifts receiv'd.
>
> *(9.634–36)*

And we are never given an example of what Adam means when he says that Eve "degrades" higher knowledge or makes wisdom look like folly — harsh words for prelapsarian female foolishness, and different from Raphael's passing and uncensorious remark that Adam himself will sometimes be "seen least wise" (8.578). Satan is astute as well as canonical in appealing so strongly to wisdom when he tempts Eve ("O Sacred, Wise, and Wisdom-giving Plant" [9.679]; cf. "a tree to be desired to make one wise" [Gen. 3:6]). Given her inexperience of deception, Eve's logic is clear enough. "His words replete with guile / Into her heart too easy entrance won" (733–34). (Again, the language of entry as of opening Wisdom's way [809, above] and of "keeping strictest watch" [363] is language used of Wisdom in Prov. 8 [2–3, 34], and it echoes back sadly and ironically against Milton's words about his blindness: "And wisdom at one entrance quite shut out" [3.50].) And Satan's temptation of Eve is far from paltry: among Christ's three temptations, it is most like the third and greatest, as the third is the greatest for Milton himself — the desire for more wisdom, including the wisdom of words. (If snakes can speak, thinks Eve, what might not I do? Suppose a speaking snake arrived as muse before a writer's desk. Suppose a muse said: you need knowledge of good and evil in order to write. How intelligent Milton is about the temptation of Eve, and how unpatronizing.) Yet a twentieth-century reader may still reflect that Eve might have withstood temptation better if she had not been taught to defer to the wisdom of another. To put my question a little sharply: is Milton willing to give his muse what he will not give Eve — a sisterly (which is to say, co-equal) relation with wisdom? The answer seems to be, alas, yes.

It is true that in a sentence from *Tetrachordon* in 1645 Milton sounds more generous: "the wiser should govern the less wise, whether male or female."

Yet the relation of females to the Wisdom figure in the *Tetrachordon* commentary on Gen. 2:18 is curiously mixed. It is not that toiling on the hill of wisdom is assumed to be a masculine activity. It is Milton's different languages for the various "recreations" of marriage. He begins with the beautiful and powerful example of Prov. 8: "God himself conceals us not his own recreations before the world was built: 'I was,' saith the Eternal Wisdom, 'daily his delight, playing always before him.'" But later language falls off sadly: "Whereof lest we should be too timorous . . . wisest Solomon among his gravest proverbs countenances a kind of ravishment and erring fondness in the entertainment of wedded leisures." Even if *erring* can also mean "right wandering" etymologically, there remains a coy naughtiness in Milton that sounds like a fumbling with Spenserian language. (Spenser knows what he is doing when he uses terms like *erring fondness*—Milton's unhappy paraphrase for the *ravishment* of Prov. 5:19–20.) It is very unlike Milton, and although brief, makes one wish for the clarity and cleanliness of some good, witty Shakespearean bawdiness. Something in Milton is uneasy in this passage, where we may hear his own wisdom from its best through to its worst.

The practical problem of governing fallen music and governing the melic powers of poetry is an old one. Logos as word and right reason usually takes precedence. There is classical authority for this: "words contribute an *ethos* to sounds, placing them in the relation of the rational soul to body."[18] In questions of practical morality, the effects of music are all-important. Ambrose "believed that psalm singing effected remission from sin,"[19] but fears of even holy music's distraction are much more common. "For centuries after Augustine the leaders of the Church, following his lead, attempted to suppress the expressive claims of melody and rhetoric."[20] Or at least to ensure that the expression was means, not end, and means to a true end. (Milton says: "May I express thee," not "May I express myself.") Augustine's beautiful meditation on his own susceptibility to music ("melos omnes cantilenarum suavium") is the *locus classicus* of this fear of music's distracting power (*Confessions* 10.33). Music may be a good teacher, as in Calvin,[21] but it needs governing. Thus also Cato's rebuke to the enraptured but dilatory listeners to Casella's lovely song (Dante, *Purg.* 2.106–33). Thus also Browning's David, who moves out of the lyric mode into prophetic logos, leaving melos behind. "Then the truth came upon me. No harp more—no song more!" (*Saul*, l. 237). (Browning, like Dante, is, of course, writing poetry with powerful melic effects, even as he moves from "song" to "truth.") The translators of the Bay Psalm Book put the matter bluntly: "we have respected . . . conscience rather than elegance, fidelity rather than poetry."[22]

All this sounds oddly modern, if we follow recent forms of the temptation story — for example, the seduction of logos by melos and trope, in Paul de Man's witty and provocative account, where even mimesis "dodges," metaphor is "wily" and wreaks "mischief," paronomasia is "dangerously seductive," and "euphony is probably the most insidious of all sources of error."[23] Or we may follow Derrida's play about words, with words, in words. Or we may desire (unwisely, I think) a bifurcation of the word into logic and song or play, with logical processes left to male writing, as the heir to a patriarchal tradition.[24] The division I have been sketching is very old and not just post-Cartesian. It is well illustrated by interpretations of Wisdom in Prov. 8:22 – 31, and especially by interpreters' frequent discomfort with a Wisdom who plays, in any sense of the word. (Neither Milton nor Barth is so unjoyous.) One sees why Derrida refuses to govern the word *viens* (come) by any system, when he reads the end of the Apocalypse (Rev. 22:17): "Le 'viens' décide, si on peut dire; pas de règle (juridique, morale ou politique) pour décider à qui il faut répondre et quel 'viens' préférer."[25]

We might leave the matter there and simply conclude that Milton finds one use for the Wisdom figure when he wants to ground his art in the Logos, and another use for the Wisdom figure when he wants to mediate the Logos through males to females.[26] But that seems simplistic, especially when Milton implicates Adam as fully as Eve in the fall from wisdom. We might more usefully reflect on how Milton himself went back to the doctrine of the Logos and wrestled with it. For his "traditional, masculine poetic inspiration" is not always traditional, and his "subservient female muses" sometimes question subservience.[27] Milton's well-known anti-Trinitarianism — that is, his restlessness with the orthodox doctrine of the Logos — is connected with the question in my title. So also is his attraction to the ante-Nicene Fathers. It is there that one finds diverse meditations on wisdom literature, the figure of Wisdom, and the Logos.[28] It is there that one would start if one wished to reform the doctrine of the Logos, reform it so as to enlarge it, using scriptural hints of music and poetry. And this would be easier to do with a subordinationist or modal doctrine of the Trinity. Whether Milton was attracted to Origen or Eusebius, or to a wider range of theologians,[29] I think the attraction is related to his love for music and poetry at their best. Similarly, I think Coleridge's attraction to the Alexandrian Fathers, especially Origen,[30] is part of his love of poetry, as is also his interest in the doctrine of the Logos. For Coleridge's famous definition of imagination and fancy properly belongs in his fresh consideration of the Logos, that never-written "treatise on the Logos or communicative intellect in Man and Deity" (*Biographia Literaria*, ch. 13).

As for my second question, whether in Milton's art there is a hierarchical or else a sisterly harmony, I think the Miltonic answer would be yes to both. Certainly, Milton indicates that, in some contexts, song and trope and charm need governance by reasonable wisdom, whether wisdom is male or female. But some of Milton's words in *Tetrachordon*, like his invocation to book 7, offer another vision. The "recreations of God" may seem at first a lesser activity than life's serious business, and, as allegory, may seem only to trivialize marriage. Yet, on reflection, the word *recreation* need not be "vacation" (as in Karsten Harries's "poetry . . . a vacation from reality").[31] For the implicit pun in the word *recreation* is hard to avoid, especially when Prov. 8 is about creation. It is as if God and humans recreate themselves continually through true play — a beautiful notion of play, both unfallen and fallen. Coleridge uses the same notion, without the pun, in his famous definition of imagination: "a repetition in the finite mind of the eternal act of creation in the infinite I AM . . . in order to re-create." By "true" play, I intend neither concept nor precept, nor art in its "expressive claim" or as "consolation."[32] I intend art in its authority, for this is its challenge (as Adam knew of Eve: "Authority and Reason on her wait"). We can understand this only if we know what Geoffrey Hill means when he says that the poet's "truthtelling" *is* his craft, when it effects "the atonement of aesthetics with rectitude of judgment."[33] There is a "true" play and a "false" play, apart from (although perhaps related to) conceptual or doctrinal truth. Many of us now, especially the daughters of Eve, are enjoying the discomfiture of "Adamic" wisdom in language. But to opt for a simple reversal, in which language's "Eve-like" functions dominate, only reinscribes the old division. We might better reconsider the old division itself and muse again on the ancient figure of a Wisdom who rejoices and plays.

TWELVE

The Poetics of Modern Punning: Wallace Stevens, Elizabeth Bishop, and Others

By second nature, as well as by family custom and the accident of historical timing, Wallace Stevens was a paronomastic.[1] Aged 15, he punned on *condescension*, complaining to his mother of condescension from fellows in their twenties but surmising that 11-to-14-year-olds regarded his company as an "ascension."[2] And aged 72, he wrote to a friend about Reinhold Niebuhr, "an admirable thinker . . . but a dull writer": "Notwithstanding his name, he is far from being Rhine Wein."[3] He was born to paronomasia. His father was a punster: "Dear Wallace — just what election to the Signet signifies I have no sign. It is significant . . ." and so on to a total of eleven puns (*L*, 26 [21 May 1899]). It was part of the times. Stevens's father was named Garrett Stevens, his mother's maiden name was Zeller, and, yes, when they married in 1876, a local Pennsylvania newspaper commented that Stevens's father had "furnished his house complete from 'Zeller' to 'Garrett'" (*SP*, 6).

Yet in the nineteenth century, although puns were immensely popular, their presence in serious poetry was another matter. Lewis Carroll and Edward Lear perhaps, but poetry properly so called? It was a time whose taste favored the line of wit less than the line of vision, when the claims of charm poetry were paramount as against the claims of riddle poetry. As Northrop Frye observes in his essay "Charms and Riddles," "Charm poetry . . . dominated taste until about 1915, after which a mental attitude more closely related to the riddle began to supersede it, one more preoccupied with the visual and the conceptual."[4] Paronomasia is related to charm verse, to follow Frye's argument, and also Andrew Welsh's in his *Roots of Lyric*,[5] but charm verse does not generate, does not display, obvious wordplay — quips, quibbles, riddles — as in the metaphysical poets or Christopher Smart, let alone James Joyce. The paronomasia of Donne is more spectacular than the paronomasia of Spenser, even though some techniques and functions are similar.

So also, some techniques and functions are similar in the work of Wallace Stevens and Elizabeth Bishop. (Bishop lived a generation after the high moderns, including Stevens; he was born in 1879 and she in 1911.) But one would want to begin by saying that Bishop's kind of wordplay usually follows a Spenser-Herbert line (she was devoted to the work of George Herbert). Stevens's kind of paronomasia occasionally does so (for example, in his visionary poems). But Stevens the witty and wicked paronomastic is the heir to Donne, to Byron, to Carroll, to Hopkins, and the like.

The *Oxford English Dictionary*, in good nineteenth-century fashion, takes a low view of wordplay. Its definitions of *pun* and of *paronomasia* are more neutral, although, as it happens, they were published earlier (1909 and 1904 respectively; see the introduction to the *OED*). The section including the term *word-play* was not published until 1928, but despite Eliot and Pound and Joyce and Stevens — perhaps because of them — it is very stern: "a playing or trifling with words; the use of words merely or mainly for the purpose of producing a rhetorical or fantastic effect" (*play, sb.* 7.b). The three definitions are not altered in the second edition of the *OED*.

It is true that paronomasia has often excited warnings in rhetorical handbooks, chiefly about its overuse or its low status. "Marry, we must not play, or riot too much with them [i.e., words], as in *Paranomasies*," Ben Jonson says in 1641 (*Timber; or Discoveries*). Or, in 1593, Henry Peacham: "This figure [paronomasia] ought to be sparingly used"; antanaclasis "may fall easily into excesse" (*The Garden of Eloquence*). Or, in 1730, César Dumarsais: "On doit éviter les jeux de mots qui sont vides de sens"; for him, Augustine provides a proper pattern (*Traité des tropes*). To which Pierre Fontanier later adds that paronomasia is better in Latin than in French: "ces jeux de mots ont en général moins de grâce dans notre langue que dans celle des Latins" (*Des figures du discours* [1827]). Quintilian, referring to Cicero, says that wordplay is "non ingratae, nisi copia redundet" ("not unattractive save when carried to excess," as the Loeb translation has it; 9.3.74). At the other end of a scale of significance, paronomasia might be built into the language by divine decree in order to teach us. As Augustine says: "it happened not by human design but perhaps by divine decision [etsi non humana industria, iudicio fortasse divino] that the grammarians have not been able to decline (or conjugate) the Latin verb *moritur* [he dies] by the same rule as other verbs of this form. . . . The verb cannot be declined in speech just as the reality which it signifies cannot be declined (that is, avoided) by any action" (*De civitate Dei* 13.11).[6] Ernst Robert Curtius offers more examples in his *European Literature and the Latin Middle Ages*.[7] And, to leap forward to an English poet who admired Augustine, Coleridge delighted in wordplay of every type and purpose.[8] The mid to late nineteenth century could not plead precedence for its low view of this rhetorical device.

I have used the term *paronomasia* throughout as a general synonym for punning and for wordplay. That is, I have not distinguished such categories as, say, antanaclasis. Nor do I distinguish the pun (low humor, below the salt) from wordplay (a superior wit), as, for example, Freud distinguishes them.[9] Leo Spitzer noted in 1950 how the later term *pun* (used from 1662, says the *OED*) has come to include a whole series of earlier rhetorical figures for wordplay.[10] Similarly with the modern use of *paronomasia*, which has become an umbrella for wordplay in general.

In treating paronomasia, it is possible to analyze types of puns, the most familiar division being between homonymic and semantic puns. It is possible to place paronomasia in a general context, as Frye and Welsh do, where it is associated with very early forms of writing, both charm and riddle. It is possible to consider paronomasia in relation to nonliterary contexts — for example, logical or linguistic or psychological or, I dare say, neurological contexts. How is punning related to logical thought or, more widely, to rational thought? The answer, I suppose, would be: as Homer to Plato, to take that ancient quarrel as a pattern. How is paronomasia related to linguistic skills as they develop in an individual or in the practice of a society? Roman Jakobson observes: "In a sequence in which similarity is superimposed on contiguity, two similar phonemic sequences near to each other are prone to assume a paronomastic function."[11] How is paronomasia revealing psychologically? Freud, of course, is very fond of interpreting it. As for a neurological context, I am thinking of Oliver Sacks and the workings of memory, since punning develops very early in children and has mnemonic force. I am assuming that I don't need to spend time on the various types of argument that defend wordplay.

My own interest lies in the area of poetics. Here, I think that a simple homonymic pun, one without further reverberation, would be classified as a scheme rather than a trope. But puns can move toward tropes when they begin to tell fables about themselves. It is these fables, including their use of etymology, that interest me especially in the poetics of paronomasia.

I want to begin with one aspect of such fabling, and how it helps us to read twentieth-century poetry. The following question seems to me a useful one for reader and writer both. What words come with so venerable a history of paronomasia that no self-respecting modern poet can use them without making choices? That is, poets may use these words if they wish, but they must decide what to do about the standard paronomasia — whether to distance it, or merely to acknowledge it, or to carry on with it. I'm not, of course, talking about entire huge classes of possible puns, but rather about certain words where specific paronomasies (Jonson's handy word) have been used so often and/or so memorably that the words carry a punning sense. It takes great skill to extend the fabling history of such words. New puns are a delight, but re-capping or re-dressing altogether an old fable offers more challenge and more riches.

Let me start with the common word *turn* and the suggestion that a poet cannot use the word at the beginning or end of a line without thinking about the original descriptive energy of the word. Consider the following stanza from Bishop's poem "Twelfth Morning; or What You Will":

The fence, three-strand, barbed-wire, all pure rust,
    three dotted lines, comes forward hopefully
across the lots; thinks better of it; turns
        a sort of corner . . .[12]

Bishop has, in fact, given us not just one but a whole family of etymological connotations. The fence turns, turns the corner of a lot and those "lots" offer a variation of the standard pun on *stanza*, meaning "room," of which more in a moment. Those are fenced lots, so that the fence can turn with the line:

"turns / a sort of corner." Well, so it is, there on the page, a sort of corner. And there it is, I think: this word that cannot be used at the beginning or end of a line without remembering the tradition of wordplay on *turn*. "Turn," which is what *verse* means etymologically. "Turn," which is what *trope* means etymologically. *Turn*, which in enjambment describes what the reader is doing, albeit with an eye rather than the etymological leg of enjambment, as it walks the line, and strides or limps or hops over the end of the line, and back, westward, to the start of the next line.

Stevens uses the word repeatedly at the beginning of a line in his well-known 1916 poem "Domination of Black":

> I heard them cry — the peacocks.
> Was it a cry against the twilight
> Or against the leaves themselves
> Turning in the wind,
> Turning as the flames
> Turned in the fire,
> Turning as the tails of the peacocks
> Turned in the loud fire,
> Loud as the hemlocks
> Full of the cry of the peacocks?

If the word *turn* appears in mid-line, that, I think, is another matter. We should need a stronger signal for our paronomastic antennae to start waving.

Are there other such common words? I think so. The word *leaves*, for example, also has an extended paronomastic family: (1) leaves of a tree (the common topos links them with the dead: Homer through Virgil through, in English, Milton and Shelley and so on); (2) leaves of a book; and (3) that which is left, or leavings. These are standard, and a poet can go on from there. Or a poet may decline the paronomasia on *leaves*, but never in ignorance. An uninvited paronomasia is apt to commit a solecism.

In a stanzaic poem, the word *room* anywhere in the line wants testing, just in case the old pun on the Italian *stanza* is at work. Thus in Stevens's "Six Significant Landscapes," no. 6 (1916):

> Rationalists, wearing square hats,
> Think, in square rooms,
> Looking at the floor,

Looking at the ceiling.
They confine themselves
To right-angled triangles.
If they tried rhomboids,
Cones, waving lines, ellipses —
As, for example, the ellipse of the half-moon —
Rationalists would wear sombreros.

"Square rooms"? We first read a conceptual analogy, then see that Stevens has not written a "square-room" stanza. That is, his stanza doesn't look square on the page, nor is it schematically square, for I suppose a square stanza is symmetrical, say four-by-four, a tetrameter quatrain. At least, that's what John Hollander suggests:

Why have I locked myself inside
This narrow cell of four-by-four,
Pacing the shined, reflecting floor
Instead of running free and wide?[13]

Modern poets are not the only ones to play on the word *room* in this standard manner. Hollander's "narrow cell" compacts two of Wordsworth's punning tropes for *stanza*, here a sonnet stanza: "Nuns fret not at their convent's narrow room; / And hermits are contented with their cells." Wordsworth's sonnet also speaks of "the Sonnet's scanty plot of ground."[14] (Lewis Carroll might say of it: "I measured it from side to side, / Fourteen lines long and five feet wide.") These are figures of right-angled rooms or plots, whether square or rectangular. If you look at Stevens's stanza, you will see that he has curved the unjustified right margin so that it is itself a half-moon ellipse or, it may be, a sombrero. This kind of punning on *stanza* belongs also to a class of visual wordplay; Stevens's poem is almost a shape poem.

But then, so is Bishop's stanza or fenced lot. Look again, and you will see a visual mimesis. The fence, or "three dotted lines," comes forward as if in an optical illusion such as Wittgenstein's famous example of the duck and the rabbit. Here are three lines of print, and behold, a mimesis of the fence and a prolepsis of what Bishop's own lines will turn into at the end: an ellipsis, three dots, a kind of fence at the end of the stanza.

Stevens also punned on the marks for ellipsis in several letters to his wife: ". . . (Notice my Frenchy way of punctuating? Très chic, n'est-ce pas?) . . ."

(16 Aug. 1911).[15] Then, four days later: "I fell asleep over a French book and had the most delightful dream. . . . [*sic*]."[16] The next pause offers five dots, a progression of points (*L*, 171). Two years later, "The cats have grown very large!!! . . . ." (*L*, 179 [7 July 1913]). Stevens implies they'd been eating birds, so that the nine dots may have to do with the nine lives of felines. This, by the way, is before Beckett's punctuating pun in his title, "Dante . . . Bruno. Vico . . . Joyce" where each dot (not counting the period) stands for a century. For wordplay on the two dots that constitute an umlaut, here is James Merrill in his poem "Lost in Translation":

> The owlet umlaut peeps and hoots
> Above the open vowel.[17]

I've been speaking of common words charged with a history of etymological suggestiveness (*turn*, *leaves*, *room*) and also of visual paronomasia. Are there some less common words that require etymological or paronomastic awareness when we read twentieth-century poetry? I think so. Take the words *immaculate* and *maculate*.

Here is the opening of Bishop's poem "Seascape":

> This celestial seascape, with white herons got up as angels,
> flying as high as they want and as far as they want sidewise
> in tiers and tiers of immaculate reflections;
> the whole region, from the highest heron
> down to the weightless mangrove island
> with bright green leaves edged neatly with bird-droppings
> like illumination in silver . . .
> it does look like heaven.

I pass by the ambiguity of "got up" meaning both "costumed" and "ascended." This pun opens up, in the most delicate way, the argument for a naturalistic origin for angels (like white birds, like swans, as Stevens suggests in *Notes Toward a Supreme Fiction*). Bishop like Stevens is not a believer, but she is usually quieter about her skeptical strain. "Got up," then, so that they can fly "in tiers and tiers of immaculate reflections," up to the highest heaven, if that echo sounds faintly in "the highest heron." *Immaculate* is here used in an etymologically pure way (from *macula*, or spot), meaning perfectly unspotted. Bishop delicately evokes older doctrinal uses, again as with "got up," setting them aside. (I'm also reminded of Dante's heaven in Bishop's "tiers and tiers of immaculate reflections" — of his *di bianco in bianco* (from tier to tier) playing against his *tanto bianco* (so white) in a flying passage in the *Paradiso* [31.16, 14].)

And this is surely the point of the line about the "pure-colored or spotted breasts" of the "big symbolic birds" in her later, powerful poem "Brazil, January 1, 1502":

> A blue-white sky, a simple web . . .
> And perching there in profile, beaks agape,
> the big symbolic birds keep quiet,
> each showing only half his puffed and padded,
> pure-colored or spotted breast.
> Still in the foreground there is Sin. . . .

"Pure-colored or spotted": this is the language of ornithological field guides. It would sound peculiar to describe a song sparrow or a wood thrush as having a maculate breast. But it is, or should be, impossible to miss that history of *immaculate* and *maculate*, which enables us to read the symbolism of the big symbolic birds.

As for Stevens, he was more irritated than Bishop with the language of whiteness, perhaps because he was more vulnerable. Pure poetry, if not doctrinally immaculate poetry, appealed strongly to him when he was young, and he reacted with proportionate bitterness later. See especially *The Man with the Blue Guitar*:

> The pale intrusions into blue
> Are corrupting pallors . . .
>
> . . . .
>
> The unspotted imbecile revery,

> (xiii)

Unspotted is the Germanic word corresponding to *immaculate*. Stevens earlier in this sequence calls the moon "immaculate," which may just make us smile when we recall its spots. In *The Man with the Blue Guitar*, many a kind of whiteness is punningly evoked and dismissed. Words like *immaculate*, Stevens implies, can themselves be lunatic ("imbecile") or even "corrupting." Wordplay here enters an entire field of association, reminding us to test our whitest, unspotted, immaculate, moony, candid, pure ideals and idealization. We need to remember this when we read Stevens's canto on whiteness in *Notes Toward a Supreme Fiction* (1.3). The word *immaculate* does not itself remain immaculate in Stevens.

Eliot also liked the punning possibilities of the word *immaculate*, at least in the form of *maculate*, which he used for "apeneck Sweeney":

> The zebra stripes along his jaw
> Swelling to maculate giraffe.

Stripes to spots, that is, and also distinctly spotted. "Still," as Bishop would observe, "Still in the foreground there is Sin," perhaps a shade relentlessly in this 1918 poem ("Sweeney Among the Nightingales").

Another example of paronomasia may owe its modern prominence to Eliot, and that is the pun on Latin *infans* (unspeaking) and English *infant*. Here is Eliot in 1919, in "Gerontion":

> The word within a word, unable to speak a word.

Eliot's allusion to a sermon by Lancelot Andrewes is well known, as is Andrewes's punning paradox that the infant Christ is the Word who is "infans" or unable to speak.[18] The paradox of *fans atque infans* is listed in Lewis and Short, a dictionary in which Stevens said he delighted.[19] He adapted the double pun in the paronomasia of a fan and an infans in the poem "Infanta Marina." The lovely infanta is appropriately one of his muse figures — that is, one who enables him to speak even if she herself is "infans," waving her fan, some palm tree metamorphosed into a Florida infanta. Later infants in Stevens may also carry this paronomasia: "It is the infant A standing on infant legs" (1949, *CP*, 469). "Infant, it is enough in life / To speak of what you see" (1946, *CP*, 365).

Bishop is too good a wordsmith not to be aware of such histories. She acknowledges this at the end of her poem "Over 2000 Illustrations and a Complete Concordance" (the reference is to a large Bible):

> Open the heavy book. Why couldn't we have seen
> this old Nativity while we were at it?
> — the dark ajar, the rocks breaking with light,
> an undisturbed, unbreathing flame,
> colorless, sparkless, freely fed on straw,

> and, lulled within, a family with pets,
> —and looked and looked our infant sight away.

"Infant" first because of the Nativity scene that is seen and not seen. Bishop once saw it in the old Bible, but has not seen it in her actual travel in biblical lands. "Our infant sight": a sight of an infant, of the infant. But sight itself is also infant in the sense that sight is always "infans," or unspeaking. We translate it into words. Yet how can we look and look our infant sight away? In different senses. As when we look away to our heart's content (Bishop's repeated *look* works to prolong this moment of looking). Or "look away" in the sense of removing "infant sight," averting our eyes? And if removing sight, then what follows? Speech, words? Or grown-up sight, and what would that grown-up sight be? In this simply worded but intricate paronomasia, Bishop has laid out our possible responses to the Nativity scene. It's remembered from a book. It's not to be seen by traveling to the area where it happened. It's desired. It might fulfill desire and at the same time necessarily translate desire into something ordinary and familiar, so that we would be back where we started in one way if not another.

Have the moderns invented new types of puns, as distinct from extending the repertoires of older types? If the portmanteau word is Lewis Carroll's invention, then the answer is yes. A portmanteau word is a paronomasia that presents the technique and the result all at once. Here is how puns work, it seems to say, and here is a new one, a neologism. " 'Twas brillig and the slithy toves . . . ," etc. "Slithy"? *Slimy* and *lithe* come into our minds, thanks to Humpty Dumpty. They came into Stevens's mind too, but he decided to take Lewis Carroll one step back. Why not simply say "ithy"? As in "Analysis of a Theme":

> We enjoy the ithy oonts and long-haired
> Plomets, as the Herr Gott
> Enjoys his comets.

Ithy as in "slithy"? Or is it *ithy* with a short *i*? The short *i* seems to invite *mythy* and *pithy*, words that are more serious than "slithy-ithy" words, portentous words, comets as omens. We recall Jove's "mythy mind" in Stevens's well-known 1915 poem "Sunday Morning." And we recall E. H. Gombrich's persuasive play on the associations of *pong* and *ping* in his *Art and Illusion*.[20] A long-*i*'d *ithy* seems to call for more squiggly or whooshing Lewis-Carroll words: *slithy, slimy, writhing, scything.* (Although there are, to be sure, *lithe* and *blithe.*) But then there is the prefix *ithy,* from Greek *ithus,* or straight, and not at all squiggly, as in *ithyphallic* (the only example in the *Concise Oxford*), which described the phallus carried in festivals of Bacchus, as well as the meter used for Bacchic hymns, or generally for licentious poems (the trochaic dimeter brachycatalectic). An "oont," by the way, is a camel.

There is a similar phenomenon in Stevens's late poem "Long and Sluggish Lines":

> . . . Could it be that yellow patch, the side
> Of a house, that makes one think the house is laughing;
>
> Or these — escent — issant pre-personae: first fly,
> A comic infanta among the tragic drapings,
>
> Babyishness of forsythia, a snatch of belief,
> The spook and makings of the nude magnolia?
> · · · · · · · · · · · · · · · · · · ·
> Wanderer, this is the pre-history of February,
> The life of the poem in the mind has not yet begun.

Stevens's syntax tells us how to read the suffixes *-escent* and *-issant.* So does the *Concise Oxford Dictionary,* at least for *-escent,* "forming adjs. denoting onset of a state or variation of colour etc. (deliquescent, effervescent, florescent, iridescent) . . . pres. part. . . . of vbs. in -escere." The suffix *-issant,* on the other hand, makes no appearance in any Oxford dictionary, or in *Webster's* either. But then, I have not been able to find any word at all with this suffix, apart from one coined by Stevens himself: "The grackles sing avant the spring / Most spiss — oh! Yes, most spissantly. / They sing right puissantly" ("Snow and Stars"). This is also from a pre-spring poem, a rather ill-tempered one (grackles are not happy birds in Stevens). Stevens's seemingly invented suffix is itself a prehistory of words, if we accept his own coinage as the first blooming *-issant* word that we have in English. *Spiss,* although obsolete, is listed in *Oxford* and *Webster's;* it means "thick, dense, close," including close intervals in music. Florio gives a form of it. But then we might hear a long *i* in *-issant,* and hence a family of French words in this Ur-paronomasia.[21]

Paronomasia through neologism: this is one type of paronomasia that

Bishop does not use, for she is not given to neologisms, whereas Stevens delights in them. His play with neologisms and with unusual words (*oonts*) makes us listen for the paronomastic force of any unknown words as a way of defining them. It's a useful training. Such paronomastic testing of the unknown, together with the paronomastic history of the known, works to make us aware of the possible paronomasia in all our words — for all that, in our syllables, letters, and punctuation marks as well. Letters? Stevens's Alpha and Omega in his "An Ordinary Evening in New Haven," for example. Or Anthony Hecht's recent brilliant pun on the "voiceless thorn," both the plant protuberance that breaks your skin and the Anglo-Saxon letter for a breathed rather than voiced *th* sound (*thorn* not *the*):

> And the wind, a voiceless thorn
> goes over the details,
> making a soft promise
> to take our breath away.[22]

An audible paronomasia may be noticed here: try sounding out *th*, as in a soft wind, then stopping, as directed in the breathtaking pun of the enjambed last line. Hecht's crows are morticians; they do not "caw" but call out *cras* or "tomorrow," as Latin crows did. Language so tested and so paronomastic displays its own vitality. Words do have a life of their own, and paronomasia makes us acutely aware of this.

Stevens's instinct for wordplay was part of his general delight in the history of words. Bishop also delighted in the diachronic life of words, their etymological family history, their various cognate relatives, and so on. In her work, words tremble with the energy of their own histories, and the potential for paronomasia is always there. Sometimes her wordplay is made obvious, laid out for us. Sometimes it is hidden but it will rarely if ever be riddling. The subtleties and challenges are not combative, and the poems can be read without realizing how rich they are. Riddling paronomasia stops you short.

Nor does Bishop experiment with the limits of wordplay. At least, this is what I think Stevens is doing in *The Comedian as the Letter C*, that difficult personal Bildungsroman. Yet her fewer and quieter examples of paronomasia are as remarkable as Stevens's own.

Stevens's paronomasia, especially in his early work, was also part of his revolt against the gentility and piety of the times, what he sardonically called "the grand ideas of the villages" in "The Man Whose Pharynx Was Bad." In the last fifteen or twenty years of his life, this shifted, as he centered his work increasingly on "the possibility of a supreme fiction, recognized as a fiction, in which men could propose to themselves a fulfilment" (L, 820 [1954]). The supreme fiction was to be, in effect, the heir and successor to Christianity. Bishop stays away from such questions. But she is like Stevens in working paronomastically to undo some effects of her religious heritage.

Andrew Welsh in his *Roots of Lyric* writes that "If Hopkins' oracle [in the poem 'Spelt from Sybil's Leaves'] is one form of poetry particularly suited to the play of language through various kinds of punning, perhaps the richest development of all the powers in the poet's language is the poetry of religious paradox."[23] We know this also from Herbert, and many a writer before and after Herbert. But if a wordplay can affirm religious paradox, it can also undo religious paradox. Stevens knows this full well, and a whole taxonomy of paronomastic undoing (or what he would call "decreation") could be deduced from his work.

Yet another type of wordplay is at work in Bishop's poem "Twelfth Morning; or What You Will," a particularly interesting type, which might be called allusive, although older readers would have found the adjective redundant, since one meaning of the word *allusion* used to be "a play upon words, a pun" (*OED*, 2; the illustrative quotations range from 1556 to 1731). James Merrill, by the way, has remarked that modern poets may sometimes even substitute wordplay for allusion: "The lucky 18th century reader — having read literally *tous les livres* — could be trusted to catch every possible allusion. This is no longer the case; some of us substitute word-play to make our texts resound."[24]

In Bishop's poem, allusive paronomasia allows her to talk back to Eliot and to extend the fabling paronomastic history of the word *turn*. For consider Eliot's use of the verb *turn*, notably in "Ash-Wednesday," where *turn* at the end of a line comes close to being an Eliot signature ("Because I do not hope to turn again . . ."). Consider Eliot's "Journey of the Magi," the best-known twentieth-century poem in English on the subject of the Three Kings. And then consider Bishop's poem, set on the Feast of the Epiphany or the Three Kings, and centered on a black boy called Balthazár. Eliot: "three trees on the low sky, / And an old white horse galloped away in the meadow." Bishop: "the black boy Balthazár, a fence, a horse." "The fence, three-strand . . . the big white horse." If this were Eliot's poem, the number three in the three-strand fence would work differently. It would turn triune, perhaps trinitarian, an emblematic numerological punning. And Bishop's later question would sound much different:

> Don't ask the big white horse, *Are you supposed*
> *to be inside the fence or out?* He's still
> asleep. Even awake, he probably
> remains in doubt.

If this were Eliot's poem, you would know for sure whether the horse were inside the fence or out, or, worse, sitting on the fence. Bishop does not foreground any of these effects. She keeps doctrinal and political matters peripheral to the main matter, which is song on this day of the epiphany, and a poor child in a small town in a remote area—rather like the original epiphany, we are given to understand. But her different paronomasia on *turn* itself turns Eliot's many turnings, alerting us to the different uses of the number three and of the white horse in her poem.

Bishop carries on other examples of wordplay from Eliot and Stevens, both of whom are gifted allusive paronomastics.[25] Bishop has heard what they are doing and signals that she wishes to do something different. To make such a challenge is easy but to live up to it is extraordinary. Bishop does so.

I want to end with an example from Stevens that I heard only recently, thanks to Bishop, who herself heard and repeated and enlarged this pun, speaking back to Stevens. Here is the opening stanza of part 3 of Stevens's 1942 masterpiece *Notes Toward a Supreme Fiction*:

> To sing jubilas at exact, accustomed times,
> To be crested and wear the mane of a multitude
> And so, as part, to exult with its great throat. . . .

"Crested?" I have previously recognized the metaphor of the multitude as a lion and the intricate wordplay on *tuba-jubilate*, for one meaning of *juba* is "crest."[26] But I did not consider etymology sufficiently. The etymon for *crest* is Latin, *crista*, a crest, as on a bird or animal. Stevens thereby suggests another origin for the word *Christian* than the actual Greek origin, where Christ signifies "the anointed one," the equivalent of the Hebrew Messiah.

He is using false etymology to suggest what is for him a true origin of *Christian* — that is, a naturalistic origin. False etymology can be just as useful for poetic fables as true etymology.[27] Stevens's punning is genial enough; he is now past the satires of the 1920's and early 1930's. And he is writing on the third note to the supreme fiction, "It Must Give Pleasure." Bishop heard all this, I think. In "Brazil, January 1, 1502," she enlarges the etymological pun, and she is much sharper than Stevens.

> Just so the Christians, hard as nails,
> tiny as nails, and glinting,
> in creaking armor, came and found it all. . . .
> Directly after Mass, humming perhaps
> *L'Homme armé* or some such tune,
> they ripped away into the hanging fabric. . . .

Bishop has overgone Stevens, a rare feat. Here, not just one but all three Latin meanings of *crista* are at work: crest, as on a helmet, for Bishop is at pains to emphasize the armor;[28] crest, as on a bird, by analogy with the bird-women at the end; and crest, as in sexual use. Nor is Bishop's wordplay genial. It sets all the Latinate uses against the Greek origin for the name of Christ, as Brazilian history itself would do, all too often, false etymology here becoming a true fable of false dealing.

A decade or so ago, we would have been considering the deconstructionist challenge to older views of paronomasia. Now we are more likely to be considering a historicist challenge. Both concur in limiting the functions of wordplay, as of all formal effects. It is the writers themselves who know the true seriousness in which paronomasia may partake, the true sense of *serio ludere*, the sense in which North Africans listened to Augustine's sermons, some sixteen hundred years ago. "The African, particularly, had a Baroque love of subtlety. They had always loved playing with words; they excelled in writing elaborate acrostics; *hilaritas* — a mixture of intellectual excitement and sheer aesthetic pleasure at a notable display of wit — was an emotion they greatly appreciated. Augustine would give them just this."[29] We, who seem to have so much trouble with the space between *serio* and *ludere*, have something to learn from these ancient Africans, as from our modern poets.[30]

THIRTEEN

Riddles, Charms, and Fictions in Wallace Stevens

No man though never so willing or so well enabl'd to instruct, but if he discerne his willingnesse and candor made use of to intrapp him, will suddainly draw in himselfe, and laying aside the facile vein of perspicuity, will know his time to utter clouds and riddles.

— MILTON, *Tetrachordon*

But not yet have we solved the incantation of this whiteness, and learned why it appeals with such power to the soul.

— MELVILLE, *Moby-Dick*

Among the many riddling poems Wallace Stevens has given us are some that are riddles structurally. That is, they cannot be read with much beyond pleasurable puzzlement until we have found the questions for which the poem provides answers. One example, published in the last year of Stevens's life, is "Solitaire Under the Oaks" (1955):

> In the oblivion of cards
> One exists among pure principles.
>
> Neither the cards nor the trees nor the air
> Persist as facts. This is an escape
>
> To principium, to meditation.
> One knows at last what to think about
>
> And thinks about it, without consciousness,
> Under the oak trees, completely released.[1]

The key to this compact little poem is Descartes: René Descartes and *des cartes*, the cards with which we play card games. The wit lies in the questions and answers implicit in the poem. What card game would a Cartesian, would M. Cards himself play? Why, solitaire, of course. We all know that our problems as *solitaires* — isolating self-consciousness, separation of nature into thinking self and outer object — stem from Descartes's principle "Cogito ergo sum." Solitaire is the quintessential Cartesian card game. But what has M. Descartes forgotten "In the oblivion of cards"? Answer: trees and air and indeed the cards themselves (which is to say, himself) as facts rather than as principles. Yet the card game of solitaire does offer compensating escape to *principium*, to meditation, as in Descartes's *Principia philosophiae* and *Les Méditations*. One escapes the burden of consciousness as long as one exists within this card game, thinking according to its rules.

I am not interested here in Stevens's view of Descartes. (It has more to do with the Descartes of Coleridge and of Valéry, I think, than with the seventeenth-century Descartes.) I am interested in the function of the riddle-poem. Itself a game, this little riddle simultaneously enacts a game and comments on other games, both small and large — solitaire and Cartesian philosophy and poetry too. In its play with paradoxes of outside and inside, it suggests that there are multiple ways to think of a player and a game, or of a reader and a text. Poetry comes closest to game in riddle-poems, those "generic seeds and kernels, possibilities of expression sprouting and exfoliating into new literary phenomena," as Northrop Frye says of both riddles and charm poems.[2] And "those who want to study the relation between form and function in a contemporary setting" may well "turn . . . to the rigid context of games."[3] The topography of riddles and charms has been finely mapped by Frye in his 1976 essay "Charms and Riddles"; my exploration here proposes to extend that map a little farther.

Games in riddle-poems may be multiple in less logical ways, as my second example is meant to demonstrate. What question do we ask to bridge the gap between title and couplets in an opaque poem of 1950, "The Desire to Make Love in a Pagoda" (*OP*, 91)?

> Among the second selves, sailor, observe
> The rioter that appears when things are changed,
>
> Asserting itself in an element that is free,
> In the alien freedom that such selves degustate:

In the first inch of night, the stellar summering
At three-quarters gone, the morning's prescience,

As if, alone on a mountain, it saw far-off
An innocence approaching toward its peak.

We begin by noting the double sense of the title: the desire (felt by a human) to make love in a pagoda, and the desire felt by a pagoda to make love. We note also the different senses of *peak*, and reflect that the act of making love has a peak physiologically and emotionally, and that pagodas are "strange buildings which come to a point at the end," as Ruskin says. We recall the old trope of the body as the temple of the Lord, and remember that a pagoda is for most of Stevens's readers a foreign or "alien" temple. Finally, we read the second line as if the noun clause were written by Lewis Carroll. "Rioter," "when things are changed," is anagrammatically a near-complete "erotic," which we might expect in a poem about a desire to make love. These preparations are sufficient for a reading of the poem as the gently witty, erotic, multilayered verse that it is: on desires of the body and of feelings; on primal desires for morning, which a temple might desire, as in love; on the desire to make riots or anagrams of letters, and to trope. The riddle takes the following form. Query: Is the body a temple? A temple of the Lord? Answer: Sometimes it is a pagoda. We begin with a sailor and a rioter and an anagram, but by the time the wordplay culminates in *peak*, only six lines later, Stevens has left behind the mode of Lewis Carroll. This is a riddle-poem whose games can touch as well as amuse the reader.[4]

These two examples are built as riddle-poems. More often, Stevens will include a riddle as part of the larger argument of a poem. For example, why does Jerome beget the tubas in *Notes Toward a Supreme Fiction* (3.1)?

To sing jubilas at exact, accustomed times,
To be crested and wear the mane of a multitude
And so, as part, to exult with its great throat,

To speak of joy and to sing of it, borne on
The shoulders of joyous men, to feel the heart
That is the common, the bravest fundament,

> This is a facile exercise. Jerome
> Begat the tubas and the fire-wind strings,
> The golden fingers picking dark-blue air . . .

In his letters, Stevens's answer to my question is carefully and courteously straightforward and also carefully limited: "Jerome is St. Jerome who 'begat the tubas' by translating the Bible. I suppose this would have been clearer if I had spoken of harps" (*L*, 435 [12 Jan. 1943]). But why tubas and not simply harps? It is true that through his translation of the Bible into Latin, Jerome begat sundry *tubae*; that he begat the *jubilas* of line 1, as in *Jubilate Deo*, the best-known plural *jubilas*; that he begat the association of *exult* and *jubilas* through his several pairings of forms of *exultare* and *jubilare*. It is also true that he gave us the sound association of *tuba-jubilate* in the Vulgate, to say nothing of Jubal and Tubalcain, whom we also know from the English Bible.[5] (Joyce exploited the sound association three years before Stevens: "jubalant tubalence," "tubular jurbulance.")[6] But there is another reason. Stevens owned a Lewis and Short Latin dictionary, whose use gave him "delight," as he testified to Robert Frost when making Frost a present of one.[7] There he would have found two meanings for the word *juba*: "the flowing hair on the neck of an animal, the mane," and "crest." These are precisely the tropes of Stevens's second line, in a happy mingling of nonsense-echo and metaphor, the metaphor being "A multitude is a lion." Stevens's huge Christian lion—not so much the Church triumphant as the Church rampant—is related to an earlier lion in *Notes* (1.4) and also to the lion that iconography commonly places beside St. Jerome. After all this, how could Jerome beget only harps? He begat the tubas not only through orthodox biblical association, but also for the good poetic reason that they rhyme with *jubas* (in a proper Latin feminine accusative plural ending too), and together the two words offer heterodox associations for the word *jubilas*, whose power we might otherwise reverence unduly.

I offer these examples partly as cautionary tales, for I think that sometimes Stevens's seeming obscurity and nonsense are in fact examples of wit we have not yet come to appreciate, riddles whose sibylline ideas of order we have not yet pieced together. To christen a questing, mountain-climbing lady Mrs. Uruguay has a good deal more point when we recall that the capital of Uruguay is Montevideo, as Frye once noted. To marry her to a Mr. Alfred Uruguay also has a certain point when we recall that the most famed Alfred in modern poetry has a surname Prufrock, and begins his poem thus:

> Let us go then, you and I,
> When the evening is spread out against the sky
> Like a patient etherised upon a table;

To which famous simile, Stevens's opening line to "Mrs. Alfred Uruguay" mischievously replies in an Eliot ragtime rhythm:

> So what said the others and the sun went down.

It does not do to underestimate the capacities for riddling and general word-play of a poet who can pun on the words *artichoke* and *inarticulate*: "a dream they never had, / Like a word in the mind that sticks at artichoke / And remains inarticulate" (*OP*, 47) — "rather an heroic pun," as its inventor endearingly remarked (*L*, 366 [27 Aug. 1940]).

If all Stevens's riddles worked as these and many others do, we would be dealing with a fine, formidable wit,

> Logos and logic, crystal hypothesis,
> Incipit and a form to speak the word
> And every latent double in the word,
>
> Beau linguist.
>
> > (*Notes* 1.8)

Our problems as readers come when Stevens's hypotheses are clouded, when the latent doubles in the word refuse to become patent and remain half-shadowed, figurae without fulfillment. I have offered readings of some of Stevens's riddles using as means of interpretation puns, logic, well-known tropes, Latin equivalents, nonsense-rhymes, iconography, literary antecedents. Although these riddles stand in varying relations to the arguments of their poems, and although their effects differ, they may all be read coherently. The interpretive devices I have mentioned satisfy our desire as readers that consistent if multiple answers be possible for riddles in texts.

But Stevens sometimes moves toward more problematic kinds of riddle. I am not thinking so much of impenetrable lines, which await a wise reader, as of lines where the riddles appear only partly soluble, and the problem becomes not only how to answer the riddle but also how to read the answer. Such lines include sinister-metamorphosis or horrid-metamorphosis poems like "Oak Leaves Are Hands"; *metamorphorid* is Stevens's fine portmanteau word for the process. They also include lines in which Stevens engages in intertextual wordplay. For example, in *Esthétique du mal*, part 5, what are the "obscurer selvages"? "For this . . . we forego / Lament, willingly forfeit the ai-ai / Of parades in the obscurer selvages." We can answer this question only so far. Selvages are edges, of course, and so belong in this canto of limits and bars. They may be more precisely placed, however, by reading them against the first five lines of the opening canto of Dante's *Inferno*. There Dante finds himself in a dark wood, "una selva oscura," and the noun *selva* is repeated in line 5, where its sounds at once expand into *selvaggia* — "esta selva selvaggia": "selva oscura . . . selva selvaggia," "oscura . . . selvaggia," obscure selvage. *Selvaggia*, however, is cognate with our word *savage* and not with the word *selvage*. Eliot makes use of etymology in "The Dry Salvages," third of the *Four Quartets*, published three years before Stevens's poem. The Dry Salvages are a small group of rocks off Cape Ann, Massachusetts, as Eliot tells us; the name, he guessed, was originally *les trois sauvages*. (See chapter 8, "The Senses of Eliot's Salvages.") By retaining the old name, New Englanders have kept it somewhat closer to its Italian cognate, *selvaggia*. In Eliot's poem, there is an implicit play on *salvages* (the rocks), *savage*, *salvage* (flotsam and jetsam), and I think *salvation* (which has the same Latin root as *salvage*) — play that includes the metaphor of the rock of salvation and allegories of traveling. I read Eliot's title as interwoven in this wordplay, and as echoing the "selva . . . selva selvaggia" of the beginning of Dante's journey.

Stevens echoes sound but dislocates denotative meaning, as he summons the ghost of a Dantean topos only to decenter it. For Dante's "selva oscura" is not in the middle of life's way for Stevens — neither as doctrinal allegory nor as personal allegory nor as a place for poetry. As allegory, it is on the edge of things, peripheral to Stevens's earthly vision. Even more on the edge — and thus the "obscur*er* selvages" — is Eliot's "The Dry Salvages." Yet, having answered this riddle, we find problems in reading the answer. Is this simply ironic distancing? If so, what is the angle of difference between Stevens's troping and Dante's, Stevens's troping and Eliot's? Or is this what John Hollander calls metaleptic echoing?[8]

Another example of a problematic riddle is the passage about the Arabian in *Notes* 1.3. Here the relation of the reader to text, even of the interior "we" to its own text, shifts as we read and reread the canto. I should like to pause over these lines and to look at the different relations of reader and text, for I think they may tell us something about the functions of riddles, and of charms as well. Here is the entire canto:

> The poem refreshes life so that we share,
> For a moment, the first idea . . . It satisfies
> Belief in an immaculate beginning
>
> And sends us, winged by an unconscious will,
> To an immaculate end. We move between these points:
> From that ever-early candor to its late plural
>
> And the candor of them is the strong exhilaration
> Of what we feel from what we think, of thought
> Beating in the heart, as if blood newly came,
>
> An elixir, an excitation, a pure power.
> The poem, through candor, brings back a power again
> That gives a candid kind to everything.
>
> We say: At night an Arabian in my room,
> With his damned hoobla-hoobla-hoobla-how,
> Inscribes a primitive astronomy,
>
> Across the unscrawled fores the future casts
> And throws his stars around the floor. By day
> The wood-dove used to chant his hoobla-hoo
>
> And still the grossest iridescence of ocean
> Howls hoo and rises and howls hoo and falls.
> Life's nonsense pierces us with strange relation.

We are not surprised to find a "Coleridgean idealization of poetry"[9] (ll. 1–12) in a meditation upon a supreme fiction, but the presence of what appears to be nonsense-verse in such a meditation is startling, and its relation to lines 1 to 12 a problem for commentators. If lines 13 to 20 are pure nonsense[10] with no affective function,[11] why does Stevens say in line 21 that life's nonsense pierces us? We can hardly exclude nonsense-verse from life's nonsense when we have just been given several lines of it. And whether lines 13 to 20 are read affectively or not,[12] what connection is there with the canto's first part? And what does the movement from the Coleridgean lines into the "hoobla" lines have to do with a supreme fiction?

At least two different types of wordplay run through this canto. The first is wordplay that makes sense; the second is closer to the uses of nonsense-verse. One proliferates from the English word *candid* and the Latin word *candidus* and dominates the first part. The other plays with Coleridgean echoes, which are submerged in the first part and surface in the second. *Candidus* in Latin, like *candid* in English, means white, but a dazzling white as against a lustreless white (*albus*). It has been used in Latin of the moon, the stars, day; of swans and snow; of Dido's beauty; of gods and persons transformed to gods. It also means "spotless" and is thus synonymous with *immaculate* in Stevens's canto. Figuratively, of discourse, it means "clear, open, perspicuous," and therefore the opposite to riddle or *aenigma*, which is in rhetorical tradition an "obscure allegory"[13] and into which Stevens moves in line 13. Until then, he weaves an entrancing web out of multiple meanings and associations of *candid* and *candidus*.[14]

Simultaneously, we may hear an uncanny echoing of Coleridge when we read this canto as a type of riddle poem. Thus: Stevens has transposed the dove's conventional English-language sound of *coo* to *hoo*. If we similarly transpose the Arabian's sounds, we hear *coobla-coobla-coobla-cow*. Then we don't. We hear *coobla-can*, and we begin to hear a nonsense refrain, much like something out of James Joyce: Kubla Khan but hoobla how? This refrain suggests that lines 13 to 20 function at least in part as a riddle whose answer is Coleridge's "Kubla Khan." Once we have begun to hear this echo, other Coleridgean echoes proliferate. We ask ourselves if it is nonsense to hear subliminal assertions of power in the homonyms for *do* and *can* in the opening line of "Kubla Khan": "In Xanadu did Kubla Khan. . . ." And to read in Stevens's canto that the poem brings back a power again that gives a can-did kind to everything. Of course it is. But in the realm of nonsense riddle, this is how we read.

Outside this realm, back in the realm of rational discourse, we recall that "Kubla Khan" came to Coleridge "without any sensation or consciousness of effort," to quote his phrase, and comes as close as any poem to showing the "pure power" of the imagination. We recall also that the Khan could simply decree a stately pleasure-dome, while Stevens must work toward a supreme fiction, which "must give pleasure." "Kubla Khan" in this reading is at least one of the poems, and I think the prototypical poem, that refreshes life in the ways suggested in lines 1 to 12 of Stevens's canto.

Lest this riddle-reading appear too arbitrary, I should observe that Stevens engaged in wordplay with "Kubla Khan" elsewhere. In 1923, in "Academic Discourse at Havana," he invented a "mythy goober khan," which is a peanut stand (*khan* as "building" we are likely to know from *The Arabian Nights*). But "goober khan" functions chiefly as a parody — "a peanut parody / For peanut people" — through its unmistakable echo of "Kubla Khan." (I read the entire poem as a forerunner of *Notes* 1.3, for it ends with sleepers awakening and watching moonlight on their floors, and comments of itself that it "may . . . be / An incantation that the moon defines.") In 1942, the year of *Notes*, Stevens opened his weird and haunting "Oak Leaves Are Hands" with a parody of the opening lines of "Kubla Khan," as Helen Vendler has noted:[15] "In Hydaspia, by Howzen, / Lived a lady, Lady Lowzen . . ." Coleridge is present in other ways in the work of Stevens at this time. Among Stevens's essays, he appears only in a quotation in a 1942 essay and in the 1943 essay "The Figure of the Youth as Virile Poet," where Stevens calls Coleridge "one of the great figures."[16] In a letter of 1942, Stevens makes use of Coleridge's phrase "willing suspension of disbelief," along with William James's "will to believe," in a discussion crucial to an understanding of *Notes* (*L*, 430 [8 Dec. 1942]). In *Notes* itself, he echoes part of Coleridge's definition of the primary imagination (3.8).[17] Coleridge is pretty clearly one of the ancestral voices with whom Stevens does battle, or records past battles, in *Notes*. A "Kubla Khan" riddle, given other parodies of the great Khan's name and poem, and given Coleridge's place in *Notes*, does not seem to me an overly arbitrary reading.

How do lines 13 to 20 function in Stevens's debate with Coleridge? They work, I think, as a reversal of lines 1 to 12, and their first function is to demonstrate how disabling such a reversal may be. "Hoobla-how?" sings or plays or challenges the Arabian, and the phrase is "damned" because one answer is: Kubla Khan but you cannot. The voice of this canto's first part talks about a power in which the reader feels invited to share as part of a communal "we." To give a "kind to everything" is to bring about unity and kinship, a process quite unlike "strange relation." Power in the second part is exercised by the Arabian certainly, but it is a power that excludes the reader in the sense that we cannot agree on even an approximate common stance for reading lines 13 to 20. If the first part shows us the power of the human imagination, just as "Kubla Khan" does, the second part shows us the helplessness of that same imagination, just as the longer "Kubla Khan" we do not have also and most painfully does. (Coleridge's preface to "Kubla Khan" makes a useful gloss on this canto; the return to "his room" and to a dissipated, fragmented vision is, I think, one source for Stevens's Arabian lines. Yet one hardly likes to bring a hoobla-how-Kubla-Khan riddle too close to the memory of Coleridge, even in fancy.)

We can work out the reversal: suggestions of white magic to suggestions of black; radiance to night, with eerie moonlight and broken constellations; openness to riddle; the future as immaculate end to the future as something cast — a context of fate rather than destiny. The visual becomes vague or erratic; the oral reduces itself to the same limited series of sounds as if the Arabian made the memory of the wood-dove chant to his own tune and allied himself with the ancient continuing hooing of the ocean. Language, once glowing with power and moving outward in its ex-prefixes, becomes fitful and nothing to read by or into. The Arabian splits fores and casts, and into the split he throws the future. By line 20, the salt ocean has prevailed over the freshening of line 1. Incantatory multilingual echoes cry through this line, with its monosyllabic equivalent of a Latinate ululate-undulate wordplay, and an implicit French-English pun on *houle* (sea-swell) and *howl*.[18] "Oh! Blessed rage for order . . . The maker's rage to order words of the sea." But the Arabian with his damned words is master now, the moon at its most unpropitious (the connection is presumably through the figure of the crescent).[19] Against the human *will* and *can* of lines 1 to 12, another voice asks, "how?" The puns move away from vanished chant and down toward incantation:[20] adnominatio to paronomasia to monotonous echo. How, hoo, who, indeed.

The movement to wood dove and then to ocean is toward losses other than the loss of poetic power, one of love and the other (I think) in death. A sequence of "gross, grosser, grossest" is implied in the superlative form of the adjective at the end; iridescences may also be of the moon and of doves,[21] and if we use the word *gross* in the sense of "material," we may see here a logical sequence of downward imagery (moonlight, bird, ocean) and of loss (of poetic power as the least fleshly, then of love, finally of the body itself). I think also that the memory of the erotic dove merges with some memory of the poetic dove who broods creatively over the abyss — descendant of the biblical and Miltonic bird of the Holy Ghost through Wordsworth's "brooding mind" to Joyce's "Coo" and Stevens's chanter of *hoobla-hoo*. The poetic voice has now lost the voice of the dove; the operative forces are the Arabian and the howling, hooing sea. The three realms here (moon, woods, ocean) are those of the triform goddess (Luna, Diana, Hecate) if we accept the ocean as Stevens's form of the underworld. The chanting of *hoobla* and *how* and *hoo*, a circle woven thrice as in the charm-poems of Theocritus and Virgil, resounds like some mage's spell to undo the white and shining enchantment of the first part.

Stevens's riddling here verges on the type of poetry Frye calls charms, poetry whose rhetoric "is dissociative and incantatory," uses repetitive devices ("refrain, rhyme, alliteration, assonance, pun, antithesis"), and seeks to "break down and confuse the conscious will."[22] Charms and riddles are two different kinds of play with language; "Magic would disrupt Nonsense," Elizabeth Sewell argues. But the two may converge: "the game or the dream, logic or irrationality, may lead us to the same point in the end."[23] For "charms and riddles . . . are psychologically very close together, as the unguessed or unguessable riddle is or may be a charm."[24] That is what I think we have here: a riddle-and-charm poem with two contrasting parts. "Like primitive astronomers, we are free to note recurrences, cherish symmetries, and seek if we can means of placating the hidden power: more for our comfort than for theirs."[25] But there is minimal comfort, if any, in the dwindling symmetries the reader can ascertain in Stevens's nonsense-lines. The moon has come down from heaven and brought a most uncandid charm, one potentially damning and disabling.

What Stevens accomplishes here is a systematic undoing of his first world, and with it all such "immaculate," idealized first worlds — childhood or erotic or religious paradises — and perforce all idealized theories of poetry. The strategies of undoing dominate the first cantos of *Notes*, and "Kubla Khan," with its magical transformations of biblical and Miltonic paradises[26] and with its yearning poet, serves Stevens's purposes wonderfully well. Such an undoing may be disabling, as it is, for example, in a lunar sequence in *The Man with the Blue Guitar* that moves from "immaculate" (vii) through "unspotted" (xiii) to "the spot on the floor" (xv). But for Stevens such an undoing may also be a defense. I have read "we say" as "we find ourselves saying" and so have followed the voice of the poem into the power of the fiction of the Arabian. But Stevens's cryptic "we say" also bears the sense of "it is we who say." As soon as we read not "an Arabian . . . with his damned hoobla-hoobla-hoobla-how," but "it is we who say an Arabian . . . with his damned hoobla-hoobla-hoobla-how," another response to his riddle becomes possible: not the accuser saying Kubla Khan but you cannot, but rather the self saying Kubla Khan and I cannot. This is to acknowledge poverty but not helplessness. It is a defensive strategy against the authority of words, including the words of supreme fictions, say, *candid* or *candidus*. Riddles and charms do not merely assert that we are makers of our own words, but demonstrate this by showing how words may be reversed and fictions undone. Stevens's nonsense-lines read to me like an archetypal riddle-and-charm poem, the precise opposite of the archetypal "original spell to keep chaos away,"[27] the Word of God or Logos.

"To indulge the power of fictions and send imagination out upon the wing is often the sport of those who delight too much in silent speculation," Imlac says in *Rasselas* (ch. 44). "Then fictions begin to operate as realities." He is speaking of an astronomer, who is persuaded he has the power to control the weather, the sun, and even the planets, and so could if he wished to do just what Stevens's astronomer does. The astronomer is for Imlac an admonitory example of the hazards of taking fictions for realities. Imlac's idea of what constitutes a fiction differs from Stevens's, of course; his religious beliefs are not to him fictions. For Stevens, they are, and Stevens was sensitive to the hazards as well as the benefits of all belief, including poetic belief: "Suppose the poet discovered and had the power thereafter at will and by intelligence to reconstruct us by his transformations. He would also have the power to destroy us" (*NA*, 45 [1943]). This would be to make art, including sacred art, into magic, and the poet, including the writer of scripture, into an arch-magician and arch-riddler. For Stevens, it is a necessary knowledge that we say and therefore can unsay all our fictions, including our most august stories. Riddles and charms, which by definition are distanced from referential discourse, can make this point very clearly. We not only can unsay all our fictions, but must, for this is how one part of the imagination works, as Stevens says in 1947 in what I read as comment on canto 1.3 of *Notes*:

> It must change from destiny to slight caprice . . .
>   . . . move to find
> What must unmake it and, at last, what can,
> Say, a flippant communication under the moon.

(CP, 417–18)

We are by now so familiar with the ways of deconstruction that my argument thus far appears to claim simply that Stevens is a modern poet. For example, my first reading of *Notes* 1.3.13–20 would be seen by Derrida as an example of nonradical "illegibility," that "non-sense" (*le non-sens*) still "interior to the book, to reason or to logos." My second reading would open the possibility of "radical illegibility" (*l'illisibilité radicale*) or the deconstruction of the traditional doctrine of logos, reason, and the book.[28] Yet the implications of these readings may be disquieting for the reader and lover of fictions. If we deconstruct the old, unifying Coleridgean theories of the imagination, as it seems we must, do we lose the power of illusions, the ability to suspend disbelief? Do all our fictions become Arabian fictions of nonsense, powerful within themselves but without much power over us? Or mirrors of another imagination, Coleridge's perhaps, as the sea mirrors the moon and the moon mirrors a greater light? We seem to be caught. When we are knowledgeable enough and defensive enough about the ways language works, how far can it then affect us? This is a question that John Bayley raises in another context,[29] and it lies behind speculation about the end of narrative. For Stevens, there is the further question: how can we then create or hear a supreme fiction?

Riddles and charms can show us in a nutshell three relations of reader to text. Readers may enter and share the assumed power of the text, answering riddles and feeling exquisite enchantments (in other terms, playing the game or dreaming happily). They may enter the assumed power of the text, unable to answer riddles and feeling sinister enchantments (in other terms, becoming the played-with or experiencing nightmare). Or, they may step outside the blessing and damning power of words, observing that we make the rules of the games and (as we now say) "privilege" the text. But insofar as we still use words, or they us, what power do they then retain?

It takes the whole of *Notes* to answer that question fully. Two parts of the answer are pertinent here. The first is suggested in Stevens's final line to *Notes* 1.3: "Life's nonsense pierces us with strange relation." Not "relations," as we might expect, but "relation," which includes more pointedly than the plural noun a relation that is a fiction. The word *pierce* is unexpected too. It is a powerful word in Stevens:[30] one use makes it a function of speech ("the acutest end / Of speech: to pierce the heart's residuum" [*CP*, 259]); another use makes it an effect of illusion, and here we need to remember that there is benign as well as harmful illusion for Stevens[31] "the laborious human [of *Notes* 2.5] who lives in illusions and who, after all the great illusions have left him, still clings to one that pierces him" (*L*, 435 [12 Jan. 1943]). In *Notes* 1.3, for all the possible defense in the clause "we say," Stevens does not end defensively. He ends with a piercing or wounding, even by nonsense-language, even by the *hoo* we hear the ocean saying, even in the full knowledge that we say these things ourselves. If we read the poem's last line as in part Stevens's gloss on his own nonsense-lines, then he is putting before us the possibility of words as not only a power to bless and damn, a power against which we must defend ourselves, but also a power to pierce and to which we cling because (not although) it pierces us. In *Notes* 3.8, Stevens asks: "Am I that imagine this angel less satisfied?" Are we who say the riddle and charm of the Arabian less pierced? Only if we defend ourselves completely against the power of all fictions. And a self that cannot be pierced by words cannot be healed or refreshed by them either.

How words "wound" has been explored by Jacques Derrida and more recently by Geoffrey Hartman.[32] This canto suggests another pattern for such speculation through its echoing of religious diction, including the language of grace in line 1 and the language of sacrifice in line 21. Stevens may be said to prefigure here the only version of the incarnate Word that he could accept: the human imagination reentering and being wounded by a world of language that it has itself created. This is, in effect, what happens in Poe's story "The Power of Words," and Stevens admired Poe.

A further answer to my question is suggested by *Notes* 3.8, a companion piece to canto 1.3 and part of the beautiful climactic development of the whole poem. Here the assertive statement that the poem "satisfies / Belief" becomes interrogative: "What am I to believe?" Satisfaction is implied but limited: "Am I that imagine this angel less satisfied?" "Is it I then that . . . am satisfied." All the sentences are interrogative, although one modulates through its clauses into a sufficiently assertive mood to drop the question mark. This canto does not send us "winged by an unconscious will." "I" both sees as spectator and experiences as angel, and sees his experience, of a movement downward "on his spredden wings," a movement protracted and without landing, a suspension. The time of fulfillment is not in terms of undefined beginning and end, but is specifically limited: an hour, a day, a month, a year, a time. *Ex*-words here (*expressible, external*) are limited in comparison with the outward movement — the ex-ness, so to speak — of such words in 1.3 (*exhilaration, excitation*). We might suppose that a movement

from first-person plural to first-person singular, from assertive to interrogative mood, from winging our way from immaculate beginnings to immaculate ends to seeing and being a falling angel, from extended to modified
adjectives, from excited participation in power to a multiple stance where
power is questioned — that all these limitations would make for a lesser
canto. But this is not what happens. Stevens's enchanting first world is presented anew here in strength. His canto both enacts and comments on "that
willing suspension of disbelief for the moment, which constitutes poetic
faith." Coleridge's definition and Stevens's canto are powerful and live for us
not in spite of their careful limiting but because of it. Stevens's "I am" claims
no more than he can sustain: "I have not but I am and as I am, I am."

At the end of this canto, the Cinderella story reverses the angelic moment,
as the Arabian's story reverses the world of *candid* and *candidus*, the two
reversals being very different. It also reverses the Miltonic and biblical world
of the aspiring Canon Aspirin in the three preceding cantos (5–7). *Candid* is
used only once elsewhere in Stevens's poetry (*candor* never again) in a way
that associates it with *canon* and *canonical*.[33] When we note that a candidate may also be an Aspirant (*OED*, s.v. *candidate*, 2.a), the candid-Canon-
canonical association appears firm. In 1909, aged 29, Stevens noted the Cinderella story in his journal in a one-word entry: "pumpkin-coach."[34] The
entry follows immediately on these lines:

> What I aspired to be,
> And was not, comforts me —

The lines, unidentified, are from Browning's "Rabbi Ben Ezra," so that
Browning's rabbi must take his place as another of the aspirers who make up
that compound ghost, Canon Aspirin. For all Stevens's love for the white
worlds and aspiring figures of a biblical, Miltonic, Coleridgean, and Browning heritage — rather, because of his love — their power has to be undone,
whether by riddle or by charm or by fairy tale. Only then can Stevens lead us
toward the exquisite fiction of his fat girl in the final canto of *Notes*. Only then
can he write at all, can he "patch together" (Stevens's revisionary version of
the word *compose*). For *Notes* ends with a Stevensian poet who

> Patches the moon together in his room
> To his Virgilian cadences, up down,
> Up down. It is a war that never ends.

FOURTEEN

The Function of Riddles at the Present Time

The impetus for this essay came from an oddity I observed over ten years ago, as follows. Although deconstructionists are highly wary of most rhetorical figures, there is one figure they do not mistrust. On the contrary: they adore her, they desire her, they remain faithful to her. She alone is not deconstructed. Her name is enigma — traditionally, the riddle.[1] Paul de Man casts most rhetorical figures as a gallery of dubious females: "As for metaphor, the mischief wreaked by this wiliest of Pandora's boxes. . . . The dangerously seductive powers of paranomasis. . . . euphony is probably the most insidious of all sources of error." But when he speaks of lyric poetry as "an enigma which never stops asking for the unreachable answer to its own riddle," he sidesteps any queries about this rhetorical figure. Enigma remains exempt.[2]

"Deconstruction," to follow Geoffrey Galt Harpham, "seems to have sprung from a passage in Nietzsche's *Beyond Good and Evil* which describes a 'new species of philosopher' who '*want* to remain a riddle' . . . (no. 42)."[3]

Enigma does not possess the status of metaphor as a rhetorical figure, but she is just as ancient in rhetorical treatises. We might say that enigma is to deconstruction as metaphor is to so-called logocentrism.

In this pleasure in enigma, deconstruction is part of a larger historical movement. For enigma has undergone a dramatic reversal of fortune from her nineteenth-century woes. The nineteenth century could be impatient with riddles and enigmas, at least in the wrong places. Ruskin, for example, was irritated when Goethe and others spoke darkly in enigmas about those moral precepts that he, Ruskin, saw so clearly in their work:

> It is a strange habit of wise humanity to speak in enigmas only, so that the highest truths and usefullest laws must be hunted for through whole picture-galleries of dreams, which to the vulgar seem dreams only. Thus Homer, the Greek tragedians, Plato, Dante, Chaucer, Shakespeare, and Goethe, have hidden all that is chiefly serviceable in their work, and in all the various literatures they absorbed and reembodied, under types which have rendered it quite useless to the multitude.[4]

Pierre Fontanier omits the figure of *énigme* altogether from his *Figures du discours*, but then for Fontanier an allegory must first of all be *transparente*, which leaves no room for obscure allegory, a common definition of the figure of enigma from Quintilian onward.[5] "Riddle Redundant" was the title of an 1883 parody of Browning's "Wanting is — What?"[6] The riddle or enigma was widely assumed to be antipathetic to lyric poetry. The assumption is illogical but pervasive.

In the late nineteenth and twentieth centuries, enigma came into her own. As Northrop Frye puts it: "Charm poetry, shown at its subtlest in Keats and Tennyson and at its clearest in Poe and Swinburne, dominated taste until about 1915, after which a mental attitude more closely related to the riddle began to supersede it."[7] Mallarmé's remark is well known: "Il doit y avoir toujours énigme en poésie, et c'est le but de la littérature" (There must always be enigma in poetry; it is the aim of literature). Not revelation, but enigma, although for Valéry the enigmas of Mallarmé were precisely a revelation.

But of course the question is: *what* riddle, *what* enigma in any given use? For obviously they differ in kind. The deconstructionists who adore enigma do not have in mind that most famous of biblical enigmas, the apostle Paul's in 1 Cor. 13, the chapter on charity or love: "For now we see through a glass darkly" (ἐν αἰνίγματι [*en ainigmati*], 1 Cor. 13:12).

In what follows, I want to outline a proposed anatomy of the enigma or riddle considered as masterplot — that is, considered in the sense that Paul, and often the deconstructionists, speak of enigma. The word *masterplot* is taken from Terence Cave's book *Recognitions*, he in turn taking it from Peter Brooks.[8] I am thinking of the literary riddle rather than the folk riddle — that is, "riddles composed by conscious literary artists," to quote the folklorist Archer Taylor,[9] or used in literary works. Riddles that appear in, say, *Oedipus Rex* or *Pericles* or *Emma* or the Alice books may also be folk riddles, but we do not read them primarily as such.

I also want to draw together the various significations of the word *riddle*. Here, for example, is the definition of *riddle* from the *Oxford English Dictionary* (both editions): "(1) A question or statement intentionally worded in a dark or puzzling manner, and propounded in order that it might be guessed or answered, esp. as a form of pastime; an enigma; a dark saying. (2) *trans.* Something which puzzles or perplexes; a dark or insoluble problem; a mystery." The word *enigma* divides in a similar, although more embattled, way. The *OED*, like other lexicons, separates verbal riddles from larger enigmas. But Sophocles did not when he set the Sphinx on the road to Thebes. Nor did W. S. Gilbert in *The Gondoliers* (a very different genre), when he wrote: "Life's perhaps the only riddle / That we shrink from giving up." Nor did Plutarch (a different genre again) when he said that Homer died of chagrin at being unable to answer a riddle. The illustrative quotations in the *OED* make it clear that riddles tend to be either very small in duration and apparent use, or else very large. Riddles seem to dislike the middle ground, including the middle ground of familiar mimetic writing. They simplify and condense, as do two other primitive genres, the charm and the proverb.

In pulling together the meanings of riddle, I am not thinking so much of what folklorists call neck-riddles — the kind where your life depends on setting or answering a conundrum. Neck-riddles turn up in *Pericles* and also in *Monty Python and the Holy Grail*, that fine spoof of the convention. I am thinking more of two master riddles, what I want to call Pauline riddling and Oedipal or Sphinxine riddling. These constitute my first two types of enigma. By Pauline riddling, I mean riddle as in Paul's "For now we see through a glass darkly; but then face to face" — thus the Authorized Version, drawing on the

Geneva Bible. Tyndale's 1534 translation reads: "Now we see in a glass even in a dark speaking," "a dark speaking" being a common translation of *aenigma* in its Greek or Latin form. Luther's 1522 translation reads: "Wir sehen jetzt durch einen Spiegel in einem dunkeln Wort." Latin Bibles repeat the Greek word in its Latinate form: "Videmus nunc per speculum in aenigmate, sed tunc facie ad faciem." The text is so familiar that I need hardly observe that this is the kind of enigma that will end in revelation, in light, in the dispersal of cloud, in the clarifying of the obscure, in the answering of the inexplicable, in the straightening of the labyrinthine, and so on through many a well-known trope for enigma. Light comes with our death, in God.

Such lexis of the riddle is standard, although not always observed as such. See, for example, Donne on the atheist's soul: "Poor intricated soul! Riddling, perplexed, labyrinthical soul!" (sermon 48 [1628/29]). Tennyson knows the lexis well: "dawn's creeping beams . . . dissolved the mystery / Of folded sleep" ("A Dream of Fair Women," ll. 261–63) —*folded* as in the Latinate *involve* (see the Sibyl's "dread enigmas," *obscuris vera involvens*, in *Aeneid* 6.98–100 [Loeb ed.]); *dissolved*, not a firm *resolve* as in Eliot's "Resolving the enigma of the fever chart" ("East Coker," pt. 4).

Pauline riddling provided an authoritative masterplot in Christendom for centuries, and not only for the verbal disciplines. Newton's work on the enigmas of the Book of Revelation was not inimical to his work in physics but consistent with it. As John Maynard Keynes put it:

> He looked on the whole universe and all that is in it as a *riddle*. . . . He regarded the universe as a cryptogram set by the Almighty — just as he himself wrapt the discovery of the calculus in a cryptogram when he communicated with Leibniz. . . . He *did* read the riddles of the heavens. And he believed that by the same powers of his introspective imagination he would read . . . the riddle of past and future events divinely fore-ordained.[10]

Nor was Newton atypical. To quote Frank Manuel:

> It is still difficult for some of us to appreciate the continued fascination of great European intellects of the seventeenth and eighteenth centuries with the interpretation of Daniel and the Apocalypse. . . . Many of the scientists and apologists of science in Newton's circle . . . tried their

hands at the exposition of a prophecy, and the number of such works composed in England during Newton's adult life is staggering.[11]

Riddles remain today, but that once-authoritative masterplot has radically altered, if not largely vanished.

Oedipal or Sphinxine riddling moves downward to darkness: it is Pauline riddling turned upside down. Not the Epistle to the Corinthians but the man from Corinth, Oedipus. I have asked myself whether Paul might have had in mind the connection of Corinth with famous riddles when he used a form of the word αἴνιγμα in his letter to the church at Corinth. (He had Num. 12:8 in mind, but why just here, to this congregation?) There are reasons this might be so, and Paul's enigma does reverse Oedipal/Sphinxine riddling. Oedipus begins by answering the famous neck-riddle of the Sphinx. If you don't answer her riddle, she kills or eats you, a graphic rendering of the inside-outside logic of the figure of enigma. But Oedipus has more than one riddle to answer, and the story of *Oedipus Rex* ends in darkness and blinding. Paul reverses the inside-outside logic. We already see as *in aenigmate*, with an enigma, but then we shall see face to face. Sight, not blindness; the riddle solved by God, not by us; light eventually though not in this life. Greeks like Plato and Aristotle distrusted what was obscure and riddling, to follow W. B. Stanford, because such things were "relics of the dark days when the utterances of Sphinx or Oracle or Seer were too often things to be dreaded."[12] Paul, I assume, is designing a Christian enigma that moves out from the enigma of Num. 12:8, and moves against a dark, oracular enigma, like those of the mystery religions, or, darker, those of *Oedipus Rex*.

It is, I think, precisely because the Sphinx's riddle and biblical riddling constitute two contrary types that Dante juxtaposes them in the closing cantos of the *Purgatorio*. "And perhaps my prophecy [this is Beatrice speaking], obscure as Themis and Sphinx, persuades you less because, after their fashion, it darkens your mind; but soon the facts . . . will solve this hard enigma" (*Purg.* 33.46–50, trans. Singleton; "buia . . . attuia . . . enigma forte"). So also Milton contrasts the Sphinx's riddle and biblical riddling at the end of *Paradise Regained*. Satan, having vainly tempted Christ, falls in a prolepsis of his final fall,

> And as that *Theban* monster that propos'd
> Her riddle, and him who solv'd it not, devour'd,

That once found out and solv'd, for grief and spite
Cast herself headlong from th'*Ismenian* steep,
So struck with dread and anguish fell the Fiend.

(4.572-6)

My type-2 enigma is not so much Oedipal as Sphinxine in the work of Dante and Milton and elsewhere. That is, it uses *Oedipus Rex* rather than the full Oedipus story.[13] I make the distinction because one dominant form of Oedipal enigma in our day is, I suppose, Freud's masterplot. If it also follows the pattern of a fall, of light versus darkness, of outside versus inside, the context is very different from that of Sphinxine riddle as conceived by Milton, Dante, and, I think, Paul. For Oedipus is partly a wisdom figure, a master interpreter of riddles, and so known for centuries. Oedipus as master interpreter makes a figure for psychoanalysis itself, insofar as it reads enigmas rather than being read by them.

To return to my title and its predecessors: what critical writing corresponds to these two riddle types, Pauline and Oedipal/Sphinxine? Here, I am aware of leaping from story to interpretation, but I follow Terence Cave when he argues that the distinction between masterplot as narrative and masterplot as interpretive method is overcome, "in theory at least, by positing that interpretation is indeed a narrative (a meta-narrative) and that allegory is simply the form in which narrative most openly declares its diegetic [narrative] hand. Allegory then becomes the narrative of narrative."[14] Enigma as condensed allegory (and in rhetorical handbooks, it is regularly classified as a species of allegory) might be called the Ur-form of this.

Contemporary criticism following a Pauline-type riddle would be that of, say, Piero Boitani in his *The Tragic and the Sublime in Medieval Literature*.[15] And especially that of Northrop Frye. Frye's criticism is sometimes said, and justly so, to follow a romance or quest pattern. But the quest pattern it follows is that of Pauline enigma. For criticism following the pattern of Oedipal or Sphinxine riddling, we would turn to Freudian critics: to the work of Peter Brooks, who calls Freud's patternings a masterplot for our fictions in his *Reading for the Plot: Design and Intention in Narrative*. Preeminently, we would turn to the work of Harold Bloom, at least in its middle stage, his work being dialectically related to that of Frye.

The desire of deconstructionists, I take it, is to evade the circle implied by their very term *logocentrism*, including criticism along what might be called the Frye-Bloom axis. If we look for a type of enigma for deconstruction, we would look for the riddle with the "unreachable answer," to use de Man's words. The radical form would be the unanswerable riddle. Not the riddle whose answer we do not know, or even whose answer we shall never know, but the riddle that has no answer. The self-enclosed riddle, the self-mirroring riddle. This constitutes my type-3 enigma. In the latter part of the nineteenth century and through much of the twentieth century, the only alternative to Pauline enigma has often been seen as this type of random, unanswerable, and hence threatening enigma. We are still, I think, working through the sense of such a threat, as witness our occasional fear or bafflement or nostalgia. Even Frank Kermode allows the word *disappointment* in the last sentence of *The Genesis of Secrecy*:

> World and book, it may be, are hopelessly plural, endlessly disappoint-ing; we stand alone before them, aware of their arbitrariness and im-penetrability, knowing that they may be narratives only because of our impudent intervention and susceptible of interpretation only by our her-metic tricks. Hot for secrets, our only conversation may be with guard-ians who know less and see less than we can; and our sole hope and pleasure is in the perception of a momentary radiance, before the door of disappointment is finally shut on us.[16]

And Paul Ricoeur, in the conclusion to *Le Temps et le récit*, returns to the ancient topos of contemplating "[le] mouvement souverain des astres."[17] The word *souverain* links Ricoeur with the Psalmist as with Coleridge: the Psalmist who writes, "The heavens declare the glory of God" (Ps. 19:1), and Coleridge at the end of the *Biographia Literaria*: "It is Night, sacred Night! the upraised Eye views only the starry Heaven . . . only to preserve the Soul steady and collected in its pure Act of inward Adoration to the great I AM, and to the filial WORD that reaffirmeth it from Eternity to Eternity, whose choral Echo is the Universe."[18]

Ricoeur's move at the end toward "the lyricism of meditative thinking [which] goes right to the fundamental without passing through the art of narrating"[19] I find especially interesting. Not only does this allow him an end-run around narrative, and the return to something close to mystical apprehension, but he also thereby moves to that family of genres, the lyric, which is itself partly rooted in enigma. For myself, I doubt that tropes can escape a masterplot, even though they may not make use of the narrative form. Lyrics too partake of a masterplot.

The new historicism takes many forms, but it is fair to say, I think, that it does not participate in Pauline riddling or in type-3 deconstructionist riddling. How far its own enterprises are related to end-directed plots interests me. (The whole question of translating end-directed plots into uses on this middle earth is, of course, a large and important one.)

As for feminist criticism, my three riddle-types can readily be mapped in familiar figures:

Type 1:   Enigma as resolved in or by a Beatrice or a Madonna (old-style).

Type 2:   Enigma as propounded by the Grecian Sphinx, the female who kills or eats you if you can't answer her question.

Type 3:   The unanswerable enigma that all women are, as we know.

It is time to come to Wallace Stevens on enigma. For some years, I read Stevens's kind of enigma in his late work as a variation on my type 3, the unanswerable riddle. But I now think it constitutes a fourth type, rather harder to define. In Stevens's 1943 essay "The Figure of the Youth as Virile Poet," we (a Stevensian "we") are moved to make a declaration of independence from any muse external to ourselves, like Milton's Urania or his greater muse, the Holy Spirit: *"No longer do I believe that there is a mystic muse, sister of the Minotaur. This is another of the monsters I had for nurse, whom I have wasted. I am myself a part of what is real, and it is my own speech and the strength of it, this only, that I hear or ever shall."*[20]

This declaration sounds like a deconstructionist formulation, and is so read. What interests me especially is Stevens's revised version of this speech at the very end of his essay. We might suppose he would sweep away Minotaurs and labyrinths and muses, together with the whole *le-pli* family of riddling, folded, implicated, inextricable, labyrinthine words. Not so. Here is the revision, now spoken by the young poet himself (*NA*, 67): *"Inexplicable sister of the Minotaur, enigma and mask, although I am part of what is real, hear me and recognize me as part of the unreal. I am the truth but the truth of that imagination of life in which with unfamiliar motion and manner you guide me in those exchanges of speech in which your words are mine, mine yours."* Stevens has reinvented, even invoked, this mysterious female. She is no longer mystic, no longer a monster, but still — note — sister of the Minotaur, and now "inexplicable," now an "enigma," now a "mask." The familiar sister of the Minotaur is, of course, Ariadne, "la tua sorella," as Dante calls her (*Inferno* 12.20). She is the rescuer from labyrinthine riddles with a devouring monster at the center. She holds the thread, the clue. Stevens at first sounds as if he has laid waste both the Minotaur and some Ariadne, and so he has, in the form of both the labyrinthine riddle and the standard rescue plot.

But his alternative is not the unanswerable enigma, my type 3. Nor does he turn his back on end-directed plots. A sister of the Minotaur has returned as mask and enigma, and explicitly as guide. "Mask" as persona is easy enough. But "enigma"? That's also easy enough in one sense: the mystery of creation, and so on.

Yet Stevens's own figurings of enigma are so intelligent and precise that I doubt he wants to end his essay on so ready and general a thought. To trace the figure of enigma through Stevens's work is a large task. Here we might simply turn to his 1954 poem "The Sail of Ulysses." Its last six lines read thus (*OP*, 131):

> *The great sail of Ulysses seemed*
> *In the breathings of this soliloquy,*
> *Alive with an enigma's flittering . . .*
> *As if another sail went on*
> *Straight forwardly through another night*
> *And clumped stars dangled all the way.*

The very short version of this poem (24 lines as against 172) includes all six lines just quoted. Five of the six lines have their words slightly altered, the exception being the line on enigma, "Alive with an enigma's flittering . . ." (see "Presence of an External Master of Knowledge"). I want to call this type of enigma Sibylline, because of Stevens's Sibyl figure in the poem. The ancient Sibyls were riddlers, of course, first classical riddlers, then transformed into Christian prophetesses. Stevens's late Sibyl is descended from these, but different in kind. She descends more immediately from his 1943 inexplicable enigma and mask. She is an everyday Sibyl; she is like the ordinary or commonplace or plain sublime of Stevens's 1949 poem "An Ordinary Evening in New Haven."

"What is the shape of the sibyl? Not,
For a change, the englistered woman. . . .
It is the sibyl of the self
. . . . the sibyl's shape
Is a blind thing fumbling for its form,
A form that is lame, a hand, a back,
A dream too poor, too destitute
To be remembered, the old shape
Worn and leaning to nothingness,
A woman looking down the road,
A child asleep in its own life.
As these depend, so must they use."

Stevens writes this sibyl against the famous twentieth-century sibyl who lives in the antechamber to *The Waste Land* — writing, as he put it elsewhere, of plain reality, not grim reality (*L*, 636 [3 May 1949]).

"Alive with an enigma's flittering": what criticism would this enigma be like? The enigma of that flittering sail, the sail of Ulysses, voyaging, in a poem written by a man of 74. Not sailing toward the Mount of Purgatory in an angel-winged boat. For Stevens says at the start that Ulysses is sailing under the "middle stars." Not sailing past the Pillars of Hercules on a thanatos voyage, nor (it appears) on a perpetually curving dualistic course, whether eros-thanatos or challenge-response. Not sailing randomly or round and round: "straight forwardly," says Stevens.

The male figure for this type-4 enigma is Ulysses, many-wiled Odysseus, a favorite figure for Stevens himself from his youth to his old age. The female figure for this type-4 riddle would be a Wisdom figure, but of this earth, and so neither Athena (who is Odysseus's patron) nor the eternal Sophia. She would be the woman who corresponds to Ulysses, a many-wiled woman — perhaps, as in Stevens, a Penelope or an ordinary Sibyl.

In a 1992 review, Denis Donoghue argued that "when readers lost interest in 'first and last things' and set about a political program of one kind or another," interest in work like Frye's went into eclipse.[21] It seems to me that we still have a problem with end-directed reading in that we desire it and yet find it difficult to imagine alternatives to the dominant ones we have known. The deconstructionist questioning of ends, useful as it often is, can itself become an end. The historicist questioning of ends, valuable and necessary as a test, is hazardous if it divorces political or social short-term goals from long-term vision. Does it help to say "long-term things," as with Stevens, rather than "first and last things"? Does it help to think of a type-4 enigma? It seems useful in any case to think again about what assumptions lie behind those sometimes trivial little words *riddle* and *enigma*.

FIFTEEN

The Flying Griphos: In Pursuit of Enigma from Aristophanes to Tournesol, with Stops in Carroll, Ariosto, and Dante

This is a story of a quest, a quest that began when I nearly burst out laughing in the reading-room of the Houghton Library at Harvard. The cause was the *Etymologicon Linguae Latinae* (Amsterdam, 1695) of Gerardus Johannes Vossius (1577–1649), where I was checking entries concerning riddles and enigmas, including the rather specialized term *griphus*. (The word comes into Latin from Greek γρῖφος and usually signifies certain kinds of crossword-puzzle-type riddles such as anagrams.) "Griphus Latinis," said Vossius, "quod Graecis αἴνιγμα, quemadmodum scribit Agellius [Gellius], lib. XII, cap. vi . . . [et] lib. I, cap. ii" (Griphus in Latin writers is what the Greeks call *aenigma*, of which Gellius writes in bk. 12, ch. 6 [and] bk. 1, ch. 2 [of his *Noctes Atticae*]). A paragraph of synonyms and other sources followed.

Why I decided to check the Latin word for "griffin" just then, I am not sure, but there it was, on the facing page in this edition, transliterated from the Greek γρύψ, along with something more: "Gryps . . . Dicitur & *gryphus.* . . . Avis est fabulosa," etc. (Gryps . . . is called also gryphus . . .

A fabulous bird, etc.). Lewis and Short's *Latin Dictionary* confirmed what I had noticed: "griphus . . . an intricate or puzzling question, a riddle, enigma (post-class. and very rare)." And in the next column: "gryps . . . (gryphus) . . . a fabulous four-footed bird, a griffin." The *Oxford English Dictionary* also offered both *griph* and *gryph*: "griph *Obs.* . . . also in L. form griphus . . . A puzzling question; a riddle, enigma"; "gryph(e *Obs.* Also . . . griph(e. [A perversion of GRIPE, after L. gryphus. . . .] 1. A griffin. . . ."

That was when I nearly laughed out loud, because the possibilities of a pun on *griphus/gryphus* (*riddle/griffin*) suddenly flashed on me. They did so chiefly because of Dante and his Griffin at the end of the *Purgatorio*, of which more later.

Lewis Carroll and his Gryphon arrived shortly afterwards, cheering presences, for there was my pun, flourishing in 1865, in chapter 9 of *Alice's Adventures in Wonderland*, "The Mock Turtle's Story." The Gryphon is discussing education:

> "I went to the Classical master, though. He was an old crab, *he* was."
> "I never went to him," the Mock Turtle said with a sigh. "He taught Laughing and Grief, they used to say."
> "So he did, so he did," said the Gryphon, sighing in his turn; and both creatures hid their faces in their paws.

Latin and Greek, Laughing and Grief: all familiar, and strange too. The whole matter of translating and learning is caught here: into and from and between Latin and Greek, into and from and between laughing and grief, together with crossings of the two pairs. Then, as happens in Carroll, there is the unexpected larger resonance, when we reflect on the curious connecting of laughing and grief. And then the third pun.

For what else is a laughing grief but a *griph-* (pronounced as in the first syllable of *griphos*), and how odd that the root of the Greek word for a joking riddle should sound the same as the English word for sorrow. And how odd that Latin *gryphus* should be the same word in some spellings for both a riddle and a fabulous creature. Personified figures of enigma are quite rare, the Grecian Sphinx being the best known, I suppose. The Griffin qualifies nicely. It's also a hybrid creature (foreparts of an eagle, hindparts of a lion), enigmas themselves being hybrid things.[1]

Certainly John Tenniel sensed the doubleness of the pun and the creature. In his first illustration, the Gryphon is sleeping, solitary and fierce, as if it were inhabiting its legendary mountain near the Hyperboreans and guarding its hoard of gold from the one-eyed Arimaspians. ("If you don't know what a Gryphon is, look at the picture," says Carroll.) But in the next two illustrations, the Gryphon is shown with Alice and the Mock Turtle, sitting on its hind quarters and dancing on its hind legs. It is a doleful domestic pet or stuffed animal, although its dolefulness is deceptive. The Gryphon is not given to taking things seriously, including the imperious Red Queen and the sad Mock Turtle. "What fun! . . . It's all her fancy, that. . . . It's all his fancy, that." He's a pun, after all — one that Alice Liddell's father, of Liddell and Scott's *Greek-English Lexicon*, would have recognized.

The other cheering presences were Ariosto and his hippogryph in *Orlando Furioso*, for the name *hippogryph* is itself a contradiction in terms. Griffins are the traditional enemies of horses, so much so that Virgil's Damon (*Ecl.* 8.27) can describe a detested love-match as impossible, as heralding a time when *iungentur iam grypes equis* ("griffins soon will mate with horses"). The quotation is regularly cited in connection with Ariosto's creature. It's as if some beast were called a *wol-amb*, half wolf and half lamb. Either we're in some paradise where wolf and lamb dwell together, or we're faced with a riddle. Surely Ariosto's hippogryph is playing with the *griphus/gryphus* pun. After all, the word *griphus* had just reentered Latin at about this time.

The word γρῖφος (*griphos*) is not rare in Greek, as *griphus* is in Latin. It goes back to Aristophanes, the earliest citation in Liddell and Scott being from line 20 of *The Wasps*, first produced in 422 B.C. Douglas M. MacDowell's 1971 edition notes, "This is the earliest instance of the word, and the earliest mention of the custom of posing riddles at drinking-parties. Neither is heard of again until the middle of the fourth century, in Antiphanes 74, 124, 194; these fragments of Middle Comedy are preserved in Ath. [Athenaeus] 448b–459b, where riddles are discussed and quoted at length."[2] Here is the passage from Aristophanes, translated by Moses Hadas:

SOSIAS: I dreamt, too, an extraordinary dream. But tell me yours first.

XANTHIAS: A big eagle, I thought, flew down into the market place,
Grabbed a bronze shield in his talons, carried it to the sky —
Then I saw it was Cleonymus who'd thrown it away.

SOSIAS: Cleonymus is a perfect riddle [γρῖφον].

XANTHIAS: How?

SOSIAS: A man asks at table, What beast is it throws its shield away
Alike on earth, in heaven, on sea?

XANTHIAS: Something terrible will happen to me — such a dream!

SOSIAS: Don't worry, nothing terrible, I swear it.

XANTHIAS: A man throwing his shield away *is* terrible. Tell your dream.

SOSIAS: Mine's big, about the whole ship of state.[3]

The Loeb edition[4] says of lines 15–19 (ll. 2–4 above), "The big eagle changes into bulky Cleonymus" (Cleonymus is the Sir John Falstaff of Aristophanes' comedies). It also notes "a play on ἀσπίς [aspis] = (1) a shield, (2) a snake," and refers the reader to *The Acharnians*, line 88, where there is a play on the words for *gull* and *phoenix*. Could not the Cleonymus-eagle of *The Wasps* be (or be also) a Cleonymus-griffin? Or a griffin manqué, having discarded his lion parts? MacDowell notes in his introduction that Aristophanes was "happy to use [as puns] words which are only similar," here γρῖφος and γρύψ. That is, could my pun be some 2,400 years old rather than 130 or 480 or nearly 700 years old?[5]

Whatever the answer, the word was rare in Latin and then disappeared altogether from general use in the Latin of the Middle Ages. It does not turn up in standard lexicons such as the *Catholicon* (1286) of Balbus[6] and the *Glossarium mediae et infimae Latinitatis* of Charles du Cange. Nor is it listed in the *Summa Britonis* of William Brito (d. 1356) or the *Promptorium Parvulorum* (ca. 1440); the 1483 *Catholicon Anglicum* lists only *enigma* under *Rydellynge*.

In the early sixteenth century, as far as I can make out, the word *griphus* (often spelled *gryphus*) reentered Latin, where it led a vigorous life. Exactly where and through whom this happened, I am not altogether sure, although northern Italy is the most likely place and Calepino the most likely person. Ambrogio Calepino of Bergamo (1435–1511) did not include *griphus* or *gryphus* (signifying "riddle") in the first editions of his influential *Dictionarium* — not as a separate entry, that is. Later editors would list the word separately, first as *gryphus* and by 1559 as *griphus*.[7] In the first edition of the *Dictionarium* (Reggio Emilia, 1502), Calepino himself included the word at

the end of the entry for *grypes* (griffin): "Gryphi vero ut Gellius inqt aenigmata sunt" (Griffins in a different meaning, as Gellius says, are enigmas). An
entry under *gryppos* gives a further definition as *sermo implicitus* (puzzling
diction), again citing Gellius. So there it was in one paragraph, the griffin-
riddle pun, for anyone wanting it, including Ariosto.

Ariosto, who lived from 1474 to 1533, published an early 40-canto version
of *Orlando Furioso* in 1516; the hippogryph was there from the start. He
began working on the poem about 1503 to 1505. Then there was Lilio
Gregario Giraldi of Ferrara (1479–1552), who like Calepino studied Greek,
and who put together a collection of riddles in which he discussed both
aenigmata and *griphi*. (But I have not seen or seen listed editions before
1551.) Someone, doubtless Calepino, was reading and annotating Gellius
late in the fifteenth or early in the sixteenth century. Someone also saw the
pleasures of this pun. Was it Calepino himself or was it the younger Ariosto
reading Calepino? I'd like to have been present when someone else burst out
laughing at the thought.

In 1538, Thomas Elyot included *gryphus* in the first edition of his Latin-
English dictionary, and it came with a double signification: "Gryphus, a grype
or gryffon. also a captious, an insoluble, or diffuse argumente, a ryddyll."
Aenigma is defined as simply "a derke question, harde to be understanded."
Perhaps Elyot wished to separate a griphus-riddle with its fine punning
possibilities from an enigma-riddle in the sense of a large, solemn mystery.
Robert l'Estienne (Stephanus), in his 1552 *Dictionariolum Puerorum Tribus
Linguis* . . . , listed: "Aenigma . . . a darke and obscure sentence, harde to
coniecte or gesse, A question and sentence insoluble . . ."; "Griphus . . . a
darke & obscure question or sentence and hard to bee copied." Richard
Huloet, *Abecedarium Anglico-Latinum* (1552), entered *gryphus* under "Riddle
or captious question." Thomas Cooper, *Thesaurus Linguae Romanae et Britan-
nicae* (1565), listed *aenigma* as "a darke or harde question: a ryddle," and
griphus as "a nette: a riddle: an intricate or dark sentence." John Rider's
Bibliotheca Scholastica (1589) gives both *aenigma* and *gryphus*, with *scrupus* for
good measure,[8] under "A Riddle, or darke sentence." As for the remarkable
and influential Greek scholar Joachim Camerarius (1500–1577), he was
using both words by 1545 in his *Elementa Rhetoricae* ("Multae sunt formae
aenigmatum & gryphorum" [pp. 326–27]).

The word *griph* (sometimes *gryphe* or *griphus*) even came into English for a while, although most of the *OED*'s quotations (1652–1796) refer to classical riddles. But the word survives to this day as a suffix of *logogriph*, literally, "word-riddle," whose signification is much the same as that of *griph*. *Logogriph* simply spells it out. *Logogriphus* was used by J. C. Scaliger in his posthumous 1561 *Poetices Libri Septem*. I have found no earlier use. (Presumably, the title of one section of the *Carmina* (1395), "Aenigmata et Logogryphi," by Philip of Harveng (d. 1183) was added by a later editor [J. P. Migne, *Patrologia Latina*, vol. 203].) And while *griphus* does not come over into French, Italian, Spanish, or Portuguese, *logogriphus* does in vernacular forms, and also survives to this day. Although the term is specialized, it even turns up in standard desk dictionaries like Cassell's Italian and Chambers' English dictionary. Bishop Hall provided the first recorded English use in 1597–98. (He disdained logogriphs, as did Ben Jonson 40 years later.) The first recorded French use was by Naudé in 1623 (*Trésor de la langue française*, citing Littré),[9] so that the *OED*'s "logogriph . . . ad. F. *logogriphe*" may be mistaken.

As for Professor Tryphon Tournesol, the recent biography by Albert Algoud of this forgotten man in the history of science (*Le Tournesol illustré: Éloge d'un oublié de l'histoire des sciences* [Belgium: Casterman, 1994]) suggests another line of enquiry. Carpaccio's 1506 painting, "Le miracle de saint Tryphon" (reproduced on p. 12) distinctly shows that *le dragon* is *un griffon*. And the illustration from Christophe's *L'idée fixe du savant Cosinus* (reproduced on p. 6) displays a large blue griffin. Christophe (Georges Colomb, 1856–1945) wrote a 284-page book on *L'énigme d'Alésia: Solution proposée d'après Livre VII de 'Commentaires' de César*—clearly a man after my own heart.

And Dante's great, mysterious Griffin, drawing the chariot in that extraordinary procession, beheld by Beatrice in rapt contemplation? After all this, a *griphus/gryphus* pun at the end of the *Purgatorio* sounds impossible, so strong are the comic connections. Yet Dante did not know Greek literature except for what was available to him in translation. And our sense of generic fitness must not be imposed on him, for both historical and aesthetic reasons. In the recent *Cambridge Companion to Dante*, Joan Ferrante notes his punning,[10] while Giuseppe Mazzotta's *Dante's Vision and the Circle of Knowledge* (1993) includes a section on "Theologia Ludens."[11]

The word *griphus*, although very rare in the Middle Ages, was nonetheless available to Dante in Gellius.[12] Gellius mentions the word, in its Greek form (*griphos*), twice; the example in book I, chapter 2, was the one available to Dante, as only the first four books of *Noctes Atticae* were known at this time. There, the term is used by a braggart of the Stoic school, claiming that he alone can unravel (*dissolvere*) tricks of logic of the genus *griphos*. So there the word was for Dante, a strange term from the Greek (as the pagan author Gellius said) but also a kind of enigma that could contain the world.

To me, the strongest reason for a personified riddle figure just here in Dante's poem is that his entry into Paradise is the most extraordinary poetic treatment of enigma that I know. But all that is another story.

PART FOUR

Practice

Ghost Rhymes and How They Work

Throughout his extraordinary poem *The Mystery of the Charity of Charles Péguy*, Geoffrey Hill works with near rhyme rather than full rhyme (off rhyme rather than true, some say). His 100 stanzas or century of stanzas ("the cortège of the century" [1.30]?) are rhymed *abab*, *abba*, or *aabb*, so that there are 200 rhyming effects. Of these, only some 20 are full rhymes. The rest explore an impressive range of near-rhyme possibilities.

Near rhyme is an area in which twentieth-century poetry is very active. It was Wilfred Owen, we are told, who demonstrated what might be done with near rhyme,[1] and Owen's presence can be felt in Hill's poem. (So can the presence of Yeats and Eliot, also war poets, although in very different ways.) Of course, the technique was there for the taking: in some seventeenth-century poems, and more immediately in Emily Dickinson and Gerard Manley Hopkins. But the influence of Dickinson and Hopkins was delayed in the twentieth century; Owen had more immediate effect. In this kind of rhyme, new work of the first order is being done in English.

Our sense of rhyme is sometimes bedeviled by the following allegories about full rhyme and near rhyme. Full rhyme shows confidence, faith in the order of some system, and so on, whereas near rhyme shows lack of confidence and uncertainty about our faith, country, vocation, personality, sexuality, and so on. These are very pretty allegories, and also so much nonsense. What near rhyme does prevent more than full rhyme is an either-or pattern of troping a rhyme. Near rhyme does not readily allow the closeness of "harmony" or the distance of "antithesis." It suggests a scale or spectrum between the two rhyme words, and it invites the reader to consider their relations in more detail. It invites the reader to consider the matter of relation itself.

About seven years ago, I observed the following effect of near rhyme, which I have been testing intermittently ever since. A near rhyme has the possibility of four terms rather than two, because each of the rhyme words on the page pulls the other a little in its own direction. Near rhyme can thus suggest a possible full rhyme that is not there, and yet is there as a ghost. Sometimes the ghost appears only to subside, because it makes no sense, and we move back to the given rhyme words. But the possibility of one or two ghostly rhymes is there for the taking.

Definition

- Rule of thumb: In many cases of near rhyme (with one exception), there are two potential ghost rhymes in the form of the two full rhymes that are not there. A near rhyme thus has the possibility of three or four terms.

- Example:

> . . . Thus the bereaved soul returns
> upon itself, grows resolute at chess,
> in war-games hurling dice of immense loss
> into the breach; thus punitively mourns.

(Hill, *The Mystery of the Charity of Charles Péguy*, part 4)

In the near rhyme *chess* and *loss*, there are two potential ghost rhymes, *less* and *choss*. *Less* has meaning and so functions as a ghost rhyme. (For the ways it is working, see below.) *Choss*, however, is meaningless, so that no ghost appears.

- Exception: The one case where this does not work is pararhyme, Owen's term for rhymes like *loss* and *lass*. Where the initial and final consonants are repeated, and the vowel varied, there is no possibility of a ghost rhyme.

Four Short Illustrations

(1) W. B. YEATS, "UNDER BEN BULBEN"

Swear by what the sages spoke
Round the Mareotic Lake
That the Witch of Atlas knew,
Spoke and set the cocks a-crow.

What are the possible ghost rhymes of this *a(a)b(b)* quatrain? To the rhyme of "spoke . . . Lake," we add the ghost rhyme *spake*. To the rhyme of "knew . . . crow," we add *know*, then *crew*. Having done this, we recognize that every one of the three ghost rhymes in this poem about ghosts shifts the verb tense from present to past or from past to present. Yeats, who knew so much about ghosts and spirits, must have been entirely aware of this effect, in his poem about past ghosts who inform the present, written by a man designing his own future ghostly voice for the time when his present will have become our past.

(2) ELIZABETH BISHOP, "THE ARMADILLO"

Last night another big one fell.
It splattered like an egg of fire
against the cliff behind the house.
The flame ran down. We saw the pair. . . .

(*The Complete Poems*, *1927–1979*)

One ghost rhyme sounds out loudly in this stanza, the ghost of *pyre* behind the "fire. . . . pair" rhyme, these fire balloons being potential funeral pyres for animal life. The other ghost rhyme, *fair* (*fare*, too) is quieter, comes with multiple punning implications, and provides complicated tonal effects.

(3) JAY MACPHERSON, "IN TIME OF PESTILENCE"

She is sick: and shall she heal?
Well she may, the world is foul.

(The Boatman [1957])

Ghost rhymes here play the words *feel* and *howl* against the "heal? . . . foul"
rhyme, both words powerful ghosts in context.

(4) ANTHONY HECHT, "THE COST"

Hecht's poem has twelve six-line stanzas, each working with three rhymes,
abacbc. Most of the rhymes are full rhymes, with occasional small variations.
But the following variation is not small. Trajan,

Honored by Dante, by Gregory the Great
        Saved from eternal Hell,
Swirls in the motes kicked up by the cough and spate
        Of the Vespa's blue exhaust,
And a voice whispers inwardly, "my soul,
        "It is the cost, the cost,"

Like some unhinged Othello, who's just found out
        That justice is no more. . . .

(Collected Earlier Poems [1990], p. 108)

Soul following *Hell* calls forth *sell* or *cell*—most appropriate ghosts for "The
Cost," which takes its title from Othello's torment, and works against such
thought.

Some Examples Unfolded

(1) ELIZABETH BISHOP:

yes, and there Peter's tears
run down chanticleer's
sides and gem his spurs.

("Roosters," 97–99)

Bishop wrote this poem in triplets, rhymed *aaa/bbb*, and so on. Many of the triplets use full rhyme, some use near rhyme, but hardly any ghost rhymes appear. Bishop certainly knew how to use ghost rhymes, for there are two loud ones in her poem "Wading at Wellfleet." Marianne Moore calls Bishop's near rhymes "impeccable,"[2] and she chose this illustration from the poem:

The sea is "all a case of knives."

Lying so close, they catch the sun,
the spokes directed at the shin.

The two ghost rhymes on "sun . . . shin" are *shun* and *sin*, the first evidently just right. (I still remember reading in childhood about those terrible Assyrian chariots with knives attached to their turning wheels.) The shin instinctively shuns those knives, even in imagining them; the ghost rhyme is a warning voice. *Sin* is not so evidently just right, for Bishop's poem, unlike her great original, George Herbert's "Affliction (IV)," does not encompass questions of sin and grace. She is not thinking in those terms. Nonetheless, *sin*, the quieter of the two ghosts, recalls Herbert and so widens the context of war, for "Wading at Wellfleet" is certainly a war poem. In "Roosters," a fable of forgiveness is taken from the Gospels and juxtaposed with a militaristic war fable. Similarly, in this poem, words of an older world and an older kind of judgment on warring (both military and psychic) echo in this ghost rhyme. Herbert, who clearly knew something of what I feel (this ghost seems to say), would judge it in other terms, I know, I know — terms I cannot accept, but shall not completely forget.

As for the ghost rhyme in the stanza from "Roosters" quoted above, it resonates with exceptional effect. The ghost rhyme is, of course, *spears*. A line that opens with *sides* and ends with *spurs* (and then a ghostly *spears*), in a fable centered on the Crucifixion, cannot but evoke the memory of the wounding of Christ. Bishop twice quotes from the Gospels in this poem. What we hear in this stanza is not a quotation from the Gospels, as in stanza 28, but an echo in a ghost rhyme recalling the Gospels: "One of the soldiers with a spear pierced his side" (John 19:34, itself using an internal rhyme on *spear*).

The conjunction of *tears* and *spears* and *chanticleer's* hardly needs comment. But one small postscript might be added. How many readers hear one dominant *tears/spears* echo when they read these words? I do, but I find it hard to judge whether this is me or Bishop. It's Blake, of course, in "The Tyger":

> When the stars threw down their spears,
> And water'd heaven with their tears,
> Did he smile his work to see?
> Did he who make the Lamb make thee?

Blake's stanza and its poem and counterpoem resonate with implication. For Bishop's two contrary fables of roosters bear some resemblance to Blake's two contrary fables of lamb and tiger. Read "The Tyger" alongside Bishop's stanzas on fighting roosters who become figures of militarism and aggression. Read "The Lamb" alongside her stanzas on Peter's thrice-crowing cock, which becomes an emblem of forgiveness in many a sculpted form, and beyond. One of Bishop's questions is essentially the same as Blake's in the last two lines of his "spears . . . tears" stanza. It is not that her contraries are innocence and experience, for matters of forgiveness belong to an adult world beyond childhood innocence; they concern goodness, not innocence. But perhaps Bishop is asking how or whether we can translate the radicals of innocence and experience. Not simple, as her last stanza makes clear.

(2) GEOFFREY HILL:

Here are the first lines of Hill's opening poem, "Genesis," in his collection *For the Unfallen*:

> Against the burly air I strode,
> Where the tight ocean heaves its load,
> Crying the miracles of God.

The ghost rhyme of *goad* sounds out after the last line, appropriately as the rest of the poem makes clear. The word itself is biblical, where it can be an instrument of killing. The words of the wise are also goads figuratively in the often-quoted final chapter of Ecclesiastes. Between these two alternatives, killing and curing, lies the more usual meaning of *goad* as a synonym for *spur*. The senses in which God might be a goad move across this entire scale of meaning. In the poem's last section, again rhyming an *-ode* word and God, the ghost rhyme of *goad* approaches even before we ride across the end of the line and find the word *spurs*:

> On the sixth day, as I rode
> In haste about the works of God,
> With spurs I plucked a horse's blood.

An example from *The Mystery of the Charity of Charles Péguy* raises more than one matter of ghost rhyming:

> and in the fable this is your proper home;
> three sides of a courtyard where the bees thrum
> in the crimped hedges and the pigeons flirt
> and paddle, and sunlight pierces the heart

The rhyme scheme here is *aabb*. Do ghost rhymes tend to sound out more loudly if they occur in adjacent lines? I think so. (See also the lines by Macpherson quoted earlier.) The ghost rhyme on "home . . . thrum" is *hum*, to my ear a loudly echoing ghost. Because bees usually hum, Hill's *thrum* sounds as if it ought to be *hum*. (*Thrum* means to play a musical instrument idly or monotonously — our hearing of the busy bee, and not the way it hears itself.) Then too, we associate *m* sounds with bees, as in "the murmuring of innumerable bees." But we need a little more from the closing lines of Tennyson's exquisite song:

> The moan of doves in immemorial elms,
> And murmuring of innumerable bees.

> (*The Princess* 7.206–7)

Bees and doves or pigeons all come with *m* sounds, humming or moaning. Hill also has a mid-line near rhyme of *crimped*, and does it matter that a ghost rhyme of *crumb* sounds faintly in this word? Surely yes. Crumbs belong in the courtyard for those pigeons. And then, for those who read Virgil (taught by the "terse teachers of Latin" from this same part?) or those who follow Tennyson's own remark on his lines,[3] there is Virgil's once-famous first eclogue, where

> hinc tibi, quae semper, vicino ab limite saepes
> Hyblaeis apibus florem depasta salicti
> saepe levi somnum suadebit inire susurro;
> hinc alta sub rupe canet frondator ad auras:

> nec tamen interea raucae, tua cura, palumbes,
> nec gemere aëria cessabit turtur ab ulmo.

> (*Ecl.* 1.53–58, Loeb ed.)[4]

Here are bees, and in a hedge too, soothing us to slumber, as the Loeb translation has it. And wood pigeons as well as turtledoves cooing and moaning. Hill, with his hedges and his flirting and paddling pigeons, is in fact closer to Virgil than his great predecessor, for Tennyson writes out Virgil's amorous turtledoves. (Or does Tennyson disperse them into the narrative of *The Princess?*) In all three, Virgil, Tennyson, Hill, the associations of sense and sound evoke a heart-stopping pastoral landscape that is a home, contrasted with a hostile place.

The example quoted on p. 224 is from part 4 of Hill's poem. Here the ghost rhyme of *less* on a "chess . . . loss" near rhyme is easy to hear. *Less* hovers about the word *loss*, so that, first, there is a haunted oxymoron of "immense loss"; second, *less* affects the first end-word, *returns*, the returns of loss themselves partaking of less; and third, *less* extracts from the rhyme-word *mourns* the pun on *more* in a *less/more* paradox.

Puzzling ghost rhymes in Hill's poem (4.13–16) can repay attention. What are sheep doing in a bookshop? A curious memory of Alice and the White Queen intervenes here.

> This is no old Beauce manoir that you keep
> but the rue de la Sorbonne, the cramped shop,
> its unsold *Cahiers* built like barricades
> its fierce disciples, disciplines and feuds. . . .

Memories of French rural landscape do include "clear sheepbell-sound," as we find in the next section. This shop that is no *manoir* nonetheless contains remembered sounds of a Beauce *manoir*. Once you have put words on the page, even if you say "This is no *x*," you have recalled *x*. So it is that the ghost rhyme of *sheep*, following "keep . . . shop," comes rightly to notice. Carroll's sheep-shop lives in our ears partly because of that very pararhyme, to say nothing of the way in which Carroll acts out the metamorphosis of one word into the other. How nearly it affected him may be guessed from the fact that he almost breaks his own given fictional bounds in describing the sweetness of a pastoral moment on the river. Sheep, for all their meekness, can be powerfully evocative.

(3) W. H. AUDEN:

An example from Auden's "Law Like Love" illustrates complications that may arise from different pronunciation. It also illustrates Auden's impeccable ear, and a craft so masterly that it can smile at technical problems in the very exemplifying of them. Most of the rhymes in this poem are full rhymes, but something happens in stanza 4, the judicial-law stanza:

> Law, says the judge as he looks down his nose,
> Speaking clearly and most severely,
> Law is as I've told you before,
> Law is as you know I suppose,
> Law is but let me explain it once more,
> Law is The Law.

Until now, all rhymes have been full, but here we have an *abcac(b)* with *-ly* and *Law* in a near rhyme. All well and good, but look what the proximity of *more* does to *Law*. Auden wrote this poem after he had moved to the United States. A North American ear hears some English pronunciations of *law* as something like *lawr*. Not *lore* but then not an American *law* either. Lest we think Auden has not heard this, we might note the start of stanza 8:

> If we, dear, know we know no more
> than they about the Law. . . .

This is a long stanza rhyming *aa bb cc*, and so on, and every other rhyme is full. I fancy Auden smiled over this one, smiling at the ways we variously pronounce the word *law*. Smiling also, it may be, at the fables this little near rhyme can provide, including prejudicial fables. It is not just the pronunciation of *law* that varies from place to place.

Testing

It is time to test this rule of thumb by way of contrary evidence. Rather than build up corroborative examples, can we follow the scientist's method of testing a hyposthesis by noting where and how it does *not* work? Or appears not to work.

What about the internal near rhyme on *dice* in my opening example from

Hill? I can only go so far in reading it.[5] But the ghost rhyme on *loss* in this stanza cannot ignore a one-line ghost rhyme on "dice . . . loss" that sounds out *lice*. Is this an error? Or a deliberate near-grotesqueness? Hill's poem does not shirk the physical brutality of warfare in the 1914–18 Great War. And the misery of it, including dangerous trench life — squalid trench life, too, including lice. If the ghost rhyme distracts, is it so very inappropriately after all? Only if we visualize war's chess or dice games as a huge heroic canvas, allegorized, sanitized, as Hill will not his canvas.

Comment and Corollaries

COMMENT

1. The terms *near rhyme* and *off rhyme* are unhappy ones, insofar as their implied opposites, *full rhyme* and *true rhyme*, sound so much better (see T. V. F. Brogan, "Near Rhyme," in the *New Princeton Encyclopedia of Poetry and Poetics* [1993]). Can anyone devise a better term?

2. Older prosodists, including George Saintsbury, disdained near rhyme. ("I've re-read all of Saintsbury's book on prosody just for fun," Elizabeth Bishop wrote to Robert Lowell as she prepared to teach. "It is a marvelous book, I think, all three volumes — so *funny* — and quite good until he meets Swinburne."[6] Amateur poets, admiring Bishop, tend to avert their eyes from her sheer mastery of craft, and as for finding these volumes funny . . . !) As late as 1950, it was possible to argue that near rhyme should be used only sparingly,[7] an argument that the last generation of poets has shown to be nonsense. How far did the term itself influence such judgment?

3. Robert Pinsky's recent translation of Dante's *Inferno* offers a fine test, because Pinsky answers the question of how to adapt Dante's *terza rima* by using near rhyme in the *aba bcb cdc* pattern. The poem makes a particularly interesting case, because evidence suggests Pinsky is not working especially with ghost rhymes as I have defined them. But as we might expect, the tact of a good poet's ear prevails. There are very few examples where a ghost rhyme might be obtrusive, and a number of examples where ghost rhyme strengthens the story. The poem is instructive, first, because Pinsky's great variety of near rhyme covers a wide scale, like Hill's, but a looser scale. A number of examples outside pararhyme do not offer the possibility of ghost

rhyme. It's thus important to remember that the rule of thumb reads: In *many* cases of near rhyme. . . . Pinsky's effects remind a critic to keep hypotheses in their proportionate place. Second, Pinsky's example suggests that Hill (and Bishop?) may be entirely aware of the effect of ghost rhyme and ways of working with it. Certainly the proportion of telling ghost rhymes in *The Mystery of the Charity of Charles Péguy* is unusually high, compared with that in Pinsky's *Inferno*.

COROLLARIES

The examples above suggest several corollaries to my opening definition:

1. That ghost rhymes are likely louder when they occur in adjacent lines.
2. That internal rhymes may enter into the cave of echo we are exploring, though usually not as strongly as end-rhymes.
3. That a word's signification and its field of association matter in ghost rhymes. That is, where such denotative and connotative meanings are readily available, as with bees (*hum*), a ghost rhyme will sound out more forcefully.
4. That a word's acoustic sound and associations also matter for ghost rhymes (*hum*).
5. That ghost rhymes that allude to other poems will have special force, bringing into our ears' hearing the voices of the dead, ghosts in another sense.
6. That it is worth testing what happens when the ghost rhyme changes a part of speech (see W. K. Wimsatt, "One Relation of Rhyme to Reason").[8]
7. That pronunciation matters in rhyme, and may itself even provide a ghost rhyme.

These corollaries are all worth noting, but they are not unique to ghost rhyme. All of them pertain to full rhyme as well. What corollaries might apply to ghost rhymes alone? The following, I think:

1. That, as these ghosts do not appear on the page, we may hear homonyms for some ghost rhymes, so that a few ghost rhymes are

multiple rather than single (*sell* and *cell*). The possible terms for a ghost rhyme still remain four, but a ghost may come with extra shadows, like Banquo and his progeny.

2. That the ghost rhyme on the second word of a near rhyme has temporal priority. In the opening example, we first hear *less* and only come to hear *choss* later or on rereading.

Richard Wilbur has a splendid thought from a poet's work table:

> It is precisely in its power to suggest comparisons and connections — unusual ones — to the poet, that one of the incidental merits of rhyme may be said to lie. Say to yourself *lake*, *rake*, and then write down all the metaphors and other reconciliations of these terms which occur to you within one or two minutes. It is likely to be a long list, extending from visual images of wind furrowing the water, to punning reminiscences of Lancelot and Guinevere.[9]

As with the full rhyme of *lake/rake*, so also with near rhyme and its possible ghosts. An inept poet will pay no attention to these ghosts hovering about near rhymes. A good poet will make sure that unwanted ghost rhymes are not allowed to distract the reader. A good poet can also put ghost rhymes to work, sometimes with very fine fabling effects.

SEVENTEEN

Methought as Dream Formula in Shakespeare, Milton, Wordsworth, Keats, and Others

In book 5 of *Paradise Lost*, when Eve recounts her distressing dream to Adam, she uses the word *methought* four times in 66 lines. It opens and closes her dream, and it is important in the carefully shaped grammar of the forbidden fruit:

> . . . methought
> Close at mine ear one call'd me forth to walk
> With gentle voice, I thought it thine. . . .

> And on, methought, alone I pass'd through ways
> That brought me on a sudden to the Tree
> Of interdicted Knowledge. . . .

> . . . the pleasant savory smell
> So quick'n'd appetite, that I, methought,
> Could not but taste. . . .

> . . . suddenly
> My Guide was gone, and I, methought, sunk down,
> And fell asleep; but O how glad I wak'd
> To find this but a dream!
>
> $(5.35-37, 50-52, 84-86, 90-93)$[1]

Adam, responding to Eve's troubled mind, echoes the word *methought*, but shifts the tense:

> Some such resemblances methinks I find
> Of our last Ev'ning's talk, in this thy dream,
> But with addition strange.
>
> $(5.114-16)$

Adam's word *methinks* belongs to his waking judgment, and the sense of the verb pulls toward "I think" or "I judge," as in reasoning more than in speculation or visionary narrative. So also with the illustrative quotations for *methinks* (from 1560 to 1871) listed in both editions of the *Oxford English Dictionary*, and with most examples of other present-tense forms from 888 on (*methinketh, methink, my think*). The word *methinks* has an unexpected history, for it is the only long-surviving form of the obsolete verb *to think*, signifying "to seem, to appear" (from Old English *Þync(e)an*). Hence the words *methinks* and *methought*, where *me-* is a form of the dative, as in "it seems to me." *To think* in its modern sense comes from Old English *Þenc(e)an*, and signifies "to conceive in the mind, etc." (*OED*, B.I), "to call to mind, take into consideration" (II), "to be of opinion, deem, judge, etc." (III). Any crude notion of a subject-object split following Descartes's work is brought up short by this very early and very intelligent range of signification for the process of "thinking."

Paradise Lost uses the present tense, *methinks*, three times in all. In the two other uses, both in book 10, the meaning of judgment dominates, although judgment is informed by some visionary sense, whether infernal or human. "Methinks I feel new strength within me rise," says Sin after the fall (l. 243, as if in parody of Milton's sentence in the *Areopagitica*, "Methinks I see a noble and puissant nation rousing herself . . ."). "Then let us seek / Some safer resolution, which methinks / I have in view," says Adam to Eve (1028–30).

The past form of this verb is another matter. Both editions of the *OED* define *methinks* as follows, with *methought* simply listed under "past tense": "It seems to me. (Used with dependent clause or parenthetically.)" But the quotations in the *OED* suggest that the past tense is strongly associated with visionary response, for most of them are about dreams. They include Cover-dale's 1535 translation of the dream of Gideon in Judg. 7; Henry More's "I dreamed thus. Methought I was . . ." (1651); Pope's adaptation of Chaucer's dream-vision in *The Temple of Fame* (1711); and Tennyson's "Dream of Fair Women," v. 14 (1832). Under *me thoughts* is listed a line from Clarence's account of his dream in *Richard III*.

Eve's dream is a dream of temptation, insinuated by Satan into her sleeping hours. Her word *methought* is emphasized in different ways: one *methought* rhymes internally with *thought* and *brought* in the two adjacent lines; two others are placed at the end of the line. *Methought* introduces a complex layered effect into Eve's dream narrative, already complex by definition since falseness is still unknown to Adam and Eve. *Methought* not only hovers finely between waking and sleeping responses; it also hovers finely between the two verbs *to think*, one already obsolete. The *OED* notes, "The original meaning [of our verb *to think*] may . . . have been 'to cause (something) to seem or appear (to oneself).' " In some examples, there is "no difference of import" between the two verbs (see *think*). But dream narrative offers the possibility of exploiting the full range of difference between the two verbs.

Before book 5, *methought* is used only once in *Paradise Lost*, again by Eve, and again of temptation.

> . . . what could I do,
> But follow straight, invisibly thus led?
> Till I espi'd thee, fair indeed and tall,
> Under a Platan, yet methought less fair,
> Less winning soft, less amiably mild,
> Than that smooth wat'ry image; back I turn'd,
> Thou following cri'd'st aloud, Return fair *Eve*. . . .

> *(4.475–81)*

How much judgment is present in this *methought*? If there is some, Eve comes to think it an unripe judgment, "unexperienc't thought" (4.457). In this *methought*, she is still influenced by the Ovidian mirror-vision of herself, no dream, yet dreamlike in its doubling of the self, its mesmerizing attraction, and its appeal to instinct. Following the logic of these uses of *methought* in books 4 and 5, we might suppose that the word should be associated with tempting dreams and false visions. But no. As in Coverdale's dream of Gideon, *methought* may be used of true dreams in *Paradise Lost*. Thus in book 8:

> On a green shady Bank profuse of Flow'rs
> Pensive I sat me down; there gentle sleep
> First found me, and with soft oppression seiz'd
> My drowsed sense, untroubl'd, though I thought
> I then was passing to my former state
> Insensible, and forthwith to dissolve:
> When suddenly stood at my Head a dream,
> Whose inward apparition gently mov'd
> My fancy to believe I yet had being,
> And liv'd: One came, methought, of shape Divine,
> And said, thy Mansion wants thee, *Adam*, rise,
>
> . . . .
>
> . . . I wak'd, and found
> Before mine Eyes all real, as the dream
> Had lively shadow'd.
>
> *(8.286–96, 309–11)*

The word *methought* appears some 40 lines later, when Adam, having named the creatures, still feels a lack. Here, the word moves between judgment and dream-story, reason and instinct.

> . . . but in these
> I found not what methought I wanted still;
> And to the Heav'nly vision thus presum'd.
>
> *(8.354–56)*

Some 100 lines later, *methought* again traces a dream, and a dream from which Adam will wake to find it truth:

> Mine eyes he clos'd, but op'n left the Cell
> Of Fancy my internal sight, by which
> Abstract as in a trance methought I saw,
> Though sleeping, where I lay. . . .
>
> *(8.460–63)*

Adam's use of *methought* for volition and for dream-narrative beautifully balances Eve's. Within the chronology of *Paradise Lost*, we end with Eve's discordant and troubled *methought*. But within the arrangement of Milton's narrative, a felicitous "methought" in book 8 counteracts the earlier association, as Milton builds pathos in preparation for book 9. The final use of *methought* comes after the Fall, when Adam attempts prayer to God and finds a sense of confirming response:

> Methought I saw him placable and mild,
> Bending his ear; persuasion in me grew
> That I was heard with favor. . . .

> (*11.151–53*)

The reader who has followed Milton's senses of *methought* will recognize how Adam's *methought* is working here. Judgment and dream-story, reason and instinct, experience and innocence: these same contraries, now fallen, have lost their fruitful tension, and henceforth will commonly work against each other. Dream and vision, true or false, will no longer come clear in the light of God's presence. That presence itself will be veiled and distanced except on the rarest occasions.

Milton's use of this verb reminds us not to make too neat a division between its two chief functions. Acts of ordinary cognition and judgment are sometimes far removed from dream-narrative. At other times they are not, and in some areas they may never be.

Milton, I think, took over the word *methought* as a dream formula from Shakespeare. In turn, later writers appear to have been influenced by Shakespeare's and Milton's use of this formula, so that the word regularly introduces visionary material. At least, this is true of enough good writers that a clumsy use of the word argues for an indifferent ear. It is not that the word *methought* cannot be used casually, still less that it cannot be used of simple cognition. It is that the word needs control. A writer needs to make very clear whether any given use is casual or weighted. And any emphatic use should show an awareness of the Shakespeare-Milton inheritance. *Methinks* requires less control, but it does require some, notably where it (rather than the more usual *methought*) functions as a dream formula.

There are two memorable dream-uses in Shakespeare's work, as well as a full spectrum of mixed uses, where ordinary cognition and dream-experience approach each other. The two memorable uses are in Bottom's dream from *A Midsummer-Night's Dream* and in Clarence's dream from *Richard III*:

> TITANIA: My Oberon, what visions have I seen!
> Methought I was enamor'd of an ass. (*4.1.76–77*)
>
> BOTTOM [AWAKING]: . . . I have had a most rare vision. I have had a dream, past the wit of man to say what dream it was. Man is but an ass, if he go about t'expound this dream. Methought I was — there is no man can tell what. Methought I was, and methought I had — but man is but a patch'd fool, if he will offer to say what methought I had. The eye of man hath not heard, the ear of man hath not seen, man's hand is not able to taste, his tongue to conceive, nor his heart to report, what my dream was. (*4.1.204–14*)[2]
>
> CLARENCE: Methoughts that I had broken from the Tower. . . .
> Methought that Gloucester stumbled. . . .
> O Lord, methought what pain it was to drown! . . .
> Methoughts I saw a thousand fearful wracks. . . .
> Methought I had, and often did I strive. . . .
> I pass'd (methought) the melancholy flood. . . .
> With that (methoughts) a legion of foul fiends. . . .
>
> KEEPER: I am afraid (methinks) to hear you tell it. (*1.4.9–65*)

In *Richard III*, *methought* does not appear again until Richard dreams in act 5 and lies about his dream: "Methought the souls of all that I had murther'd . . ." (5.3.204; and see 230).

The word is used elsewhere in Shakespeare of dream or vision: in *The Tempest*, in *Macbeth*, elsewhere in *Midsummer Night's Dream*, in *Hamlet*, in *Cymbeline*, and in *Henry IV, Part II*. It is also used of heightened actual perception, where one perceives as in a dream or a vision. What one perceives may be so, or not so, or it may be in the realm of figuration where something is and is not so at once. Thus, the word is used of the judgment of faces and of bearing, where intuition informs reasoning processes, and the audience senses a denouement at hand. "Methought he was a brother to your daughter," says Orlando of the disguised Rosalind (*As You Like It* 5.4.29). "Methought thy very gait did prophesy / A royal nobleness," says the duke of Albany of the disguised Edgar (*King Lear* 5.3.176–77). Shakespeare can also parody this kind of intuitive apprehension, as in *Coriolanus*: "He had, sir, a kind of face, methought — I cannot tell how to term it" (4.5.155–56). Similarly, in the state of falling in love, or in some kinds of figure like hyperbole, the word is appropriate, introducing as it does the authority of dream or vision. "O, when mine eyes did see Olivia first, / Methought she purg'd the air of pestilence" (*Twelfth Night* 1.1.18–19). "Methought I lay / Worse than the mutines in the bilboes" (*Hamlet* 5.2.5–6), where Hamlet appears not to be dreaming but to be in the oppressive state of being unable to sleep or wake, a prey to fancy, here true fancy.

What Milton adds to the Shakespearean usage is a powerful sense of the dialectic of true as against false dreams. Shakespeare provides a map, a taxonomy of uses. Milton concentrates on the either-or of true or false dream, remembering, among other things, the long biblical tradition of dream-interpretation. How powerful the dream formula could be for Milton, we may surmise from its use as the opening word in a poignant dream-poem of his own: "Methought I saw my late espoused saint. . . ."

It is Milton's use of *methinks* in the *Areopagitica* that influences Dryden in *Annus Mirabilis*. We can hear the cadences of one of Milton's best-known sentences when Dryden also introduces an inspiring vision with the word *methinks*: "Methinks already, from this chymic flame, / I see a city. . . . Already, lab'ring with a mighty fate / She shakes the rubbish from her mounting brow / And seems to have renew'd her charter's date" (*Annus Mirabilis*, l. 1169). Among later writers, Pope unobtrusively tells his readers that he too has heard what Shakespeare and Milton have done with this verb. All three uses of *methought* and many uses of *methinks* in his poetry are in association with dream material. Cary, on the other hand, translating Dante's *Divine Comedy* into Miltonic language, shows no sign of having heard this formula. *Methinks* and *methought* are used carelessly. There is no clear sign whether to read the words casually or to weight them. There is no resonance from their use, no signaling of a pull between ordinary and heightened perception, no signaling of a problem in interpreting true and false, no care with the placing of the word in the line for purposes of emphasis.

Not so with the major Romantic poets, all of whom show they have heard and understood Shakespeare's and Milton's use of this word, although only Keats and Wordsworth, I think, grapple with Milton's dialectic of dream, vision, and fancy. Wordsworth's use, as we might expect, is of special interest, notably in *The Prelude*. *Methinks* and *methought* do not appear in the 1799 version of *The Prelude*. But they are used in the 1805 and 1850 *Prelude*, and with evident care. *Methought* appears in the introductory passage:

> For I, methought, while the sweet breath of heaven
> Was blowing on my body, felt within
> A correspondent breeze, that gently moved
> With quickening virtue. . . .
>
> *(1.33–36 [1850 version])*[3]

The word *methought* itself gently moves Wordsworth and the reader to recall Milton's *methought*s, Wordsworth having directly alluded to Milton in line 14. The context requires us to recall Adam's dreams, especially his dream of God in the act of creation.

The word is repeated in line 74, of an envisioned dwelling: ". . . reached the very door / Of the one cottage which methought I saw" (1.73–74 [1850]). ("And saw, methought, the very house and fields / Present before my eyes" [1.84–85 (1805)].) The force of this image is emphasized in Wordsworth's added lines in the later version:

> No picture of mere memory ever looked
> So fair: and while upon the fancied scene
> I gazed with growing love, a higher power
> Than Fancy gave assurance of some work
> Of glory there forthwith to be begun,
> Perhaps too there performed. . . .
>
> *(1.75–80)*

"Fancy" belongs in Milton's world of *methought* — that is, in dreams; it can be true, prophetic fancy as in Adam's dream, or false, delusive fancy as in Eve's. There is little doubt which Wordsworth has in mind here, given that his vision takes place in "a green shady place" (62 [1850]), as Adam's does "on a green shady bank."

Methought is used only twice more in *The Prelude*, and in both versions. In 9.454 (1850), "Sometimes methought I saw a pair of knights," and in 12.166–

67 (1850), of Mary Wordsworth, "methought / Her very presence such a sweetness breathed. . . ."

One use of *methinks* is of special interest. In book 8 of the 1850 *Prelude*, Wordsworth again, as in 1.74, comments on the mental process at work. This time, the word *methinks* appears only in the 1850 version:

> Philosophy, methinks, at Fancy's call,
> Might deign to follow him through what he does
> Or sees in his day's march. . . .

> *(249–51)*

Methinks here suggests judgment, but also a lively imaging, as if Wordsworth envisaged a personified Philosophy following the shepherd to learn of him. The word is finely placed in mid-line between philosophy and fancy, and so balanced, as Milton balances it, between two different (although not separate) powers of the mind. That this balancing is deliberate may be inferred not just generally from the care we expect of a good poet when shaping a line; it may also be inferred from the fact that Wordsworth changed the position of *methought* in 1.74 and 9.454 between 1805 and 1850, so as not to break the flow of the line. The effect there is to lessen emphasis. Here, he plainly wants emphasis.

Keats's use of *methought* in *Endymion* suggests a debt to Shakespeare rather than Milton, and reminds us to check our reading of this word by context and by other echoes. It is Bottom's dream we are hearing when *methought* introduces the dream account in 1.578, and is repeated in lines 598 and 637.[4] In *The Fall of Hyperion: A Dream*, the word *methought* opens the dream-story of Hyperion:

> Methought I stood where trees of every clime,
> Palm, myrtle, oak, and sycamore, and beech,
> With plantane, and spice-blossoms, made a screen. . . .

> *(1.19–21)*

Later the word measures the effects of time, and of old Saturn's voice:

> For by my burning brain I measured sure
> Her silver seasons shedded on the night,
> And every day by day methought I grew

More gaunt and ghostly. . . .
Methought I heard some old man of the earth
Bewailing earthly loss. . . .

(1.393–96, 440–41)

In *The Fall of Hyperion, methought* is not just an allusive echo of Eve's dream
but also an allusive echo of all Milton's *methoughts*. (Other echoes of *Paradise
Lost* in the poem bear out this wider sense.) If this is so, it calls for a reading of
The Fall of Hyperion that accommodates not just echoes of deceptive dreams
but also echoes of true dreams. The dream-language, in other words, would
be read as equivocal. Even as Keats is echoing Miltonic dreams and visions,
he is questioning a Miltonic dialectic of true versus false dreams.[5]

Methought as dream formula is not confined to poetry, although the art of
poetry allows a subtler placing and weighting of the word. Addison, for
example, in the *Spectator*, introduces dream material in this way:

> The different Opinions which were started on this Occasion, pre-
> sented to my Imagination so many new Ideas, that by mixing with those
> that were already there, they employed my Fancy all the last Night, and
> composed a very wild extravagant Dream.
>   I was invited, methought, to the Dissection of a *Beau's Head* and of a
> *Coquet's Heart*. . . .

> *(No. 275 [15 Jan. 1712])*

The causes of dreams are here accounted for in terms close to Milton's. In
No. 524, a dream is introduced by the formula "Methought I was . . ."
(31 Oct. 1712, unsigned). Johnson also uses the formula: "I had lately a
very remarkable dream. . . . Methought I was in the midst of . . ." (*Rambler*
No. 44 [18 Aug. 1750]). Lamb's essay on "Witches, and Other Night Fears"
provides a dream-test for aspiring poets:

> Methought I was in that country, but the mountains were gone. The pov-
> erty of my dreams mortifies me. There is Coleridge, at his will can con-
> jure up icy domes, and pleasure-houses for Kubla Khan . . . when I
> cannot muster a fiddle. . . . the poor plastic power, such as it is, within
> me set to work, to humour my folly in a sort of dream that very night.
> Methought I was upon the ocean billows at some sea-nuptials, riding and

mounted high, with the customary train sounding their conches before me (I myself, you may be sure, the *leading god*), and . . . just where Ino Leucothea should have greeted me . . . the billows . . . landed me in the wafture of a placid wave or two, alone, safe and inglorious, somewhere at the foot of Lambeth palace.

The degree of the soul's creativeness in sleep might furnish no whimsical criterion of the quantum of poetical faculty resident in the same soul waking. An old gentleman, a friend of mine, and a humourist, used to carry this notion so far that when he saw any stripling of his acquaintance ambitious of becoming a poet, his first question would be, "Young man, what sort of dreams have you?"

As the nineteenth century passed, *methought* came to be of less interest to poets, to judge from the work of Tennyson and Browning and Whitman and Dickinson. Perhaps it had come to sound too formulaic. For all of Tennyson's interest in dreams and visions, he appears to use *methought* in only two of his nondramatic poems. But its use in "The Holy Grail" (1869) is striking, and shows his grasp of the history of the word. Lancelot's face is read through this formula, a use that may recall some Shakespearean examples: "methought I spied / A dying fire of madness in his eyes" (764–65). A few lines later (843), Tennyson uses the word as part of his subtly layered presentation of Lancelot's mixed vision of the Grail. (He may be drawing on Malory's "that him thought.")[6] In the late poem "Akbar's Dream" (1892), *methought* introduces a metaphor rather than a dream (74), but a metaphor of the visionary mental effect of certain doctrines.

Browning uses *methought* five times in all, three times of dream material. In "The Pied Piper of Hamelin" (1842), it appears just before the dream vision vanishes in the wash of the Weser (144). In "Parleying with Charles Avison" (1887), the word introduces a sudden visual fancy, a mistaken perception (13); the effect is close to simile. In book 9 of *The Ring and the Book* (1868–69), Browning's use is as striking as Tennyson's at the same date. Again, there is a layered presentation, layers of irony this time, with speaker quoting historian quoting dreamer: "I dreamed I dreamed; and in that mimic dream / (Impalpable to dream as dream to fact) / Methought I meanly chose to sleep no wink . . ." (1086–88). Considering all the speeches using *methinks* in *The Ring and the Book*, it is a good question whether Browning is not playing ironically with the word throughout. Neither Whitman nor Dickinson uses *methought* at all. Poe does, at midcentury, in "The Raven," to move the poem from foreboding to nightmare: "Then, methought, the air grew denser . . ." (79). Among prose writers, Charlotte Brontë provides one example, reminiscent of Milton's *Areopagitica*, in *Villette* (1853): "In my reverie, methought I saw the continent of Europe, like a wide dream-land, far away" (ch. 6).

It is Henry James who helps us to date the decline of *methought*. In 1870, in the serial version of "A Passionate Pilgrim," the word is used to imply judgment informed by intuition: "I read in her glance, methought, that she was interested." In 1884, James revised the sentence: "I thought I read in her glance that she was interested." In 1885, he again revised the sentence: "It began to be plain enough that she was interested." The 1908 New York Edition followed the 1885 version but deleted *enough*.[7] Can we say that some time between 1870 and 1885 *methought* began to sound dated? Perhaps so, if we keep in mind that Browning used the word in 1887 and Tennyson in 1892. Still, both these uses are restricted.

Methinks and *methought* are no longer current, even in poetic diction. They already had an archaic flavour, although they were judged possible for poetic use, at the time of the first edition of the *Oxford English Dictionary*. The *terminus ad quem* for this verb is 1906 (see the historical introduction, pt. 8). The second edition of the *OED* retains "Now *arch.* and *poet.*," which is surely an error. The *Concise Oxford* knows more about poetry when it simply says "arch."

When we reflect on changes in diction, we often emphasize the growth of our word-hoard. Yet we also lose words from the common tongue, words with useful functions. Something is lost in James's deletion of *methought* in 1884 and later. Shakespeare and Tennyson used *methought* of an intuitive judgment in reading countenances, and the very word could evoke a series of instructive examples. "It began to be plain" loses the history of *methought* and hence the kind of judgment involved, even if it gains a sense of how a thought gradually progresses. *Methought* functioned for centuries as a generic signal indicating likely dream narrative, one of those opening formulas considered by Alastair Fowler in his *Kinds of Literature: An Introduction to the Theory of Genres and Modes*.[8] As dream formula, *methought* also encouraged the widening of our notions of "thought" beyond purely rationalist kinds and degrees of thinking. But then, the two old forms of the verb *to think* already encouraged a wide and imaginative view of our mental processes, including "thinking."[9] There was certainly no lack of interest in dreams and intuitive thinking in the later nineteenth century. Quite the contrary. Freud's *The Interpretation of Dreams* was published in 1900. But the dream formula *methought*, which had held from Shakespeare to the Romantics and later, slipped into the realm of the archaic just when the interest in dreams started to take its modern form.

EIGHTEEN

Reading a Poem: On John Hollander's "Owl"

Suppose we start with grammar, assuming we've already glanced at the look of "Owl" on the page (pp. 269–72 below), as if through the eyes of May Swenson. Here is the way she begins to read a poem:

> I like to see the poem first as a shut box or package to be opened, within which is an invention whose particular working I hope to discover. Something can be felt about it even before beginning to read: its profile on the page, its regular or irregular pattern of stanzas, length of lines, their symmetry, its wide or thin shape, its look of bulk or lightness.[1]

So here, we observe a one-word title: a noun, no article, and so more like Bishop's "Sandpiper" than Frost's "The Oven Bird." Then quatrains, 24 of them, each shorter in its third and more in its fourth line; the pulse iambic and 5 5 4 3 (pentameter twice, tetrameter, trimeter), the rhyme *abab*. Each stanza, in little, looks and listens like an owl, narrowing down to its fourth line, listening to the sounds and silences both — the sounds of the full end-rhymes, assonance, mid-line rhyming, schematic echoes, and so on; and the silences resonating in the vacant space left by one fewer foot in the third line, then two in the fourth, an effect especially noticeable in the end-stopped lines. This stanza form is (I believe) John Hollander's own,[2] and it teaches us how to listen better. Owls hunt with their ears as well as their eyes, and with only their ears if necessary.

In starting with grammar, I am simply choosing one partner in the dance of grammar, rhetoric, and dialectic that constitutes all writing. I shall touch on lexical questions and two senses of voice, before turning to the heart of the matter, the poem's figuration and fable, then end with some remarks on "Owl" as part of all Hollander's work and also as a poem of our moment.

The grammar, then, and first the syntactic variety of the sentences. T. S. Eliot wrote in 1918 that technique is not simply "what may be learned from a manual of prosody. This is making technique easy. . . . Technique is more volatile; it can only be learned, the more difficult part of it, by absorption. Try to put into a sequence of simple quatrains the continuous syntactic variety of Gautier or Blake."[3] Something of Hollander's distinctive voice in both poetry and prose lies in his great command of grammatical structures, including his syntactic variety. "Owl" is strongly predicative in style (note the complex syntax, and the remarkably high use of participles, past and present). The sentences give the effect of generating themselves, especially through their parallel grammatical constructions, where the last term in a double or triple set is likely to be modified by a clause or phrase — the whole sentence ramifying and exfoliating, as if we were watching a zoological or genealogical tree grow under our eyes. (See, for example, the parallel participles in the last line of stanza 4 and stanza 5: "Taking heed . . . you more than see." Or consider how one participle leads to another in stanzas 15 through 17, beginning with "Trembling . . .").

Such syntactic energy gives a quick, vital rhythm to the sentence — a fast pace, given the richness of thought, hints, implications. A pace sometimes slightly nervous, curbing and steadying its own energies, partly through the regular beat of the simple rhyme scheme and quatrain. It seems to me that the forward propulsion of both the grammar and dialectic is steadied, directed, by the rhetorical schemes — that rhetoric here offers what I want to call something like a discipline of simplicity. This is a function we may not associate with rhetorical schemes, those "surface patterns of words" that "carry no meanings per se."[4] In Roman Jakobson's terms — and his discussion

of parallelism was really the only thing that helped with what I was hearing —
in Jakobson's terms, what I am hearing is the pull between a regular, simple
parallelism of stanza form and a much-varied, complex parallelism of syntax.[5]
It would be interesting to look at Hollander's considerable work with the
quatrain over the past decade and more, and inquire further about this play of
grammar and rhetoric.

The poem even tropes on grammatical conventions themselves: see stanza
6, "Medusa's visage gazed our bodies to / Literal stone unshaded." Normally
the verb *to gaze* does not take a direct object, but then Medusa's gaze is not
normal, and certainly takes — rather, makes — a direct object. Your object,
should you meet her, is to gaze only indirectly. Hence the very nice double
antecedent of the word *shaded*. Hence also, in the same stanza, "astonishing
our thought," where the root stoniness of *astonishing* (given the Medusa
legend) accounts again for the unusual direct object. (Minerva's shield or
breastplate is sometimes adorned with the head of Medusa, by the way.)

Hollander's command of lexis is extraordinary but unobtrusive; no word, I
think, requires the dictionary, although many invite it. *Sky-eyed*, for instance
(st. 9), offers a very fine solution to the traditional epithet γλαυκῶπις, used of
Athena's and Minerva's eyes, and associated with her owl.[6] (See Gustav
Klimt's 1898 *Pallas Athene*, where the matched pairs of eyes, goddess's and
owl's, look out at the viewer from the same level.) *Sky-eyed* encompasses all
the different translations, "shining" or "flashing" and "blue-or-grey-or-
green-coloured," together with a sense of the widest scrutiny. Or see the
phrase, "patient agency" (st. 18): "With patient agency the beak and claws /
Of fierce sublime awareness pluck it clean. . . ." The root meaning of *patience*
(from Latin *patere*) is "to suffer," as in the passion of Christ. (Hence Eliot's
"We who were living are now dying / With a little patience" [*The Waste Land*,
pt. 5], and Adrienne Rich's "They said, *Have no patience*" ["Snapshots of a
Daughter-in-Law"].) In "Owl," it's the word *agency* that calls up this etymology. Patience modifies agency, not just grammatically, and not just in the
primary sense of *patience*. This agency of beak and claws knows what it is both
to do and to suffer, *agere et patere*, or, rather, suffers in the very doing. The
phrase quietly claims the widest scope for the fierce agency of owl wisdom.
We who experience its beak and claws occasionally are not likely to think of
this at the time.

Or, another effect, note the choice of rhyme words in the opening stanza, all four lines being enjambed, and all four end-words signifying something about enjambment: how it comes *between* the paces of our poetic walk, how we *wait* for meaning in the next step, meaning *unseen* until we round the curve of the poetic line, how we instinctively *interrogate* what waits for us after an enjambed line.

One small lexical parenthesis, about the phrase "the cold, freeing North" (third last st.). This could not be written quite as is by a Canadian poet, who would need to signal just how the word *freeing* is at work. I hear distracting echoes of "the true North strong and free" (national anthem), plus bits of argument about the mystic north, hard primitivism, and climatic theories. (The North is to Canadians much as the West is to Americans.) I also hear parodies, for example, "Make me over, Mother Nature. . . ."[7] It interests me that for some groups, although not for others, certain words in a poem need signaling — *green* for an Irish poet, I suppose, and so on.

There is not time to do justice to various matters of voice, so I shall just touch on two aspects:

1. "Voice" as tone (and so allied with what James Merrill wonderfully called "manners").[8] "Owl" is a didactic poem, although never we-versus-they, never "I thank Thee I am not as other creatures, even as these poor rodents." The poem erupts in wit from time to time (and who altogether trusts humorless didactic writing?), from the "laid-back south" with its erotic holly to my favorite, "Drunk with the Milky Way, our eyes / Are on the Wagon now." The Wagon as the Big Dipper would hardly do here — although come to think of it, dippers I've encountered dip water. By any name, of course, this constellation points to the Pole Star.

2. "Voice" as in the figure of birdsong for the voice of the poet. "Owl" is not of the majority party of songbirds (lark, thrush, etc.). But then, the division is not simple. For one thing, ornithologists define bird vocalizations by form and function, and so may well speak of owl hoots as "songs" (unless in fact they're alarm calls, flight calls, etc.). For another, as Hollander knows, songbirds can also sing lessons, and a lot more. (See, among many examples, Bishop's superbly troped song of the white-throated sparrow in "North Haven" (*"repeat, repeat, repeat; revise, revise, revise"*).

It is time to come to the remarkable figuration of the poem. I'll start with a general observation. "Owl" bears in the following way on the whole mimetic question of descriptive language as against figurative, what others might call the actual owl as against the troped or fabled owl. I am struck by the sharp sense of owlness in this poem. Hollander tropes chiefly on two characteristics of the order of owls, the Strigiformes, including the owl of Minerva, the European little owl, or *Athene noctua*, for those interested, as I was:[9] (1) the fact that most owls are awake and hunt at night, and (2) their unusual eyes, which are fixed in the front of the head, so that they "see only forward," compensating "for this limitation of field by being able, unlike other birds, to turn [the] head . . . backward."[10] The owl's eyes, that is, "take their head with them" (st. 4), as ours often do not, alas. "Owl" is not centered on the natural history of a creature, as perceived in a given time and place, yet for me the effect is to heighten awareness of the natural world, so that I find myself wanting to see an owl move its head again, just as I set about observing an actual waxing dusk after reading stanza 2.[11] Which is to say, the languages of the actual world and of the troped or fabled or emblematic world may be different (or more precisely, differentiated by us) but are not inimical. Painting the world as fabled does not cut us off from the natural world; it may even help us to see it, because, I suppose, it's true that "we're made so that we love / First when we see them painted, things we have passed / Perhaps a hundred times nor cared to see."[12]

I make the point for itself and also to extend it to the reading of fables and figures in relation to history. The temper of the times just now readily translates the mimesis of fable and figure into the mimesis of history, but not vice versa. I hear each informing the other.

I want to approach the remarkable figuration and fictive power of this poem by asking (as I often ask new poems) what surprises it offers. In a general way, it is full of surprises. Some smaller ones we take in stride, smiling, say, at the surprise of "merely charming" (used of the grumpy medieval owl). The surprise lies not so much in the usual puns on Latin *carmen* ("song") and on *charm* as "spell" or the double sense of *merely*, as in the thought of the poet John Hollander uttering such a phrase at all. (But then he also once said, "Cave canem, Watch out, I may sing.") The poem is full of such smaller surprises thanks to its own attentiveness: attentiveness to concepts, as for example, the concept of "fixity" (see st. 5), here defended against any knee-jerk adulation of words like *process*; the fine reminder in passing of "the mind's great heart" (also st. 5); and the precision of the term *inferences* (not *implications*) in "Squirming with the life of being / Inferences and notions" (st. 17). Attentiveness to scheme: say, the alliterative scheme of *ill-illumined* (st. 3), "badly lit," that is, but with an unusual sense of *badly*; "ill-ill-" says this compound, as if it were extracting the *ill* in *illumine*, and adding to the ululation of the echoic words *owl* and *howl*—and shall we ever slide over the word *illumine* so easily again? Or the scheme of echo in "*Keep knowing forth*" (third last st.), where the unusual wording makes us hear "going forth" or "showing forth," as if knowing involved both movement and manifesting. Wisdom itself involves movement etymologically, for all that, as the compound *lantern-wise* in stanza 4 reminds us, for *-wise* here is what remains today of the Old English word *wise* from the verb *wisian* ("to show the way, to make 'wise'").

But the poem's greater surprises take us past close reading and into larger matters. For me, they come in the movement of the central fable: in the relation of bird to prey, and of both to us. Here this didactic poem takes on unexpected emotional force. (I think, by the way, that the emotional force of indirection in Hollander's work is sometimes underread; we have almost forgotten what indirection is these days.) "Owl"'s greater surprises come right after the midpoint, with the question, "Where in day's vastnesses does truth reside?" Well, not so hard a question given all the earlier questioning of high noon. But who would have guessed that truth would be "with the poor blind prey / Trembling with prescience or cold / Waiting . . . ," and so on? Most of us would surely write this fable, casually attaching truth to wisdom, would we not? And the poem closes on this same conjunction, owl and prey, and on what *silences* might mean as part of a reply to this modern invocation, including the fact that a good poem comes to rest, not on dead silence, but on the live, resonating silence following a poem that does not leave with its last leaf.

As with all first-person fables or parables, the "I" or "we" becomes who-ever reads the poem, and readers will read their own interior and occasional owl of wisdom and poor blind prey each a little differently. As we shall read what we are at night each a little differently, but not so as to exclude the shadowed, unclear, darker parts of our entire selves and worlds: something of a dream-life, something of our less pleasant selves, something of eros and thanatos.

So read, the poem takes its place with all Hollander's work on shadows, shading, shades as ghosts, and especially memory, which is a constant subject and way of being in his work. (This owl speaks to the listener *and* the remem-berer [l.5]; it can see backward as well as forward; the poem itself sometimes make us read retrospectively [see ll. 6–7]; and the very root of Minerva's name is said to mean "memory" [one reason I can think of for using her rather than Athena].) "Keeping faith with," which is what the owl does (st. 5), turns up elsewhere in Hollander's work,[13] and the word *trembling* ('the poor blind prey / Trembling" [st. 15]) has a resonance throughout, from the recent poem "Arachne," where Athena herself trembles, back to an early poem called "The Fear of Trembling." The fear of the Lord is said to be the beginning of Wisdom, biblical wisdom, and I found myself asking what relation the owl of Minerva has to the great figure of Wisdom in the Old Testament as in the Hebrew Scriptures: Wisdom who plays before and dur-ing creation, Wisdom sought throughout the sapiental books. After all, Hol-lander's work began under the aegis of wisdom literature, with the finely troped title and epigraph of his first collection, *A Crackling of Thorns*, even if he did turn a little against the troping (as in the "cackling" of laurels), or rather move from wood and flame to kettle to pot (as in "The Mad Potter," but then, a potter is both a biblical figure and a near-anagram for a "troper" — see the headless Alice-in-Wonderland trope of the first stanza). Wisdom like shadow and memory is a constant in Hollander's work.[14] And biblical wisdom may just touch the owl's own language here, in *"knowing* [going/showing] *forth,"* where the mostly archaic word *forth* carries a biblical resonance. Not so much *going forth* (such phrasing is common in Shakespeare too) but rather *showing forth*, present in the 1611 English Bible (seven times in the Psalms ["Open thou my lips, and my mouth shall shew forth thy praise" (Ps. 51:15), etc.], twice in Isaiah, once in Proverbs and once in the New Testament), but absent altogether in Shakespeare.[15]

Then, too, the didactic that runs throughout Hollander's work as poet, essayist, and editor places him as if in a line of inheritance from the great rabbis, those for whom teaching was temperamentally congenial and some-thing more. The energy of the rabbinical strain works against any elegiac pull of the fable in "Owl," even if the owl of Minerva does take wing at dusk, and even if we widen this time between owl-light and darkness to a cultural dusk as well as an individual dusk. It seems to me that the fable does not turn out Hegelian, in that it stays on middle earth. Nor does it turn out Yeatsean. A Yeatsean movement would go back down to the laid-back south, in an Eros vision. I don't find here the up-and-down movement of an Eros-versus-heavenly-Logos vision, as, for example, in Yeats's "Dialogue of Self and Soul" or the end of "Vacillation." This a poem whose directives and directions are both important. Its turn northward and its movements along middle earth (st. 20: "Down-to-tree, then, if not -to-earth") are more like late Stevens, like the wisdom of the commonplace in "An Ordinary Evening in New Haven" or the northward gaze of "The Auroras of Autumn." Yet in the end they bring me back to the sapiental books, because I think I could make the case that Hollander's body of poems as a whole tropes on these books: Ecclesiastes, Proverbs, the Song of Songs. But this needs more thought.

As for our own historical and cultural moment, "Owl" speaks to it in more ways than one. Most obvious is the simple mention of the shadowed byways of wisdom when our maps show only information highways. Second, I have already mentioned our loss when we read fable by the light of history, and not history by the dark of fable. Third, there is the whole matter of attentiveness, which leads into our own cultural moment through some remarks by Geoffrey Hill in a 1986 interview:

INTERVIEWER: You have described reading a poem as "an act of passionate attention." But how many people are capable of bringing such attention to bear?

HILL: I think that nearly everyone is capable of passionate attention of some kind, but the nature of present-day culture is such that this passionate attention is devoted to things other than reading. A great deal of passionate attention goes into pigeon-fancying, fishing and model-railways. These admirable pursuits are regarded as bring worthy of passionate attention, at the same time as energy and devotion in the making or reading of poems is regarded as marginal and eccentric.[16]

Or, in a wider scope, here is Auden, quoted in Anthony Hecht's recent book on him: "Choice of attention — to attend to this and ignore that — is to the inner life what choice of action is to the outer. . . . As Ortega y Gasset said: 'Tell me to what you pay attention, and I will tell you who you are.' "[17] Which is one way of answering the owl's "Who?"

Finally, I want to end with "Owl" 's "execution highly wrought," for in its very execution, this poem exemplifies its own fable. As such, it is a standing rebuke to our current verbal slovenliness. As such, it tells us that aesthetic choices are in themselves moral choices, that rhetorical decisions are moral decisions.[18] Most of us stand convicted in our words of the sin of sloth. Hollander's fine little fable, like Auden's 1946 Phi Beta Kappa poem, offers a most necessary tract for the times.

NINETEEN

Teaching Poetry: Accurate Songs, or Thinking-in-Poetry

The logical faculty has infinitely more to do with Poetry than the Young and the inexperienced, whether writer or critic, ever dreams of.

— WILLIAM WORDSWORTH[1]

What makes the new poetry so bad is its failure to realize that there is no sound poetry without intelligence.

— JAMES WRIGHT[2]

[T]he evil of thinking as poetry is not the same thing as the good of thinking in poetry.

— WALLACE STEVENS[3]

Suppose we reverse things. Instead of asking how we can teach poetry, suppose we ask how it can teach us. What might we learn from Wallace Stevens, for example, about the art to which he was devoted — was "faithful," to use his word? Some of Stevens's lessons are so advanced that only the best poets and critics will recognize them. But he can also teach us something obvious yet perhaps startling: that thinking matters crucially when we read good poetry. Again and again, he emphasizes this, as do others, for example, Wordsworth and James Wright in my first two epigraphs. Here is Stevens, offering advice to a young writer and friend:

> True, the desire to read is an insatiable desire and you must read. Nevertheless, you must also think. . . . [T]here is no passion like the passion of thinking which grows stronger as one grows older, even though one never thinks anything of any particular interest to anyone else. Spend an hour or two a day even if in the beginning you are staggered by the confusion and aimlessness of your thoughts.

(*L*, 513)

We need to remember this when we hear Stevens saying, "The poem must resist the intelligence / Almost successfully" (*CP*, 350). *Resist*, not ignore or flee. *Almost* successfully, but not altogether successfully. How long was Stephen Hawking's *A Brief History of Time* on the best-seller list? And why was this, if not that people were hungry to know, to think about, what physicists make of our universe? At 26, Stevens noted "the capable, the marvellous, poetic language; and the absence of poetic thought. . . . We get plenty of moods (and like them, wherever we get them). . . . But it's the mind we want to fill" (*L*, 92). At 65, he wrote that "supreme poetry can be produced only on the highest possible level of the cognitive" (*L*, 500).

As a long-term goal in teaching Stevens, or teaching any poetry, I like to show how all good poetry requires thinking. This means combating several stereotypes: first, the stereotype where thinking is what you do in mathematics or the physical and biological sciences or philosophy or psychology; second, the stereotype of an easy division between thinking and feeling, where poetry is assigned to feeling, and judgments about feeling go unexamined; third, the stereotype where poetry is divided between "content" (associated with thought, themes, arguments that are *already in existence*) and "form" (associated with ornament, purple passages, hyperbole, etc., that "express" what is already in existence); fourth, the stereotypes that prevent too many people from simply enjoying art, and this includes the enjoyment of thinking about it. I'll say a word or two about these long-term goals before some particular remarks about Stevens in the classroom.

1. Let's start with the atmosphere in which most teachers of literature work. Here's how Northrop Frye described it in 1975, and it doesn't seem to have changed much since. Teachers of literature are

> harassed and bedeviled by the dismal sexist symbology surrounding the humanities which [they meet] everywhere, even in the university itself, from freshman classes to the president's office. This symbology . . . says that the sciences, especially the physical sciences, are rugged, aggressive, out in the world doing things, and so symbolically male, whereas the literatures are narcissistic, intuitive, fanciful, staying at home and making the home more beautiful but not doing anything really serious, and are therefore symbolically female. They are, however, leisure-class females, and have to be attended by a caste of ladies' maids who prepare them for

public appearance, and who are the teachers and critics of literature
in schools and universities.[4]

The tendency to assign thinking, serious thinking, to any subject but the arts
or humanities is all part of this. So are fallacies of accuracy. I used to say,
"Words are not as accurate as numbers," until it struck me that this was a
meaningless statement. For what did I mean by *accurate*? I meant accurate as
in 2 + 2 = 4. So all I was really saying was that words are not accurate in the
same way that numbers are accurate, which is not exactly news. It may sound
odd to use the word *accurate* in connection with poetry, but it was Stevens's
word: "My dame, sing for this person accurate songs" (*Notes Toward a Supreme Fiction* 1.9). And Proust once observed: "In literature 'almost-parallel'
lines are not worth drawing. Water (given certain conditions) boils at 100
degrees. At 98, at 99 the phenomenon does not occur. It is better, therefore,
to abstain"[5] — if, that is, the author can't get it exactly right. Getting something just right in a poem: this can produce as much pleasure and knowledge
as getting something just right in baseball. Getting just the right spin on a
word or a group of words.

Baseball may help. Logically considered, it makes less sense than poetry.
Grown men taking a stick of wood to a small object, and racing against a set
of arbitrary rules? But it's intensely human, this exercise of physical and
mental skill, and beautiful to watch when seemingly preternatural ability
looks effortless. We know from our own softball games how gifted those
major-league players are, and good commentators help us realize this. So
with poetry. We all use words. Still, there's not much to encourage us to use
them really well, let alone play games with them or write occasional poems. If
we played softball games with words, and also regularly heard the major-
league word-players, with good commentators. . . . It's a nice thought. And
nobody supposes for a moment that baseball players don't think, even if they
don't think in philosophical concepts or chemical numbers. They think in
baseball: thinking-in-baseball, we might call it. Thinking-in-poetry is what
poets do.

Movies may help too, except that there are so many third-rate ones
around. We have higher standards in baseball by far. But movies have the
advantage of being one art form that students are relaxed about and will
reflect on. That includes questions of technique. Why this shot and not that
one? What precisely makes Griffith or Chaplin or Renoir or Hitchcock or X,

Y, Z so good? I've watched a number of student films from a very good film school. You can trace the progress in learning the mechanics of filmmaking. But the real challenge is different. It's *thinking*, imaginative thinking. It's avoiding the pitfalls of novelty or hyperbole or overambitious claptrap. It has to do with a sense of proportion, a sense of shaping. It has to do with attention, passionate attention, to details. It has to do with an active, examining, alive self, a thinking self, as against the passive self who just accepts without thinking whatever it's fed by the TV or movie or computer screen.

2. As for thinking and feeling, there is one great hazard in separating them. We are accustomed to rigor and discipline in thinking. We prize it, we strive for it. But we usually do not think of rigor or discipline in connection with feeling. Our terminology for speaking of the emotions can be reduced to notions like "expression" and "suppression." As if these were the only alternatives or indeed were simple matters. Worse, "expression," any expression, becomes a good in itself, in the ignorant antipuritanism of pop psychology. What happens, T. S. Eliot asked, when our feelings are separated from our thinking, and both from our senses, so that the three function in different compartments? What happens to our capacity to feel? To use our senses? To think? "Instead of thinking with our feelings . . . we corrupt our feelings with ideas; we produce the public, the political, the emotional idea, evading sensation and thought. . . . Mr. Chesterton's brain swarms with ideas; I see no evidence that it thinks."[6]

3. As for content and form, the first time that the content-form metaphor turns up in a class, I stop things. Time to examine this metaphor, which is nearly always based on a container-and-contained model. "Content" is the milk or beer or important substance, what sometimes gets wrongly called the "philosophy" of A or B. (Here insert growls from good philosophers and good poets alike.) "Content" can be poured into all kinds of containers. The container or form is just what's convenient or pretty. One way to shake up this stereotype is to remember an Aristotelian notion of form, as in: the form of an oak tree is contained in an acorn. The form of an adult is contained in an infant. Form suddenly becomes something vital in these examples of the oak tree or the human being. Similarly with poems.

4. Enjoying, and this includes enjoying thinking. Here is where I usually start when teaching Stevens, in order to get students to relax with the work. Just listening to poems can help. I read myself or else play a record of Stevens

reading. What poems? There are poems of immediate sense appeal, there are funny poems, there are quirky poems, there are protest poems. Try a few of the early Florida poems: "Nomad Exquisite," "Indian River," "Fabliau of Florida." You could include "Frogs Eat Butterflies . . ." or an early seashore poem, "Hibiscus on the Sleeping Shores." You could illustrate what Stevens is *not* doing by reading a bit of the hilarious mock-poem "Le Bouquet" from *Bowl, Cat and Broomstick* (*OP,* 174). "Six Significant Landscapes," no. 6, is funny, centers on suggestive analogy, curves itself on the page like its theme, and uses the familiar hat metaphor. (Putting on your thinking cap. Putting on x hat for x job.) It can also start a class thinking about thinking. There are other possible groupings, a seasonal one, for example. A *New York Times* column once claimed that nobody wrote poems about February. Is that so? See Stevens's "Poésie Abrutie." Other possibilities would be river and seashore poems, starry-night poems, poems of ghosts and shades, love poems, and so on.

Any one of these groups will lead on to later work, and thereby show how Stevens enlarges his subjects as he goes on. Stevens's great river or seashore poems would include the challenging poem "The Idea of Order at Key West," as well as "Somnambulisma" and the intensely moving poem of Stevens's late years "The River of Rivers in Connecticut." But all this comes later.

Enjoying includes the pleasure we take in exactness. As for example, why this word and not that one? W. H. Auden is said to have given his students an exercise in which he blanked out several words in a poem they didn't know and asked them to fill in the blanks. I regularly use this exercise myself. (You have to play fair, keeping enough key words.) It's fun to look for poems that use different effects. For example, "Nomad Exquisite," with its utterly unexpected alligator. Or the third section of "Someone Puts a Pineapple Together," with its dozen one-line pineapple likenesses. Or "The Plain Sense of Things," especially the start of stanza 4. (Here the surprise is not in a single word or a fresh metaphor but in the force of logic.) This exercise helps to show readers their own presuppositions and sometimes their stock responses. (There's a handy essay by I. A. Richards on stock responses,[7] and see also Christopher Ricks's opening chapter in his *T. S. Eliot and Prejudice.*)[8]

All this can lead to the pleasure of dictionary exercises, the best dictionary by far being the generous multivolume *Oxford English Dictionary.* For any assigned poem, all students should know precise lexical meanings. For key words, they should pay attention to all the information in the *OED*: the word-root, cognates, and especially usage as in the illustrative quotations. These last help to give the connotations or associations of words, which are just as important as denotations. And we need to remember that poets help make dictionaries; they don't just follow them. On Stevens's unusual words, there's a useful essay by R. P. Blackmur.[9] There's also Stevens's own wonderful remark: "Personally, I like words to sound wrong" (*L*, 340). He did like throwing curveballs.

From enjoyment, to single words, to combinations of words. (And actually words in a poem never exist in isolation but always in relation.) Yeats once wrote that he only began to make a language to his liking when he sought a "powerful and passionate syntax."[10] Watching sentence structure, our own and others, is always instructive. (Students may need a little teaching about basic grammar if their schools have deprived them of it — which is like depriving math students of the multiplication table.)

Here's one exercise that's fun. Consider James Merrill's observation about writing workshops:

> Last winter I visited a workshop in which only one out of fifteen poets had noticed that he needn't invariably use the first-person present active indicative. Poem after poem began: "I empty my glass . . . I go out . . . I stop by woods . . ." For me a "hot" tense like that can't be handled for very long without cool pasts and futures to temper it. Or some complexity of syntax, or a modulation into the conditional — *something*. An imperative, even an auxiliary verb, can do wonders. Otherwise, you get this addictive self-centered immediacy, harder to break oneself of than cigarettes. That kind of talk (which, by the way, is purely literary; it's never heard in life unless from foreigners or four-year-olds) calls to mind a speaker suspicious of words. . . . He'll never notice "Whose woods these are I think I know" gliding backwards through the room, or "Longtemps je me suis couché de bonne heure" plumping a cushion invitingly at her side.[11]

Exercise: test this in Stevens. And yes, there are surprisingly few first-person present active indicatives, one being in the third of the "Six Significant Landscapes." But then, Stevens does seem to be saying something Merrill-like to the "I" who talks this way. (See the ants.) From here, students can go on to think about person in Stevens. Who *are* "we" and "he" and, and? (Students might think about the use of all those at-first-anonymous *he*'s and *she*'s in modern short stories in contrast to the properly introduced *he*'s and *she*'s in nineteenth-century fiction.) There are also matters of verb tense, active and passive voice, grammatical moods, and so on.

Of course, there's much more, and especially the large question of rhythm. Hearing poetry read aloud helps to develop the ear, and this should continue throughout a course. Students often don't hear the rhythms of poetry — of a phrase, a line, a stanza. (John Hollander's lively and instructive *Rhyme's Reason* is invaluable for this.)[12] Try reading "The River of Rivers in Connecticut" or the first two stanzas of "Credences of Summer."

Sooner or later, the question of feeling will come up, often in the form of feeling versus thought or ideas. "Domination of Black," an extraordinary early poem, is a useful case in point. Here is what Stevens said about it, as he directed the reader away from "ideas": "I am sorry that a poem of this sort has to contain any ideas at all, because its sole purpose is to fill the mind with the images & sounds that it contains. . . . You are supposed to get heavens full of the colors and full of sounds, and *you are supposed to feel as you would feel if you actually got all this*" (L, 251; emphasis added). Teachers could try blanking out the word *afraid* at the end of the poem, and asking students to surmise what feeling they are "supposed to feel." And then to work out just how we know that such a feeling has developed rather than, say, a "delightful evening" feeling. (Stevens, in fact, wrote a funny poem under that title.) Students might also be interested in thinking about different kinds of fear. See especially the six different sentences offered by Wittgenstein, all using the clause "I am afraid," together with his comment: "To each of these sentences a special tone of voice is appropriate, and a different context."[13]

Or take the feeling of rage, and the word *rage*. Take also the word *order*, and do a dictionary exercise with both these words. Consider likely rhythms for matters of rage and of order. Likely subjects, likely settings, other poetry on these two subjects. (Try Shakespeare, via a concordance.) Then turn to "The Idea of Order at Key West," beginning with the title.

Tracing the line of thought in a poem is always necessary, and should become a matter of course, just as hearing the rhythm, hearing the sentence structure, hearing the range of diction, hearing the exact form of verb and pronoun, and so on, should become matters of course. Even if a poem has a minimal line of thought, we should register this (*x* is a minimal-thought poem, working with *abc*). Everyone is suspicious of paraphrases, but such suspicion should not banish the ever-useful précis, which should be tested, every word, against the actual words of the poem. Is it adequate? (Given that it's never meant to be a substitute for the poem.) Should it be modified? How? (Where I live, students used to be trained in the invaluable art of writing a précis. That has mostly gone, so that some students have trouble following an argument, and hence of recognizing what's at stake, if anything.)

See, for example, the implicit argument in "Tea at the Palaz of Hoon" (*CP*, 65):

> Not less because in purple I descended
> The western day through what you called
> The loneliest air, not less was I myself.

"Not less was I myself"? Why say this? What's the logic? The day and the place ("The western day," "there") will turn out to be extraordinary, but why this opening response? Has someone said, "You were less yourself that day"? Do we ourselves say, "I was less myself that day"? No, the usual expression is simply, "I wasn't myself that day," period. That's how we often take care of extraordinary days and experiences, ones that don't fit into our regular routine, ones that are better (or worse) than usual. And so we guard ourselves against our other selves, the other better (or worse) selves. Not so Stevens. This means he can go on to say: "And there I found myself more truly and more strange."

Stevens talked about how we all carry within us a trunkful of characters (*L*, 91). "Hoon" was his strange, true, sublime self (early style), and he was not about to say, "I wasn't myself the day I had tea at the palaz of Hoon — or maybe was Hoon himself, serving tea." (For poetry as tea, see his lovely little poem "Tea.") And so we learn to think a bit before we say, "I wasn't myself that day." Weren't we, now?

Thinking extends to the logic of figures. Take, for example, angels. "Am I not, / Myself, only half of a figure of a sort . . . ?" asks Stevens's late angel, in a wicked pun ("Angel Surrounded by Paysans" [*CP*, 496]). There are angels galore in Stevens, a far better selection than the impoverished angels of modern movies, those broadly comic figures with standard properties attached — haloes and wings, "tepid aureoles," said Stevens of such haloes.

"Tepid"? "I suppose that I shall feel sorry about paysans and tepid by the time this reaches you but they suit me very well today," Stevens wrote to a journal editor (*L*, 650). "Tepid" is fine for a bath sometimes, but not for a cup of tea and not for most feelings and not for churches. (See Revelation, the last book of the Bible: "So then because thou art lukewarm, and neither cold nor hot, I will spue thee out of my mouth" [3.16].) An aureole or halo ought to be glowing, gold, or white-hot surely. A halo that is lukewarm to the touch is a property rejected by Stevens's necessary angel.

There are early angels in Stevens, but he is mostly anxious to shed them. "Trees, like serafin" is a simile in "Sunday Morning" (*CP*, 66), as if the highest order of angels, the seraphim, were being explained away in naturalistic terms. And sure enough, in "Evening Without Angels" (*CP*, 136), Stevens is explicit:

> Why seraphim like lutanists arranged
> Above the trees? And why the poet as
> Eternal *chef d'orchestre*?

It is "light / That fosters seraphim and is to them / Coiffeur of haloes, fecund jeweller." Stevens is still fighting the same battle. "Sad men made angels of the sun. . . ." For him, "Bare earth is best. Bare, bare, / Except for our own houses." The reasoning is clear, and the type of argument is common enough.

At some point, Stevens decided not to fight angels but to reimagine them. After all, they do seem to have appealed to the human imagination for a long time. Rather than lopping off angels and demons — which leaves their force in the hands of others — why not reinvent them? "Bare earth" is fine, but no angelic equivalents at all? This is poverty, Stevens came to think. And so they start to return, the angels, most remarkably in 1942 in *Notes Toward a Supreme Fiction*: the tired angels, the goatish angels, the angel on a pond in a park, the angel in the name of Nanzia Nunzio, the capital-*A* Angel who listens to Stevens, the Miltonic angel who leaps downward and never lands, the angels whose functions Stevens takes over in the end. *Notes* is for advanced students, although teachers might like to try one or two cantos with junior students; Nanzia Nunzio is lots of fun.

Then there is the later "Angel Surrounded by Paysans" (1949), where Stevens invents "the angel of reality . . . the necessary angel of earth." He liked this angel well enough to use it as a title for his collected essays in 1951. Here is his comment on the creature: "in Angel Surrounded by Paysans the angel is the angel of reality. This is clear only if the reader is of the idea that we live in a world of the imagination, in which reality and contact with it are the great blessings. For nine readers out of ten, the necessary angel will appear to be the angel of the imagination and for nine days out of ten that is true, although it is the tenth day that counts" (*L*, 753).

Students often find it nearly impossible to read this angel without turning it into its contrary: an angel of imagination, after all, and an angel of heaven, after all. Our habits of thinking about all this are deeply ingrained. It takes discipline of thought to be able to imagine an angel of reality. Or discipline of imagination to be able to think of an angel of reality.

Either way, we hear Stevens writing accurate songs. We hear thinking-in-poetry. We understand more fully how Stevens can write that "the evil of thinking as poetry is not the same thing as the good of thinking in poetry" (*NA*, 165).

Reference Matter

Owl

John Hollander

Now that the owl-light — in the time between
Dog and wolf, as some call it — ends, we wait
    As you alight on an unseen
        Branch to interrogate

The listener and the rememberer;
Lost outlines heighten — as last colors fade —
    The sounder darkness you confer
        Upon the spruce's shade.

Deluded by the noonlight's wide display
Of everything, our vision floats through thin
    Spaces of ill-illumined day:
        How we are taken in

By what we take in with our roving eyes!
Your constant ones, if moved to track or trace,
    Take their head with them, lantern-wise
        Taking heed, keeping face

In the society of night, and keeping
Faith with the spirit of pure fixity
    That sets the mind's great heart to leaping
        At what you more than see.

Medusa's visage gazed our bodies to
Literal stone unshaded: your face, caught
    In our glance widely eyes us through,
        Astonishing our thought.

You who debated with the nightingale
The rectitude of northern wisdom, cold
    Against the love-stuff of the tale
        The laid-back south had told;

And yet who stood amid the lovely, thick
Leaves of the ivy, while in all their folly
    The larks and thrushes sought the prick
        And berries of the holly;

You who confounded the rapacious crow
Thus to be favored by the great sky-eyed
    Queen of the air and all who know,
        Now ever by her side;

With silent wing and interrogative
Cry in lieu of a merely charming song,
    You sound the dark in which you live
        Perched above right and wrong.

Resonance is not vacancy: although
He could hear nothing in your hollow howls
    But woe and his own guilt, Thoreau
        Rejoiced that there were owls.

Scattered and occasional questionings
With here and there too late a warning shout,
    Wisdom arises on the wings
        Of darkness and of doubt.

Where in day's vastnesses does truth reside?
In noon's uncompromising light and heat
    When even our own shadows hide
        Under our very feet?

Or in the hidden center of the quick
Resilient dark on which your narrowed sight
    So pointedly alights to pick
        Not the day, but the night,

Its fruitful flower, petaled a hundredfold?
Oh it is there, truth, with the poor blind prey

Trembling with prescience or cold
　　Waiting for how your way

Of well-tuned suddenness and certitude
Tight-strung and execution highly wrought
　　Leads to the pounced-on object, food
　　　　For something beyond thought,

By overlooking nothing, overseeing
In all the stillness hidden, tiny motions
　　Squirming with the life of being
　　　　Inferences and notions.

With patient agency the beak and claws
Of fierce sublime awareness pluck it clean
　　Deriving what for us are laws
　　　　Governing the unseen.

Under torn canvas we put out to sea
Trusting, though puzzled by what glows above,
　　To something like philosophy
　　　　To be the helmsman of

Life (but whose life?). Your lessons of the land,
Down-to-tree, then, if not -to-earth, indict
　　Our helplessness to understand
　　　　Just what we are at night.

Immensities of starlight told us lies
Of what and where we are; but, we allow,
　　Drunk with the Milky Way, our eyes
　　　　Are on the Wagon now,

Fugitive slaves, leaving despair for dread
As if in search of the cold, freeing North,
　　Keep gazing steadily ahead
　　　　Keep on Keep knowing forth

You urge us, as your silences address
The power that Minerva chose you for:
　　Great-winged, far-ranging consciousness
　　　　Now come to rest in your

Olympian attentiveness that finds
The affrighted heartbeat on the ground, perceives
   The flutter of substances, the mind's
      Life in the fallen leaves.

Notes

ABBREVIATIONS

CP   *The Collected Poems of Wallace Stevens* (New York: Knopf, 1954)

L   *The Letters of Wallace Stevens* (New York: Knopf, 1966)

L&S   C. T. Lewis and C. Short, *A Latin Dictionary* (Oxford: Clarendon Press, 1879)

NA   Wallace Stevens, *The Necessary Angel: Essays on Reality and the Imagination* (New York: Knopf, 1951)

Notes   Wallace Stevens, *Notes Toward a Supreme Fiction*

OED   *The Oxford English Dictionary*

OP   Wallace Stevens, *Opus Posthumous (1957)*, rev. ed., ed. Milton J. Bates (New York: Knopf, 1977)

SP   Holly Stevens, *Souvenirs and Prophecies: The Young Wallace Stevens* (New York: Knopf, 1977)

FOREWORD

1. Stephen Jay Gould, "For Want of a Metaphor," in *The Flamingo's Smile: Reflections in Natural History* (New York: Norton, 1985), 151.

2. Oliver Sacks, *The Man Who Mistook His Wife for a Hat and Other Clinical Tales* (New York: Harper & Row, 1987), 87.

3. Richard Wilbur, "The Bottles Become New, Too," *Quarterly Review of Literature* 7 (1953): 189.

4. Paul Cézanne, 26 Sept. 1897, in *Letters*, ed. John Rewald (London: Bruno Cassirer, 1941), 261.

5. James Merrill, *Recitative: Prose by James Merrill*, ed. J. D. McClatchy (San Francisco: North Point Press, 1986), 60.

6. Geoffrey Hill, *The Lords of Limit: Essays on Literature and Ideas* (New York: Oxford University Press, 1984), 2.

7. Václav Havel, from a speech of 25 July 1989, trans. A. G. Brain, *New York Review of Books*, 18 Jan. 1990. "The Power of the Powerless" is in Havel's *Living in Truth*, ed. Jan Vladislav (London: Faber & Faber, 1986), 36–122.

INTRODUCTION

1. Northrop Frye, *The Anatomy of Criticism: Four Essays* (Princeton: Princeton University Press, 1957). In what follows, I have drawn on my essay "Anatomies and Confessions: Northrop Frye and Contemporary Theory," *Recherches sémiotiques/ Semiotic Inquiry* 13, no. 3 (1993): 13–22.

2. As the subtitle is the only remnant of the original title, its mendacity is all the more interesting. Frye's original and preferred title was "Structural Poetics: Four Essays." See John Ayre, *Northrop Frye: A Biography* (Toronto: Random House, 1989), 252–54.

3. The introduction begins with a revised version of Frye's essay "The Function of Criticism at the Present Time," *University of Toronto Quarterly* 19 (1949): 1–16; the title is from Arnold.

4. Frye's 1986 remark from a review of Paul de Man should be read alongside his remark on the isolated work of art: "All dominant ideologies are structures of author-ity, and, unless they are merely tyrannies enforced by terror, they are aesthetic struc-tures as well." "In the Earth, or in the Air?" review of *The Rhetoric of Romanticism*, by Paul de Man, *Times Literary Supplement*, 17 Jan. 1986, 51–52.

5. See Raymond Williams, "Base and Superstructure in Marxist Cultural The-ory," in his *Problems in Materialism and Culture: Selected Essays* (London: Verso, 1980), 31–49. I am being a little mischievous; Frye and Williams start from different as-sumptions. But the similar areas of detachment and concern (Frye's terms) are worth noting.

6. Hill, "Lives of the Poets," *Essays in Criticism* 34 (1984): 265.

I. ELIOT, KEYNES, AND EMPIRE

1. Hugh Kenner, "The Urban Apocalypse," in *Eliot in His Time: Essays on the Occasion of the Fiftieth Anniversary of "The Waste Land,"* ed. A. Walton Litz (Princeton: Princeton University Press, 1973), 23–49; quotation at 35.

2. See, e.g., *The Divine Comedy*, trans. J. A. Carlyle and P. H. Wicksteed (New York: Modern Library, 1932), *Paradiso* 27, n. 11.

3. "Virgil and the Christian World," broadcast from London, 9 Sept. 1951, re-printed in *T. S. Eliot: Selected Prose*, ed. John Hayward (Harmondsworth, Eng.: Pen-guin Books, 1953), 97.

4. And perhaps earlier. "I hope to get started on a poem I have in mind" (Eliot to John Quinn, 5 Nov. 1919); he hopes "to write a long poem I have had on my mind for a long time" (Eliot to his mother, 18 Dec. 1919); quoted in *The Waste Land: A Facsimile and Transcript of the Original Drafts including the Annotations of Ezra Pound*, ed. Valerie Eliot (London: Faber & Faber, 1971), xviii.

5. T. S. Eliot in the *Transatlantic Review* 1 (Jan. 1924): 95.

6. T. S. Eliot in the *International Journal of Ethics* 27 (1916): 117.

7. Stephen Spender, *T. S. Eliot* (New York: Viking Press, 1975), 117–18.

8. T. S. Eliot in the *Criterion* 2 (1924): 491. H. Stuart Hughes, *Oswald Spengler: A Critical Estimate* (New York: Scribner, 1962).

9. T. S. Eliot, "A Sceptical Patrician," *Athenaeum* (23 May 1919): 361–62. On the use in "Gerontion" of material from the beginning of ch. 18 of *The Education of Henry Adams*, see F. O. Matthiessen, *The Achievement of T. S. Eliot*, 3d ed. (London: Oxford University Press, 1958), 73.

10. T. S. Eliot, "Kipling Redivivus," *Athenaeum* (9 May 1919): 297–98. For the 1941 essay, see *A Choice of Kipling's Verse*, made by T. S. Eliot, with an essay by Rudyard Kipling (London: Faber & Faber, 1941).

11. T. S. Eliot in the *Little Review* 5 (1918): 46.

12. T. S. Eliot, *The Waste Land*, ed. Valerie Eliot, xviii; the two quotations are from letters of 20 Feb. to Eliot's mother.

13. And for that matter, in "Gerontion," although "Gerontion" was ready for publication on 25 May 1919 (*The Waste Land*, ed. Valerie Eliot, xvi) and Keynes wrote his book in Aug.–Sept. 1919 (Roy Harrod, *The Life of John Maynard Keynes* [London: Macmillan, 1951], 288). Quotations from *The Economic Consequences of the Peace* are from the first U.S. edition (New York: Harcourt, Brace, & Howe, 1920), 5–6, 7, 32, 56, 64, 48, 49, 51, 297. Later references are to 33, 5, 268.

Keynes was fond of poetry and was reading *The Waste Land* soon after its first appearance in the October 1922 issue of the *Criterion*. Sir Roy Harrod remembers "coming into his rooms in the autumn of 1922, to find that he was reading aloud *The Waste Land* by T. S. Eliot, a poet of whom I had so far not heard. His reading was intelligent and moving, and served to win one's admiration for this strange new form of expression" (*Life of John Maynard Keynes*, 29). Early in 1923, Keynes, as the new chairman of the board of the *Nation* and *Athenaeum*, strongly supported Eliot for the position of literary editor, against much opposition from fellow directors (Michael Holroyd, *Lytton Strachey: A Critical Biography* [New York: Holt, Rinehart & Winston, 1967–68], 2: 368–89). I do not know when Eliot first met Keynes; Clive Bell recalls first meeting Eliot in 1916 when he came for dinner to Gordon Square, where Bell was living with Keynes, but Keynes was out that evening (Clive Bell, *Old Friends* [London: Chatto & Windus, 1956], 119).

14. Eliot, *The Waste Land*, ed. Valerie Eliot, xii.

15. Holroyd, *Lytton Strachey*, 2: 365. Recent work by David Bradshaw shows that Eliot had read Major C. H. Douglas's social credit theories of monetary reform by 24 March 1920. "His book is interesting, but fearfully difficult and obscurely written," Eliot wrote. See David Bradshaw, "T. S. Eliot and the Major: Sources of Literary Anti-Semitism in the 1930s," *Times Literary Supplement*, 5 July 1996, 14–16, which goes on to consider Douglas's influence on Eliot, including the influence of his anti-Semitism, evident by 1922.

16. Ezra Pound quoted by William Empson, *Essays in Criticism* 22 (1972): 419.

17. Cleanth Brooks, in *Modern Poetry and the Tradition*, reprinted in *The Waste Land: A Casebook*, ed. C. B. Cox and Arnold P. Hinchcliffe (London: Macmillan, 1968), 136.

18. The perennial power of money and the craft of bartering are central themes in both *The Golden Bowl* and *Heart of Darkness*.

19. Spender, *T. S. Eliot*, 118. On the "present decay of eastern Europe" that Eliot perceived (head note to pt. 5 of the notes to *The Waste Land*), see, e.g., Keynes, *Economic Consequences of the Peace*, 4: "But perhaps it is only in England (and America) that it is possible to be so unconscious. In continental Europe the earth heaves and no one but is aware of the rumblings. There it is not just a matter of extravagance or 'labor troubles'; but of life and death, of starvation and existence, and of the fearful convulsions of a dying civilization." Or ibid., 250n.: "For months past, the reports of the health conditions in the Central Empires have been of such a character that the imagination is dulled, and one almost seems guilty of sentimentality in quoting them. But their general veracity is not disputed."

20. St. Augustine, *The City of God*, trans. Henry Bettenson, ed. David Knowles (Harmondsworth, Eng.: Penguin Books, 1972); all quotations in English are from this edition.

21. Spender, *T. S. Eliot*, 121–22.

22. Northrop Frye (who calls Eliot's poem "intensely Latin") mentions the symbolism of fishing in the Gospels in connection with *The Waste Land* (*T. S. Eliot* [Edinburgh: Oliver & Boyd, 1963], 67, 71).

23. Joachim du Bellay, *Défense et illustration de la langue française* (1549), bk. 2, ch. 8.

24. Augustine, *De civitate Dei*, ed. J. E. C. Welldon (New York: Macmillan, 1924).

25. On the theme of *peregrinatio*, the status of a *peregrinus*, and his sense of exile, see Peter Brown, *Augustine of Hippo* (Berkeley: University of California Press, 1967), 323–34.

2. SCHEMES AGAINST COERCION

1. Geoffrey Hill, "Poetry as 'Menace' and 'Atonement,'" in his *The Lords of Limit: Essays on Literature and Ideas* (Oxford: Oxford University Press, 1984), 2.

2. W. K. Wimsatt, "One Relation of Rhyme to Reason," in his *The Verbal Icon: Studies in the Meaning of Poetry* (Louisville: University of Kentucky Press, 1954), 152–66.

3. Note also the following observation about *abidance*: "An instance of the Romance vb. -affix -*ance*: — L. -*antia*, added to an Eng. vb. in imitation of such words as *subsidence, observance, continuance*, which are adoptions of actual or possible Fr. words" (*OED*, s.v. *abidance*).

4. T. S. Eliot in the *Times Literary Supplement*, 27 Sept. 1928; quoted in Christopher Ricks, *The Force of Poetry* (Oxford: Oxford University Press, 1984), 342 n. 48.

5. John Hollander, *Melodious Guile: Fictive Pattern in Poetic Language* (New Haven: Yale University Press, 1988), 6.

6. Richard Wilbur, "The Bottles Become New, Too," *Quarterly Review of Literature* 7 (1953): 191.

7. Roman Jakobson, *Language in Literature* (Cambridge, Mass.: Harvard University Press, 1987), 82, 81.

8. The introductory notes are one, or two, or one or two. The verbal equivalents do give five notes, though: "Old (poor) Sam (Bill, Tom) Peabody, Peabody, Peabody" or "Sweet sweet (Hard times) Canada Canada Canada."

9. I often hear fewer or more than five notes, and one excellent observer on the Ottawa River said the autumn song was regularly short. See Malcolm Macdonald, *The Birds of Brewery Creek* (London: Oxford University Press, 1947), 293–94.

10. Roger Pasquier, *Watching Birds: An Introduction to Ornithology* (Boston: Houghton Mifflin, 1977), 112. See also Christopher Leahy, *The Birdwatcher's Companion* (New York: Hill & Wang, 1982): "Different geographical races often sing distinctive variations of the basic song of their species — one often hears birdwatchers from out of state say, 'That doesn't sound like our Song Sparrow.' . . . relatively subtle individual variations of the 'basic' song seem to be more the rule than the exception" (660–61).

11. Moschus, "The Lament for Bion," ll. 99–105, in *The Greek Bucolic Poets*, trans. J. M. Edmonds, Loeb ed. (Cambridge, Mass.: Harvard University Press, 1960), 453.

12. Pasquier, *Watching Birds*, 112–13.

3. FABLES OF WAR IN ELIZABETH BISHOP

1. Adapted from Ben Jonson, "To the Reader," on Shakespeare.

2. See Elizabeth Bishop, *One Art: Letters*, ed. Robert Giroux (New York: Farrar, Straus & Giroux, 1994), 36–39, and David Kalstone, *Becoming a Poet: Elizabeth Bishop with Marianne Moore and Robert Lowell* (New York: Farrar, Straus & Giroux, 1989), 42, 55–56.

3. *Recitative: Prose by James Merrill*, ed. J. D. McClatchy (San Francisco: North Point Press, 1986), 22.

4. See, however, Victoria Harrison, *Elizabeth Bishop's Poetics of Intimacy* (Cambridge: Cambridge University Press, 1993), 77–79, and passim.

5. Kalstone, *Becoming a Poet*, 45.

6. Marcel Proust, *La Prisonnière*, vol. 6 of *A la recherche du temps perdu* (1923; Paris: Gallimard, 1954), 95: ". . . turns their slates iridescent like a pigeon's throat."

7. Emily Dickinson, *The Complete Poems of Emily Dickinson*, ed. Thomas H. Johnson (Boston: Little, Brown, 1960), 675. (Johnson's numbering is standard for Dickinson's poems.)

8. I am indebted to the Canadian historian J. L. Granatstein for this information.

9. Bishop, *One Art: Letters*, 38.

10. Elizabeth Bishop, letter to Marianne Moore, 4 Feb. 1936, quoted in Lorrie Goldensohn, *Elizabeth Bishop: The Biography of a Poetry* (New York: Columbia University Press, 1991), 156.

11. See Susan Schweik, *A Gulf So Deeply Cut: American Women Poets and the Second World War* (Madison: University of Wisconsin Press, 1991), 213–41.

12. Quoted in Samuel Hynes, *The Auden Generation: Literature and Politics in the 1930s* (Princeton: Princeton University Press, 1972, 1976), 176.

13. Ibid., 193.

14. Bishop, *One Art: Letters*, 55–56.

15. Kalstone, *Becoming a Poet*, 35.

16. *Surreal*, from a critic, is often a word of bewilderment rather than a precise term having to do with surrealism. "I have disliked all of his [Max Ernst's] painting intensely and am not a surrealist," Bishop wrote in 1946 (*One Art: Letters*, 134), although she later mentions that the frottage of some Ernst prints influenced "The Weed" (ibid., 478). Bonnie Costello has some very helpful remarks on surrealism, frottage, and "The Monument" in her *Elizabeth Bishop: Questions of Mastery* (Cambridge, Mass.: Harvard University Press, 1991), 26–28, 218–23.

17. Hynes, *Auden Generation*, 226.

18. Quoted in Goldensohn, *Elizabeth Bishop*, 129.

19. Elizabeth Bishop, letter of 17 Oct. 1940, *One Art: Letters*, 96.

20. Anthony Hecht, "Retreat," in *Collected Poems* (New York: Knopf, 1990), 128.

21. Bishop, *One Art: Letters*, 388. She wrote "Brazil, January 1, 1502" late in 1958, sending it to Lowell on New Year's Day, 1959 (see Kalstone, *Becoming a Poet*, 194). Gombrich's book, the A. W. Mellon Lectures in the Fine Arts for 1956, was published in 1960.

22. Ernst Robert Curtius, *European Literature and the Latin Middle Ages*, trans. Willard R. Trask (Princeton: Princeton University Press, Bollingen, 1953 [1948]), 545, 562.

23. Kalstone, *Becoming a Poet*, 194.

4. FAULKNER, TYPOLOGY, AND BLACK HISTORY IN *GO DOWN, MOSES*

1. "Afterword," in *Literary Uses of Typology*, ed. Earl Miner (Princeton: Princeton University Press, 1977), 385.

2. "Introduction," in *Typology and Early American Literature*, ed. Sacvan Bercovitch (Amherst: University of Massachusetts Press, 1972), 3.

3. Northrop Frye, *Anatomy of Criticism: Four Essays* (Princeton: Princeton University Press, 1957), 14.

4. Erich Auerbach, "Figura," in *Scenes from the Drama of European Literature*, trans. R. Manheim (New York: Meridian, 1944), 11–76.

5. For the decline of this method in the eighteenth and nineteenth centuries, see especially Hans Frei, *The Eclipse of Biblical Narrative* (New Haven: Yale University Press, 1974).

6. For such Messianic texts, see A. C. Charity, *Events and Their Afterlife: The Dialectics of Christian Typology in the Bible and Dante* (Cambridge: Cambridge University Press, 1966), 113. On the historical background of the intertestamental period, see James Barr, *Old and New in Interpretation: A Study of the Two Testaments* (London: SCM Press, 1966), 117–29.

7. In Samuel Mather's *Figures or Types of the Old Testament* (1673; see the index). But his nephew Cotton Mather "combined the allegorical sense with the typological reading of the two testaments" (Mason I. Lowance, Jr., "Cotton Mather's *Marginalia* and the Metaphors of Biblical History," in *Typology and Early American Literature*, ed. Bercovitch, 160).

8. Charity, *Events and Their Afterlife*, 153; see also 60.

9. See the *Encyclopedia of Religion and Ethics*, ed. James Hastings (Edinburgh: Clark, 1908), 12: 500–504, s.v. *typology*. Cf. the philosopher and poet Francis Sparshott on the progressive God of progressive revelation: "But He's so sensitive to trends: / Instructed by the Stoics, / He turned to world-soul, snubbed old friends, / Abandoned false heroics" ("Mysterious Way: After the *Hebrew Origins* of T. J. Meek," from *A Divided Voice* [Oxford: Oxford University Press, 1965], 54–55).

10. Northrop Frye, *The Great Code: The Bible and Literature* (Toronto: Academic Press, 1982), 85.

11. K. J. Woollcombe, "The Biblical Origins and Patristic Development of Typology," in *Essays on Typology*, ed. G. W. H. Lampe and K. J. Woollcombe (London: SCM Press, 1957), 40.

12. Ibid., 42. For arguments against the strict demarcation of typology from allegory, see Barr, *Old and New in Interpretation*, 103–48.

13. Ursula Brumm, *American Thought and Religious Typology*, trans. John Hoagland (New Brunswick, N.J.: Rutgers University Press, 1970), 207–21.

14. William Faulkner, *Go Down, Moses* (1942; New York: Vintage Books, 1973), 380–81. All subsequent references are to this edition. Page numbers are given in parentheses in the text.

15. William Faulkner, *The Sound and the Fury* (1929; New York: Vintage Books, 1954), 423, 211.

16. *Faulkner in the University: Class Conferences at the University of Virginia, 1957–58*, ed. Frederick L. Gwynn and Joseph L. Blotner (1959; New York: Vintage Books, 1965), 18.

17. *William Faulkner: Three Decades of Criticism*, ed. Frederick J. Hoffman and Olga W. Vickery (New York: Harcourt, Brace & World, 1960), 78.

18. Cf. Theodore Ziolkowski, "Some Features of Religious Figuralism in Twentieth-Century Literature," in *Literary Uses of Typology*, ed. Miner, 360–61.

19. See, e.g., Thomas Virgil Peterson, *Ham and Japheth: The Mythic World of Whites in the Antebellum South* (Metuchen, N.J.: Scarecrow Press and American Theological Library Association, 1978); and David Brion Davis and James M. McPherson in *The Antislavery Vanguard: New Essays on the Abolitionists*, ed. Martin Duberman (Princeton: Princeton University Press, 1965), 4–5, 158–59. On early uses of the Hamitic myth, see William McKee Evans, "From the Land of Canaan to the Land of Guinea: The Strange Odyssey of the 'Sons of Ham,'" *American Historical Review* 85 (1980): 15–43.

20. William Faulkner, *Absalom, Absalom!* (1936; New York: Modern Library, 1964), 282.

21. Ibid., 167: ". . . not the heritage of Ham, not the mark of servitude but of bondage; the knowledge that for a while part of his blood had beene the blood of slaves." On the "doomed dark brothers" of Scripture as identified with the Indians, see Bercovitch, *The American Jeremiad* (Madison: University of Wisconsin Press, 1978), 75n. See also James Hugo Johnston, "Indian Relations," in his *Race Relations in Virginia and Miscegenation in the South, 1776–1860* (1937 thesis; Amherst: University of Massachusetts Press, 1970), 269–92. See also *Interpreting Southern History: Historiographical Essays in Honor of Sanford W. Higginbottom*, ed. John B. Boles and Evelyn Thomas Nolan (Baton Rouge: Louisiana State University Press, 1987). I am indebted to Michael Wayne for introducing me to a number of these titles.

22. See Albert J. Raboteau, *Slave Religion: The "Invisible Institution" in the Antebellum South* (New York: Oxford University Press, 1978), 246–65, for a fine account of the typology and uses of spirituals.

23. Robert Penn Warren, "The South, the Negro, and Time," in *Faulkner: A Collection of Critical Essays*, ed. id. (Englewood Cliffs, N.J.: Prentice-Hall, 1966), 263.

24. Isa. 53:3, from a passage widely read as messianic prophecy; cf. Gal. 4:14.

25. Eugene Genovese, *Roll, Jordan, Roll: The World the Slaves Made* (New York: Pantheon Books, 1974), 253.

26. *Narrative of the Life of Frederick Douglass, an American Slave* (1845; New York: Penguin Books, 1982), 90.

27. Regina Schwartz, "Joseph's Bones and the Resurrection of the Text," *PMLA* 103 (1988): 120. Faulkner, I am arguing, implicitly raises just this question in connection with Ishmael and Esau. (There is a brief reappearance of a rejected brother in the next generation [Gen. 48:14–19], but the theme is not developed.)

28. See Herbert Marks, "Pauline Typology and Revisionary Criticism," *Journal of the American Academy of Religion* 50 (1982): 71–92. See also Richard B. Hays, *Echoes of Scripture in the Letters of Paul* (New Haven: Yale University Press, 1989).

29. Beyond works cited here, see Elizabeth Fox-Genovese and Eugene Genovese, "The Divine Sanction of Social Order: Religious Foundations of the Southern Slaveholders' World View," *Journal of the American Academy of Religion* 55 (1987): 211–33; and John B. Boles, "The Discovery of Southern Religious History," in *Interpreting Southern History*, ed. Boles and Nolan, 510–48.

30. For recent historical work on the Southern family, see Drew Gilpin Faust, "The Peculiar South Revisited: White Society, Culture, and Politics in the Antebellum Period, 1800–1860," in *Interpreting Southern History*, ed. Boles and Nolan, 107–8.

31. "The most important events of the world require to be traced to the secrets of families, and thus the marriages of the patriarchs give occasion for peculiar consideration" (*Aus Meinem Leben: Dichtung und Wahrheit*, trans. John Oxenford as *The Autobiography of Johann Wolfgang von Goethe* [Chicago: University of Chicago Press, 1974], 1: 138).

32. *Faulkner in the University*, ed. Gwynn and Blotner, 167.

33. It is important to recognize that Faulkner is not offering a simple reversal in which the outcast brother becomes the hero. This would follow the plotting of some of the Romantics, notably Byron, as Frye observes. See Frye, *The Great Code*, 180–82, and also his *A Study of English Romanticism* (New York: Random House, 1968), 30–31.

34. Cited in Peterson, *Ham and Japheth*, 51–52. On the uses of Sir Robert Filmer's *Patriarcha* (1680, written ca. 1640), see C. Vann Woodward, *American Counterpoint: Slavery and Racism in the North-South Dialogue* (Boston: Little, Brown, 1976), 134–38.

35. *Mary Chesnut's Civil War Diary*, ed. C. Vann Woodward (New Haven: Yale University Press, 1977), 31 (1861). Page numbers are given in parentheses in the text following.

36. Leah was, after all, foisted on Jacob in lieu of Rachel; Bathsheba was married, and Nathan's great reproach against David is that he arranged to have her husband killed. (The example of Sarah and Hagar would have been painful to Mary Chesnut because of Sarah's long barrenness.)

37. Elizabeth Fox-Genovese, *Within the Plantation Household: Black and White Women of the Old South* (Chapel Hill: University of North Carolina Press, 1988), 366.

38. For example, Johnston, *Race Relations in Virginia and Miscegenation in the Old South*; Genovese, *Roll, Jordan, Roll*, 413–31; Joel Williamson, *New People: Miscegenation and Mulattoes in the United States* (New York: Free Press/Macmillan, 1980); Bertram Wyatt-Brown, *Southern Honor: Ethics and Behavior in the Old South* (New York: Oxford University Press, 1982), 307–24.

39. Cited in Herbert G. Gutman, *The Black Family in Slavery and Freedom, 1750–1925* (New York: Pantheon Books, 1976), 45.

40. Genovese, *Roll, Jordan, Roll*, 252–55.

41. Woodward, *American Counterpoint*, 73–77.

42. *The Complete Poems of Emily Dickinson*, ed. Thomas H. Johnson (Boston: Little, Brown, 1960), no. 597, pp. 293–94. The reference is to Moses, whom God allowed to see the promised land from Mount Nebo, but not to enter it.

5. "A SEEING AND UNSEEING IN THE EYE"

1. André Provos, *Journal of Canadian Fiction* 28 (1980): 204.

2. Antonine Maillet, *La Sagouine* (Ottawa: Lemeac, 1974), 191–92. "Yer nationality, they ask you. . . . Hard to say. We live in America, but we ain't Americans. Nope, Americans, they work in 'em factories in the States, and in summer, they come around, visitin' our beaches in their white trousers 'n speakin' English. . . . Us, we live in Canada; so we figure we mus' be Canadians. Well, but that ain't true either, cause the Dysarts . . . they also live in Canada [but] they're English, 'n us, we're French. . . . can't say that: the French folks is the folks fr'm France, *les Français de France*. . . . We're more like French Canadians, they told us. . . . Well, that ain't true either. French Canadians are those that live in *Québec*. They call 'em *Canayens* or *Québécois*. . . . For the love of Christ, where do we live? In *Acadie*, we was told, 'n we're supposed to be *Acadjens*. . . . [but] them censors, the way they sees it, seems *l'Acadie* ain't a country, 'n *Acadjen* ain't a nationality. . . . we told 'em to give us the nationality they wanned. So, I think they put us down with the Injuns. . . . Sure, they says you're a full fledged citizen; but they can't name yer nationality. Maybe you ain't in the way, but you don't have yer place in the country." Antonine Maillet, in *La Sagouine*, trans. Luis de Céspedes (Toronto: Simon & Pierre, 1979), 164–66. Other translations from the French in this chapter are my own.

3. Northrop Frye, *The Bush Garden: Essays on the Canadian Imagination* (Toronto: Anansi, 1971), ii.

4. Cf. Mavis Gallant: "I suppose that a Canadian is someone who has a logical reason to think he is one," from *Home Truths* (Toronto: Macmillan, 1981), xiii.

5. Northrop Frye, *Bush Garden*, iii.

6. Alastair Fowler, *Kinds of Literature: An Introduction to the Theory of Genres and Modes* (Cambridge, Mass.: Harvard University Press, 1982).

7. Helen Vendler, ed., "Introduction," in *The Harvard Book of Contemporary American Poetry* (Cambridge, Mass.: Harvard University Press, 1986), 14–15.

8. Wallace Stevens, "A Postcard from the Volcano."

9. Hector de Saint-Denys-Garneau, "Spectacle de la danse," in *Regards et jeux dans l'espace*, in *Poésies complètes* (Montreal: Fides, 1949), 39. "My children, you dance badly. / It has to be said that it's hard to dance here, / in this lack of air, / here without

space, which is everything in dance. / You don't know how to play with space, / and you play in it / (not chained) / you poor children who cannot play."

10. Anne Hébert, *Poèmes* (Paris: Editions du Seuil, 1960), 71.

11. Recent interest in the sinking of the *Titanic* elicited a letter to the *New York Times* recounting the heroism of Ida Straus, who chose to go down with her husband rather than take her place in a lifeboat. Americans were being informed of a piece of their history that many a Canadian student knew very well from Pratt's poem.

12. *Recitative: Prose by James Merrill*, ed. J. D. McClatchy (San Francisco: North Point Press, 1986), 28.

13. *The Complete Prose of Marianne Moore*, ed. Patricia C. Willis (New York: Penguin Books, 1986), 265.

14. Carl Berger, "The True North Strong and Free," in *Nationalism in Canada*, ed. Peter Russell (Toronto: McGraw-Hill, 1966), 3–26.

15. George Woodcock, "Introduction," in *Canadian Writers and Their Works: Essays on Form, Context, and Development*, ed. Robert Lecker et al., vol. 7 (Toronto: ECW Press, 1985), 9.

16. Margaret Atwood, "Northrop Frye Observed," in *Second Words: Selected Critical Prose* (Toronto: Anansi, 1982), 403.

17. Robert Kroetsch, at the "Ritratto di Northrop Frye" conference, University of Rome, May 1987.

18. John Bayley, "Up from Under," *London Review of Books*, 18 Feb. 1988, 9.

19. Ibid.

20. I am indebted to the historian Ramsay Cook for this information.

21. The context is fully given in Geoffrey Hill's *New and Collected Poems* (Boston: Houghton Mifflin, 1994).

22. Seamus Heaney, "The Sense of Place," in his *Preoccupations: Selected Prose, 1968–1978* (New York: Farrar, Straus & Giroux, 1980), 135.

23. Marie-Claire Blais, "Introduction," in *The Oxford Book of French-Canadian Short Stories*, ed. Richard Teleky (Toronto and Oxford: Oxford University Press, 1983), xiii.

24. Judith Wright, "Landscape and Dreaming," *Daedalus* 114 (1985): 31, 55.

25. Northrop Frye, interview in *Scripsi* 4 (1986): 224.

26. The phrase "a seeing and unseeing in the eye" is taken from Wallace Stevens, *Notes Toward a Supreme Fiction*, 1.6.

27. Alice Munro, "Menesteung," in *Friend of My Youth* (Toronto: McClelland & Stewart, 1990), 60–61.

6. QUESTIONS OF ALLUSION

1. Leslie Marmon Silko, in *Critical Fictions: The Politics of Imaginative Writing*, ed. Philomena Mariani (Seattle: Bay Press, 1991), quoted in the *New York Times Book Review*, 29 Dec. 1991, 27.

2. Margaret Atwood, in *University of Toronto Quarterly* 61 (1992): 382.

3. John Milton, *The Reason of Church Government Urged Against Prelaty* (1641–42), pref. ii. Arguments that citation confers authority need to take care not to confuse intent with effect. See, for example, Stefan Moraweski, "The Basic Functions of

Quotation," in *Sign, Language, Culture*, ed. A. Greimas and Roman Jakobson (The Hague: Mouton, 1970), 690–705.

4. Gian Biagio Conte, *The Rhetoric of Imitation: Genre and Poetic Memory in Virgil and Other Latin Poets*, trans. Charles Segal (Ithaca, N.Y.: Cornell University Press, 1986), 29. He notes Gérard Genette's useful work on sorting out terminology, and getting rid of ideological overtones associated with the word *intertextuality*.

5. Carlo Ginzburg, "Morelli, Freud and Sherlock Holmes: Clues and Scientific Method," *History Workshop Journal* 9 (1980): 5–36.

6. Christopher Ricks, "Allusion: The Poet as Heir," in *Studies in Eighteenth-Century Literature*, vol. 3, ed. R. F. Brissenden and J. C. Eade (Toronto: University of Toronto Press, 1976), 209–40; id., "Tennyson Inheriting the Earth," in *Studies in Tennyson*, ed. Hallam Tennyson (London: Macmillan, 1981), 66–104; id., "Austin's Swink," *University of Toronto Quarterly* 61 (1992): 297–315; John Hollander, *The Figure of Echo: A Mode of Allusion in Milton and After* (Berkeley: University of California Press, 1981). Among various recent surveys, Ubo J. Hebel's *Intertextuality, Allusion, and Quotation: An International Bibliography of Critical Studies* (New York: Greenwood, 1989) offers a reasonably full listing.

7. See Hollander, *Figure of Echo*, ch. 3, "Echo Schematic."

8. Conte is rightly uncomfortable with the narrowness of Michael Riffaterre's syllepsis as the proposed figure for allusive practice (*The Rhetoric of Imitation*, 30). On the overdetermination of aleatory as against obligatory reading in Riffaterre, and the apparent weakness of semiotics in the area of probability, see my *Poetry, Word-Play, and Word-War in Wallace Stevens* (Princeton: Princeton University Press, 1988), 87.

9. James Merrill, in *University of Toronto Quarterly* 61 (1992): 390.

10. Tennyson quoted in Ricks, "Tennyson Inheriting the Earth," 66.

11. See, e.g., Conte, *Rhetoric of Imitation*, 36–39, and Philip Hardie, *Virgil's "Aeneid": Cosmos and Imperium* (Oxford: Clarendon Press, 1986), 233–37.

12. For example, E. H. Gombrich's well-known study of schemata, *Art and Illusion: A Study in the Psychology of Pictorial Representation* (Princeton: Princeton University Press, 1960).

13. *University of Toronto Quarterly* 61, no. 3 (1992), special issue on allusion, passim.

14. Marilyn Butler, in *Rethinking Historicism: Critical Readings in Romantic History*, with Marjorie Levinson, Jerome McGann, and Paul Hamilton (Oxford: Blackwell, 1989), 83.

15. D. C. Masters, *The Winnipeg General Strike* (Toronto: University of Toronto Press, 1950), 126.

16. Dietrich Bonhoeffer, *The Cost of Discipleship* (London: SCM Press, 1948; abridged from the original, *Nachfolge*, first published in Munich in 1937), 32–33.

7. THE LANGUAGE OF SCRIPTURE IN
WORDSWORTH'S *PRELUDE*

1. All quotations from Wordsworth are from *The Prelude: A Parallel Text*, ed. J. C. Maxwell (1971; New Haven: Yale University Press, 1981), and *The Prelude, 1798–99*,

ed. Stephen Parrish (Ithaca, N.Y.: Cornell University Press, 1977). Unless otherwise identified, quotations are from the 1850 *Prelude*.

2. W. J. B. Owen, ed., *The Fourteen-Book Prelude* (Ithaca, N.Y.: Cornell University Press, 1985), note to line 267.

3. How *hoc* and *opus* were pronounced in Wordsworth's day, I do not know. Sliding from the Latin into the English *opus* might offer the chance of sliding from a short to a long *o*, hence to an abridged *hoc-opus-* "opus" in the form of *hope*. The *OED* offers both long and short pronunciations for the *o* of *opus* in English (*o* as in *no* and *o* as in *pot*).

4. *The Fourteen-Book Prelude*, note to 9.362–63.

5. Wordsworth, letter of 22 Nov. 1831, in *Letters of William and Dorothy Wordsworth*, 2d ed., vol. 5: *1829–1834*, ed. Alan G. Hill (Oxford: Clarendon Press, 1979), 454.

6. *William Wordsworth: The Borders of Vision* (Oxford: Clarendon Press, 1982), 449 n. 43.

7. Coleridge, *Collected Letters*, ed. Earl Leslie Griggs (Oxford: Clarendon Press, 1956–71), 3: 490.

8. Wordsworth, letter [Jan. 1815], in *Letters*, ed. Hill, 5:454.

9. *William Wordsworth: Selected Poems and Prefaces*, ed. Jack Stillinger (Boston: Houghton Mifflin, 1965), 537.

10. See esp. Geoffrey Hartman, "The Poetics of Prophecy," in his *The Unremarkable Wordsworth* (Minneapolis: University of Minnesota Press, 1987), 163–81. I am here offering evidence that Wordsworth did often work with "the precise verbal content" of scripture, as against Hartman's argument on p. 178. On Wordsworth's earlier sense of death, see Alan Bewell, *Wordsworth and the Enlightenment: Nature, Man, and Society in the Experimental Poetry* (New Haven: Yale University Press, 1989), 187–234. My argument throughout works with the apparent intentionalities of Wordsworth's poems.

11. Wordsworth, letter, 15 Mar. 1829, in *Letters*, ed. Hill, 5: 54.

12. Geoffrey Hartman, *Wordsworth's Poetry, 1787–1814* (1964; New Haven: Yale University Press, 1971).

13. Alan Bewell, letter to the author.

14. Harold Bloom, *Ruin the Sacred Truths: Poetry and Belief from the Bible to the Present* (Cambridge, Mass.: Harvard University Press, 1989), 129. For "filthy rags" as a metonymy, see also George Eliot, *Middlemarch* (1872), bk. 1, ch. 26: "the consciousness at once of filthy rags and the best damask."

15. "Vaudracour and Julia" (1820), ll. 573, 618 ("overblest"), in both cases used of Vaudracour. The revision of "such inheritance of blessedness" to "such inheritance of blessed fancy" is instructive. Wordsworth places "Vaudracour and Julia" insistently in the realm of fancy, fascination (605), Arabian fiction (607), enchantment (617), and the like, and I can ascertain no biblical allusion or echo. In fact, the lack of interest in Julia's sufferings compared with Vaudracour's is almost embarrassing. See *The Thirteen-Book Prelude*, ed. Mark L. Reed (Ithaca, N.Y.: Cornell University Press, 1991), bk. 9.

16. Preface, 1815, in *William Wordsworth: Selected Poems and Prefaces*, ed. Stillinger, 486.

17. See *The Love Letters of William and Mary Wordsworth*, ed. Beth Darlington

(Ithaca, N.Y.: Cornell University Press, 1981), 50, 59, 60, 67, 77, 80, 82, 130 ("I am the blessedest of all Women" [Mary, 6–7 May 1812, alluding to the prophecy to her namesake]), 134, 142, 148 ("I am the blessedest of Men, the happiest of husbands. . . . 'I chiefly who enjoy so far the happier lot, enjoying thee, preeminent, &c'" [William, 9–13 May 1812, quoting Milton's Eve in *Paradise Lost* 4.445–47]), 197, 201, etc.

18. Edwin Stein, *Wordsworth's Art of Allusion* (University Park: Pennsylvania State University Press, 1988), 10.

8. THE SENSES OF ELIOT'S SALVAGES

1. T. S. Eliot, "Charybde et Scylla," *Annales du Centre universitaire méditerranéen* (Nice) 5 (1951–52), quoted in Christopher Ricks, "A Note on 'Little Gidding,'" *Essays in Criticism* 25 (1975): 153.

2. Helen Gardner, *The Composition of "Four Quartets"* (London: Faber & Faber, 1978), 121. The quotations following are from pp. 120–21.

3. Northrop Frye, *T. S. Eliot* (Edinburgh: Oliver & Boyd, 1963), 86.

4. Helen Gardner, *The Art of T. S. Eliot* (1950; New York: Dutton, 1959), 170.

5. Morison is cited in Gardner, *Composition*, 53. The phrase "leaden periphrases" is A. D. Moody's in his *Thomas Sterns Eliot, Poet* (Cambridge: Cambridge University Press, 1979), 222.

6. Perhaps through Cowper's Miltonic lines, "So wither'd stumps disgrace the sylvan scene, / No longer fruitful and no longer green" ("Conversation," 50–51). See A. V. C. Schmidt, "T. S. Eliot and William Cowper: A New Waste Land Source," *Notes and Queries*, n.s., 29 (1982): 347.

7. Cited in Mary T. Reynolds, *Joyce and Dante: The Shaping Imagination* (Princeton: Princeton University Press, 1981), 208.

8. Otway (*OED*, s.v. *savage*, 5d, 1680) hears the force of Milton's phrasing, but not the Dantean resonance: "I, methinks, am Salvage and forlorn, / Thy presence only 'tis can make me blest." Johnson, incidentally, adds to *salvage* (wild) the note: "It is now spoken and written savage."

9. A. Bartlett Giametti is the exception; he makes a brief connection between Dante and *Paradise Lost* 9.1085–90 in his *The Earthly Paradise and the Renaissance Epic* (Princeton: Princeton University Press, 1966), 345. Carey and Fowler see *Paradise Lost* 9.1085–90 as "the archetypal poem of retirement" and note that "Adam's guilty impulse to retirement is by no means approved of by Milton" (*Poems of John Milton*, ed. John Carey and Alastair Fowler [Harlow: Longmans, 1968], note to 9.1085–90). But Adam's guilt seems to me more radical than impulsive, not only because of the Dantean echoes, but also because of the echo in Adam's "cover me" of "cover us" from Hosea (10:8) and Luke (23:30). The context is a day of judgment, not retirement.

10. Helen Gardner notes the echo of Dante's *nodo* (*Paradiso* 33.91) in Eliot's "knot" in "Little Gidding," 5 (*Composition*, 224).

11. Denis Donoghue, *The Ordinary Universe: Soundings in Modern Literature* (New York: Macmillan, 1968), 257.

12. See A. D. Moody's persuasive suggestion that Eliot's *juvescence* in "Gerontion" is derived from *iuvare*, to help (*Thomas Stearns Eliot*, 67).

13. John Freccero, "Manfred's Wounds and the Poetics of the *Purgatorio*," in

Centre and Labyrinth: Essays in Honour of Northrop Frye, ed. Eleanor Cook et al. (Toronto: University of Toronto Press, 1983), 79–81. Dante's farewell echoes and revises the farewell of Orpheus to Eurydice in *Georgics* 4.525–27. But even as Virgil fades, so also, paradoxically, does the finality of the farewell. *Salute* means necessary separation from Virgil, but it implies no universalism to say that *salute* has also meant, and may mean again, some mitigation of that separation. Both distancing Virgil, yet blessing him, Dante's *salute* is one more mark of his poetic maturing.

14. Wallace Stevens, letter of 23 Apr. 1950, in *L*, 677.

15. Incidentally, in his work at the Hartford Accident and Indemnity Company, Stevens was responsible for a "salvage department" among others (Peter Brazeau, *Parts of a World: Wallace Stevens Remembered* [New York: Random House, 1983], 31). I do not know whether, in his work at Lloyds Bank, Eliot also was.

16. Donoghue, *Ordinary Universe*, 263.

17. Christopher Ricks, "Tennyson Inheriting the Earth," in *Studies in Tennyson*, ed. Hallam Tennyson (London: Macmillan, 1981), 84. For metaleptic echo, see Hollander, *The Figure of Echo: A Mode of Allusion in Milton and After* (Berkeley: University of California Press, 1981), 113–32.

18. Ricks, "Tennyson Inheriting," 104.

9. WALLACE STEVENS AND THE KING JAMES BIBLE

1. Wallace Stevens, entry of 19 Apr. 1907, in *L*, 102. Quotations from Stevens's poetry are taken from his *Collected Poems* (New York: Knopf, 1954) and may be found through the title index.

2. Wallace Stevens, *Opus Posthumous*, rev. ed., ed. Milton J. Bates (New York: Knopf, 1989), 187, 202.

3. Stevens adapted Simone Weil's term *décréation* in his essay "The Relations Between Poetry and Painting," in *NA*, 174–75. The term is not synonymous with *deconstruction*.

4. John Hollander, in *Poetry East* 13–14 (1984): 28.

5. See esp. Christopher Ricks, "Allusion: The Poet as Heir," in *Studies in Eighteenth-Century Literature*, ed. R. F. Brissenden and J. C. Eade (Toronto: University of Toronto Press, 1976), 209–40; and id., "Tennyson Inheriting the Earth," in *Studies in Tennyson*, ed. Hallam Tennyson (London: Macmillan, 1981), 66–104.

6. See my *Poetry, Word-Play, and Word-War in Wallace Stevens* (Princeton: Princeton University Press, 1988), passim.

7. Joan Richardson, *Wallace Stevens: A Biography*, vol. 1 (New York: Beech Tree Books, 1986), 525.

8. Geoffrey Hill, *The Lords of Limit: Essays on Literature and Ideas* (New York: Oxford University Press, 1984), 16.

9. James Joyce, letter of 30 July 1929, in *Selected Letters of James Joyce*, ed. Richard Ellmann (New York: Viking Press, 1975), 346.

10. See, e.g., Alastair Fowler, *Kinds of Literature: An Introduction to the Theory of Genres and Modes* (Cambridge, Mass.: Harvard University Press, 1982), 192.

11. See Helen Cooper, "The Goat and the Eclogue," *Philological Quarterly* 53 (1974): 363–79.

12. Cited in Fowler, *Kinds of Literature*, 177.

13. On this connection, see Charles Berger, *Forms of Farewell: The Late Poetry of Wallace Stevens* (Madison: University of Wisconsin Press, 1985).

10. BIRDS IN PARADISE

1. *CP*, 486. For Stevens's love of Goethe, see *L*, 457.

2. On the problem of tone here, see Harold Bloom, *Wallace Stevens: The Poems of Our Climate* (Ithaca, N.Y.: Cornell University Press, 1977), 332–34.

3. It is also now common on ordinary evenings in New Haven, from spring through fall, though this was not true before the 1950's. ("The mocking-bird is rarely heard here," said Thoreau in the Conclusion to *Walden*.) See Roger F. Pasquier, *Watching Birds: An Introduction to Ornithology* (Boston: Houghton Mifflin, 1977), 229.

4. Jefferson quoted in Leo Spitzer, "*Explication de Texte* Applied to Walt Whitman's 'Out of the Cradle Endlessly Rocking," *ELH* 16 (1949): 242.

5. Anon [Richard Lewis], "Description of the Spring: A Journey from Patapsco in Maryland to Annapolis, April 4, 1730," *Gentleman's Magazine* 2 (1732): 669.

6. *The Arabian Nights*, trans. Richard Burton (1885–88), note on the "thousand-voiced," Third Kaladar's Tale (Sixteenth Night).

7. John Ruskin, *Fors Clavigera*, pt. 4, letter 42 (June 1874): "this dying England taught the Americans all they have of speech, or thought, hitherto. What thoughts they have not learned from England are foolish thoughts; what words they have not learned from England, unseemly words; the vile among them not being able even to be humorous parrots, but only obscene mocking birds." Ruskin may be drawing on the old tradition, long preceding 1649, of a rhetorical "mock bird."

8. "Evangeline," 2, in *The Poetical Works of Longfellow* (London: Oxford University Press, 1904), 162. Though the context is here paradisal ("the Eden of Louisiana"), Gabriel remains absent. But Longfellow refrains from developing the possible ironies of the mockingbird's "derision."

9. A collection of singing birds may be found in Frank Doggett, "Romanticism's Singing Bird," *Studies in English Literature* 14 (1974): 547–61.

10. For example, Geoffrey Hartman, "Evening Star and Evening Land," in his *Fate of Reading* (Chicago: University of Chicago Press, 1973), 163, 164.

11. This is a modifying of David Perkins's ironic reading in his *Quest for Permanence: The Symbolism of Wordsworth, Shelley and Keats* (Cambridge, Mass.: Harvard University Press, 1959), 257. I think Eliot implies that we cannot but deceive ourselves to some degree about our "first world." See also A. D. Moody, *Thomas Stearns Eliot, Poet* (Cambridge: Cambridge University Press, 1979), 185–86.

12. Harold Rosenberg quoted in John Hollander, *The Figure of Echo: A Mode of Allusion in Milton and Later* (Berkeley: University of California Press, 1981), 72n.

13. On the use of *lemon* and *citron*, as well as the relation of this canto to the entire sequence, see my "Directions in Reading Wallace Stevens: Up, Down, Across," in

Lyric Poetry: Beyond New Criticism, ed. Chaviva Hosek and Patricia Parker (Ithaca, N.Y.: Cornell University Press, 1985), 298–309.

14. Cf. Francis Sparshott: "This fundamental ambiguity in the notion of imitation, between imitating a person in action and manufacturing an imitation flower (or whatever), haunts the theory of the fine arts from its beginnings in Plato, who . . . uses the Greek word *mimeisthai* to mean 'depict,' although its ordinary meaning was 'mimic' or 'enact'" (*The Theory of the Arts* [Princeton: Princeton University Press, 1982], 540 n. 51). For an intricate exploration of the territory between kinds of mimicry and kinds of traditionally Platonic mimesis, see Jacques Derrida, "The Double Session," which works through a reading of Mallarmé's "Mimique" (in his *Dissemination*, trans. Barbara Johnson [Chicago: University of Chicago Press, 1981; first published as *La Dissémination* (1972)], 172–285).

15. The *mac-* part of the nonsense compound can also function this way, if we hear *mac–maquillage–make-up* associations, as "to mimic" is in some sense to "make up." Arthur Symons (in *London: A Book of Aspects*, in *Selected Writings*, ed. Roger Holdsworth [Cheadle: Carcanet, 1974], 91–92) uses *maquillage* as a synonym for *make-up*, although the *OED* does not admit it. The echoing of *mac–maquillage* occurred to me before I read Symons, because of Anne Hébert's poem "Le Tombeau des rois": "Le masque d'or sur my face absente / . . . L'ombre de l'amour me maquille" ("The golden mask over my absent face / . . . Love's shadow makes me up"). Symons's contrast of "illusion," "delightful imposition," and "make-up," to the "everyday" fits very well into Stevens's argument in "An Ordinary Evening in New Haven."

16. Cf. Gombrich's exuberant and persuasive experiment with *ping* and *pong* in his *Art and Illusion: A Study in the Psychology of Pictorial Representation*, 2d ed. (Princeton: Princeton University Press, 1969), 370–71. Stevens repeatedly experiments with such effects. *Click-clack* is figuratively appropriate for machinelike reasoning; thus Stevens in 1942, "reason's click-clack" (*CP*, 397).

17. Spitzer, *"Explication de Texte,"* 235.

18. Hart Crane, A. R. Ammons, and Amy Clampitt are the three. For Crane's turning of Whitman, see Hollander, *Figure of Echo*, 123. For Crane's turning of Keats, see Amy Clampitt, "Keats at Margate" (*What the Light Was Like* [New York: Knopf, 1985]), which implicitly links Crane's "bottom of the sea" with Keats's "bottom of the sea" (*The Letters of John Keats*, ed. Hyder Edward Rollins [Cambridge, Mass.: Harvard University Press, 1958], 14 Sept. 1817), and Keats with Whitman by the use of *Paumanok*. For Ammons, see the end of this essay.

19. *Leaves of Grass*, ed. Sculley Bradley and Harold W. Blodgett (New York: Norton, 1965), 246–53. All quotations from Whitman's poetry are from this edition. See my *Poetry, Word-Play, and Word-War in Wallace Stevens* (Princeton: Princeton University Press, 1988), 125–29.

20. There is both classical and Thomist authority for this. Fancy figures in Adam's own dreams (*Paradise Lost* 8.294, 461).

21. *John Milton: Complete Poems and Major Prose*, ed. Merritt Y. Hughes (Indianapolis: Bobbs-Merrill, 1957), 257. All quotations from Milton's poetry are from this edition.

22. *Complete Poems*, ed. Jack Stillinger (Cambridge, Mass.: Harvard University Press, 1982), 279–83. All quotations from Keats's poetry are from this edition.

23. This sequence might be compared with Coleridge's conversation with Keats six weeks before Keats supposedly wrote this ode: "Nightingales, Poetry — on Poetical Sensation — Metaphysics — Different genera and species of Dreams — Nightmare — a dream accompanied by a sense of touch — single and double touch — A dream related" (*Letters of John Keats*, 3 May 1819). Apropos of dreams and touch, we should note how skillfully Milton keeps from us, and from Eve, the knowledge whether she touched or tasted the forbidden fruit in her dream. A stimulating argument centered on Coleridge's use of Milton's nightingales, with some implications for Keats, may be found in Fred W. Randel, "Coleridge and the Contentiousness of Romantic Nightingales," *Studies in Romanticism* 21 (1982): 33–55.

24. The formulation is Hollander's in *Figure of Echo*, 90.

25. I include the prologue to bk. 9, although it is not formally an invocation.

26. Janet Adelman observes how both Milton's and Eve's "night visitants inspire dreams of flying, of attaining more than mortal power" ("Creation and the Place of the Poet in Paradise Lost," in *The Author in His Work: Essays on a Problem in Criticism*, ed. Louis Martz and Aubrey Williams [New Haven: Yale University Press, 1978], 53). To me, the two night spirits do not appear "uncomfortably close," given the power of Milton's dialectic. When that goes, the old contraries crumble, although not of course the old problem. All this I think Keats knew.

Milton's dialectic of true and false may also be seen in his use of the word *mock*, which supports Arnold Stein's argument that "the work of pruning and viniculture opposes, with precisely chosen terms, the work of Satan's dream" (*The Art of Presence: The Poet and Paradise Lost* [Berkeley: University of California Press, 1977], 151–52). The "mockery" of unfallen vegetation (4.628) is different in kind from demonic mocking and mimicking.

Clearly, I would agree with Stuart M. Sperry's argument that Eve's dream informs "The Fall of Hyperion" (*PMLA* 77 [1962]: 77–84) and I would put back Keats's meditation on Milton and dreams to the spring of 1819. Jack Stillinger, in the introduction to the *Complete Poems*, provides a compact and useful discussion of Keats on dreams and dreaming; in *The Hoodwinking of Madeline and Other Essays on Keats's Poems* (Urbana: University of Illinois Press, 1971, passim), he concentrates on the contrast of dreaming and actuality. I have difficulty with the erotic part of Willard Spiegelman's argument in his "Keats's 'Coming Muskrose' and Shakespeare's 'Profound Verdure'" (*ELH* 50 [1983]: 347–62), but he usefully reminds us of the influence of *A Midsummer Night's Dream* on Keats generally and on this ode in particular.

27. On the way the poem's verbal texture makes us aware of basic dimensions and movement, see Isabel MacCaffrey, *Paradise Lost as Myth* (Cambridge, Mass.: Harvard University Press, 1959), 64. On the connection of such movement with Milton's voice and perspective, see Anne Davidson Ferry, *Milton's Epic Voice: The Narrator in Paradise Lost* (Cambridge, Mass.: Harvard University Press, 1963), 24. Roger Sundell notes that it is Milton's prospective song that flies in the first invocation, he himself attaining flight only in bk. 3 ("The Singer and His Song in the Prologues of Paradise Lost," in *Milton and the Art of Sacred Song*, ed. J. Max Patrick and Roger H. Sundell [Madison: University of Wisconsin Press, 1979], 65–82).

28. Milton's confident lines should not cause us to assume he was "unconcerned with the dangers . . . of falling like Bellerophon," as Arnold Stein points out (*Art of*

Presence, 5). George de F. Lord reads Milton's "inner strife" here movingly ("Milton's Dialogue with Omniscience in *Paradise Lost*," in *Author in His Work*, ed. Martz and Williams, 48–49).

29. A. R. Ammons, *Sphere: The Form of a Motion* (New York: Norton, 1974), 30.

30. This interesting argument is put forward by Kenneth Gross: ll. 39–40 "compare the poet's flight not to the presumptuous ascent of Pegasus but to that of the ever-flying but more terrestrial bird of paradise, bound to the atmosphere if not to the surface of the world" (" 'Pardon Me, Mighty Poet': Versions of the Bard in Marvell's 'On Mr. Milton's Paradise Lost,' " in *Milton Studies* 16, ed. James D. Simmonds [Pittsburgh: University of Pittsburgh Press, 1982], 90).

31. See George de F. Lord's sense of a Keatsean presence in these lines and in the invocation to bk. 7 ("Milton's Dialogue with Omniscience," 48). And note the fancy-wings-fall-false conjunction (together with wine and mirth) in the newly fallen Adam and Eve (9.1008–11, 1068–70):

> As with new Wine intoxicated both
> They swim in mirth, and fancy that they feel
> Divinity within them breeding wings
> Wherewith to scorn the earth: but that false Fruit . . .
>
> . . . .
>
> . . . that false Worm, of whomsoever taught
> To counterfeit Man's voice, true in our Fall,
> False in our promis'd Rising. . . .

On the echo from Adam's fallen words, see Hollander, *Figure of Echo*, 36–37. Milton, I think, learned the power of an echoing and terminal *forlorn* from Spenser; after Milton, it came to seem almost de rigueur to place *forlorn* at the end of the line. Keats, working with effects of enjambment and refrain, uses Miltonic allusive echo, but Spenserian technique, to toll the poem back from Spenserian romance. The Spenserian source is the January Eclogue, with its two echoing plays on *forlorne*.

See also Geoffrey Hill, *The Lords of Limit: Essays on Literature and Ideas* (New York: Oxford University Press, 1984), 5: "The echo [of *forlorn* in Keats] is not so much recollection as a revocation; and what is revoked is an attitude towards art and within art. The menace that is flinched from is certainly mortality . . . but it is also the menace of the high claims of poetry itself. 'Faery lands forlorn' reads like an exquisite pastiche of a Miltonic cadence: 'Stygian caves forlorn' ('L'Allegro' 3); 'these wilde Woods forlorn' (*Paradise Lost* IX.910)."

32. This fits what we know of Whitman's reading, on which see Floyd Stovall, *The Foregrounding of Leaves of Grass* (Charlottesville: University Press of Virginia, 1974).

33. See Gombrich, *Art and Illusion*, 186–89.

34. On the themes of death and dreams in Whitman, see Stephen E. Whicher, "Whitman's Awakening to Death: Toward a Biographical Reading of 'Out of the Cradle Endlessly Rocking,' " in *The Presence of Whitman*, ed. R. W. B. Lewis (New York: Columbia University Press, 1962), 52–71.

35. The description of the bird's eggs (l. 25) is accurate, although critics seem curiously uninterested in this fact.

36. Walter Ong, quoted by Donald Wesling in "Difficulties of the Bardic," *Critical Inquiry* 8 (1981): 77.

37. Gerald L. Bruns, "Intention, Authority, and Meaning," *Critical Inquiry* 7 (1980): 302.

38. Northrop Frye, "Approaching the Lyric," in *Lyric Poetry*, ed. Hosek and Parker, 34.

39. Paul de Man, "The Epistemology of Metaphor," 13, in *On Metaphor*, ed. Sheldon Sacks (Chicago: University of Chicago Press, 1979), 11–28.

40. For metaphorical echo, see Hollander, *Figure of Echo*, 62–112, and note esp. 67–68, on the Miltonic echoes in Keats's "Ode to Psyche." For metaleptic echo, see 113–32.

41. "Lucky lot" is Golding's translation, "happy state" is that of Sandys, and Sir Samuel Garth's collaborative edition adds "that all might envy."

42. This is not listed as a debt to Ovid in the standard editions of Milton, but I find it persuasive, especially in the light of Louis L. Martz's study of Milton's revisions of Ovid. He observes that Milton converts "Ovid's sense of endless change . . . into change that has a higher, a teleological design" (*Poet of Exile: A Study of Milton's Poetry* [New Haven: Yale University Press, 1980], 231).

43. Carey and Fowler, in a note to *Paradise Lost* 8.282, write that "throughout *Paradise Lost* happiness is a resonant and often ironic term." Of course, the line may be read in other ways. If we read hearing formulaic echoes, we may hear a variation on the formula, I envy not *x* because I am doing it differently or better. Herbert's "I envy no man's nightingale or spring" may be at work here, especially as Herbert is considering truth and fiction in poetry. De Selincourt notes in his edition of Keats's *Poems* that Bridges compares Browne's *Britannia's Pastorals* 1.3.164, "Sweet Philomela . . . I do not envy thy sweet carolling," but the profession of nonenvy is common.

James R. Chandler, in his valuable "Romantic Allusiveness" (*Critical Inquiry* 8 [1982]: 473–74), does not read 1.6–7 as I do, for I hear apposition: "But being too happy in thine happiness, — / [Being too happy] That thou. . . ." But I agree that the syntax surprises slightly.

44. To this we owe one of the finest moments of black farce in English drama, when Lucifer lasciviously considers Eve: "I could (so variously do my passions move) / Enjoy and blast her in the act of love" (John Dryden, *The State of Innocence* 3.1). Lucifer seems to have Semele in mind.

45. See Horace, *Epistles* 2.2.76–78, for a *locus classicus* of the connection of poetry, the grove, Bacchus, sleep, and shade; and note the use of Bacchus in the quotation from Longfellow above.

46. Helen Vendler, *The Odes of John Keats* (Cambridge, Mass.: Harvard University Press, 1983), 90.

47. "Whither thou goest I will go; and where thou lodgest I will lodge: thy people shall be my people, and thy God my God: where thou diest, will I die, and there will I be buried: the Lord do so me, and more also, if ought but death part thee and me" (Ruth 1:16–17). In Cary's Dante, which Keats read, Ruth is the "meek ancestress of him, who sang the songs / Of sore repentance" (*Paradiso* 32.8–9). Perhaps Keats thought she didn't want to be.

48. See, e.g., John Bayley, "Intimacies of Implication," *Times Literary Supplement*,

7 May 1982, 499–500; Cynthia Chase, "'Viewless Wings': Intertextual Interpretation of Keats's 'Ode to a Nightingale,'" in *Lyric Poetry*, ed. Hosek and Parker, 208–25; and Vendler, *Odes of John Keats*, 307. Sometimes the Miltonic phrase is ignored (Bayley, p. 500) and sometimes the Shakespearean echo is called an allusion, which it seems in process of becoming. Eamon Grennan, who drew attention to the echo from *Measure for Measure* in 1975, distinguishes between "direct allusion" and "verbal echoes" in his "Keats's Contemptuous Mundi: A Shakespearean Influence on the 'Ode to a Nightingale,'" *Modern Language Quarterly* 36 (1975): 274, 276.

49. For a beautiful re-hearing of a Keats-Whitman topos, see Amy Clampitt, "Keats at Margate," in her *What the Light Was Like* (New York: Knopf, 1985): "all that / traffic in the perilous."

50. James Thomson's lines "Bear me, Pomona . . ." from "Summer" (661 ff.) are cited by more than one editor of Goethe, but not Thomson's Miltonic source.

51. Milton's play with etymology in these beautiful lines goes unremarked; the correct etymology is assigned to Milton's own singing voice.

52. This is to be distinguished from the pattern of Frye's "modal grandfather," on which see his *Anatomy of Criticism: Four Essays* (Princeton: Princeton University Press, 1957), 62, and also W. Jackson Bate, *The Burden of the Past and English Poetry* (London: Chatto & Windus, 1971), 21–22. The subject index to Freud's *Collected Works*, ed. James Strachey, contains no entry under *grandparent*, *grandfather*, or *grandmother*. I have avoided the masculine terminology common in many discussions of allusion.

53. Thomas M. Greene, *The Light in Troy: Imitation and Discovery in Renaissance Poetry* (New Haven: Yale University Press, 1982), 19.

54. Christopher Ricks, "Allusion: The Poet as Heir," in *Studies in the Eighteenth Century*, ed. R. F. Brissenden and J. C. Eade (Toronto: University of Toronto Press, 1976), 209–40, passim; and id., "Tennyson Inheriting the Earth," in *Studies in Tennyson*, ed. Hallam Tennyson (London: Macmillan, 1981), 104.

55. A. R. Ammons, "Hermit Lark," *Worldly Hopes* (New York: Norton, 1982), 25–26.

56. See Hollander, *Figure of Echo*, 105, on Eliot's debt to Whitman. (But he is mistaken about the thrush in "Marina," which is a wood thrush, whose very different song I hear imitated in Eliot's words of calling at the end of the poem.) I have long assumed that Eliot chose a Quebec thrush partly because of the pun on the French name of the bird. Charles Tomlinson has excellent commentary on Eliot's use of birds and birdsong in his *Poetry and Metamorphosis* (Cambridge: Cambridge University Press, 1983), 23–47 passim.

57. "Stevens and Keats's 'To Autumn,'" in *Wallace Stevens: A Celebration*, ed. Frank Doggett and Robert Buttel (Princeton: Princeton University Press, 1980), 171–95.

11. MELOS VERSUS LOGOS, OR, WHY DOESN'T GOD SING?

1. This raises questions about the canon, but such questions are not to my purpose here. Christ sings in the apocryphal Acta Johannis (cited in Leo Spitzer, *Classical and Christian Ideas of World Harmony* [Baltimore: Johns Hopkins Press, 1963], 27–28).

Wyclif reports that "thei seyn that angelis heryen god bi song in hevene" but he has a low view of such speculation (cited in John Hollander, *The Untuning of the Sky: Ideas of music in English Poetry, 1500–1700* [Princeton: Princeton University Press, 1961], 251). God sings in some other traditions, for example, Egyptian and Indian. In the classical pantheon, lesser gods like Amphion create by song; Zeus speaks.

2. C. A. Patrides, *Milton and Christian Tradition* (Oxford: Clarendon Press, 1966), 45.

3. John Milton: *Complete Poems and Major Prose*, ed. Merritt Y. Hughes (Indianapolis: Bobbs-Merrill, 1957). All quotations from Milton's poetry are from this edition.

4. "As to the eighth chapter of Proverbs, it appears to me that it is not the Son of God who is there introduced as the speaker, but a poetical personification of Wisdom" (Milton, *De Doctrina Christiana* 1.7, tr. Bishop Sumner, in *The Student's Milton*, ed. F. A. Patterson [New York: Appleton-Century-Crofts, 1933], 973).

5. This remains true no matter how Wisdom is related to the Logos (e.g., whether helping to create the Logos as in pre-Philonic Jewish Alexandrian philosophy, or identified with the Logos as in Philo, or separate because created as in Pico). Milton's interest in origins may be labeled patriarchal and simply dismissed, but the dismissal, if not the label, seems to me to do violence to the historical imagination.

6. Karl Barth, *Die Protestantische Theologie im 19. Jahrhundert* (Zurich: Evangelischer Verlag, 1947), 52; in the selections translated as *Protestant Thought: From Rousseau to Ritschl* (New York: Simon & Schuster, 1959), 50.

7. Milton argues on the ground of the Hebrew language in *De Doctrina Christiana* 1.7.

8. W. B. Hunter, "Milton's Muse," in *Bright Essence*, ed. W. B. Hunter, C. A. Patrides, and J. H. Adamson (Salt Lake City: University of Utah Press, 1971), 154.

9. Harris Francis Fletcher, *Milton's Rabbinical Reading* (Urbana: University of Illinois Press, 1930), 113, 113–14n. In the major rabbinical commentaries of Rashi, Ibn Ezra, and Gersonides, there is no development of the notion of play as music. Hunter suggests a reading of Milton's "play" as music by conflating Prov. 8 and Ps. 33, and also arguing from the word *pulsate* for "play." It seems simpler to work from the original Hebrew. Musical playing need not exclude playing as "some kind of physical activity" (Hunter, "Milton's Muse," 154) — the usual reading of this problematic text. One may agree with Hunter, and with Robins (below), that Milton's Muse is Christ as Logos, but that leaves the question of why Milton bothered with Urania at all.

10. "The Exhoration to the Greeks," in *Clement of Alexandria*, trans. G. W. Butterworth, Loeb ed. (London and New York: Heineman and Putnam's, 1919), 13–15, 17. On "how it is possible for man to become a god," see p. 23. The translator may have had Prov. 8 in mind in "before the foundation of the world," but Clement does not use the Greek of the Septuagint for the word *foundation*. Song is ᾆσμα, as in Ps. 149:1 in the Septuagint. The "heavenly Word" uses a form of Urania's name: οὐράνιος λόγος. I do not know how widespread this phrase is in Greek patristic literature; it would be one logical source for Milton's Urania. On the Uranian Aphrodite or Heavenly Beauty, see Hunter, "Milton's Muse," 151–53.

11. Ernst Robert Curtius, *European Literature and the Latin Middle Ages*, trans. Willard R. Trask (Princeton: Princeton University Press, 1953), 235–45. Wisdom figures in the Excursus on Calderón (xxiii), especially in the remarks on children's play

as "willed by divine Wisdom itself" (p. 562). Curtius does not mention the likely reason for this, which is the text in Proverbs.

12. Northrop Frye, "Charms and Riddles," in his *Spiritus Mundi: Essays on Literature, Myth, and Society* (Bloomington: University of Indiana Press, 1976), 129.

13. William Oram remarks on Milton's "increased distrust of pagan myth and . . . intensified awareness of the spiritual danger, for fallen man, of attempting to locate the sacred in created things" ("Nature, Poetry, and Milton's Genii," in *Milton and the Art of Sacred Song*, ed. J. Max Patrick and Roger Sundell [Madison: University of Wisconsin Press, 1979], 63–64). Similarly, his austerity about magical things.

14. The echo was identified by Bishop Newton and has been used to infer a political allegory, but the general appropriateness goes unnoticed.

15. See Gershom Scholem, *On the Kabbalah and its Symbolism* (New York: Schocken Books, 1965), 104–9, on the notion of a feminine element in God. On various Gnostic readings of Sophia, see Hans Jonas, *The Gnostic Religion*, 2d ed. (Boston: Beacon Press, 1963), passim.

16. This important argument is taken from Mary Nyquist. For a full treatment, see her "Textual Overlapping and Dalilah's Harlot-Lap," in *Literary Theory/Renaissance Texts*, ed. Patricia Parker and David Quint (Baltimore: Johns Hopkins University Press, 1986), 341–72.

17. Reason for Milton includes right choice as well as logic.

18. Hollander, *Untuning of the Sky*, 397. But see also Augustine: "So men who sing like this — in the harvest, at the grape-picking, in any task that totally absorbs them — may begin by showing their contentment in songs with words; but they soon become filled with such a happiness that they can no longer express it in words, and leaving aside syllables, strike up a wordless chant of jubilation" (quoted in Peter Brown, *Augustine of Hippo* [Berkeley: University of California Press, 1967], 258).

19. Cited in James Kugel's authoritative study, *The Idea of Biblical Poetry: Parallelism and its History* (New Haven: Yale University Press, 1981), 149.

20. James Anderson Winn, *Unsuspected Eloquence: A History of the Relations between Poetry and Music* (New Haven: Yale University Press, 1984), 55. For an excellent account of how Christian thought altered prevailing attitudes toward *mousikē*, see 30–73.

21. John Calvin, *Institutes of the Christian Religion*, 3.20.31–33, trans. Henry Beveridge (London: James Clark, 1957), 2:180–83. But see the anti-pietistic and non-Platonic tribute to Mozart in Barth's *Church Dogmatics*, vol. 3: *The Doctrine of Creation*, pt. 3 (Edinburgh: Clark, 1960), 297–99. Barth hears Mozart's music as entirely creaturely, and also profound because it embodies the "no" as well as the "yes" of creation.

22. Quoted in *The American Puritans: Their Prose and Poetry*, ed. Perry Miller (New York: Anchor Books, 1956), 322.

23. Paul de Man, *Blindness and Insight: Essays in the Rhetoric of Contemporary Criticism*, 2d ed. (Minneapolis: University of Minnesota Press, 1983), 285.

24. On this, see Christopher Norris, "Reading as a Woman," *London Review of Books*, 4 Apr. 1985, 8–11; more generally, see K. K. Ruthven, *Feminist Literary Studies* (Cambridge: Cambridge University Press, 1984), ch. 4, "Gynocritics," 93–128.

25. *Les fins de l'homme: À partir du travail de Jacques Derrida* (Paris: Galilée, 1981), 483.

26. As in the notorious lines, "Hee for God only, shee for God in him" (4.299), a

line I have always read as un-Protestant and even un-Christian. Un-Protestant because Protestant thought so vehemently objects to any mediator other than Christ. Un-Christian because Milton here outdoes the apostle Paul's analogy in Eph. 5 and ignores his once-famous text, "There is neither Jew nor Greek, there is neither bond nor free, there is neither male nor female: for ye are all one in Christ Jesus" (Gal. 3:28). My word *un-Christian* is more polemical than historical. But I think it is important not to make Paul into a straw man by ignoring such visionary texts as Gal. 3:28.

27. The phrases are from Maureen Quilligan's *Milton's Spenser: The Politics of Reading* (Ithaca, N.Y.: Cornell University Press, 1983), 225–26, and Sandra M. Gilbert and Susan Gubar, *The Madwoman in the Attic: The Woman Writer and the Nineteenth-Century Imagination* (New Haven: Yale University Press, 1979), 210.

28. Clement, Origen, and Hippolytus, as well as Didymus and Chrystostom, wrote commentaries on Proverbs. Augustine and Jerome use Prov. 8:22–31 only sparingly, in order to establish the doctrine of the Trinity.

29. For Origen, see Harry F. Robins, *If This Be Heresy* (Urbana: University of Illinois Press, 1963). For Eusebius, see A. S. P. Woodhouse, *The Heavenly Muse: A Preface to Milton*, ed. Hugh MacCallum (Toronto: University of Toronto Press, 1972), 165–75. Patrides observes that Milton was likely to have read widely in "the formidable array of theologians from the patristic age to the Reformation and the late Renaissance" (p. 4).

30. Cf. Thomas McFarland, *Coleridge and the Pantheist Tradition* (Oxford: Clarendon Press, 1969): "Coleridge . . . works rather in the counter-tradition of Origen" (317); "Coleridge was very sympathetic toward Alexandrian thinkers" (360).

31. As part of an argument toward another conception of poetry, in Karsten Harries, "The Many Uses of Metaphor," in *On Metaphor*, ed. Sheldon Sacks (Chicago: University of Chicago Press), 86.

32. For "expressive claim," see the quotations from Winn, *Unsuspected Eloquence*, 206, above. For "consolation," cf. Iris Murdoch: "Plato feared the consolations of art. . . . To present the idea of God at all, even as a myth, is a consolation, since it is impossible to defend this image against the prettifying attentions of art. Art will mediate and adorn, and develop magical structures to conceal the absence of God or his distance" (*The Fire and the Sun: Why Plato Banished the Artists* [London: Oxford University Press, 1977], 83). But see also her remark: "as if the artist could indeed penetrate the creative reverie of the Demiurge where truth and play mysteriously, inextricably mingle" (ibid.). Even so, the division between truth and play makes me uneasy. Deconstructive play tries to break this division; we may say, paradoxically, that deconstruction recreates itself through play.

33. Geoffrey Hill, *The Lords of Limit: Essays on Literature and Ideas* (New York: Oxford University Press, 1984), 10. Cf. Milan Kundera on the "wisdom of the novelist" in "Man Thinks, God Laughs," *New York Review of Books*, 13 June 1985, 11–12.

12. THE POETICS OF MODERN PUNNING

1. I have made a noun out of the *OED*'s adjective *paronomastic*. Or should I call Stevens a "paronomasian"?

2. Wallace Stevens, letter of 23 July 1985; in *L*, 5. Unless otherwise indicated,

quotations from the poetry are from Stevens's *Collected Poems* (New York: Knopf, 1954) and may be located through its title index.

3. Wallace Stevens, unpublished letter, 13 Aug. 1952, to Barbara Church, Huntington Library. Quoted by permission of the Huntington Library.

4. Northrop Frye, *Spiritus Mundi: Essays on Literature, Myth, and Society* (Bloomington: University of Indiana Press, 1976), 142.

5. Andrew Welsh, *Roots of Lyric: Primitive Poetry and Modern Poetics* (Princeton: Princeton University Press, 1978).

6. St. Augustine, *The City of God*, trans. Henry Bettenson, ed. David Knowles (Harmondsworth: Penguin Books, 1972), 521.

7. E. R. Curtius, *European Literature and the Latin Middle Ages* (Princeton: Princeton University Press, 1953), 299–301, trans. Willard R. Trask, from *Europäische Literatur und lateinisches Mittelalter* (1948).

8. Cf. Owen Barfield, "Coleridge's Enjoyment of Words," in *Coleridge's Variety: Bicentennial Studies*, ed. John Beer (London: Macmillan, 1974), 204–18.

9. Freud's "puns" are *Kalauer*, and James Strachey says the term is wider than the English *pun*. "Calembourges" is offered in brackets. From *Jokes and Their Relations to the Unconscious* ("The Technique of Jokes"), vol. 8 of *The Standard Edition of . . . Sigmund Freud*, trans. and ed. James Strachey (London: Hogarth Press, 1905), 45.

10. Leo Spitzer, "Puns," *Journal of English and German Philology* 49 (1950): 952–54.

11. Roman Jakobson, "Linguistics as Poetics," in his *Language in Literature*, ed. Krystyna Pomorska and Stephen Rudy (Cambridge, Mass.: Harvard University Press, 1987), 86.

12. Quotations from Elizabeth Bishop are taken from *The Complete Poems, 1927–1979* (New York: Farrar, Straus & Giroux, 1983).

13. John Hollander, "Others Who Have Lived in This Room," in his *Time and Place* (Baltimore: Johns Hopkins University Press, 1986), 37. The allusion works both thematically and schematically.

14. William Wordsworth, *The Poems*, ed. John O. Hayden, vol. 1 (New Haven: Yale University Press, 1977), 586–87.

15. Wallace Stevens, unpublished letter, Huntington Library. Quoted by permission of the Huntington Library.

16. Wallace Stevens, unpublished portion of a letter, 20 Aug. 1911 (*L*, 171), Huntington Library. Quoted by permission of the Huntington Library.

17. James Merrill, *From the First Nine: Poems, 1946–1976* (New York: Athenaeum, 1984), 352.

18. See T. S. Eliot, "Lancelot Andrewes," in *Selected Essays* (London: Faber & Faber, 1951), 349–50. See also K. K. Ruthven, "The Poet as Etymologist," *Critical Quarterly* 11 (1969): 9–37, esp. 18.

19. See my *Poetry, Word-Play, and Word-War in Wallace Stevens* (Princeton: Princeton University Press, 1988), 40 n. 24. See also Richard Howard's richly paronomastic and allusive and funny poem on Stevens and Frost and the Lewis and Short Latin lexicon, ". . . Et Dona Ferentes," in his *Like Most Revelations* (New York: Pantheon Books, 1994), 94–98.

20. E. H. Gombrich, *Art and Illusion: A Study in the Psychology of Pictorial Representation*, 2d ed. (Princeton: Princeton University Press, 1969), 370–71.

21. This French alternative was suggested by members of the Symposium on Paronomasia, chaired by Inge Leimberg, Münster, July 6–8, 1992. Given Stevens's pleasure in the French language, it is very likely.

22. Anthony Hecht, "Crows in Winter," from his *The Transparent Man* (New York: Knopf, 1990), 65.

23. Welsh, *Roots of Lyric*, 251.

24. James Merrill, under "Comments," *University of Toronto Quarterly* 61 (1992): 390.

25. See chs. 8 and 9 above, and also my *Poetry, Word-Play, and Word-War in Wallace Stevens*, ch. 4 and passim.

26. "Riddles, Charms, and Fictions in Wallace Stevens," pp. 187–201 in this volume.

27. Cf. the numerous examples given by Ruthven, "Poet as Etymologist."

28. To Inge Leimberg, I owe the observation that the "arma Christi" would include those very "nails" figuring in Bishop's description of tapestry and her metaphor of armor. The connection with the nails of the crucifixion is made by Bonnie Costello in her *Elizabeth Bishop: Questions of Mastery* (Cambridge, Mass.: Harvard University Press, 1991), 148; Leimberg's suggestion helps to confirm this. To Maria Elisabeth Brockhoff, I owe the persuasive argument that Bishop's word *fabric* is punning musically, as in German *Gewebe* (fabric) in the musical sense. The soldiers also "ripped away into the hanging fabric" of the Mass, tearing out from its entire *Tongewebe* the original secular song "L'Homme armé" — tearing out not simply the melody, but tragically, the militarism.

29. Peter Brown, *Augustine of Hippo* (Berkeley: University of California Press, 1967), 254.

30. For further discussion of this essay, see *Connotations* 2 (1992): 99–102, 201–4, 295–304; and 3 (1993): 90–94, 95–98, 99–102.

13. RIDDLES, CHARMS, AND FICTIONS
    IN WALLACE STEVENS

1. *OP*, 137.

2. Northrop Frye, "Charms and Riddles," in his *Spiritus Mundi: Essays on Literature, Myth, and Society* (Bloomington: Indiana University Press, 1976), 123.

3. E. H. Gombrich, *Art and Illusion: A Study in the Psychology of Pictorial Representation*, 2d ed. (Princeton: Princeton University Press, 1969), 119–20.

4. There is an actual pagoda in Reading, Pennsylvania. See further my *Poetry, Word-Play, and Word-War in Wallace Stevens* (Princeton: Princeton University Press, 1988), 299.

5. *Biblia Sacra* (Vulgate), Ps. 99 (100): 2 (*Iubilate Deo*), Ps. 80 (81): 2 (*Exsultate . . . iubilate*), Ps. 97 (98): 4 (*Iubilate . . . cantate, et exsultate, et psallit*), Zacharia 9: 9 (*Exsulta . . . Iubila*), Ps. 97 (98): 6 (*In tubis . . . et voce tubae . . . Iubilate*), and Gen. 4:21, 22.

6. James Joyce, *Finnegans Wake* (1939; New York: Viking Press, 1961), 338, 84.

7. Wallace Stevens, letter of 16 July 1935, Dartmouth College Library. Quoted by permission of Holly Stevens and Dartmouth College Library. Cf. *L*, 275, 4 Mar. 1935.

8. "Echo Metaleptic," in *The Figure of Echo: A Mode of Allusion in Milton and After* (Berkeley: University of California Press, 1981), 113–32. *The Figure of Echo* is essential reading for anyone who talks about echoing, as I do in this essay. It came into my hands after this essay had gone out of them.

9. Harold Bloom, *Wallace Stevens: The Poems of Our Climate* (Ithaca, N.Y.: Cornell University Press, 1976), 182.

10. I use the term *pure nonsense* — that is, self-contained nonsense with no apparent affective function — where others simply use *nonsense*. Cf. John M. Munro, "Nonsense Verse," in *The Princeton Encyclopedia of Poetry and Poetics*, ed. Alex Preminger (Princeton: Princeton University Press, 1974); Elizabeth Sewell, *The Field of Nonsense* (London: Chatto & Windus, 1952); and Michael Holquist, "What Is a Boojum? Nonsense and Modernism," *Yale French Studies* 43 (1969): 145–64.

11. Cf. Hugh Kenner, "Seraphic Glitter: Stevens' Nonsense," *Parnassus: Poetry in Review* 5 (1976): 153–59, and Irvin Ehrenpreis, "Strange Relation: Stevens' Nonsense," in *Wallace Stevens: A Celebration*, ed. Frank Doggett and Robert Buttel (Princeton: Princeton University Press, 1980), 233–34.

12. For an affective reading, see Bloom, *Wallace Stevens*, 181–83.

13. Cicero, *De or.* 3.43; Quintilian, *Inst. or.* 8.6.52. On *aenigma* in relation to the structure of allegory, see Angus Fletcher, *Allegory: The Theory of a Symbolic Mode* (Ithaca, N.Y.: Cornell University Press, 1964), under *aenigma*, passim.

14. Cf. William Empson on the word *candid*, in *The Structure of Complex Words* (London: Chatto & Windus, 1951), 307–10.

15. Helen Vendler, *On Extended Wings: Wallace Stevens' Longer Poems* (Cambridge, Mass.: Harvard University Press, 1969), 151.

16. After quoting at length an anecdote from *Biographia Literaria*, Stevens goes on to say: "As poetry goes, as the imagination goes, as the approach to truth, or, say, to being by way of the imagination goes, Coleridge is one of the great figures." Coleridge's definitions of poetry are for Stevens "valid enough," although those definitions "no longer impress us primarily by their validity" (*NA*, 40, 41).

17. Cf. Bloom, *Wallace Stevens*, 169.

18. Exploited by Eliot in *Dans le restaurant* ("Oubliait les cris des mouettes et la houle de Cornouaille"), but lost, or much submerged, in the revised English version (*Waste Land*, pt. 4), where Eliot alters the acoustical effect to a whisper. For nightmare associations of *hoo*, cf. Eliot, *Sweeney Agonistes*: "You've had a cream of a nightmare dream and you've got the hoo-ha's coming to you. / Hoo hoo hoo." Stevens's associations with the word *hoo-ing* in *The Man with the Blue Guitar* are pejorative (*L*, 789 [12 July 1953]).

19. "There are several things in the NOTES that would stand a little annotating. For instance, the fact that the Arabian is the moon is something that the reader could not possibly know. However, I did not think it was necessary for him to know" (*L*, 434 [12 Jan. 1943]).

20. Cf. Northrop Frye: "There is a perilous balance in paronomasia between verbal wit and hypnotic incantation" (*Anatomy of Criticism: Four Essays* [Princeton: Princeton University Press, 1957], 176).

21. Cf. "the moon . . . with its dove-winged blendings" (*CP*, 119), and "she . . . bathed the dove in iridescence" (Ruskin, *Love's Meinie*, pt. 2).

22. Frye, "Charms and Riddles," 126.

23. Sewell, *Field of Nonsense*, 40, 43.

24. Frye, "Charms and Riddles," 137–38.

25. Hugh Kenner, said not of Stevens but of Beckett, in *Samuel Beckett: A Critical Study* (London: John Calder, 1961), 10.

26. Cf. Thomas MacFarland, in *New Perspectives on Coleridge and Wordsworth: Selected Papers from the English Institute*, ed. Geoffrey Hartman (New York: Columbia University Press, 1972), 203. On "Kubla Khan" as a model for other nonsense verse, see Kenner, "Seraphic Glitter," and James Rother, "Wallace Stevens as a Nonsense Poet," *Tennessee Studies in Literature* 21 (1976): 86–87.

27. Frye, "Charms and Riddles," 129.

28. Jacques Derrida, *Writing and Difference*, trans. Alan Bass (Chicago: University of Chicago Press, 1978), 77.

29. John Bayley, "Tropes and Blocks," *Modern Language Review* 73 (1978): 748–54.

30. Cf. Bloom, *Wallace Stevens*, 194.

31. "Poetry as a narcotic is escapism in the pejorative sense. But there is a benign escapism in every illusion. . . . Of course, I believe in benign illusion. To my way of thinking, the idea of God is an instance of benign illusion" (*L*, 142 [18 Feb. 1942]).

32. Derrida, "Edmund Jabès and the Question of the Book," in *Writing and Difference*, 64–78, and Geoffrey H. Hartman, "Words and Wounds," in *Saving the Text: Literature/Derrida/Philosophy* (Baltimore: Johns Hopkins University Press, 1981), 118–57.

33. "From the Journal of Crispin," in *Wallace Stevens: A Celebration*, 43: "His town exhales its mother breath for him / And this he breathes, a candid bellows-boy, / According to canon."

34. *SP*, 220.

14. THE FUNCTION OF RIDDLES AT THE PRESENT TIME

1. The rhetorical figure of enigma is "usually identified with *riddle*," as Angus Fletcher says (*Allegory: The Theory of a Symbolic Mode* [Ithaca, N.Y.: Cornell University Press, 1964]), 8 n. 14.

2. Paul de Man, *Blindness and Insight: Essays in the Rhetoric of Contemporary Criticism*, 2d ed. (Minneapolis: University of Minnesota Press, 1983), 285, 186.

3. Geoffrey Galt Harpham, *The Ascetic Imperative in Culture and Criticism* (Chicago: University of Chicago Press, 1987), 264.

4. *Munera Pulveris*, pt. 3, "Coin-Keeping," sec. 87, in *The Works of John Ruskin*, ed. E. T. Cook and Alexander Wedderburn (London: George Allan, 1912), 17: 208.

5. Pierre Fontanier, *Les figures du discours* (1827, 1830; Paris: Flammarion, 1977), 114.

6. Anonymous, *Punch*, 21 Apr. 1883.

7. Northrop Frye, "Charms and Riddles," in his *Spiritus Mundi: Essays on Literature, Myth, and Society* (Bloomington: Indiana University Press, 1976), 142.

8. Terence Cave, *Recognitions: A Study in Poetics* (Oxford: Clarendon Press, 1988); Peter Brooks, *Reading for the Plot: Design and Intention in Narrative* (New York: Knopf, 1984).

9. Archer Taylor, "The Riddle," *California Folklore Quarterly* 2 (1943): 143.

10. John Maynard Keynes, *The Collected Works of John Maynard Keynes*, vol. 10: *Essays in Biography*, ed. D. E. Moggridge (Cambridge: Cambridge University Press, 1971), 366.

11. Frank Manuel, *The Religion of Isaac Newton* (Oxford: Oxford University Press, 1974), 88–89.

12. W. B. Stanford, *Greek Metaphor: Studies in Theory and Practice* (Oxford: Blackwell, 1936), 24.

13. I am indebted to Anthony Hecht for this observation, and for noting how the full story of Oedipus ends with something closer to Pauline enigma.

14. Cave, *Recognitions*, 230 n. 8.

15. Piero Boitani, *The Tragic and the Sublime in Medieval Literature* (Cambridge: Cambridge University Press, 1989).

16. Frank Kermode, *The Genesis of Secrecy: On the Interpretation of Narrative* (Cambridge, Mass.: Harvard University Press, 1979), 145.

17. Paul Ricoeur, *Temps et récit*, vol. 3: *Le temps raconté* (Paris: Editions du Seuil, 1985), 391.

18. *Biographia Literaria*, ed. James Engell and W. Jackson Bate, vol. 7 of *The Collected Works of Samuel Taylor Coleridge*, Bollingen ser., no. 75 (Princeton: Princeton University Press, 1983), pt. 2, 247–48.

19. Ricoeur, *Temps et récit*, 3: 273.

20. *NA*, 60.

21. Denis Donoghue, "Mister Myth," *New York Review of Books*, 9 Apr. 1992, 25–28.

15. THE FLYING GRIPHOS

1. E. G. Stanley has drawn my attention to the fact that the bird *grifo(n* is in Spanish a term of abuse: "also the son of a black woman, and a mulatto" (Delpino's *Dictionary*). For another prejudicial use of the griffin's nature, note the signification in the *OED* of *griff* (also *griffin*) as a mulatto in U.S. usage (giving the origin, from Littré, as Buffon). But *Webster's* definition is the same as the Spanish above, although with sex unspecified, and *Webster's* adds a second definition of "a person of mixed Negro and American Indian blood."

2. Aristophanes, *The Wasps*, ed. Douglas M. MacDowell (Oxford: Clarendon Press, 1971), 130.

3. Aristophanes, *The Complete Plays of Aristophanes*, trans. Moses Hadas (New York: Bantam Books, 1962), 145.

4. Aristophanes, *The Wasps*, in *The Acharnians, The Knights, The Clouds, The Wasps*, trans. and ed. Benjamin Bickley Rogers (Cambridge, Mass.: Harvard University Press, Loeb ed., 1924).

5. Aristophanes, *Wasps*, ed. MacDowell, 14. Note the remarks by Georg Curtius,

in *Principles of Greek Etymology* (London: Murray, 1886), trans. Augustus S. Wilson and Edwin B. England from *Grundzüge der Griechischen Etymologie*, 4th ed.: "γρῖφος has no quite certain etymology. The most probable comparison . . . seems to me . . . that with ῥίψ (gen. ῥίπ-ος) and Lat. *scirp-u-s*, OHG. *sciluf*" (1: 127).

6. For information about Latin, Latin-English, and English-Latin dictionaries, from Balbus on, see De Witt T. Starnes, *Renaissance Dictionaries: English-Latin and Latin-English* (Austin: University of Texas Press, 1954).

7. For editions of Calepino, see Albert Labarre, *Bibliographie du Dictionarium d'Ambrogio Calepino* (Baden-Baden: Editions Valentin Koerner, 1975). For prompt and cheerful help with my search through editions of Calepino, I am indebted to librarians at the following institutions: Columbia University (Rare Book Library), Harvard University (Houghton Library), The Johns Hopkins University (Milton S. Eisenhower Library, Special Collections), University of North Carolina at Chapel Hill (Rare Book Collection), University of Pennsylvania (Special Collections), Philadelphia Library Company, University of Texas at Austin (Humanities Center), University of Toronto (Renaissance and Reformation Centre Library and the Thomas Fisher Rare Book Library), Yale University (Beinecke Library). The library and staff of the Pontifical Institute of Medieval Studies, University of Toronto, were also most helpful. Throughout, I am indebted to A. G. Rigg for checking my Latin translations.

8. For *scrupus*, see *scirpus* in L&S (the spelling varied a good deal during the Renaissance). This word, says Gellius, is what the Greeks call *aenigma* (see L&S), although it seems to me more like an attempt to invent a Latin term corresponding to *griphos* in meaning. The word turns up in Renaissance use, but is less favored than *griphus*. The primary meaning of *scirpus* is "a rush, a bulrush," and the transferred meaning (from woven rushes), "a riddle." Similarly with *griphus*, where the first meaning is "a net," as with Greek *griphos* ("a fishing-basket, creel"). Note also the English word *riddle*, meaning both "an enigma" and "a coarse sieve." The brain's process of solving riddles is here likened to sifting or draining or panning out what you don't want from what you do, as you search for answers.

9. *Trésor de la langue française*, ed. Paul Imbs (Paris: Editions du Centre national de la recherche scientifique, 1979). (The *Trésor* follows W. von Wartburg, *Französisches Etymologisches Wörterbuch*, fasc. 44 (1950), V, 399/2.) The word is not to be found in Edmond Huguet's *Dictionnaire de la langue française du seizième siècle* (Paris: Didier, 1946). The *OED* may have its possibly mistaken view about the English word as an adaptation of the French on such evidence as the fact that *The Great French Dictionary*, ed. G. Mieze (London, 1688), explains the word s.v. *logogrife*, but has no entry in the English-French part. I owe this last surmise to E. G. Stanley, from whom the sentence is quoted, as I also owe the information about von Wartburg.

10. Joan Ferrante, "A Poetics of Chaos and Harmony," in *The Cambridge Companion to Dante*, ed. Rachel Jacoff (Cambridge: Cambridge University Press, 1993), 153–71.

11. Giuseppe Mazzotta, *Dante's Vision and the Circle of Knowledge* (Princeton: Princeton University Press, 1993).

12. Note the single and anomalous listing of *griphus* (*gliphus*), meaning "enigma" and dated ca. 1000 A.D., in *A Revised Medieval Latin Word-List from British and Irish Sources*, ed. R. E. Latham (London: Oxford University Press, 1965). E. G. Stanley, to my pleasure, has also drawn my attention to a single quotation from Peter of Blois

(twelfth century) in *A Dictionary of Medieval Latin from British Sources*, ed. D. R. Howlett, fasc. 4 (London: Oxford University Press, 1989), s.v. *griphus*.

16. GHOST RHYMES AND HOW THEY WORK

1. D. S. R. Welland, "Half-Rhyme in Wilfred Owen: Its Derivation and Use," *Review of English Studies*, n.s., 1 (1950): 226–41, argues that Owen's use of near rhyme stems from French practice as propounded by Jules Romains.

2. *The Complete Prose of Marianne Moore*, ed. Patricia C. Willis (New York: Penguin Books, 1986), 407.

3. Tennyson compared l. 58 of *Ecl.* 1. See *The Poems of Tennyson*, ed. Christopher Ricks, 2d ed. (Berkeley: University of California Press, 1987), 2: 288.

4.

> Behold! yon bordering fence of sallow trees
> Is fraught with flowers; the flowers are fraught with bees:
> The busy bees, with a soft murmuring strain,
> Invite to gentle sleep the labouring swain.
> While from the neighbouring rock, with rural songs,
> The pruner's voice the pleasing dream prolongs,
> Stock doves and turtles tell their amorous pain,
> And, from the lofty elms, of love complain.
>
> ("Pastoral I," in The Works of Virgil, trans. John Dryden
[London: Frederick Warne, n.d.])

5. For Peter Dale, this internal rhyme harms the rhythm. See his note, "Some Thoughts on Rhyme in *The Mystery of the Charity of Charles Péguy*," *Agenda* 30 (1992): 32–34. My arguments here and in "Schemes Against Coercion" address some of the same difficulties that Dale finds in Hill's rhyme effects.

6. Elizabeth Bishop, *One Art: Letters*, ed. Robert Giroux (New York: Farrar, Straus & Giroux, 1994), 440.

7. Welland, "Half-Rhyme in Wilfred Owen."

8. W. K. Wimsatt, "One Relation of Rhyme to Reason," in *The Verbal Icon: Studies in the Meaning of Poetry* (Louisville: University of Kentucky Press, 1954), 152–66.

9. Richard Wilbur, "The Bottles Become New, Too," *Quarterly Review of Literature* 7 (1953): 191.

17. *METHOUGHT* AS DREAM FORMULA

1. Quotations are from *John Milton: Complete Poems and Major Prose*, ed. Merritt Y. Hughes (Indianapolis: Bobbs-Merrill, 1957).

2. Quotations are from *The Riverside Shakespeare* (Boston: Houghton Mifflin, 1974); square brackets have been deleted.

3. Quotations are from William Wordsworth, *The Prelude: A Parallel Text*, ed. J. C. Maxwell (1971; New Haven: Yale University Press, 1981).

4. Quotations are from *John Keats: Complete Poems*, ed. Jack Stillinger (Cambridge, Mass.: Harvard University Press, 1982).

5. The same process, I have argued elsewhere, is at work in the Miltonic echoes in "Ode to a Nightingale." See "Birds in Paradise: Revisions of a Topos in Milton, Keats, Whitman, Stevens, and Ammons," pp. 139–55 in this volume.

6. See *The Poems of Tennyson*, 2d ed., ed. Christopher Ricks (Berkeley: University of California Press, 1987), 3: 488.

7. *The Tales of Henry James*, ed. Maqbool Aziz (Oxford: Clarendon Press, 1978), 2: 67, 474, 609.

8. See Alastair Fowler, "Opening Formulas and Topics," in *Kinds of Literature: An Introduction to the Theory of Genres and Modes* (Cambridge, Mass.: Harvard University Press, 1982), 98–105.

9. In "The Syntax of Dreaming in Old English Biblical Narrative," a paper written for Roberta Frank, Centre for Medieval Studies, University of Toronto, Carin Ruff has expertly extended this investigation of *methought* as dream formula into medieval dream-vision narratives.

18. READING A POEM

1. May Swenson, in *The Contemporary Poet as Artist and Critic*, ed. Anthony Ostroff (Boston: Little, Brown, 1964), 12.

2. See George Saintsbury, *Historical Manual of English Prosody* (London: Macmillan, 1910), 209–10, on Tennyson's variations on the quatrain; his 5 5 5 3 iambic quatrain rhymed *abab* is taken up by Yeats in "The Double Vision of Michael Robarts," pt. 1, but Yeats varies it to 5 5 3 3 with irregular feet. Variations on the English "elegiac" stanza (iambic 5 5 5 5 quatrain rhymed *abab*) mostly change the alternate lines. For a general survey to the mid nineteenth century, see Jakob Schipper, *A History of English Versification* (Oxford: Clarendon Press, 1910). No such stanza is found in Hardy, to follow Dennis Taylor, *Hardy's Metres and Victorian Prosody* (Oxford: Clarendon Press, 1988), "Metrical Appendix," 207–66, and a quick glance through Auden has turned up no example.

3. T. S. Eliot, "Professional, Or . . . ," *The Egoist*, Apr. 1918, 61.

4. John Hollander, *Rhyme's Reason: A Guide to English Verse*, 2d ed. (New Haven: Yale University Press, 1989), 1, and *Melodious Guile: Fictive Pattern in Poetic Language* (New Haven: Yale University Press, 1988), 6.

5. Roman Jakobson, "Poetry of Grammar and Grammar of Poetry," in his *Language in Literature*, ed. Krystyna Pomorska and Stephen Rudy (Cambridge, Mass.: Harvard University Press, Belknap Press, 1987), sec. 1, 121–28.

6. On Athena, see Homer, *Odyssey* 1.44, variously translated as "flashing-eyed" and "grey-eyed" (see Loeb text and note) and also "owl-eyed" (see W. B. Stanford's edition, although he suggests "bright-eyed" as the preferred choice). On Minerva, see L&S, s.v. *glaucopis* = γλαυκῶπις (gray-eyed, an epithet of Pallas Athene's), the owl. The *Oxford Latin Dictionary* (1982) translates the word as "flashing-eyed." I say "apparently of Minerva's" because I haven't found an actual Latin example. Francis Sparshott writes: "I don't suppose *anyone* in the 8th century B.C. and after had the *least* idea of what γλαυκῶπις had originally meant, but I shall always think of it as 'owl-

faced,' bearing in mind the owl with its huge eyes in the Athenian drachma" (letter to the author, 13 Aug. 1996, after reading poem and commentary). On the "mere Volksetymologie" that connects γλαύξ with this epithet, see D'Arcy Wentworth Thompson, *A Glossary of Greek Birds*, new ed. (London: Oxford University Press, 1936), 76. Hugh Kenner briefly discusses the epithet in *The Pound Era* (Berkeley: University of California Press, 1971), 45.

7. From F. R. Scott, "The Call of the Wild," in *The Blasted Pine: An Anthology of Satire, Invective and Disrespectful Verse*, ed. F. R. Scott and A. J. M. Smith (Toronto: Macmillan, 1962), 59–60.

8. James Merrill, *Recitative: Prose by James Merrill*, ed. J. D. McClatchy (San Francisco: North Point Press, 1986), 33.

9. Thompson, *A Glossary of Greek Birds*, 76–80.

10. Roger F. Pasquier, *Watching Birds: An Introduction to Ornithology* (Boston: Houghton Mifflin, 1977), 101.

11. What the poem says about lost outlines is true; the jury is still out on last colors.

12. Robert Browning, "Fra Lippo Lippi."

13. For example, ". . . to keep/Faith, perhaps, with the City," in "Movie-Going" (*Movie-Going* [New York: Atheneum, 1962]), 2, and elsewhere.

14. For example, from *Powers of Thirteen*: "unwisdom's buzz-saw" (no. 111) or "the Law that, while being laid down, had been cut up / Into bits with some sort of saw" (no. 152).

15. The count is based on James Strong's *Exhaustive Concordance of the Bible* (New York: Methodist Book Concern, 1890), under forms of *shew*, and a visual scanning of Marvin Spevack's *The Harvard Concordance to Shakespeare* (Cambridge, Mass.: Harvard University Press, Belknap Press, 1973), together with a computer scanning of Shakespeare's works. There are over 800 uses of *forth* in the 1611 Authorized or King James Version, and some 500 uses in Shakespeare.

16. "Interview: David Sexton Talks to Geoffrey Hill," *Literary Review*, Feb. 1986, 28.

17. W. H. Auden, "Pride and Prayer," *The Episcopalian* (Mar. 1974), cited in Anthony Hecht, *The Hidden Law: The Poetry of W. H. Auden* (Cambridge, Mass.: Harvard University Press, 1993), 387.

18. For me, it is not a question of "investing" rhetoric with moral rigor, as one very good critic remarked of Hollander's work; David Lehman also comments on the rabbinical in Hollander. See his "The Sound and Sense of the Sleight-of-Hand Man," *Parnassus* 12, no. 1 (1984): 190–212.

19. TEACHING POETRY

1. William Wordsworth, letter of 24 Sept. 1827, in *Letters of William and Dorothy Wordsworth*, 2d ed., vol. 4: *1821–1828*, ed. Alan G. Hill (Oxford: Clarendon Press, 1978), 546.

2. James Wright quoted in J. D. McClatchy, *White Paper on Contemporary American Poetry* (New York: Columbia University Press, 1989), 16.

3. *NA*, 165.

4. Northrop Frye, "Expanding Eyes," in his *Spiritus Mundi: Essays on Literature, Myth, and Society* (Bloomington: Indiana University Press, 1976), 102.

5. Marcel Proust, preface to *Green Shoots*, by Paul Morand, trans. H. I. Woolf (London: Chapman, 1923), 44.

6. T. S. Eliot, "In Memory [of Henry James]," *Little Review* 5 (Aug. 1918): 46.

7. I. A. Richards, *Practical Criticism: A Study of Literary Judgment* (New York: Harcourt, Brace, 1929).

8. Christopher Ricks, *T. S. Eliot and Prejudice* (Berkeley: University of California Press, 1988).

9. R. P. Blackmur, "Examples of Wallace Stevens," in his *Form and Value in Modern Poetry* (New York: Doubleday, 1957).

10. W. B. Yeats, "A General Introduction to My Work," *Essays and Introductions* (London: Macmillan, 1961), 526.

11. *Recitative: Prose by James Merrill*, ed. J. D. McClatchy (San Francisco: North Point Press, 1986), 21.

12. John Hollander, *Rhyme's Reason: A Guide to English Verse*, rev. ed. (New Haven: Yale University Press, 1989).

13. See Ray Monk, *Ludwig Wittgenstein: The Duty of Genius* (London: Vantage, 1991), 547.

Index to Poetry

307

General Index

In this index "f" after a number indicates a separate reference on the next page, and "ff" indicates separate references on the next two pages. A continuous discussion over two or more pages is indicated by a span of numbers. *Passim* is used for a cluster of references in close but not consecutive sequence. Subentries are arranged in order of their occurrence in the text.

aboriginal peoples, 53–60 *passim*, 67, 92–93, 104, 187
l'Acadie, 78–79, 287n8
Adams, Henry, 14–15
Addison, Joseph, 244
Adelman, Janet, 289n26
allusion, 99–155 *passim*, 164, 166, 180, 191f, 193–98, 229–30; in Elizabeth's Bishop's work, 42, 177, 184–86, 227–28
Ambrose, Saint, 169
Ammons, A. R., 146, 153–54
Anacreon, 45
Andersen, Hans Christian, 49
Andrewes, Lancelot, 180
apocalyptic mode, 13–16, 21–24, 131
Aquin, Hubert, 84, 90–91
Arabian Nights, see Burton, Richard
Arcand, Denys, 90
Ariosto, Ludovico, 215, 217
Aristophanes, 215–16
Athanasius, Saint, 159
Atwood, Margaret, 88f, 94, 100
Auden, W. H., 50, 231, 255–56, 261
Auerbach, Erich, 61
Augustine of Hippo, Saint, 15, 21–24, 62, 160, 169, 174, 186, 294n18
Avison, Margaret, 86

Barth, Karl, 160–63, 170, 294n21
baseball, 259
Bateson, F. W., 126–27
Bayley, John, 90, 199, 291n48
Beckett, Samuel, 178
Bell, Clive, 275n13
Bercovitch, Sacvan, 61
Berger, Carl, 87
Berger, Charles, 287n13
Bewell, Alan, 117
Bible (Christian and Hebrew), 61–76 *passim*, 100, 103, 146–52 *passim*, 159–71 *passim*, 190, 203–12 *passim*, 227, 254; and William Wordsworth, 107–19; and Wallace Stevens, 128–38, 187–201 *passim. See also names of individual books*
birds and birdsong, 56, 57–58, 179; white-throated sparrow, 39–43; pigeon, 45–48; rooster, 50–53, 59; hoopoe, 59; mockingbird, nightingale, and thrush, 139–55; dove (Holy Ghost), 196–97; owl, 248–56, 269–72
Bishop, Elizabeth, xiii, 44–60, 86, 173–86, 225–28, 232, 248; "Poem," 1, 6–7; "North Haven," 39–43
Blackmur, Richard, 262
Blais, Marie-Claire, 92
Blake, William, 117–18, 228, 249

Source Acknowledgments

Some of this work has appeared elsewhere, as noted below. I have corrected minor errors and infelicities, altered a few titles, and slightly revised the original versions of chapters 6, 10, and 14.

Chapter 1, "Eliot, Keynes, and Empire: *The Waste Land*," as "T. S. Eliot and the Carthaginian Peace," *ELH* 46 (1979): 341–55.

Chapter 4, "Faulkner, Typology, and Black History in *Go Down, Moses*," as "Reading Typologically, For Example, Faulkner," *American Literature* 63 (1991): 693–711.

Chapter 5, "'A Seeing and Unseeing in the Eye': Canadian Literature and the Sense of Place," reprinted by permission of *Daedalus*, journal of the American Academy of Arts and Sciences, from the issue entitled "In Search of Canada," vol. 117, no. 4 (Fall 1988).

Chapter 6, "Questions of Allusion," as "Introduction," *University of Toronto Quarterly*, special issue on allusion, 61 (1992): 289–96.

Chapter 8, "The Senses of Eliot's Salvages," in *Essays in Criticism* 34 (1984): 309–18.

Chapter 9, "Wallace Stevens and the King James Bible," in *Essays in Criticism* 41 (1991): 240–52.

Chapter 10, "Birds in Paradise: Revisions of a Topos [orig. Uses of Allusion] in Milton, Keats, Whitman, Stevens, and Ammons," in *Studies in Romanticism* 26 (1987): 421–43.

Chapter 11, "Melos Versus Logos, or, Why Doesn't God Sing? Some Thoughts on Milton's Wisdom," in *Re-membering Milton: Essays on the Texts and Traditions*, ed. Mary Nyquist and Margaret W. Ferguson (London: Methuen, 1988), pp. 197–210.

Chapter 12, "The Poetics of Modern Punning: Wallace Stevens, Elizabeth Bishop, and Others," as "From Etymology to Paronomasia: Wallace Stevens, Elizabeth Bishop, and Others," *Connotations* 2 (1992): 34–51.

Chapter 13, "Riddles, Charms, and Fictions in Wallace Stevens," in *Centre and Labyrinth: Essays in Honour of Northrop Frye*, ed. Eleanor Cook et al. (Toronto: University of Toronto Press, 1983), pp. 227–44.

Chapter 14, "The Function of Riddles at the Present Time," in *The Legacy of Northrop Frye*, ed. Alvin A. Lee and Robert D. Denham (Toronto: University of Toronto Press, 1994), pp. 326–34.

Chapter 17, "*Methought* as Dream Formula in Shakespeare, Milton, Wordsworth, Keats, and Others," in *English Language Notes* 32, no. 4 (1995): 34–46.

Chapter 18, "Reading a Poem: On John Hollander's 'Owl,' " in *Philosophy and Literature* 20 (1996): 167–76.

Chapter 19, "Teaching Poetry: Accurate Songs, or Thinking-in-Poetry," in *Teaching Wallace Stevens: Practical Essays*, ed. John N. Serio and B. J. Leggett (Knoxville: University of Tennessee Press, 1994), pp. 41–50.

"Owl" is reprinted by permission of John Hollander and the *Yale Review*, where it first appeared.

Excerpts from "Poem" are from *The Complete Poems, 1927–1979*, by Elizabeth Bishop. © 1979, 1983 by Alice Helen Methfessel. Reprinted by permission of Farrar, Straus & Giroux, Inc.

Bird and Memorial, 1980 (oil on canvas, 30″ × 30″), from the Frum Collection, is reproduced by permission of Tim Zuck. (Photograph by Tom Moore.)

Library of Congress Cataloging-in-Publication Data

Cook, Eleanor
Against coercion : games poets play / Eleanor Cook.
       p.   cm.
Includes bibliographical references (p.   ) and index.
ISBN 0–8047–2937–9 (alk. paper)
1. Poetics.   2. Poetry — History and criticism.   I. Title.
PN1042.C586   1998
809.1 — dc21   97–27591
                                                      CIP

This book is printed on acid-free, recycled paper.

Original printing 1998
Last figure below indicates year of this printing:
07   06   05   04   03   02   01   00   99   98